A Perfect Storm

Milton Shain is Professor Emeritus of
Historical Studies at the University of
Cape Town and the former Director of the
Isaac and Jessie Kaplan Centre for Jewish
Studies and Research. He has written and
edited several books, including *The Roots of
Antisemitism in South Africa*. Most recently
he co-edited with Christopher Browning,
Michael Marrus and Susannah Heschel,
*Holocaust Scholarship: Personal Trajectories and
Professional Interpretations*. In 2014 he was
elected a Fellow of the Royal Society of
South Africa.

In Memory of Manya, Minya, Abe and Rita

MILTON SHAIN

A Perfect Storm

Antisemitism in South Africa, 1930–1948

Jonathan Ball Publishers

JOHANNESBURG & CAPE TOWN

© Text, Milton Shain, 2015
© Photographs, as credited individually

Originally published in South Africa in 2015 by
JONATHAN BALL PUBLISHERS
A division of Media24 Limited
PO Box 33977
Jeppestown
2043

ISBN 978-1-86842-700-0
ebook ISBN 978-1-86842-701-7

*Every effort has been made to trace the copyright holders and to obtain their
permission for the use of copyright material. The publishers apologise for any
errors or omissions and would be grateful to be notified of any corrections that
should be incorporated in future editions of this book.*

Twitter: www.twitter.com/JonathanBallPub
Facebook: www.facebook.com/JonathanBallPublishers
Blog: http://jonathanball.bookslive.co.za/

Cover: An Ossewa-Brandwag (OB) guard of honour
(courtesy North-West University Archives and Museum)

Cover design and typesetting by Triple M Design, Johannesburg
Set in 11/15pt Bembo Std

Printed by *paarlmedia*, a division of Novus Holdings

CONTENTS

INTRODUCTION

*'South Africa has a Jewish problem, and we cannot deal with it effectively, unless
we name it specifically, and face it squarely.'*
– DF Malan, House of Assembly, 12 January 1937

*'If the Jew in South Africa gets more power than he now has and becomes more
powerful economically then I ask, what future is there for the rest of the people
of South Africa.'*
– DF Malan, *Sunday Times,* 31 October 1937

The 'Jewish Question' in South Africa in the 1930s and 1940s has attracted
relatively little scholarly attention.[1] When addressed, it correctly identifies
specific factors invariably associated with the radical right. These include the
Afrikaner's existential condition, neo-Calvinism, *herrenvolk*ism, the influx
of German-Jewish refugees, attitudes towards capitalism and the structural
position of Jews in the economy.[2] It has been especially associated with the
upward mobility of Jews, as well as with the fear of radical Jewish activism
in alliance with the *swart gevaar* (black peril).[3] Patrick Furlong ties the emergence of the 'Jewish Question' specifically to the brief interregnum between
the moribund 'Pact' government (an alliance between the National and
Labour parties that governed after 1924) and the birth of the United South
African Party, better known as the United Party, in June 1934.[4] During these

I

years of political uncertainty and pessimism, complicated by a pervasive 'poor white' problem, the effects of the Wall Street crash and a devastating drought, Louis Weichardt – a rabble-rouser who had spent his youth in Germany – launched the 'South African Gentile National Socialist Movement', commonly known as the Greyshirts, in October 1933. Inspired by European fascism and Nazism, Weichardt opposed what he called 'corrupt and rotted democracy' and confidently proclaimed that the Westminster parliamentary system 'was outmoded and unsuited to South Africa's needs'.[5]

Other radical right movements subsequently mushroomed across the country, flourishing especially in the southwestern and eastern Cape Province, northern Natal and on the Witwatersrand. Doing their best to appeal to dislocated and unskilled whites, these movements consistently blamed the Jew for the country's woes. By mid-1936 six independently branded 'Shirtist' groups were in existence, some operating as breakaways, others newly created. Led for the most part by disillusioned and angry young men, these fascist clones traversed the country aping the politics of their European mentors. Filled with conspiratorial bluster, they crudely alerted South African whites to the exploitative, menacing and evil Jew.[6] Propagating fantasies, flirting with notions of 'Aryanism' and 'Nordicism', and peddling international Jewish conspiracies and other outrageous fabrications, they took advantage of enhanced rail and road communications and improved literacy to spread their toxic message. In an attempt to harness discontent, a plethora of pamphlets, broadsheets and newspapers littered the landscape with hate.

Radical right leaders in the main were marginal figures, invariably at odds with one another, often financially troubled, petty and thin on loyalty.[7] Maligned and even ridiculed in the mainstream press, on the few occasions they contested elections they performed poorly. Yet they demanded attention. More importantly, they succeeded in shifting the 'Jewish Question' from the political margins of South African public life to its centre. A diverse Jewish community was transformed by them into a uniform and menacing monolith.[8] By 1936, the leader of the opposition 'Purified' National Party, Daniel François (DF) Malan, was imitating the rhetoric of the radical right. In particular, the influx of German-Jewish refugees seeking to escape

Hitler aroused anger and concern across party lines and drove the political agenda.[9] Government bureaucrats worked to contain what they feared would be a flood of unassimilable Jewish immigrants who would threaten the status quo: the 'Jewish Question' was no longer the concern solely of fringe fascist groups.

The groundswell of anti-Jewish feeling prompted the ruling United Party – led by JBM Hertzog – to introduce stiffer educational and financial immigration requirements during the 1936 parliamentary session, followed by the passing of the Aliens Act of 1937. Widely supported and considered a political necessity, the Act effectively excluded South Africa as a refuge for German Jews, who were deemed unassimilable. Yet hostility did not subside. Nationalists now pushed for Jewish occupational and professional quotas, their propaganda underpinned by an insistence on the threat of Jewish domination in business and the professions. At the same time, they drew attention to radical Jewish activists who undermined *völkisch* ambitions and threatened to act in alliance with a restive African proletariat. These issues penetrated the debates of the 1938 general election, with the National Party and the radical right utilising the 'Jewish Question' as a stick with which to beat the United Party. By the time South Africa joined the Commonwealth war effort against Nazi Germany, the radical right – now bolstered by the *Ossewa-Brandwag* (Ox-wagon Sentinel) and *Nuwe Orde* (New Order) – made it quite clear that it envisaged no place in South Africa for the 'unassimilable' Jew.[10] National Party publications issued in the early 1940s also demonstrated the formative influence of Mussolini and Hitler on the nature of *völkisch* Afrikaner nationalism.[11]

Many questions present themselves. Why were radical right fantasists able to exert such influence, and why was a demagogic, simplistic and vulgar message able to gain such traction? Why did the National Party – and especially Malan, a man with only a hint of animus towards Jews prior to 1930 – mimic the discourse of the radical right, and why was the 'Jewish Question' such a useful vehicle for political mobilisation? What induced the United Party (strongly supported by Jews) to succumb to pressure from the National Party and the radical right and introduce legislation that halted the influx of German Jews? What was the reason to continue targeting

Jews, long after this legislation, with added calls to limit their involvement in commerce and the professions? And finally, why was European fascism, with its exclusivist orientation in which the Jew had no place, so seductive?

This study engages with these questions as it tracks and narrates chronologically the growth of antisemitism in the 1930s and 1940s and seeks to locate this growth within the broader context of South African politics and culture. It will be argued that many Nationalists, including high-ranking bureaucrats, had a visceral dislike of Jews and gave direction to a mood (shared by a not insignificant number of English-speakers) that grew substantially in the years building up to the Second World War. Antisemitism was not, as the historian Dunbar Moodie argues, a 'muted theme' during the 1938 general election, and it certainly informed the radical right during the war years. European fascism, and with it antisemitism, had demonstrable appeal.[12]

Put simply, it will be argued that Jew-hatred was not a marginal factor in South African public life during these troubled years. Indeed, awesome and nefarious power was conferred on a community that comprised a mere 4.5 per cent of the total white population.[13] Defined by the radical right as an existential danger, the Jewish community in reality posed no challenge to power and made no claims on state resources. Its modest origins dated back to the early nineteenth century, although it was only by the early twentieth century that the community had established a substantial presence, augmented by immigrants seeking to escape oppression and discrimination in the Russian empire. By the outbreak of the Great War, the Jewish population numbered about 50 000, nearly four per cent of the total white population.[14] A range of communal institutions had been founded and Jews were gradually integrating into the wider (white) society. This, however, did not demand the shedding or discarding of ethnic distinctiveness. In a country where English- and Afrikaans-speakers still saw themselves as separate 'races', there was ample room for Jewish particularism.[15] In the main Jews identified with the more urban and commercially dominant English-speaking population, although in the smaller towns many Jews interacted closely with Afrikaners.

By the mid-1920s two-thirds of Jewish working males were concentrated in trade and finance, more than three times the proportion of their non-Jewish (white) counterparts.[16] Most operated on a modest scale, though their presence on many high streets was conspicuous. In manufacturing, Jews benefited from the disruption of imports during the Great War and continued to benefit thereafter from the protectionist policies of the 'Pact' government. In addition to commerce and manufacturing, Jews also entered the professions in significant numbers. The proportion of professional Jewish men equalled that of the general white male population, and was steadily rising.[17] Jews were also overrepresented among radical groups, including the budding Communist Party of South Africa, founded in 1921; a Yiddish-speaking branch of the International Socialist League had been a forerunner of that party.[18] Jewish visibility in leftist politics indeed added yet another layer to a kit of well-worn anti-Jewish stereotypes that had accompanied the influx of Jews from the late nineteenth century: fortune-seekers, cosmopolitan financiers, rural traders, urban hucksters and wartime shirkers.[19] These stereotypes confirmed and even reinforced the widely shared European Jewish stereotype, but they were not simply its reflection. They were intimately bound up with the local stresses and upheavals resulting from the mineral revolution of the late nineteenth century and labour instability in the early 1920s. From the mid-1920s, nativist and eugenicist concerns with race, miscegenation and the 'Nordic' character of South African 'stock' amplified obsessions with the Jew.[20] These obsessions, together with the threat of Jewish economic competition and (to a lesser extent) fears of radical subversion, underpinned the Quota Act of 1930, which effectively curtailed the influx of eastern European Jews – the seedbed of South African Jewry.[21] Every nation has the right to 'maintain its own particular type of civilisation', Minister of the Interior Malan told an approving parliament in defence of the Act.[22] Tellingly, English-speakers supported the legislation, as did the press in general. 'Jews were the wrong type of immigrant,' explains Sally Peberdy, a historian of South African immigration, 'because, although white, they were of the wrong race.'[23]

Without this notion of the Jews as a race apart and the maturation of widely shared anti-Jewish stereotypes, the Quota Act of 1930 would not have received popular support. Hostility towards Jews in the 1930s and

5

1940s was not an aberration of South African thought or a moment of irrational deviation; it was premised on these stereotypes.[24] But the anger went much further. Whereas prior to the Quota Act, anti-Jewish enmity had been expressed essentially at the level of ideas, in the 1930s and 1940s it mutated into proposed action or public policy – what the historian Todd Endelman has referred to as the transformation of 'private' into 'public' antisemitism.[25] Injected into the bloodstream of South Africa's body politic, major political parties increasingly took cognisance of mounting anti-Jewish feeling.

To capture the mood and temper of the times, use has frequently been made of direct quotations. Not only does this more accurately convey the discourse about Jews, but it also gives a sense of heightened obsession over time. It should also be noted that the focus of this study is on the white population only. The African majority, as well as Asians and mixed-descent Coloureds, seldom identified Jews specifically in their struggle for political rights during the period covered. For them it was rather an issue of white exploitation and oppression.[26] For many whites, however, the Jew was identified in negative terms. Even an upturn in the economy from the mid-1930s failed to dampen a populist discourse that characterised Jews as unassimilable, exploitive and subversive, as well as an additional 'racial' challenge to a country grappling with its own sense of identity. For the first time, South Africans confronted a 'Jewish Question' in the broadest sense. Although deeply and indelibly linked to earlier ideas and stereotypes about the Jew, the transformation of 'private' into 'public' antisemitism was not simply a deepening of ideas. It was, to be sure, a product of specific factors, a set of contingencies that ultimately drove South Africa's 'Jewish Question' in the decade before and during the Second World War. It was a perfect storm.

CHAPTER ONE

AN UNABSORBABLE MINORITY

'With the nurturing of the national consciousness of South Africa there has arisen an anti-Jewish feeling that was unknown, or at any rate, unnoticed before.'
– South African Jewish Chronicle, 31 May 1930

'… it is very easy to rouse a feeling of hate towards the Jews in this country.'
– DF Malan, interview, Die Burger, 2 November 1931

'I challenge anyone here to accuse me of preaching murder and persecution – the reports you see of the affairs in Germany are lies – but if the Jew does not want to be put in his place, we shall put him there. What objection can the Chosen Race have if I recommend a policy by which they would be happily settled in their own country? What, I ask you, is wrong in that we want to assist them in that direction?'
– Louis T Weichardt, speech in the Koffiehuis, 26 October 1933

'While we are squabbling, Comrades, Ikey is rubbing his dirty greasy hands, and we are paying the price in blood and tears … Every Jew is a skunk. There is not a good Jew. They are all evil and filthy. Every mother must warn her sons of the fate which is his by the hands of Zion and send her husband and sons out to fight this evil. I urge you, Comrades, forget your animosity, and British, Boer and German, come out together as one man and fight Judaism until we have strangled the snake and it lies dead at our feet. This is a religious fight. The fight for Christianity.'
– Ray (RK) Rudman, Newcastle, 17 June 1934

BETHAL

In summer the daytime temperature in Bethal often rises above 30°C, but evening thunderstorms frequently bring welcome relief to the surrounding potato and mealie (maize) farmers who have for generations interacted with the eastern Transvaal (now Mpumalanga) town.[1] Among these men of the soil in the 1920s were a handful of Jews, most notably the 'Mealie King' of the region, Esrael Lazarus.[2] He and the other *Boerejode* (Afrikaans-speaking Jews) were exceptions among a rural community overwhelmingly dominated by Boers, or Afrikaners.[3] Nonetheless, they were well integrated with their (white) English-speaking and Afrikaner compatriots, although farming was far removed from the usual trading occupations pursued by the overwhelming majority of their coreligionists in Bethal.[4]

The community's origins went back at least to 1906, a time of reconstruction and optimism, driven by British High Commissioner Lord Alfred Milner and his 'Kindergarten', in the wake of the devastating Anglo–Boer War.[5] Its numbers, though, remained small: the *South African Jewish Year Book 1929* reported a mere 60 members of the Bethal Hebrew Congregation.[6] Yet the 'Pact' government led by the National Party's revered General James Barry Munnik (JBM) Hertzog, was determined not to alienate Bethal's Jewish vote in the upcoming by-election scheduled for 22 January 1930.

Seven months earlier, in the general election of 1929, the National Party's Tielman Roos, a shrewd and enigmatic friend of the Jews, had narrowly defeated his South African Party opponent, Hendrik Grobler, in the Bethal constituency. But Roos was in poor health and subsequently resigned as Minister of Justice in October 1929 to take up a position on the Supreme Court of Appeal. It was by no means certain that his replacement, GE Haupt, would hold the seat for the Nationalists in the by-election. The small Jewish vote was therefore important and could not be taken for granted, particularly in light of the National Party's stated intention to restrict Jewish immigration from eastern Europe.[7]

This festering issue had been on the back burner during the June 1929 election, which had been dominated by the *swart gevaar* and issues of South Africa's relationship with Britain. However, the issue was resurrected at the National Party's Orange Free State congress, held in the wake of the election, with delegates resolving 'that the time has arrived to fix a quota of immigration on the basis operating in the United States'.[8] This resolution had obvious implications for the upcoming by-elections in both Bethal and Stellenbosch, where the National Party faced a distinct possibility of losing the Jewish vote in these tightly contested seats.[9]

To secure the Bethal seat for the Nationalists and to assuage Jewish fears about restricting Jewish immigration, the National Party dispatched one of its rising stars, the forty-year-old Oswald Pirow, to the small town. The 'young gladiator of the Nationalists', as the *Cape Times* described him, was Roos' replacement as Minister of Justice.[10] The grandson of German immigrants, Pirow had been schooled in Potchefstroom, but at the age of fourteen had left for Germany before proceeding to England to read Law. At the age of twenty-three he was elected to the Inner Temple, London. He returned to practise law in Pretoria, and in 1925, one year after being elected to parliament for the Zoutpansberg seat, was appointed a King's Counsel (KC). Four years later Pirow audaciously, but unsuccessfully, mounted a challenge for General Jan Smuts' seat in Standerton. He was highly regarded and, despite his defeat at the hands of the South African Party leader, was appointed Minister of Justice as a nominated senator in the 'Pact' government. A short while later he won a by-election in Gezina, a Pretoria suburb.[11]

In a lengthy and careful address, Pirow told the voters of Bethal that the National Party had no intention of changing the immigration laws and that no plans were afoot to curtail specifically the influx of Jews from eastern Europe. He assured Bethal's Jews that the policy of the Nationalists would remain as Tielman Roos had often explained. Pirow went on to warn voters against a surreptitious propaganda campaign, launched by the South African Party, claiming that the Nationalists were hostile to Jews and against Jewish immigration. Indeed, his own experience had led him to believe that Jews were the only immigrants 'who did not become a burden on the State'.[12]

To the relief of the Jewish community, immigration from eastern Europe did not appear to be under threat, at least for the time being. 'We have no doubt that Mr Pirow's assurance will set at rest the minds of many Jews who were becoming anxious lest propaganda and agitation should drive

Oswald Pirow (left) in conversation with a member of the diplomatic corps.
(courtesy Museum Africa)

the Government to discriminate against their race,' noted the *South African Jewish Chronicle* (hereafter the *SAJC*).[13] But as a cabinet minister, Pirow's assurance must surely have been a dissembling political ploy, since it is highly unlikely that he was unaware that plans were already in the pipeline to introduce restrictive immigration legislation aimed specifically at eastern European Jews.[14]

For decades calls had been made from many quarters to curtail this immigration, and these had grown increasingly vociferous in the 1920s with the *Cape Times* leading the way. Driven by its Oxford-educated editor, the pipe-smoking and urbane Basil Kellett (BK) Long, the Cape Town daily persistently advocated curbs on undesirable immigration from countries where 'western concepts of morality' were not understood and demo-cratic ideals were unknown.[15] The replacement of South Africa's 'dominant Nordic Stock of Europeans by a stock of entirely distinct characteristics, dubious quality, and undoubted unsuitability to the economic conditions of the country' – as the *Cape Times* put it – was of great concern. Such immi-gration would have 'a profound effect upon the whole character of a white population which is initially well under two nations'.[16]

A new 'race' discourse, in which 'Russians' and 'Jews' joined 'Orientals', 'Africans', 'Europeans', 'Anglo-Saxons', 'English', 'Nordics' and 'Mediterra-neans' as racial groups, had crept into discussions about Jewish immigration. So-called moral degeneracy already occupied a prominent place in the lexi-con of South African eugenicists, and 'miscegenation' or 'cross-breeding' – primarily associated with Africans – was a fear voiced even by liberal social scientists and philosophers.[17] Such fears were encapsulated in the response of the *Star*, a Johannesburg daily, to a report on immigration by the census director, John Holloway, who in the mid-1920s had identified the influx of impoverished Lithuanian Jews as a major cause for concern. The newspaper referred to the 'fecundity' of the newcomers and the impact this would have upon the country's intellectual and physical development. Such immigra-tion, it contended, would profoundly modify the racial composition of the country and it would be far better to encourage 'Nordic immigrants', as the United States had done.[18]

THE QUOTA ACT

Only days after the South African Party had won the Bethal by-election and reduced the National Party majority in Stellenbosch, and notwithstanding Pirow's pious pre-election reassurances to the Jewish community, the 'Pact' government's Minister of the Interior, DF Malan, shocked South African Jewry with the introduction of a Quota Bill on 29 January 1930.[19] Modelled in part on the Johnson-Reed Act of 1924 in the United States, the new legislation effectively planned to halt eastern European Jewish immigration by imposing an initial limit of 50 immigrants per annum from each of a list of 'non-scheduled' or 'quota' countries that included Lithuania, Latvia and Poland.[20]

The fifty-six-year-old Malan, a Dutch Reformed Church theologian and one-time editor of the Nationalist mouthpiece, *Die Burger*, had correctly sensed an anti-immigrant mood. Educated at Victoria College (that became Stellenbosch University) and at Utrecht University in the Netherlands, Malan was schooled in a European romanticism that conflated language, state and nation. He had always been drawn to the idea of the *volk*, believing in its 'special calling and destiny', as historian Hermann Giliomee puts it.[21] Malan certainly knew that he had support across party and language lines for his plans to curtail the influx of eastern European Jews: English-speaking merchants appreciated the prospect of less competition, while the *volk* wished to limit what it considered to be a powerful and alien element that blocked its advancement and added to the country's 'racial' problems.[22] Both the English and Afrikaans press greeted the immigration restriction initiative with affirmation. 'The Bill will commend itself to most citizens of the Union and has not been introduced a day too soon', noted an editorial in East London's *Daily Dispatch* that perhaps best captured the public mood.[23]

In his careful, precise and emotionless introduction to the Quota Bill, Malan focused on the character of the immigrants entering the country. Most, he maintained, were from eastern Europe, and many did not belong to the 'producing classes'.[24] More significantly, in justifying the introduction of the Bill, Malan employed nativist assumptions that were directly influenced by literature from the United States, as well as by a domestic

DF Malan (DF Malan Collection, courtesy JS Gericke Library, University of Stellenbosch)

segregationist discourse and *völkisch* theories that conflated race and culture. The Bill, he told an approving House of Assembly, was rooted in every nation's wish to maintain its own particular identity based on the composition of its original inhabitants. The eastern European newcomers, Malan contended, undermined the character and homogeneity of the nation: 'Nations desire to preserve homogeneity, because every nation has got a soul, and every nation naturally desires that its soul shall not be a divided one. Every nation considers from all points of view that it is a weakness, if in the body of that nation, there exists an undigested and unabsorbed and unabsorbable minority, because that always leads to all sorts of difficulties.'[25]

Malan's Herderian or essentialist rationalisation – spiced with Kuyperian reasoning that challenged individualism – evinced a worldview that organically conflated culture and nation and stressed the need for 'racial homogeneity' and a 'particular type of civilisation'.[26] Evidently, eastern European Jews were 'unassimilable', a notion shared by English- and Afrikaans-speakers alike. But 'Doktor' – as the stout, unsmiling and bespectacled Malan was often called – wished to avoid being labelled an antisemite. He went out of his way to assert that the imposition of quota restrictions did not reflect negatively on those Jews already in the country. He even praised the Jewish community for its contribution to South Africa, and made it clear that Jews from England or Holland were still welcome to enter South Africa.[27] But he did warn Jews that the indiscriminate influx of eastern Europeans engendered a broad-based apprehension that was capable of turning into outright hostility.[28]

The four Jewish parliamentarians – the Labour Party's Morris Kentridge and the South African Party's Charles Robinson, Eli Buirski and Emile Nathan – were predictably angered by Malan's rationalisations. However, speakers on both government and opposition benches shared Malan's concerns. For instance, Heaton Nicholls, the well-known South African Party segregationist, spoke in much the same spirit as Malan, arguing that if the characteristics of the 'white stock' were undermined disharmony would result. In his opinion it was essential that the government maintain unimpaired the country's heritage in the interests of the future civilisation of South Africa.[29] Nicholls' party colleague, Leslie Blackwell, similarly argued that a large influx of eastern European Jews would pose a very real threat if not diluted with other more acceptable European immigrant stock: 'We do not want to keep people out because they are Jews or Lithuanians, but we do want to restrict their numbers so that they shall conform with the present ethnological conditions.'[30] The Bill has been 'unreservedly welcomed with a sigh of relief', claimed Alexander MacCallum – also of the South African Party – a statement that reflected the general sentiment in the House. As the debate wound to a close, he accurately articulated the tone of discussions when he questioned, somewhat rhetorically, why everyone was agreed upon the Bill. 'There must be good reason for the unanimity,' he suggested, a reason that 'is directly connected with the class of persons who comes to this country, but it is not directed against Jew qua Jew … The feeling is due to a lack of character, to a lack of commercial morality, and to the manner in which these immigrants conduct themselves.'[31]

Where the opposition South African Party did take issue with the administration was in regard to the way the Bill had been introduced. In his maiden parliamentary speech (memorised for the occasion),[32] the brilliant but patently nervous thirty-six-year-old Jan Hofmeyr, who would emerge as an icon of South Africa's liberal whites, ridiculed the government's subterfuge and the fact that no mention of the impending legislation had been made during the Governor General's opening address to parliament. With biting sarcasm, Hofmeyr reminded the House of Pirow's duplicitous 'eulogium on the merits of Jewish immigration' when he had visited Bethal to secure votes for the Nationalists in the by-election, as well as his excessive praise of Jewish farmers in the Bethal district. In Hofmeyr's estimation, the Bill had cast an unwarranted slur on a valued and important section of South Africa's population. Yet, ironically, for all his criticism, Hofmeyr indicated broad agreement with the maintenance of South Africa's 'racial stock'. Moreover, he expressed confidence that Jews already in South Africa would be able to escape their ghetto origins and broadly assimilate into society, as long as their numbers did not exceed immigrants from more familiar backgrounds.[33]

The South African Party's confused stance was exacerbated by the absence of its leader, former Prime Minister Jan Smuts. When the celebrated General returned from abroad in time for the second reading of the Bill, he attempted to ameliorate its harsh implications: 'Let us have an open door as long as possible and restrict the type of immigrant which we cannot digest, on lines approved of and followed by other countries like the USA, but do not let us put this black mark, this stigma, not only on these countries, but also, that is what it comes to, on these people.'[34]

It was too late. In the words of George Wilson (who wrote 'Notes in the House' for the *Cape Times*), the South African Party had endeavoured 'to dance without breaking any eggs'.[35] Even more troubling from Smuts' point of view was the fact that a number of his colleagues had used the debate to vilify Jews by rehashing a range of ugly anti-Jewish tropes that had evolved over the previous decades.[36] His concerns, however, made little difference. The Bill passed its second reading with almost unanimous opposition support.

The whole tenor of the debate surrounding the Quota Bill had revealed that the issue of immigration revolved solely around the 'Jewish Question'.[37] As the feisty Kentridge cogently explained, Malan knew that virtually all those people coming from 'non-scheduled' or 'quota' countries were Jewish. He tellingly quoted the *Friend* (of Bloemfontein) which had argued that the real object of the Bill was to 'keep out an unlimited influx of the Jewish people'.[38] Charles Robinson made a similar observation: 'Do not tell me this is merely a Bill for the exclusion of Lithuanian Jews. It sounds the death knell of any more Jews coming to South Africa. At present it is the poor Lithuanian, tomorrow it may be the Jew from Germany or France that will not be allowed to come in.'[39]

Robinson's fears would prove to be well founded. He was absolutely correct to stress that the divide between eastern European and other Jews was academic at best; concern about the very presence of Jews, as well as hostility towards an uncontrolled influx, underpinned the Bill. Hofmeyr certainly recognised this: 'Those of us who have visited many parts of this country have noted in recent years a change of feeling on the part of the non-Jewish population towards our Jewish population.' With much perspicacity, he went on to warn the House of possible conflict between Jews and non-Jews if current immigration laws were not revised.[40]

The Quota Act was passed on 11 March 1930, becoming law on 1 May, with immediate consequences for Jewish immigration, which declined dramatically.[41] Jews were predictably disillusioned and aggrieved. More than that, they were stunned. Only three weeks before the legislation was introduced, Siegfried Raphaely, President of the South African Jewish Board of Deputies – the community's representative national body (referred to hereafter as the Board of Deputies or simply the Board) – had confidently told the organisation's Eighth Congress that 'we have had absolutely no difficulty and no unpleasantness with the question of immigration'.[42] In the words of Morris Alexander, a lawyer and Jewish communal leader as well as a former Member of Parliament (MP), the Quota Bill came 'as a complete shock'.[43]

All the Jewish community could do was to organise a series of protest meetings across the country, where resolutions were passed opposing the notion that country of origin should be a determining factor in immigration legislation.[44] In addition, the Board sought an urgent interview with Malan, hoping to propose other methods of controlling immigration, but first Malan and then Prime Minister Hertzog indicated they were unable to accede to a meeting. Alexander (and a small deputation) did, however, manage to meet privately with Malan, who promised to discuss the Board's suggestions with the Prime Minister.[45]

Malan had obviously anticipated Jewish objections, but he believed the legislation was essential despite its consequences for Afrikaner-Jewish relations. That much he confided in a letter to his colleague Eric Hendrik Louw, then serving as Ambassador Extraordinary and Minister Plenipotentiary in the United States. 'For the rest of my days I will be for the Children of Israel like the Canaanite and the Philistine,' he told Louw. 'But at least something was done for the *volk* on which its life depends, and that is altogether enough for me. It is only a pity that already so much has been permitted for our country to make commercial demoralisation and exploitation a terrible and permanent reality.'[46]

WHY THE QUOTA ACT?

Eric Louw shared Malan's devotion to the *volk*. Educated at Victoria College and Rhodes University, where he obtained an LLB degree, Louw

Throughout his political career, the ambitious Eric Louw consistently exploited fears about Jews and Jewish immigration. (courtesy Archives for Contemporary Affairs, University of the Free State, Bloemfontein)

had founded and served on the chamber of commerce in the Karoo town of Beaufort West, which he represented in parliament in the mid-1920s. Smallish of stature but hugely ambitious, Louw was aware of the significant presence of Jews in both the urban and rural economy. He also understood the alienation of poor rural Afrikaners that dated back to the 1890s. Indeed, anti-Jewish generalisations abounded in the *platteland* (country districts), where Afrikaner farmers, many of whom were on the road to 'poor whiteism', projected disturbing feelings of alienation and displacement onto the alien newcomers, who were readily available as symbols of change.[47] The *smous*, or itinerant Jewish pedlar, was often seen as scheming and cunning – 'a danger and a menace to the country', as Matthys Venter told the old Cape Colony parliament in 1893 – while the Jewish shopkeeper was considered as avaricious, living by his wits and bent on exploiting the Boer.[48]

But hostility to the eastern European Jews at the turn of the century went beyond rural opposition to the *smous* and the Jewish country shopkeeper. The unkempt 'Peruvian'[49] in the urban areas, who was identified

18

with the seamier side of city life, including illicit liquor dealing and prostitution on the Witwatersrand, was an even greater source of concern, while the cosmopolitan financier was represented in the grotesque and semitic cartoon caricature 'Hoggenheimer', the mine owner. Characterised as an *éminence grise* and the personification of British imperialism and rapacious international capital in South Africa, Hoggenheimer was perceived as disturbing a rustic and idyllic harmony with his financial machinations.[50]

The anti-Jewish stereotype was embellished during the Great War of 1914–18 with accusations of Jews shirking military service and, after the Russian Revolution, the conflation of 'Russian Jews' with Bolshevism. The Rand Rebellion of 1922, a violent clash between the state and white mine workers, was construed, at least in some quarters, as a 'Bolshevik' revolt.[51] In the context of economic depression and the spread of African radicalism, 'the Jew', as understood in racial terms, emerged as an archetypical subversive. The eastern European newcomers, argued the *Natal Advertiser*, undermined liberty and were a threat to a state that had given them too much latitude. The 'sternest measures', the newspaper asserted, should be meted out to 'the low down alien' and 'the propagandists of Communism'.[52]

As we have seen, by the mid-1920s eastern European immigrants were being characterised as 'unassimilable', a notion that increasingly dominated debates surrounding immigration restriction. The emigration of English men and women from South Africa after 1924, alongside the immigration of eastern European Jews – perceived as inherently devious and immutably alien – was considered particularly disturbing, while the term 'unassimilable', reflecting the new discourse of race and culture, conveniently dodged the taint of antisemitism.

When he initiated the Quota Bill, Malan was tapping into these sentiments, as well as into the crisis facing dislocated 'poor whites', a crisis exacerbated by changes in rural production and the Wall Street crash of October 1929.[53] In his view the South African economy could be analysed in zero-sum terms: the success of upwardly mobile Jews in both the countryside and the city was understood to be at the expense of the uprooted Afrikaner, described by historian David Welsh as living like a 'foreigner among aliens'.[54] To be sure, thousands of impoverished rural

Afrikaners had 'found refuge in the ragged edges of the cities',[55] where insalubrious slums mushroomed and poor Afrikaners lived cheek by jowl with Africans and Coloureds.[56] They were like 'strangers in their own country: hesitant, fearful of using their own language in shops and businesses, and confined very largely to the humbler areas and jobs', writes the historian WA de Klerk.[57] The 'terrible distress' that was captured in a petition by unemployed whites in Vryheid, a small town in northern Natal (now KwaZulu-Natal), was indicative of a widespread crisis where, according to a report in the *Cape Argus*, the condition of wives and children bordered on starvation.[58] In fact, at the time of the Quota Act almost one in five whites – mainly Afrikaners – was living below the poverty datum line, constituting a political time bomb. For them life had become, in the words of the Afrikaans belletrist NP van Wyk Louw, 'grimmer, harsher and more naked'.[59]

Disturbingly, the Carnegie Commission investigating the 'poor white' problem (and whose findings were rooted in the vocabulary of racial science) regularly heard how Jews, through their cunning, were the source of the Afrikaner's plight. One of the commissioners – Johannes Grosskopf of Stellenbosch University, whose report constituted one of five volumes published on the question of 'poor whites' – also concluded that Jewish commercial dealings were causing great harm. 'Calm, sensible people in all parts of the country repeatedly bear this out,' he reported.[60]

AN ESCALATING ANTI-JEWISH MOOD

Whether or not the vandalisation of a synagogue in the small Orange Free State town of Brandfort in early 1930 was indicative of a more aggressive anti-Jewish mood is uncertain;[61] but what is apparent is that the 'poor white' problem, coupled with a growing Afrikaner nationalism, at a time of political and social uncertainty, ensured opportunities for those wishing to identify Jews as the reason for their misfortune.[62] An editorial in the *SAJC* on the eve of Union Day of that same year sensed the mood: 'With the nurturing of the national consciousness of South Africa there has arisen an anti-Jewish feeling that was unknown, or at any rate, unnoticed before … It was perhaps inevitable that with the growth of national feeling, these sentiments should change.'[63]

Shortly after the Brandfort incident, Joel Mann, a Lithuanian-born Jew who represented the Ladismith Division for the South African Party in the Cape Provincial Council, was described by a delegate to a National Party congress in Somerset East as an *Uitlander* (foreigner) who had used his financial muscle to secure his seat. 'They should prevent Uitlanders from working the original Afrikander population out of their property in an insidious manner,' he said.[64] Anti-Jewish sentiment was also prevalent during the Transvaal Provincial Council elections of 26 March 1930 when the National Party took umbrage at Jews who, allegedly angered by the Quota Act, were publicly supporting the opposition South African Party.[65] More disturbing was a report to the Board that the *Protocols of the Elders of Zion*, an outrageous antisemitic fabrication that suggested Jews were plotting to destroy the Christian world, was on sale at a bookstore in Cape Town, together with other examples of antisemitic literature.[66]

A few months later, Pirow complained that Jewish citizens were now 'condemning every measure of the Nationalist Government because of the passage of the Quota Bill, with resultant ill feeling between the platteland and the Jews'.[67] He returned to this theme during a speech in Lichtenburg, where he claimed certain Jews were deliberately misinterpreting the Act to stir up racial animosity.[68] Pirow's admonitions, however, did not prevent Siegfried Raphaely from mentioning the Quota Act and its unjust treatment of eastern European Jews in his Board of Deputies' 'New Year Message'.[69] A resolution condemning the Act was subsequently passed by the South African Zionist Federation at its Thirteenth Conference in January 1931.[70]

Although the intensity of Jewish public protest gradually declined,[71] Nationalist politicians continued to believe that Jews were turning away from their party.[72] Malan, the National Party's Cape Province leader, was especially concerned about developments in his own backyard, the arid northwestern Cape Province (the town of Calvinia was his parliamentary constituency). There, Willem Petrus Steenkamp, the colourful independent MP for Namaqualand and a former Nationalist, together with Louis Karovsky, had founded the *Nasionale Werkers en Boerebond* (National Workers and Farmers Union), an organisation aimed at garnering the support of workers and farmers against the National Party.[73] Karovsky had been a long-time supporter of the 'Pact' government, and Steenkamp, a *predikant* (clergyman) and a United States-trained medical doctor, was well known and hugely respected in the region. Much to his chagrin, Malan believed Steenkamp was attracting Jewish support and making mischief against the backdrop of the Quota Act and the evolving economic crisis.

After touring the sparsely populated region, Malan spelled out his concerns in an interview with *Die Burger*, claiming that Steenkamp was being aided by a group of Jews bent on revenge for the Quota Act. The fact that Jews comprised a mere handful of the region's voting population was of little importance in his eyes.[74] Fearing Steenkamp's popularity, Malan was determined to manipulate the issue by harnessing a festering anti-Jewish feeling.[75] In forthright terms, he told *Die Burger* that his party looked unfavourably on what it saw as Jewish agitation around the Act. He had visited the northwestern Cape Province, where he had found that Steenkamp was well supported by Jews because of their anger at the Quota Act. They wanted revenge for the legislation but were afraid to come out into the open and instead made use of 'men such as Steenkamp'. Malan reiterated that the Quota Act had been introduced with the interest of Jews in mind because there had been opposition to the uncontrolled influx of eastern Europeans. He issued a warning that should Jewish opposition continue, he would ensure that, at the next election, every candidate would have to give a candid reply to the question of whether or not he favoured the repeal of the Quota Act. As Malan explained, 'it is very easy to rouse a feeling of hate towards the Jews in this country'.[76]

Malan's interview in *Die Burger* suggested an appetite for political opportunism that would characterise his behaviour throughout the 1930s and 1940s. Having spoken positively about the Jews at the time of the Quota Act, he was now fully prepared to turn against them. His comments threatened to become a national political issue; the interview certainly provided good copy for opponents of the Nationalists. An editorial in the *Star* castigated the minister for threatening 'Jews as a class with an official anti-Semitic programme if they do not support the Nationalist Party'. The newspaper was unable to recall 'a cruder piece of class animus or a more undignified and improper ministerial attitude in all the chequered annals of South Africa'.[77] In similar vein, the *Friend* described Malan's warning as 'political blackmail', contending that such a statement could 'only be construed as an attempt to buy off political opposition by threats of reprisals from the Government in power ... Since when has it been a crime, punishable with dire penalties, "to fight the Nationalists," as Dr Malan puts it, by constitutional means?'[78]

Predictably, the targets of Malan's comments were outraged. 'We are free citizens in a free country where we are entitled to express our opinions freely and to vote as we choose,' Morris Alexander told the *Cape Times*. 'As a people we belong to no particular political party ... But when any individual or any government attacks our status or our self-respect as a community, we unite irrespective of party to put the matter right.'[79] Addressing a luncheon a day later, Alexander spoke of the huge contribution Jews had made to South African trade and industry, mining and agriculture and how much South Africa owed to their 'brains, energy and patriotism'. Despite the threats levelled at them, Jewish South Africans would remain faithful to South Africa – their adopted home and motherland.[80]

One week after the Malan interview appeared in *Die Burger*, representatives of the Board met with him and outlined concerns with respect to the implementation of the Quota Act. These involved government plans to advance the operational date of the Act from 1 July to 1 May, an increased cost of naturalisation, and the threatened deportation of insolvents despite promises that 'Europeans' would be exempt from such action. The deputation also pointed out that 'a venomously antisemitic book', *The Riddle of the Jew's Success* by Theodor Fritsch (known as the 'Godfather of German antisemitism'), was being advertised in England with a letter from Malan's private secretary, Willem Louw, thanking the publisher for sending a copy to the minister. Louw's letter indicated that Malan had found the book very interesting and informative and that he appreciated the publisher's interest in South Africa's problems with regard to its Jewish citizens and the proposed government solution.[81]

The Board's two-hour meeting with Malan was cordial but frank, and the subsequent correspondence between the antagonists was widely reported and published in full in the *SAJC* and the *Zionist Record*.[82] Malan refuted the Board's concerns, contending that naturalisation fees had in fact declined since the National Party had come to office,[83] and that bringing the date of implementation of the Quota Act forward was aimed at preventing a flood of Jewish immigrants from entering South Africa at the last minute, which would have been very problematic. He also denied threatening Jewish opponents of the Quota Act or indeed Jewish opponents of the National Party. But he did reiterate his contention that a large sector of the Jewish community was using the negative feelings aroused by the Quota Act to discredit the government.[84] In his view, the Act was in the interest of Jews and represented a genuine attempt to avoid the creation of yet another racial problem in South Africa.[85] He claimed that the success of the legislation was already obvious, with a reduction in tensions and a discernible softening of anti-Jewish feeling, and warned that if Jews exploited anger at the Quota Act for party political purposes, this would only increase animosity against them. Malan did, however, indicate that he was pleased that the Board denied the existence of a large body of Jews organised for the purpose of defeating the National Party on account of the Quota Act.[86]

Further editorials devoted to the matter appeared in the Jewish and general press. The *Rand Daily Mail* remained hostile to Malan's 'deplorable' threats. 'It cannot be said that Dr Malan has done a great deal to eliminate the justifiable irritation aroused by his injudicious interview,' explained the daily. 'The Jews have made, and are making, an important contribution to the building up of this country.'[87] On the other hand, both *Die Burger* and *Die Volksblad*, the latter an Afrikaans newspaper also aligned to the National Party, refrained from commenting, although they did report in detail the exchange of correspondence between the Board and Malan and, implicitly, appeared satisfied with Malan's explanations.[88] Certainly *Ons Vaderland*, a Nationalist newspaper in the Transvaal, appreciated Malan's response.[89]

Widespread antagonism towards Jews obviously presented opportunities for party political gain.[90] This explosive dynamic was recognised by the *SAJC*. With impressive foresight, the weekly warned that 'if serious attention is to be paid to Dr Malan's strictures it would seem as if the possibility of the Jew becoming a pawn in the South African political game is not too remote'.[91] The *SAJC* was not alone in its forebodings. The *Zionist Record* refused to accept Malan's justifications and rationalisations – 'this specious, this insidious, this venomous propaganda' – and wrote of 'the sinister forces of racial prejudice into which a political virus has now also been injected'.[92] Interviewed by the same newspaper, Siegfried Raphaely confirmed that the Board was extremely concerned and would watch the situation carefully.[93]

Five weeks later, the Ninth Congress of the Board noted that South African Jews were becoming increasingly worried about their safety and wellbeing in these dangerous times. The situation – unparalleled in Jewish life in South Africa – needed to be carefully monitored.[94] A warm and cordial message from Prime Minister Hertzog to Congress did not deflect concern; speaker after speaker engaged with the 'Malan incident', some even questioning the Board's decision to have met with the minister. 'Here was a country known to be free, where Jews had always enjoyed freedom,' explained one delegate, 'and now anti-Semites could turn around and say that Dr Malan, the Minister of the Interior, had declared that it is easy to arouse a feeling of hatred against them.'[95]

Despite the concerns articulated at the Board's congress, Jewish unease in fact diminished as the year progressed. Aside from the formation in Cape Town of a 'Hitlerist Club' under the leadership of fifty-six-year-old German-born Hermann Bohle, a one-time lecturer in Electrical Engineering at Bradford Technical College in England and a Professor of Electronics at the University of Cape Town, there were few anti-Jewish manifestations.[96] The aim of Bohle's club, officially the '*Landesgruppe Südafrika* of the Nazi Party', was ostensibly to inform South Africans about the 'real' intentions of Hitler.[97] With only about 20 members – mainly new arrivals from Germany – the organisation made little impact, but the Jewish community nevertheless remained vigilant.[98] It was, for example, greatly perturbed by the introduction in parliament of the Potchefstroomse Universiteitskollege vir Christelike Hoer Onderwys (Private) Bill, which raised the possibility of not including a 'conscience clause' – a move that would permit religious discrimination. For the institution in question, the clause obstructed its Calvinist principles, but the initiative clearly threatened to exclude Jews from enrolling at the college.[99]

Still smarting from the Malan episode, Jewish leaders refrained from yet another confrontation, and in a communication to Alexander, the Board's new President, Hirsch Hillman, specifically requested that Alexander and his Jewish colleagues in parliament lie low on the matter.[100] However, the pugnacious Alexander (a man who made up in intellect what he lacked in height) made it clear that the Jewish MPs would challenge the Bill: 'If we neglect our duty for fear of our enemies, we shall justly be regarded with contempt and will be playing into the hands of anti-Semites. All they would have to do in future is to threaten us, if we dare to defend ourselves, and so have a clear field for their work.'[101]

In a spirited stand, Alexander challenged the discriminating intent of the Bill, but to no avail.[102] Although many parliamentarians shared his concerns, Alexander's proposal to include a 'conscience clause' was defeated in the second reading by 63 votes to 45 and thereafter suspended until the following year.[103] During the debate, Reverend Marthinus Fick, the National Party member for Potchefstroom who had introduced the Bill, took exception to Jewish concerns and made it quite clear that South Africa was a Christian country:

> If the Jew has that suspicion of us, then we on our side also have the right to have a suspicion of him. If the Jew wishes to harm us thereby, he must bear in mind that by doing so he will get the worst of it in the matter. He must not touch the tender chord with the Afrikaner by saying that he is afraid of the word 'Christian'. As the Minister of Education has said, 95 per cent of our population has Christian tendencies. What position might not we have been in if the situation had been reversed and if the Jews had a 95 per cent majority?[104]

Fick's tone reaffirmed the reason for the vulnerability felt by Jewish leaders, which was no doubt reinforced by offensive letters concerning Jewish immigration appearing in the press.[105] Some comfort was drawn from a meeting between Prime Minister Hertzog and some of his ministers with Hillman to discuss issues of mutual concern.[106] A message from Malan to the Jewish community, published in the 1932 *South African Rosh Hashana Annual*, further assuaged Jewish sensitivities, containing as it did assurances that relations between Jews and other South Africans had in fact improved. Malan's assessment was corroborated by Kentridge, a man always alert to slights directed at the Jewish community. 'In South Africa,' he wrote, 'we have had little cause yet to complain of the evils of anti-Semitism. While unfortunately it is not entirely absent and has, on occasion, flared up, its progress has been slow and has during the past twelve months even been arrested.'[107]

Notwithstanding Malan's encouraging Jewish New Year message and Kentridge's guarded optimism, the economic, political and social turmoil in the wake of the global financial crisis provided ideal conditions for those seeking to scapegoat the Jew. Indeed, in addition to his cautiously sanguine message about declining antisemitism, Kentridge had also warned that it was necessary to 'foster the spirit of liberalism and bring about economic revival, especially as the lesson of Jewish history is that racialism, illiberalism and economic depression have always proved fertile soil for anti-Semitism'.[108]

Public attention at this time, however, was focused on the debate over the gold standard. Britain's decision to withdraw from gold in September 1931 had left South African exports hugely overvalued, but Hertzog and his fellow Nationalists were reluctant to follow the lead of the mother country. They were also tired of kowtowing to the Chamber of Mines, long seen by them as the symbol of *geldmag*, or money power, and personified in the figure of Hoggenheimer. Going off the gold standard, argued some, would also have inflationary implications. Adding fuel to the fire was the fact that subsidies to the farming industry had failed to relieve rural distress, greatly exacerbated by the worst drought in living memory.

On 16 December 1932, Tielman Roos re-entered the political arena. In a dramatic Dingaan's Day speech, the mercurial judge called for the formation of a government of national unity and the abandonment of the gold standard.[109] Drawing large and enthusiastic crowds, the former Minister of Justice moved from town to town threatening to bring down the government.[110] Although his message electrified the stock exchange, as foreign investors sought equities and short-term profits, capital fled the country in anticipation of South Africa's withdrawal from the gold standard and the recovery of sterling. Banks were now in crisis and pressure on the National Party was enormous.

Less than two weeks after Roos' initial appeal to abandon the gold standard, finance minister Nicolaas (Klasie) Havenga made the unexpected announcement that South Africa had indeed done so. The next day, in his New Year's address, a despondent and humiliated Hertzog lamented that he had been forced to yield to the 'money power' and organised finance.[111] It was an accusation built upon a long-standing Afrikaner antipathy (deeply rooted in Calvinist culture) towards the conspiratorial financial sector.[112] *Die Burger's* well-known cartoonist, DC Boonzaier, reinforced the message in three powerful cartoons, each illustrating the power of Hoggenheimer, the cigar-puffing Jew.[113] A strident anti-capitalism was now being comfortably fused with a rising antisemitism.[114]

Behind the scenes, Roos continued to plot the creation of a new national government under his leadership. Threatening enough dissident support to bring down the 'Pact' government, he did his best to draw Smuts into a proposed new government as his deputy. But Roos' initiatives backfired. Recognising growing despair and calls for devolution among his British-oriented (mainly Natalian) party colleagues, Smuts had reluctantly drawn closer to his Anglo-Boer War comrade-in-arms, Hertzog. The National Party leader, in turn, aware of tensions within his own republican-oriented ranks and the real prospect of losing the next election, agreed to crisis talks.[115] Principles were rapidly hammered out by negotiators in February 1933, and one month later Smuts was able to tell a packed public meeting in Cape Town that he and Hertzog had agreed that their parties would form a coalition to fight the forthcoming general election, set for May.[116]

Malan was unhappy with his party's decision and made it clear that he would not serve in the new cabinet. In the May election, easily won by the coalition, he was opposed in his own constituency by Antonetta Steenkamp, the wife of his Namaqualand *bête noire*.[117] Although he was successfully returned, Malan remained uneasy.[118] Coalition sat heavily with him. His eye was on a surging republican-inclined Afrikaner *völkisch* sentiment, originally nurtured under the leadership of Hertzog's breakaway National Party (founded in 1914). The more powerful republican and anti-imperial strains of this nationalism had been dampened during the 'Pact' years.[119] But these passions were now reignited and would be harnessed by Malan under more propitious circumstances. The economic crisis had subverted the status quo and had prepared the way for a reordering of the South African body politic. And this occurred at the very time Adolf Hitler was appointed Chancellor of Germany.

A RISING TIDE OF ANTISEMITISM

Even before Hitler became Chancellor in January 1933, Jews in South Africa had been monitoring the unfolding Nazi agenda through the 'Jewish World' section in the *SAJC*, which regularly reported on what it termed 'Hitlerism', effectively meaning the vicious unfolding of Nazism.[120] Articles on events in Germany and other European countries, notably Poland and Romania, reported virulent antisemitism that unequivocally demonstrated the precarious situation of European Jewry. 'We are concerned today with the fate of German Jewry,' noted a prescient editorial in the *SAJC* shortly after Hitler's accession to power. 'Tomorrow we may have to feel no less concern for other Jewries.'[121] But the weekly remained optimistic that the civilised world would not allow 600 000 German Jews to become 'the victims of the Nazi beast of prey'.[122] The *Zionist Record* was equally perturbed. On the eve of the boycott of Jewish businesses in Germany, on 1 April 1933, the newspaper expressed forebodings of imminent tragedy.[123]

While the South African Party-aligned press generally shared these concerns,[124] the Nationalist press remained equivocal. In some quarters there was sympathy for the Nazis. Aware of and often concurring with this sentiment, the government urged Jews not to react and to refrain from public comment for the time being.[125] Nevertheless the Board did issue a statement deploring the discriminatory acts against German Jews, but it made little impact on a media concerned first and foremost with domestic matters.[126] This was a period of high political drama, with ongoing threats from Malan to break away from the coalition as the National Party and South African Party moved inexorably towards fusion.

Nationalist empathy with Hitler's Germany was rooted in long-standing Afrikaner ties with that country, dating back to Paul Kruger's republic in the late nineteenth century and, more recently, to resentment at Germany's

treatment by the victors at Versailles in 1919. Many were prepared to dis-
count stories of discrimination against Jews, as well as rumours of far worse
to come. Indeed, Hertzog told an election rally in Potchefstroom that a
real revolution was in progress in Germany and 'they would find, in a few
years that it had been to the benefit not only of Germany, but of the whole
world'.[127] On the same night that Hertzog spoke in Potchefstroom, a meeting to express sympathy with Germany's Jews, convened by the mayor of
Johannesburg, Bertie Vickers, was turned into a rowdy and chaotic affair by
Nazi sympathisers,[128] while earlier in the day scurrilous anti-Jewish pamphlets were distributed around the city.[129]

Die Vaderland took exception to the Johannesburg meeting and lashed
out at Vickers for hosting the occasion. Echoing Hertzog's distrust of media
reports, the newspaper wrote of the 'alleged atrocities' in Germany and
expressed surprise that several Afrikaners participated in what it described
as an ill-considered Johannesburg demonstration. But the newspaper –
capturing a rather sinister mindset – also alluded to what it termed a far
more serious aspect: 'Apart from Israelites, our Union is also inhabited by a
large German element, and by Afrikaners approximately 65 per cent of the
blood in whose veins is reckoned to be German.' In addition, the newspaper
accused Jews of being unpatriotic or of avoiding naturalisation as South
African citizens, in which case as foreign subjects they could expect no
political status. Therefore they should desist from activities that prejudiced
other South African citizens. Failing that, there could be dire consequences
for their actions.[130]

Shortly after Die Vaderland's warning, the executive of the Board met
with the Prime Minister to place before him Jewish concerns about the
German situation. Hertzog was rather unsympathetic and once again
expressed unhappiness about persistent local Jewish agitation against Germany, including alleged calls for a boycott of German goods.[131] He also
criticised another protest meeting that had been held in Cape Town in late
May under the auspices of the mayor of the city, Henry Stephan,[132] and told
Jewish leaders that he hoped their sectional concerns would not jeopardise
government actions that were in the interest of all South Africans.[133]

Despite these differences and obvious tensions, Hertzog conveyed his greetings and best wishes to the Tenth Congress of the Board. His rather bland statement repeated the government's position: Jewish citizens, as well as those of other races, had to give the government their fullest support and cooperation, particularly at this troubled time in world history.[134] Here was a veiled reference to the alleged Jewish-led boycott of German goods. Indeed, a few weeks later, the veil was lifted in another formal statement from Hertzog that once again spelled out the government's position vis-à-vis Germany. Noting with concern the adverse reaction from some quarters in South Africa to events in Germany, the government wished to point out that Germany was 'in the throes of a revolution' and at such a time the innocent sometimes had to suffer alongside the guilty. In any event, the way in which a state chose to treat its citizens was an internal matter, and outside interference might only exacerbate the problem. As for advocating an economic boycott of Germany, this could indeed have dangerous consequences, especially in South Africa's current economically depressed times. Hertzog's statement concluded with a warning to South African Jews to desist from 'attempting to alleviate the condition of the members of their own race in Germany … and to abstain, in word and action, from anything that may harm the Union'.[135]

No doubt reflecting the Jewish community's anger, the *SAJC* was outraged that the Prime Minister's statement did not mention the victims of Nazism. Nor was there 'a single word of condemnation for any of those actions which the civilised world has condemned and which the Nazis themselves have never denied'.[136] But Hertzog had to tread a difficult line. Besides South Africa's long-standing ties with Germany, by the mid-1930s Germany was the country's third-largest trading partner.[137] Hertzog, moreover, was cognisant of a rising tide of local anti-Jewish sentiment: the hostile anti-Jewish comments that emerged in the Carnegie investigations; the attempt by local Nazis to break up an anti-German protest meeting in Johannesburg;[138] and widely disseminated anti-Jewish propaganda[139] that included a call on Christians to deal only with other Christians because Jews were dominating the professions and the economy.[140] Hermann Bohle's Landesgruppe Südafrika was now established in larger cities,[141] and a pamphlet, 'The Jew and the Farmer', informed farmers in the Orange

Free State, the northern Cape Province and the southeastern part of the Transvaal of nefarious Jewish plans on a global scale. 'The Jew is hostile to the farmer,' the pamphlet warned. 'He may cajole the farmer and fawn upon him, but all the while is working to ruin him. Why? ... Because farmers constitute a class that stands between Jewry and the completion of Communist "world-domination" (such as the Jew has already achieved in Russia).'[142] Attitudes were palpably hardening. 'The hydra-head of anti-Semitism is beginning to show its fangs in South Africa,' warned the *Zionist Record*. It exhorted its readers not to bury their heads in the sand but to confront the evil vigorously and courageously.[143]

Even more worrying than domestic anti-Jewish manifestations, however, was the known Nazi activity in South West Africa, the former German colony mandated to South Africa by the League of Nations.[144] As early as 1929, Major Heinrich Weigel had established a National Socialist party in the territory and from 1933 worked with the Nazi Party's *Auslands-Organisation* (Foreign Organisation) in Germany, headed by Ernst Wilhelm Bohle, the son of Hermann Bohle.[145] One of its objectives was to enrol *Reichsdeutsche* (German citizens) and *Volkdeutsche* (former German citizens and ethnic Germans) in the local Nazi party,[146] and both groups were targets of a concerted and successful propaganda campaign.[147] A lengthy article on the subject in the *SAJC* reported that swastikas had been painted on the premises of Jewish shops and the country flooded with antisemitic literature, printed in both English and German, emanating from Germany and distributed by local Nazis.[148] This activity was confirmed by Morris Alexander in a letter to Percy Niehaus (an executive member of the South West African administration) in which he repeated a specific case where two women and three young men in Nazi uniform were sent from Germany to organise the Nazi movement in South West Africa.[149]

Amid growing calls to clamp down on Nazi activities, the South African government began to monitor developments closely in South West Africa, and on 3 August 1933 an ordinance was passed enabling the mandate administration to take control of the situation.[150] Despite efforts by Nazi sympathisers to prevent the government from countenancing the promulgation of the ordinance, the cabinet agreed to its enactment and the government began gathering information on Nazi activity in the territory.[151] But this did not stop propaganda material rapidly finding its way into South Africa and being distributed to local sympathisers.[152]

DOMESTIC REVERBERATIONS

Further evidence of the Nazi impact on domestic politics was vividly brought home by a raucous meeting held at the Koffiehuis, a well-known Cape Town meeting place for politicians situated next to the Groote Kerk in Church Square, only a short walk from parliament. The basement venue acted as an informal Afrikaner club, a meeting place for social, cultural and political interaction. Students and writers regularly met in this agreeable setting on Saturday mornings for coffee and a chat. However, on the night of 26 October 1933 it was a less refined crowd – in fact, an exuberant gathering of about 200 – that heard a disillusioned Louis Theodore Weichardt launch the South African Christian National Socialist Movement, later popularly known as the 'Greyshirts'.[153]

The evening opened on a relatively sober note with the rather elderly chairman, Johannes van Ginkel, explaining that the movement set out to be non-partisan and wholly South African. If its intentions were in any way geared to incite race-hatred or create trouble, he certainly would not be party to it. But the tone changed markedly when the thirty-nine-year-old Weichardt – tall, trim and clean-cut – took to the floor and delivered an address more akin to a rant at a Hitlerian rally than the dulcet and gossipy tones usually heard in the Koffiehuis.

Outlining the aims of his new movement, Weichardt identified the Jews as a problem of the utmost importance to both English- and Afrikaans-speaking South Africans. His immediate target was the 'Jewish-owned press' that had been critical of National Socialism. Germany is 'just a sideline', he told an audience beginning to warm to his oratory: 'National Socialism is something so new that some people have been told and believed what I would call deliberate lies; lies concerning the occurrences in one of the most important countries of the world.' While not wanting to 'defend Germany's cause', he did wish 'to refer in some instances to what has happened in that country owing to the lies that have been circulated; tales which make it difficult for you to realise what Nationalist Socialism really stands for. Is there any sane man in the world that does not believe that Hitler would not have risen to power had not that great nation been trampled on by a certain race that will have to be brought to book?'

Now in his stride, Weichardt cut to the quick. He was opposed to persecution but, citing outrageously fabricated statistics, wondered why Jews were so massively overrepresented in the South African economy: 90 per cent of licensed hotels were in Jewish hands, as were 100 per cent of wholesale butcheries; 90 per cent of retail butcheries; 70 per cent of retailers; 100 per cent of theatres and bioscopes; 65 per cent of attorneys and advocates; 90 per cent of the press and radio; 70 per cent of the medical profession, and 100 per cent of the stock exchange, pawnbrokers and shareholders. Jews, Weichardt added, also controlled the gold mines and comprised 90 per cent of communist agitators. When he claimed that there were no 'poor white' Jews, that one per cent of carpenters and bricklayers were Jews, and that 'hard work' was for Jews 'a joke', the audience burst into laughter: 'I have travelled throughout South Africa and have found that in IDB [Illicit Diamond Buying] and IGB [Illicit Gold Buying] cases, the culprits are our people, but the ringleaders are the others.' Latching on to every word, the crowd needed little reminding who the others were; throughout the evening shouts of 'Peruvians', 'international gangsters', 'scoundrels' and 'rogues' – all derogatory references to Jews – punctuated the address.

Turning to South African politics, Weichardt vociferously blamed all political parties for not sticking to their election promises. His movement would not tolerate the present system of 'corrupt and rotted democracy.' Claiming that the Jews had won the Great War and were spoiling for another, Weichardt challenged anyone present to accuse him of encouraging violence; the reports of what was happening in Germany were fabrications, and the Jews needed to be put in their place. Amid rapturous applause he added: 'What objection can the Chosen Race have if I recommend a policy by which they would be happily settled in their own country? What, I ask you, is wrong in that we want to assist them in that direction? Healthy nationalism is nothing else but National Socialism. But a minority in this country has got the power in its hands by means of the Press, and is dragging you down to your knees.' Obviously concerned about the appellation 'socialist' in his organisation's name, Weichardt denied allegations that his movement was 'camouflaged Bolshevism' and assured his audience that it was his intention to proceed constitutionally. But it was the Jews who were stirring up hatred and were determined 'to crucify Christianity'.[154] All fired up and far from satiated, the audience posed enthusiastic questions from the floor at the conclusion of Weichardt's address. The meeting terminated with loud applause and some of the audience gave the Nazi salute.

Comment in the mainstream press was less than enthusiastic. A concerned editorial in the *Cape Times* noted that an investigation into Nazi activities was to take place in the United States and that it would be worthwhile doing the same in South Africa as a great deal of Nazi propaganda was circulating not only in the Union but in South West Africa as well. Prominent Germans, the editorial asserted, were visiting South West Africa and spreading mischievous propaganda all over the country that amounted to a particularly malignant form of antisemitism:

> Much of the language employed last night by Mr Weichardt at the Koffiehuis meeting, is an abominable abuse of the rights of free speech in South Africa. It is clownishly calculated to make appeal to the most inferior intellects, and it seeks to re-establish in this country, which has just succeeded in outgrowing a very destructive racialism of old standing a new type of racialism which is nothing more nor less than the Aryanism of Hitler, and is undoubtedly deriving its impetus and its propaganda from Nazi sources in Germany ... A certain number of Nazi fanatics in this country – some of them hailing from Germany and under the spell of Hitlerism – are conducting a very pestilent form of racial incitement against the Jewish citizens of South Africa in the collective sense as well as against individuals.[155]

The *Cape Argus* similarly castigated Weichardt, noting that while he insisted 'that the Jewish question is a sideline ... he can talk of nothing else. He employs blood-curdling threats against the Jew – but he is all against persecution and would fight anybody who advocates it. He would put the Jews "in their place" – but strictly in accordance with the dictates of justice, Weichardtian justice.'[156] Similarly scathing, the *Natal Mercury* noted rather ominously that, over the past weeks, poisonous anti-Jewish propaganda had been promoted by anonymous messages left in various places.[157]

But it was not only the English-language press that lambasted Weichardt's agenda. An editorial in *Die Burger* entitled 'Die Jode' (The Jews) considered his initiative to be a political movement foreign to the nature of South African politics: 'There is not a single abuse of which a Jew has been guilty which is not found in a wider circle. No abuse can be pinned to the Jews as a race. And if abuses must be dealt with, it is quite possible to deal with them in such a way that there is no discrimination between races.' The newspaper was confident that the Quota Act passed three years earlier had been the correct way to deal with the Jewish influx that, it suggested, underpinned Weichardt's concerns. It was also confident that there would not be a great influx of Jews from Germany, claiming quite erroneously that, because most German Jews had been born in eastern Europe, they would be blocked by the Quota Act.[158]

Reinforcing the view that the National Party would not tolerate the sort of rabble-rousing heard at the Koffiehuis, *Die Kerkbode*, the official organ of the Dutch Reformed Church, devoted an editorial to the matter of anti-Jewish propaganda.[159] Even if Weichardt's statistics showed a pre-ponderance of Jews in the economy, criminal activity could be controlled by laws that were not based on race or colour, maintained the journal. And while acknowledging that some Jewish immigrants were not a positive acquisition to the country, it reminded readers that the Quota Act had been introduced precisely for this reason. But, noted the editor, these were not the kind of Jewish immigrants who Weichardt was attacking. Rather it was successful professionals and businessmen who were the real targets of the propagandist. The editorial then went on to list a range of Jews who had contributed enormously to the country's development.[160]

These mainstream responses to Weichardt were encouraging for the Jewish community, as was an official statement published only a few days after the Weichardt launch in which Smuts – Minister of Justice in the recently formed coalition government – issued a warning about the menace of antisemitism, which encouraged ill-feeling and stoked racial prejudice. He allowed for the possibility that some charges might be personal expressions of animosity, but there were indications of an organised campaign to foster race and class hostility in South Africa. Smuts pointed to the origins and importation of antisemitic prejudices from abroad and expressed the government's determination to prevent the 'transplantation of this poisonous weed to South Africa'. He issued a warning to South Africans that, if they wished to stay out of any future trouble, they should avoid 'this movement which, under various political or economic disguises, is really of a most sinister and dangerous character …'[161]

Smuts' stern statement arose out of a meeting with a Board of Deputies delegation held three weeks before the launch of Weichardt's movement. The Board had met with him and Colonel Isaac Pierre de Villiers, the Commissioner of Police, to express the anxiety felt by South African Jews at the growth of anti-Jewish sentiment, and requesting authorities to intervene and protect the community against the poisonous lies being circulated.[162] At this meeting Smuts had promised to take action and the Board in turn had agreed to follow a policy of restraint, appealing to Jewish communal bodies and the Jewish community in general to abstain from any act of reprisal.[163] This was clearly a reference to Jewish groups supposedly organising anti-German boycotts and disrupting meetings of the radical right, both issues of concern to the government.

Although Smuts' statement went some way to pacifying Jewish concerns,[164] a special meeting convened by the Board nevertheless agreed to initiate a counter-propaganda campaign.[165] Pressure was building up from within the Jewish community, against a backdrop of ongoing anti-Jewish gatherings, pamphleteering, rumours that Johannesburg firms were dismissing Jewish employees,[166] and the flood of Nazi literature being brought into the country on German ships.[167] The elderly Reverend Alfred Philipp Bender, spiritual leader of the Cape Town Hebrew Congregation, told the *Cape Argus* that, as well as outrages in the Transvaal and other parts of South Africa, swastikas had been chalked on trees in the garden and outhouse of a prominent Jew in Port Elizabeth. He also referred to defamatory anti-

Jewish notices being pasted in public library books, on public notice boards, outside homes and on railway carriages.[168]

Only a day after Weichardt's meeting at the Koffiehuis, a pro-Nazi meeting had been held in Woodstock, at which, reported the *Cape Times*, thousands of leaflets printed in English and Afrikaans and bearing Nazi slogans had been distributed. The chairman of a meeting had urged the killing of Jews.[169] Jewish children in Cape Town were even being taunted by non-Jewish children wearing swastikas,[170] and the *Zionist Record* reported that farmers were being stoked up by outrageous accusations of Jewish responsibility for all the difficulties experienced by the farming community.[171]

Among those entering the fray was Hermann Bohle. In a lengthy letter to the *Cape Times*, he denied that his movement was receiving Nazi propaganda, although he did admit to receiving a booklet of Hitler's speeches sent to him for distribution, as well as a compilation of comments on the Versailles Treaty produced by the Hamburg-based propaganda outfit, the Fichtebund, but published in Port Elizabeth. 'Let the Jews drop all vilification of Germany and the boycott and give her a chance of settling down and finding work for millions of unemployed, and things will soon become normal,' wrote Bohle. 'Revolutions always cause hardship. The cruelties of the Hitler regime towards the Jews have been dinned into our ears, and thrown into our eyes almost daily. Has any Jew in any South African paper ever analysed the Russian Revolution, instigated principally by 271 Commissioners, of whom 232 were Jewish?'[172]

Escalating anti-Jewish feeling appeared with great regularity in many parts of South Africa.[173] In Durban, Harold Dold, the scion of a well-known family of German origin and a self-styled 'industrial' candidate in the Umbilo by-election, associated himself with the Greyshirts.[174] When asked about his attitude towards Jews during one of his campaign outings, Dold, among other antisemitic accusations, spuriously claimed that something would have to be done to prevent Jews transferring money from South Africa to another country. As Percivale Liesching in the British High Commissioner's office reported: 'No sooner had the echoes of Mr Weichardt's meeting at the Koffiehuis died away than a band of "Greyshirts" were discovered clicking their heels and sawing the air with their hands at Durban under the leadership of Mr Harold Dold.'[175]

As 1933 drew to a close, the *Zionist Record* lamented that a range of organisations was stirring up antagonism towards Jews through public meetings. This was a recent departure from hitherto more private activities – symptomatic of a new feeling of freedom to express hostile anti-Jewish sentiments without incurring official public condemnation.[176] The *Friend* too acknowledged increased public interest in the Greyshirts, with numerous letters landing on its desk both for and against the organisation. However, the newspaper expressed confidence that the government would deal with the matter.[177]

There can be little doubt that the disaffected and alienated, across language lines, sought inspiration from events in Germany. Even the stance of *Die Kerkbode* on Jew-baiting, in the wake of Weichardt's Cape Town launch, was challenged by readers who did not share its anti-Weichardt editorial line.[178] Anonymous letters to the weekly provided a taste of what was to come from within church circles, as well as a glimpse of the storm clouds on the horizon. 'Vrystater' claimed that Jews controlled the resources of South Africa and dominated the Afrikaners who were bankrupt, and he hoped God would open the eyes of the Afrikaner and that they would stop supporting the Jews.[179] 'Plattelander' was angry that *Die Kerkbode* highlighted Jewish concerns while ignoring the victimisation of Germans in South Africa, and warned that Jews posed a serious danger to the *volk*. They were responsible for the ruination of many young girls, dominated business, lived off the fat of the land and were behind the Jameson Raid, the Anglo-Boer War and Afrikaner poverty.[180]

Such criticisms were reinforced at a biennial meeting of the Dutch Reformed Church Synod in Bloemfontein only a short while after the above two letters appeared. Exception was taken to *Die Kerkbode*'s editorial stance, with the Reverend H Botha suggesting that the Church should spell out what it thought about the Jews and their influence on South Africa. The question was urgent and it was incumbent on the Church to express its opinion on the matter 'in a Christian way'.[181]

FILLING A POLITICAL VACUUM

By early 1934 a vacuum had developed in South African politics. Having left the gold standard but still in crisis, there was a discernible sense of malaise and inaction within the administration. Amid a problematic economic situation, the Hertzog-Smuts coalition appeared to provide little hope for malcontents. Huge disparities in wealth existed between English-speakers and Afrikaners, with the latter poorly represented in white-collar occupations and in the professions.[182] Anger was easily displaced onto the Jew. 'It is difficult for a non-Jew to realise the gravity of the situation which is being created,' wrote 'JS' to the *Rand Daily Mail* only a week after swastikas had been painted on the walls of a synagogue in Benoni: 'It is not so much fear of any material injury that causes distress to South African Jewry as the fact that a considerable number of hooligans throughout this country should be permitted to slander, blackguard and heap unspeakable insults on the Jewish sector of the South African population.'[183]

This danger was also recognised by the liberal South African Institute of Race Relations, which invited Morris Alexander to speak on the obviously burning question of antisemitism at its annual general meeting in Cape Town.[184] The occasion allowed the respected parliamentarian to share his views on an issue that had dominated the Jewish agenda for some time. 'This anti-Jewish propaganda is the biggest and most mischievous thing that has ever come to South Africa,' Alexander told the meeting. He hoped that the Institute of Race Relations, 'whose purpose is the establishment of inter-racial goodwill, will help to work against it'. He maintained that an outright war against Jews was going on. 'We are up against a dangerous racial campaign which goes far beyond mere bitterness …'[185]

This was dramatic language from the usually phlegmatic Jewish leader, who reiterated his concerns in an interview with the *SAJC* shortly after his speech to the Institute. Here he was even more precise about the scourge and extent of antisemitism: 'Meetings are being regularly held throughout the Eastern and Western Province, the Free State and other parts of South Africa where the vilest libels against the Jewish people are being circulated, and where naked, racial hatred is being shown in all its very worst manifestations.' Alexander spoke of one anti-Jewish organisation in the Transvaal that was advocating the cancellation of citizenship of all South African Jews. An antisemitic meeting in Stellenbosch on 5 December 1933 had been attended by 800 people and another at Moorreesburg had attracted 400 people. Frequent meetings had also been held at Parow and Malmesbury, while boycotts had been attempted in Woodstock. Some school magazines contained articles signed by pupils lauding the work of Hitler, and there were instances of schoolchildren wearing swastikas with the intent of distinguishing themselves from the Jewish children. Alexander also mentioned attempts to propagandise among 'non-Europeans', but two prominent leaders, Dr Abdullah Abdurahman and Tengo Jabavu, had indicated that they had no desire to be a part of the agitation.[186] Alexander spelt out his concerns in no uncertain way: 'The idea is being steadily fostered by our enemies that it would be a good thing to get rid of the Jews, as this would mean cancellation of all debts owed to Jews, confiscation of money in banks owed them, liquidation of their businesses and properties, all of which would become the property of themselves.'[187]

Well-attended radical right meetings, at which Jews were the chief target, continued apace during early 1934, with some ending in violence when opponents – among them young Jews – turned up to disrupt events.[188] Vrededorp, a poor Johannesburg neighbourhood, saw two ugly and violent meetings within a fortnight. 'We are going to be attacked tonight by Jews or Communists', said G Mulligan, who opened proceedings at the first mass meeting in Vrededorp, convened (outdoors) by the *Suid-Afrikaanse Nasionale Demokratiese Beweging* (South African National Democratic Movement, known as the 'Blackshirts'), another anti-Jewish movement founded by Hermanus (Manie) Wessels and Chris Havemann in December 1933.[189] The two speakers, Wessels and Havemann, told a 500-strong audience that the Jews were foreigners who were attempting 'to establish an oligarchy with Afrikaners as nothing but wage slaves'.[190] According to a report in the *Zionist Record*, Jews were denounced as 'unwanted foreigners who were contaminating the South African people and underpaying the non-Jews who sweated for them. Jews had formed a world-wide conspiracy to gain control of the wealth of the world and direct it to pernicious ends.' The newspaper reported that Mulligan had referred to the *Protocols of the Elders of Zion* to bolster his accusations of a Jewish conspiracy to overthrow Western civilisation. According to Mulligan, there was only one way to deal with Jews, and that was to follow the example of Hitler.[191]

Two weeks later, another meeting in Vrededorp organised by the Blackshirts drew an audience of some 2000 people. This time the tense crowd had sticks and stones in case of assaults. Once again, speakers attacked what they identified as the Jewish stranglehold on commerce and spoke of retrieving the birthright of English- and Afrikaans-speaking South Africans.[192] The Blackshirt programme included, *inter alia*, opposition to destructive international economic and cultural influences that were undermining national life, and demanded 'South Africa for the nationally minded Christian aryan'. The Blackshirts also adopted the principle of 'strict prevention of immigration especially that of Semitics or Asiatics' and 'the cancellation of the existing citizenship of the Jew'.[193]

These were tense days, exacerbated by events in Germany. After Weichardt's Greyshirts paraded through the streets of Port Elizabeth calling for a boycott of Jewish storekeepers, the Jewish community put out a statement requesting support from public leaders.[194] According to the *Zionist Record*'s special correspondent, Greyshirt activity had increased in the coastal city following the closure of a number of important large factories.[195] A short while later, Weichardt addressed a meeting at the city's Feather Market Hall, hosted by the Greyshirts' Port Elizabeth Division and presided over by the mayor. Ostensibly a protest against undesirable immigrants, the occasion turned nasty, with hecklers and 'Greyshirtists' engaging in bloody brawls, while others in the crowd sang 'Rule, Britannia' in response to those giving Nazi salutes.[196] 'Pandemonium reigned', reported the *Eastern Province Herald*, with blood flowing freely.[197]

This was Weichardt's first address in the 'Friendly City', and it was one redolent with antisemitism. The Greyshirt leader claimed that while he believed there had to 'be decent Jews in South Africa', he had difficulty finding them. 'A man had come to him and said that he was a decent Jew. He had answered that he hoped so; but why didn't he come forward as leader of the decent Jews and say that they as decent Jews of South Africa definitely discounted the low moral code of the other section.' This

Greyshirt mass meeting. This photograph originally appeared in *Die Suiderstem* and was reproduced in *Common Sense* in January 1941.

anecdote drew loud applause. Weichardt went on to speak about Albert Einstein, whom he claimed to have heard lecture in Berlin, describing him as nothing more than a communist and an advocate of Bolshevism. His own movement, he asserted, was bent on fighting communism. Spelling out the constitution and programme of the Greyshirts, he told the excited crowd that aliens who had entered the country from 1918 onwards would have to relinquish their South African nationality. With clever wordplay, Weichardt also made it clear that he did not 'believe in the confusion or fusion party', a reference to widespread talk that Smuts' South African Party and Hertzog's National Party were planning to move beyond a coalition and merge or fuse into a single party. His movement 'wanted the truest fusion of all South African Gentiles'; they did not want 'the Kantrovskys' who were behind the merger. Even the boycott campaign of German goods by the Jews, he claimed, was a scam to attract more business. 'It had been "Boycott Germany and buy from me."'[198]

By now the radical right, employing the symbols and rhetoric of German fascists, had attracted substantial attention in the wider community. In May 1934, the Blackshirts put out a flyer focusing on alleged Jewish economic and financial oppression of the Christian Afrikaner *volk*,[199] and the

43

general press devoted much space to the turn of events in both South West Africa and South Africa.[200] This flurry of anti-Jewish activities and meetings predictably led to Jewish leaders' calling for the invocation of the Riotous Assemblies and Criminal Law Amendment Act of 1914, section 7, which deemed it a common law offence to incite probable violence through speech or publication.[201] In the House of Assembly, the South African Party's Leila Reitz asked justice minister Smuts if the government was paying attention to 'the riots and disturbances at Port Elizabeth and Johannesburg arising out of meetings called by certain individuals at which speeches of a violently anti-Semitic nature were made'. The minister replied that the police were watching the movement closely and would take steps necessary to maintain law and order.[202]

Smuts' response confirmed the gravity of the situation, an assessment shared by a senior member of the South African Party, the Scottish-born Patrick Duncan. 'The Nazi fever is infecting us here,' he informed his close friend Lady Maud Selborne. Local Germans were 'organising themselves under a "führer" who takes orders from Hitler − or is supposed to. In this Union it also takes the form of an anti-Semitic agitation, not open but widespread, and not specially German as to its field. The Jews are beginning to take alarm and that of course adds fuel to the fire. The poor old world is full of fevers and shakes.'[203]

FROM THE PRIVATE TO THE PUBLIC

Antisemitism was moving from the sphere of ideas into the party-political realm. Certainly prior to the launch of Weichardt's South African Gentile National Socialist Movement, anti-Jewish ideas had been articulated essentially at the level of iconography and stereotypes.[204] These tropes had now become a part of public discourse and politics, no doubt fuelled by the Hitler 'revolution' and aided, at least to some extent, by propaganda from Germany. But Weichardt's rhetoric and that of others resonated precisely because a widely shared negative Jewish stereotype had been firmly laid in the preceding decades. Ideas that characterised Jews as a people apart, dominating the economy at the expense of the marginalised, were now being rehashed from platforms across the country. The message appealed in particular to young, restive and disaffected Afrikaans- and English-speakers who lacked a political home now that the 'Pact' government had crumbled and for whom the coalition was considered to hold out no prospects. The Jew was an easy and obvious scapegoat. Hoggenheimer was seen to be acting against the interests of the majority in general and the Afrikaner in particular. Suspicion of big capital ran deep and increasingly informed the outlook of Malan's Nationalists.[205] Even Hertzog, as noted earlier, had acknowledged succumbing to the 'money power' at the time of South Africa's withdrawal from the gold standard.

On the positive side, the government did not minimise the potential dangers of antisemitism. As the keynote speaker at the laying of the cornerstone of the Sea Point Synagogue in Cape Town, Smuts expressed the government's concern and assured those present that Jews would continue to enjoy equal rights and just treatment and had no reason to fear the future. Those sowing dissension, he assured them, would fail.[206] He must have recognised the fertile social conditions in South Africa for the cloning of European fascism, which he detested and feared.[207] This reality was well understood by AZ Berman, a Jewish left-wing Cape Town city councillor. He told a Zionist Socialist Party meeting that 'Nationalism such as was reflected in fascism was moulded out of the concept of unity. That was why it necessarily implied anti-Semitism ... There would always be Jews scattered all over the world regarded as "different" from the people among whom they lived. If fascism arose they were bound to be persecuted in the name of "unity".'[208]

The Jew as an outsider, an alien in the body politic, was increasingly perceived as an unwelcome component of South African society. Even a meeting hostile to the radical right – that of the Golden Valley Branch Divisional Council of the South African Party – tabled a resolution expressing its anxiety about Jewish immigration. Deeply concerned about the rise in antisemitism, it called for further restrictions on the number of eastern European Jews entering the country to prevent their posing a threat to the white population.[209] This explanation for anti-Jewish hostility would continue to inform South African discourse, particularly when it became evident that German Jews (who were untouched by the provisions of the Quota Act) were entering the country. With a serious 'poor white' problem and Afrikaner nationalism in the ascendant, antisemitism would flourish, as Berman had pointedly warned.

In June 1934 Afrikaner nationalism gained impetus with the *samesmelting*, or 'fusion', of the National Party and South African Party into the United South African National Party, better known as the United Party, or UP. The merger, formalised six months later, proved too much for the mainly Cape-based Afrikaner nationalists led by Malan and strongly supported by three parliamentarians: Nicolaas (Nico) van der Merwe (MP for Winburg), Charles Robberts (Blackie) Swart (MP for Ladybrand) and Johannes Gerhardus (Hans) Strijdom (MP for Waterberg). Angered at the turn of events, they broke ranks with the National Party to form the *Gesuiwerde* (Purified) National Party under Malan.[210] There was 'only one kind of *hereniging* [reunion] that Malan cared anything about', noted the writer and public intellectual Alan Paton. 'That was the reunion of all true Afrikaners.'[211] From now on, Malan, the dour theologian turned politician, became the face of a chauvinistic and religiously inspired Afrikaner nationalism focused on the *volk*, the protection of 'white civilisation' and, ultimately, republicanism.[212] In the eyes of the *Gesuiwerdes*, Hertzog had undermined any semblance of Afrikaner sovereignty through his compromises with the Labour Party after the establishment of the 'Pact' government in 1924. It was anticipated that the newly created United Party government would deepen that betrayal by following a pro-imperial policy orchestrated by Hoggenheimer at the expense of Afrikaner interests. The soul of Afrikanerdom was at stake.[213]

This crisis had been recognised by Afrikaner intellectuals for some time. Organised around and propelled by the *Afrikaner Broederbond* (Band of Brothers), a largely Transvaal-based Afrikaner cultural movement founded in 1918, these ethnic entrepreneurs were active in coordinating initiatives to enhance the position of the Afrikaner. The Broederbond nurtured and inspired a nascent ethno-national movement aimed at inculcating in Afrikaners a deep love for their people and their history. Although riven with dissension in its early years, the organisation gave direction to the *volk* based on Christian principles.[214] The Calvinist clergymen and academics who dominated the organisation were especially dismayed at the mounting 'poor white' problem. 'There was a growing feeling among intellectual Afrikaners,' writes WA de Klerk, 'that the problem was getting out of hand; that soon a considerable part of Afrikanerdom would, economically and spiritually, be beyond redemption.'[215]

Five years earlier, in 1929, the *Federasie van Afrikaanse Kultuurvereenigings* (Federation of Afrikaans Cultural Organisations), or FAK – 'the public face of the Broederbond' – had been established to coordinate the many Afrikaner cultural organisations that had evolved against a backdrop of economic, social and political turmoil.[216] It combined a cultural nationalism, grounded in religion and tradition, with an emergent economic nationalism, particularly in the more conservative northern provinces. For example, the *Handhawersbond* (Union of Militant Defenders) was founded in 1930 on the Witwatersrand essentially to challenge those Afrikaners who wished to emulate the ways of Englishmen. With its slogan 'opsaal' (saddle up), and its symbol a clenched fist, the Handhawersbond demanded, with some initial success in the Transvaal, that business transactions be conducted in Afrikaans.[217]

Taking their lead from their elders, Afrikaner youth too imbibed the heady nationalist atmosphere. In late 1933, a group broke away from the English-dominated National Union of South African Students (NUSAS) to form the *Afrikaanse Nasionale Studentebond* (Afrikaner National Student Union, or ANS), under the leadership of Piet Meyer, a twenty-four-year-old student at the University of the Orange Free State. 'The Bond rests on a Christian-Protestant and cultural-national foundation and acknowledges the guidance of God in the sphere of culture as in every sphere of life,' noted the new movement's constitution. When the Jewish Students' Association organised a protest against their exclusion from the body, claiming that some Jewish students might prefer the principles of the Bond to NUSAS, and that religion should not be a defining factor, the secretary of the ANS told them they welcomed the pro-Afrikaans feeling existing among some Jewish students but that its constitution could not be changed. 'The Bond strongly recommends to Jewish students that they establish their own Jewish National Student Union in South Africa, with which the Bond would be pleased to cooperate on a federal basis.'[218]

Clearly a conflation of language, state and nation underpinned the *völkisch* mission. In an almost mystical manner, the FAK combined an ethnic exclusivism that built on an imagined past and a future vision. 'I believe the FAK is more than a mere organisation or organisation of organisations,' said Nico van der Merwe. 'I believe that it is a revelation of a living national organism, a self-conscious ethnic soul which ensures unity in strife.'[219]

ONWARD FASCIST SOLDIERS

By the time Malan's 'Purified' National Party was born in the wake of Fusion, Weichardt's Greyshirts and other groups on the radical right had for months enjoyed the exhilaration of freely trumpeting a domestic fascism powerfully laced with antisemitism. Filled with bluster and intoxicated with their own rhetoric and message, these extremists did their best to bring their ideas to the centre of South African politics. Meetings became increasingly ugly and violent, with a particularly fierce fracas in Paarl after Weichardt had been refused permission under the Riotous Assemblies Act to hold a meeting there. The Greyshirt leader met with followers initially in a private house and then went on to address a gathering from a truck in a public place, at which point the police broke up the meeting. The Greyshirts then started moving back to Cape Town, only to be attacked by a large group of Jews.[220]

At another meeting in Cape Town, Weichardt made it clear that his movement was bent on a 'constitutional revolution', but unlike Hitler, who took sixteen years to attain power, his revolution would, he believed, take three. 'We stand for the White Block in South Africa,' he explained. But this excluded aliens – an obvious reference to Jews – whom, he argued, were 'trying to oust Christianity'. The secretary of the Greyshirts, Frikkie du Toit, also focused on the Jews, referring to Smuts as the 'Jew in Parliament' and the 'Jews' King'.

The rash of anti-Jewish meetings spread throughout 1934. Small towns in particular hosted radical right gatherings where talk of boycotting Jewish traders was common.[221] A school in Zeerust debated whether the Jew or the Indian constituted the greatest menace for South Africa, and photographs of Hitler were distributed by a teacher at the same school.[222] In

Dalton, a village near Pietermaritzburg, the Natal Greyshirt leader, thirty-six-year-old horticulturalist Raymond Kirch (RK) Rudman – a coarse and rabid Jew-hater – told a largely farming audience of about 300 (estimated by the *Natal Witness* at 40 per cent German, 40 per cent English and 20 per cent Afrikaans) how Jews had their 'poison fangs' into South Africa. Quoting extracts from the *Protocols of the Elders of Zion*, the Uitenhage-born Rudman described Jews as 'snakes' who wished to enslave 'the goyim'. They intended:

> to conquer the world with the slyness of the symbolic snake, whose head is represented by the Chief Jews and the body of the snake, the Jewish people themselves ... One by one this accursed race of non-believers has laid countries low. They are one hundred per cent immoral and corrupt. Their women assist them and are the surest spreaders of licentiousness into the lives of leading men of every country.

Presenting grossly exaggerated figures to illustrate disproportionate Jewish control of the economy, Rudman informed his enthusiastic audience that their country's 'maize, primary industries, wheat, fruit and wool' were controlled by the Jew, who was also responsible for the 'poor white' problem. Obsessed with conspiratorial ideas, Rudman claimed that Jews had crept into the 'highest positions in the land' and that 'their breath taints and degrades every profession'. They preached free love, incited the 'Natives' and instigated war:

> While we are squabbling, Comrades, Ikey is rubbing his dirty greasy hands, and we are paying the price in blood and tears ... Every Jew is a skunk. There is not a good Jew. They are all evil and filthy. Every mother must warn her sons of the fate which is his by the hands of Zion and send her husband and sons out to fight this evil. I urge you, Comrades, forget your animosity, and British, Boer and German, come out together as one man and fight Judaism until we have strangled the snake and it lies dead at our feet. This is a religious fight. The fight for Christianity.

Praising Hitler and the Nazis, Rudman maintained that only the Greyshirts could save South Africa. The movement, he claimed, was active in every district and had grown massively in Cape Town and Port Elizabeth.[223]

The Board sent a copy of Rudman's speech to Smuts in preparation for a scheduled meeting with him.[224] Only a month earlier, it had written to Smuts as a follow-up to the meeting held in early October 1933. 'It is my painful duty to report that the activities of the Anti-Jewish organisations are increasing in scope and intensity,' wrote Acting President Siegfried Raphaely. His sombre message was prompted by the ongoing anti-Jewish meetings in small towns: the Blackshirts had been active in Springs, Ermelo, Amersfoort, Volksrust, Wakkerstroom, Piet Retief, Moolman Stasie, Paulpietersburg and Lunsberg. On the advice of Smuts, Jews had avoided these gatherings, but, noted Raphaely, the plethora of 'manufactured figures' and the 'slanderous statements' about Jews were cause for serious concern. The erstwhile harmonious relationship between Jew and non-Jew in small towns, he lamented, was rapidly eroding. Raphaely explained that the Netherlands had introduced legislation to make the 'slander of any Race, Nationality or Creed' an offence and that the province of Manitoba in Canada, as well as New York state, had similar legislation. 'My Board, after long and careful consideration, is of opinion that the time has definitely arrived for similar legislation in the Union,' he said, and for its speedy introduction to deal promptly with the growing menace.[225]

At the Board's meeting with Smuts on 27 June 1934, the justice minister expressed disgust at Rudman's speech, describing it as 'the raving of a lunatic' that would hold no appeal for South Africans. But he also expressed concern about Jews attending radical right meetings and partially blamed them for the violence at Paarl. He advised the Board to take a dignified attitude and objected to its recommendation that the government pursue a more active policy on the matter. Counter-propaganda, Smuts believed, would play directly into the hands of the Greyshirts, and it would be far more effective to find out the source of their financial support, as in his view the change for the worse was indicative of new capital being injected into the movement. Smuts also objected to raising the matter in parliament, anticipating that it would lead to an acrimonious debate. However he did acknowledge that the position might change.[226]

Notwithstanding his apprehension about Jewish actions and refusal to take up the Board's recommendations, Smuts clearly appreciated the seriousness of the situation. In this he was not alone. On 6 July 1934, Albertus Geyer, the influential editor of *Die Burger* (now fully aligned to Malan's 'Purified' Nationalists) recorded in his diary that Manie Maritz, a firebrand Anglo–Boer War hero and leader of the 1914 Afrikaner Rebellion, had paid him a visit to secure the support of *Die Burger* in the fight against the Jews.[227] Maritz was probably acting on behalf of Weichardt, who had invited him to Cape Town. Geyer – known as the *Ysterman* (Iron Man) for his tough opposition to Fusion – was well aware of widespread support for the Greyshirts, despite their leader, whom he described as an insignificant 'Führer'. Difficult times, he wrote, had stirred a latent anti-Jewish sentiment, which he feared was capable of being ignited by the Greyshirts. This presented a sticky problem for the National Party, and he was unclear as to how it would play out. For the nationalist-inclined sector of the Afrikaner *volk*, noted Geyer in his diary, this was the greatest challenge since 1913. Obviously concerned about a major schism within Afrikanerdom, he concluded his entry with a warning that another battle, this time with the Jews, would 'be fatal'.[228]

CHAPTER TWO

THE RADICAL RIGHT

'That the "shirt" nuisance would spread sooner or later to South Africa has long
been a certainty. It ranks with jazz and measles as a highly contagious disease
of the day ...'
– Cape Argus, 27 October 1933

'... Unhappily organised political prejudice was never before so venomous as it
is today.'
– Natal Advertiser, cited in SAJC, 31 August 1934

'Everything points to the fact that the Jews' game in South Africa is up, and, if
they have any sense, they will realise the fact and try to effect compromise. But
history shows that the greed for gold and lust for power is so ingrained in the
Jewish race that they will cling to their gold and power until it is too late.'
– Professor J Kerr Wylie to Sir Carruthers Beattie, Principal, University of Cape
   Town, 18 February 1935

'Muizenberg has its usual throng of Jews of the usual unattractive type. I am
not anti-Semitic. I have many Jewish friends whom I like and admire. But
something in me revolts against our country being peopled by the squat-bodied,
furtive-eyed, loud-voiced race which crowds Muizenberg from the upcountry
trading stores. In a big population they would be lost and negligible. But we have
too many of them.'
– Patrick Duncan to Lady Maud Selborne, 10 January 1935

WEICHARDT AND THE GREYSHIRTS

Louis Theodore Weichardt was born on 23 May 1894 in Paarl, a town set in a fertile valley less than an hour's drive from Cape Town. He moved to Pretoria (in what was then the South African Republic) as an infant with his older brother, Carl, and widowed mother, Johanna.[1] In 1906 his mother married a German schoolmaster, and at the age of twelve, after attending the German School in Pretoria, Weichardt was sent to the German-medium Neu-Hannover Schule in New Hanover, a village in the Natal Midlands (now KwaZulu-Natal) established in 1858 by German cotton planter families. A year later the family moved to Germany.[2]

Little is known about Weichardt's years in Germany. According to the Board, he was briefly interned as a British subject at the outbreak of the Great War in 1914.[3] Thereafter he joined the German army, presumably influenced by his mother's German descent.[4] Contradictory reports (especially about his war years) make it impossible to establish more about his life in Germany with any certainty. Weichardt's obituary in the *Natal Mercury* reported that he had been severely wounded after three years' service in the German army,[5] but in a defamation case brought by Weichardt against the Argus Printing Company during the Second World War (for accusing him of committing treason by fighting for Germany as a Union of South Africa national),[6] an affidavit from his brother Carl indicated that Louis had been forced into the German army but had refused to take up arms, serving instead in a 'Labour Corps'. However, Weichardt's London lawyers (AF and RW Tweedie of Lincoln's Inn Fields) discovered evidence that their client did indeed fight for Germany and was arrested 'by the British Military authorities on a charge of High Treason, but owing to the intercession of relatives in South Africa he was never brought to trial'. (William A Crump & Son, acting for the Argus Printing Company, corroborated that Weichardt had fought for Germany 'with hostile intent'.) Weichardt alleged that he had subsequently been furnished with a pardon, but the Foreign Office had no such record. It would thus seem that Weichardt's war years are shrouded in mystery.[7]

We do, however, have two articles about his youth and early adult years, each obviously tendentious: 'A Short Biography of a Great Leader', by

SANP leader Louis T Weichardt, sporting Nazi regalia.
(courtesy Archives for Contemporary Affairs, University of the Free State, Bloemfontein)

Frikkie du Toit, published in the Greyshirts' bilingual weekly, *Die Waarheid/ The Truth*; and a pamphlet, 'Die Man en die Plan vir die Volk in Suid Afrika', written by the Greyshirt publicist, Isak le Grange.[8] Merging the accounts, and using interviews conducted with Weichardt by FJ van Heerden in 1972 and by Izak Hattingh in 1983, a picture emerges of an aggrieved, disillusioned and Jew-obsessed young man.

According to the 'Short Biography of a Great Leader', while Weichardt was in Germany in the years before the Great War, he had witnessed the 'havoc which the Jews, particularly those coming from Eastern countries of Europe, were everywhere playing with European and Ottoman civilisation'. They had, Weichardt asserted, profited from the Great War and had financed the communists in Italy with Jewish gold from Russia, thus reducing the country to chaos. In his travels, Weichardt also claimed to have observed the Turkish peasantry 'being bled to death by Jewish extortioners and money lenders'. In the light of these fabricated experiences, Weichardt expressed particular pleasure that 'he had the privilege of witnessing the first beginnings of the nationalist German uprising against Jewish domination'. With his own eyes he claimed to have seen the depths of demoralisation and degradation inflicted on Germany, with Jews controlling the government, the press, the professions, the universities, industry and trade, art and culture, and every other branch of national life; even the law courts, he asserted, were largely manned by Jewish judges and it was almost impossible for a German to obtain justice, while Jews could commit grievous crimes with impunity.[9]

Weichardt had remained in Germany after the war – a time of great hardship in that country – working for an export company in the Ruhr steel town of Solingen and only returned to South Africa in 1923, having experienced great difficulty obtaining a South African passport, as his had expired in 1917.[10] 'From then till 1933,' he recounts, 'I struggled, within the ranks of one of the then existing political parties, to propagate the principles of National Socialism, and found myself checkmated at every turn by powerful financial interests, predominantly Jewish.' Weichardt expressed increasing dissatisfaction with the corruption of South African politics, in which he was unable to find a place to conduct honest business due to the dominance of foreign or alien elements.

While Hitler's ascent to power and his rejection of liberal democracy might have encouraged the angry Weichardt to break away from the National Party, the real spur to action – the climax, as he put it – was the coalition between the National Party and the South African Party in March 1933, 'when the majority of the Nationalist leaders abandoned the principles for which they had hitherto professed to stand and entered into an unholy, Jew-inspired alliance with the followers of General Smuts'.[11] This he found unacceptable and, believing that nothing could be achieved under the prevailing party system, he abandoned the National Party.[12] In the same year, with the intention of combating 'the pernicious influence of the Jewish race', he founded the South African Christian (Gentile) National-Socialist Movement, with its 'Body Guard', the South African Greyshirts.[13]

In May 1934, Weichardt's movement and the Greyshirts coalesced to form the Suid-Afrikaanse Nasionale Party–South African National Party (SANP).[14] From the start, recalled Weichardt, he was assailed by the 'Jewish and the Jewish-controlled press ... with a virulence probably unparalleled in the whole of South African history'.[15] In his interview with Hattingh, he reaffirmed this pressure, claiming that Jews also put pressure on his bank manager,[16] while, according to the 'Short Biography', Jews had made several attempts on his and his wife's life and on the life of their child.[17]

From the outset, Weichardt fashioned the SANP's racist, antisemitic, and fascist philosophy, a *Weltanschauung* demonstratively drawn from European sources but grafted onto South African conditions.[18] Greyshirt members had to be obedient, acknowledge Weichardt as the leader, exercise self-discipline and always be neatly dressed.[19] The popular appellation for the party referred to the uniform shirt worn by the militant sector responsible for protecting the leader and maintaining order at political meetings.[20] Patently inspired by Hitler's successful tactics in Germany, including Brownshirt thuggery and the 'Heil' greeting, and aided and abetted by anti-Jewish literature from South West Africa as well as Nazi support from abroad, the SANP did its best to set the national agenda.[21]

With its headquarters at 166 Longmarket Street in Cape Town, the party established regional branches throughout the country. Its reach was helped by speedier rail communications, improved literacy and the spread of newspapers. Yet it would appear that, despite many meetings in small country towns, the membership of the uniformed Greyshirts countrywide never exceeded 2000.[22] Accurate figures, however, are difficult to obtain. According to the Board, the SANP as a whole – that is, not only the uniformed Greyshirts – had in excess of 4000 members in Port Elizabeth and environs alone, and claimed a membership of between 3000 and 4000 in Natal.[23]

SANP propaganda was tailored to incorporate both disillusioned English- and Afrikaans-speakers, with Weichardt himself more comfortable speaking in English.[24] Betraying an affinity with Nazi racial categories, he defined the Dutch and English as branches of 'the same great Aryan race' capable of complete assimilation. According to Weichardt, anyone trying to keep the Dutch and English apart was simply playing the Jews' game of 'Divide and Rule'.[25] Indeed, some articles in the SANP mouthpiece, *Die Waarheid/The Truth*, were in English and some in Afrikaans, demonstrating a determination to woo English-speakers and not simply to build on the anger of aggrieved, alienated and impoverished Afrikaners.[26]

Indicative of this strategy was the fact that the publication's undisclosed one-time editor was Kerr Wylie, who held the WP Schreiner Chair of Roman Law and Jurisprudence at the University of Cape Town.[27] An inveterate antisemite, the Scottish-born and -educated Wylie would become a target of Jewish concerns.[28] Under his guidance (and later that of others), *Die Waarheid/The Truth* published fascist articles from abroad as part of a general assault against Jews both in South Africa and beyond. Its tone, tailored to South African conditions, was crude and defamatory, and bore all the hallmarks of the movement's Nazi mentors.

This was evident from the start. In an editorial, 'It Has Got To Go – by Louis Weichardt', *Die Waarheid/The Truth* spelled out the leader's vision. Here he traced all South Africa's ills to one source – what he termed the international exploiters who were neither Afrikaans nor English:

> Whilst the legal, medical and dental professions, commerce, trading houses, liquor trade, etc., are from 60 to 100 per cent in the hands of the Jews, we hardly find 1 per cent of the Jews among the sweated labourers of the country. I demand that a stop be put to this domination by

the aliens. Party politicians are warned that whilst we definitely do not stand for persecution of the Jews, we are determined to put the Jew in his place. We are not going to tolerate bootlicking. Gentile South Africans – English or Dutch speaking – are no longer prepared to play second fiddle to these aliens.[29]

Demonstrating its affinity with European racism and 'Nordicism', the SANP's objective was to unite South Africa's 'Nordic peoples' and eradicate all financial and political exploitation by those 'who cannot be true citizens of the Union by reason of their National incapacity to assimilate with the Nordic peoples ...' Here the party was referring to what it perceived to be the increasing financial and political power exercised by the Jews in South Africa.[30] As far as the SANP was concerned, the Quota Act of 1930 had not gone far enough. Rather than simply curtailing Jewish immigration, the party sought, *inter alia*, to prevent Jews who entered South Africa after 1918 from being granted South African citizenship; to revoke such citizenship if already granted; to proscribe Jews holding any official position in South Africa; to treat Jews in South Africa as temporary guests; to prevent Jews from holding immovable property other than with permission of the state; and to protect South Africans against being ousted by Jews from any trade or profession.[31] Details were spelled out in the party's 17-clause programme, clause nine of which made it quite clear that Jews who had arrived after 1918 were 'unassimilable' aliens.[32]

Die Waarheid / The Truth focused endlessly on supposed Jewish domination of South Africa and the power of international Jewry.[33] It claimed to attack Jews because they 'are the organised exploiters and oppressors par excellence, and moreover their organisation is international'.[34] Alleged Jewish conspiracies abounded, the boycott of Jewish businesses was encouraged, and the notorious *Protocols of the Elders of Zion* was treated as authentic.[35] Article after article spoke of the Jews and their lies and the power of the 'Jew-Capitalists and Jew-Communists'.[36] Even the salacious dimension of Nazi antisemitism seeped onto its pages, with Jews being accused of trafficking in young girls and treating non-Jewish women as merchandise.[37] Jews were described as disciples of the devil,[38] and a vitriolic Hitler speech

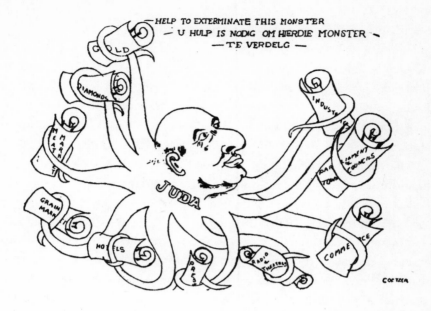

Antisemitic cartoon, illustrating supposed Jewish control of the South African economy.
(courtesy South African Jewish Board of Deputies)

at Nuremberg was praised.[39] Most importantly, the SANP's message related directly to the South African experience, claiming that 'the disastrous Anglo–Boer War of 1899–1902 was deliberately brought about by the Jewish mine magnates who circumvented Rhodes and Kruger alike'.[40] Jews were accused of inciting blacks against white civilisation, controlling the press, dominating the economy, exploiting Afrikaners and being part of a vast international conspiracy.

While antisemitism was endemic to the SANP's thinking, its major challenge was to provide an alternative ideology to communism and capitalism. Although not formally spelt out, it was fascism that informed and infused its propaganda; the swastikas alongside the newspaper's banner and the nature of the coverage make this clear.[41] Even the promised constitutional road was Hitlerian, with great emphasis on 'the Leader'.[42]

GAINING TRACTION

Shortly after Weichardt's movement had transformed itself into the SANP, Advocate Joseph Herbstein toured the platteland with a view to gauging the depth and strength of anti-Jewish hostility. The thirty-seven-year-old Jewish leader was well acquainted with the world of the rural Afrikaner, having grown up in Graaff-Reinet, a small town in the eastern Cape Province, before proceeding to Rhodes University College in Grahamstown and the University of Cape Town to complete a BA LLB degree.

Following his fact-finding trip to areas where the Greyshirts had made rapid inroads and where, historically, relations between Jews and Gentiles had been reasonably sound (although not unblemished),[43] Herbstein was interviewed by the *SAJC* on his impressions. Clearly concerned, he said that many Jewish country dwellers were angry at 'the scurrilous statements that are being made about the Jews in this country'. With a sense of guarded relief, Herbstein noted that there was only one centre where he had found evidence of the antisemitic movement having gained traction with people of influence. Instead it was those with nothing to lose who were attracted to it, as well as some businesspeople who hoped that the movement would eliminate Jewish competition. But the situation was nonetheless of some concern:

> In other centres, however, the position is by no means pleasant, because of the effect this propaganda is having on the children. An incident was related to me where, after a meeting of one of the leaders of the anti-Semitic movement with some school children, a little Jewish girl was placed in a wheelbarrow, wheeled outside the school grounds and told to go off to Jerusalem. In some towns where Jews and non-Jews have mixed equally in the social spheres, a boycott has been set up against the Jewish youth who are no longer invited to participate in the general social life such as dances and tennis tournaments and Jewish girls have had the experience of being insulted by statements made by members of the Greyshirt organisation that they did not want 'to meet any dirty Jewesses'.

Despite these revelations, Herbstein concluded that the small Jewish communities were confident that the hostility would not last.[44] Such optimism was misplaced. Anti-Jewish sentiment was in fact gaining ground, especially in the rural eastern Cape Province. Less than three months before Herbstein's tour, the town of Aberdeen – a short distance from his birthplace – had hosted a Greyshirt meeting that would result in a major legal trial which would, in due course, have international reverberations, especially in the Jewish world.

The Victorian hamlet of Aberdeen was an unlikely setting for a meeting of such consequence. Situated on the high plains of the Camdeboo in the Great Karoo, the town catered essentially to the surrounding farming community. Jewish *smouse*, mostly of eastern European origin, had traversed the district – known for its mohair and wool – from the late nineteenth century. The Aberdeen Hebrew Congregation was established in 1898 but it remained tiny, never exceeding about 20 members.[45] Yet the Jewish presence was used as a vehicle for Greyshirt propaganda by the movement's regional leader, the twenty-six-year-old Johannes von Strauss von Moltke.

The son of an English-speaking father of German origin (his grandmother was of English 1820 Settler stock), Von Moltke claimed to be a proud Christian. Born in Senekal in the Orange Free State six years after the Anglo-Boer War (in which his mother had served in the Red Cross), Von Moltke fell easily into conspiratorial thought and accusations of Jewish power. After completing standard eight he joined the Standard Bank as a stenographer. Firmly ensconced in the Nationalist and republican camp, a position he attributed to knowledge of the Anglo-Boer War imparted by his parents, he moved to South West Africa in 1925, where he worked as a clerk for the Windhoek Town Council. Subsequently he joined the firm of TW Beckett & Co as a packer before working his way up to advertising manager. Thereafter he moved to the Afrikaanse Pers group, but soon left to join *Die Burger*, where he was placed in charge of the Port Elizabeth office, only to leave that position shortly thereafter as well.[46]

Von Moltke was struggling financially when he met Weichardt in October 1933, and the two decided that 'the Gentiles must stand together' if they were to continue living in South Africa.[47] But it was handsome Harry Victor Inch, the eastern Cape Province Greyshirt leader and manager of its office in Port Elizabeth (always bedecked with a swastika-emblazoned flag) who converted Von Moltke to the Greyshirt movement.[48] Of Dutch descent, the thirty-four-year-old Inch, who had left school in standard six, was born in Cradock, not far from Port Elizabeth. Following his discharge from the South African Police in 1922, he had gone to the United States to avoid prosecution on a charge of indecency or immorality. There he became involved with the Industrial Workers of the World, a left-wing and anarchist labour movement, and as a consequence was asked to leave the country. He worked his way back to South Africa from England, settling in Port Elizabeth, where he became chairman of the South End branch of the National Party in 1929. Keenly involved in politics, he was repeatedly absent from his work at a pre-cooling plant of South African Railways, choosing instead to attend political meetings.[49]

THE GREYSHIRT TRIAL

The march of the Greyshirts into the annals of the history of modern antisemitism began on 27 March 1934, when Von Moltke claimed to have uncovered a sensational plot. Standing under a baking midday sun in the middle of Aberdeen's Market Square on a wagon decorated with four Greyshirt flags, the Greyshirt regional leader told a gathering of several hundred that he had in his possession a document taken secretly from the Western Road Synagogue in Port Elizabeth by a member of the Greyshirt movement.[50] Purportedly signed by the 'rabbi' of the synagogue and replete with Hebrew lettering that supposedly spoke to its authenticity,[51] the document, according to Von Moltke, spelled out in meticulous detail a Jewish plot to control the world. In his exposé, Von Moltke spoke of Jews' dividing and exploiting Christians and ensuring their bondage to Jews within four generations.

The speech was fully covered in *Die Rapport*, an Aberdeen weekly owned by David Hermanus Olivier.[52] A rather simple farmer turned newspaper proprietor, Olivier had met Von Moltke two days after the infamous Greyshirt meeting addressed by Weichardt at the Feather Market Hall in Port

Elizabeth almost two months earlier. The go-between once again was Inch. Harbouring clear sympathies towards the movement,[53] Olivier offered a grateful Von Moltke the opportunity to insert news of the Greyshirts in his newspaper.[54] Von Moltke's dramatic two-hour midweek speech at Aberdeen, purporting to throw 'light on the persecution of the gentiles by Organised Jewry throughout the world', was thus given front-page exposure in *Die Rapport*, leading to its increased circulation in nearby towns.[55] In the speech, Von Moltke told the gathering that he wanted the truth to be brought into the open, despite the corruption of 'the organised money powers', and warned that Christian peoples were coming under the sway of the 'International Jew'. All this preceded the climax of his tirade: the revelation of the stolen document in his possession that spelled out unequivocally that Jews were at war with Christendom.[56]

Notwithstanding the seemingly shocking revelations, an editorial in *Die Rapport* suggested that, before non-Jews took action against the Jewish plot, the accused should have the opportunity to prove their innocence by challenging the authenticity of the accusation. If this challenge was unsuccessful, 'there can only be one procedure for our Christian state: the ejection of Jews from South Africa'.[57]

On 4 April, Von Moltke repeated the accusation at another Greyshirt mass meeting in the Feather Market Hall, attended by approximately 500 people. Before quoting from the ostensibly stolen document, Von Moltke warned the gathering that what they were about to hear 'would make their blood curdle'. The audience appeared dumbstruck. 'A few seconds of intense silence prevailed throughout the Hall,' noted *Die Rapport*. Von Moltke then appealed for calm but urged the 'Nordic peoples' in the city to form a self-defence organisation to deal with 'such occult, alien organisations as are harboured in the Jewish synagogues ... If the Jews dispute the truth of the contents of this document let them prepare a charge of theft against any person; then the Judiciary of this land will be able to decide what occult movement belongs to Jewry.'[58] The message was clear: the 'Jewish state' within the South African 'Christian state' was 'affiliated to other hostile Jewish states in other Christian states throughout the world' and was working to achieve world domination.[59]

Although the speech was ignored (or perhaps boycotted) by Port Elizabeth's mainstream *Eastern Province Herald*, the Reverend Abraham Levy of Port Elizabeth's Western Road Synagogue, who had been implicated in the document, was both encouraged and assisted by the Board to institute a libel action.[60] Within days, Levy obtained an order of court restraining Von Moltke from publishing or printing 'a certain document which purports to have been removed from the Western Road Synagogue'. In an affidavit, the middle-aged Reverend demonstrated the crudities of the 'document', which he felt threatened his safety. He also indicated that he would sue the respondents for defamation.[61] Shortly after the submission of the affidavit, Von Moltke consented to the interdict and an action for defamation was set.[62]

With twenty years' service in the synagogue and ongoing involvement in important public bodies, the Reverend had every reason to feel aggrieved. 'Faintly professorial – the sort of man who would love to be left alone in his study and who is in his element on library committees rather than on the Stock Exchange' (as Ethelreda Lewis, a South African novelist who had been commissioned to cover the trial for the *Zionist Record* described him), Levy was clearly not privy to any purported worldwide Jewish plot. But more importantly, the Board, grappling with the question of incitement against Jews and badgered for months by Jewish leaders in the eastern Cape Province to attend to the Greyshirt menace in the region,[63] now saw an opportunity to discredit the Greyshirts and to expose before a court of law the fabricated nature of the *Protocols of the Elders of Zion*.

Rooted in a classic forgery that had gained currency in the early part of the twentieth century via Russian agents, the *Protocols* had been exposed by the *Times* of London as a forgery thirteen years earlier, when an investigative article by Philip Graves had revealed that the document was based on both a French satirical political pamphlet, compiled in the 1860s against Napoleon III, and a German antisemitic novel, *Biarritz*, written by Hermann Gödsche.[64] But this exposé had failed to dampen the popularity of the *Protocols*, which continued to attract attention, particularly in Germany, where Hitler's Nazi Party used the fabrication as a means of activating the conspiratorial impulses informing the radical right. The *Protocols* was

The Greyshirt trial, Grahamstown, 1934. Shown outside the courtroom are (left to right) Johannes von Strauss von Moltke, Harry Inch and DH Olivier.
(courtesy SA Rochlin Archives, South African Jewish Board of Deputies)

palpably the inspiration behind Von Moltke's accusations. Indeed, shortly after Von Moltke had sounded the alarm about a Jewish plot, *Die Waarheid/ The Truth* published a full-page account, 'Die Sionistiese Protokolle' (The Protocols of Zion), in which it described the nefarious actions of world Jewry against the 'goyim' (Gentiles).[65]

The civil claim against Von Moltke, Inch and Olivier, for an amount of £2000 each, was set for July in the Eastern Districts Local Division of the Supreme Court of South Africa in Grahamstown. The legal battle between Reverend Levy and his accusers would be of great import for those tracing the byways of conspiratorial thought sustained by labyrinthine international connections. Indeed the 'Greyshirt Trial', as it became known, resulted in the first-ever court judgment confirming the fabricated nature of the *Protocols of the Elders of Zion.*[66]

Sir Thomas Lyndoch Graham, Judge President of the Eastern Cape Province court, and Justice Clemens Gutsche, both experienced and learned jurists, presided over the libel action. Graham, an alumnus of the prestigious St Andrew's College in Grahamstown, had enjoyed a distinguished legal and political career, serving as a cabinet minister and Attorney General in the old Cape Colony before becoming Judge President of the Eastern Districts court in 1913.[67] Gutsche had been a student at Dale College – the great rival of St Andrew's – in nearby King William's Town. He too had established a fine reputation both as Professor of Law at the South African College (later the University of Cape Town) and as a judge in South West Africa. In 1930 he had taken up a position as judge in the Eastern Districts.

While the trial attracted great interest in Jewish circles, the *Zionist Record* was without doubt given to hyperbole when, on the eve of proceedings, it claimed that the case 'has aroused tremendous interest among people throughout the country, and is certain to be keenly followed by Jews as well as non-Jews in all parts of the world'.[68] For most white South Africans, it was rather the country's status within the Commonwealth, as well as ongoing battles within Afrikanerdom, that were exercising their minds. Nonetheless, the case was widely covered in the general media, albeit without editorial comment and with little sense of its international significance. Not so for the Jewish observers. 'One of the most extraordinary civil actions in the history of South African Courts and one which vitally affects the welfare of the Jewish Community in this country,' was what the *Zionist Record* told its readers.[69]

Only days before the trial began, a severe cold front reached the southern and eastern Cape Province. Grahamstown experienced its coldest weather of the winter, with snow covering the nearby mountains, but the bitter chill failed to prevent a capacity crowd attending the trial's opening. However, if the expectant voyeurs had hoped to see 'a battle between Jew and Gentile', wrote Lewis, they would have been disappointed. It was 'common knowledge', she noted, 'that a distinguished Jewish KC refused to take this case of Jew versus Gentile for fear of prejudice or bias within himself or the possibility of a loss of self-control. By refusing this brief,' explained Lewis, 'it became less a case of Jew versus Gentile than a case of man versus man.' In her view, the choice of Frederick Reynolds, KC, assisted by Will Stuart (instructed by Messrs Bell and Hutton), acting for Levy, was a masterstroke. 'I can imagine no greater blow, and probably surprise, to the defendants than to find themselves at the mercy, not of a Jewish barrister, but of an unbiased and unemotional Gentile.'[70]

The focus of proceedings was primarily the authenticity of the document, the question of whether it had been stolen, and the views of the defendants and their motives for making them public.[71] It very quickly became obvious that the document in question was inspired by the *Protocols of the Elders of Zion*, but with a particular South African twist. It purported to be a copy of detailed minutes discussing Jewish attitudes toward Christianity, as well as issues pertaining to antisemitism and the Greyshirts. Accordingly it described how, beginning with Martin Luther, Jews had manipulated Christendom and planned to destroy the Roman Catholic Church, establish world communism and a dictatorship of the proletariat. In addition, the document accused South African Jews of harbouring plans to hand the country over to the black population.

After some minor quibbles about the consolidation of charges, the corpulent and neatly attired Reynolds said he proposed to show that the entire document was fabricated. Levy gave evidence that exposed the inaccurate use of the term 'Rabbi' (he was in fact only a Reverend), as well as the falsified Hebrew lettering at the top of the document. Under cross-examination from the three defendants, who were either unable to afford legal counsel or happy to gain publicity, Levy made it clear that the accusations were invented and ridiculous. It was soon apparent that the defendants had little to support their claims. But they persisted with leading and often harsh questions based on scant knowledge of Judaism and Jewish practice, and all informed by conspiratorial thought of the highest order. Von Moltke, 'fluent in speech and aggressive in manner', as the judges described him, was particularly vicious.

Fortuitously, Nahum Sokolow, President of the World Zionist Organization, was visiting South Africa and was available for the trial as an expert witness. A journalist by profession, extremely erudite, internationally esteemed and well versed in argument, the distinguished seventy-five-year-old Zionist leader easily refuted the false and malicious allegations made in the *Protocols*. 'There was absolutely no truth in the suggestion that there was a Jewish plot to overcome the world,' he calmly told the court in a thick Polish accent. In fact, he had first heard of the *Protocols* in 1920 and, together with Ward Price of the London *Times*, had been instrumental in tracing its origin to an anti-Napoleonic pamphlet in the British Museum library. 'I have handled the original pamphlet myself,' he told the Judge President, and informed the court how the name of Herzl had been substituted for that of Napoleon III, and 'Jews' for the French clique operating against the emperor.

With measured clarity, Sokolow fielded questions from the three defendants, each of whom quoted extensively from an array of anti-Jewish literature. Their accusations that Jews dominated world affairs and the press, and were responsible for the white slave traffic and pornography, were easily dismissed.[72] When Von Moltke suggested to Sokolow that the 'Jews had levelled a pistol at the head of the British Government when putting forward the Zionist proposals', the Jewish leader told him that he was exaggerating the importance of Jews. 'Do you think we could frighten Great Britain? That is childish imagination.'

The Reverend Wolfe Hirsch, spiritual leader of the Pretoria Jewish community, gave evidence on technical aspects of the document, including the falsified Hebrew lettering, and he was followed by Rabbi Ephraim Levy of Durban, who explained the meaning of the term 'Rabbi' and its confusion with 'Reverend'. It was, however, the dignified George François Dingemans, Professor of Afrikaans for three decades at nearby Rhodes University College, who floored the defendants. In an erudite analysis of the document, the philologist and expert in Hebrew concluded that it 'is an impudent and malicious forgery', the 'product of a mind distorted by blind malice and hatred, an attempt to poison the minds of gullible people'. Inch struggled to understand why a Christian professor who admitted to 'having no Jewish blood in his veins or his family' was so sympathetic to Jewry. Unable to cope with what for them was cognitive dissonance, both Inch and Von Moltke insisted that Dingemans was indebted in some way to the 'Kahal', or international 'Jewish Government'.[73]

There was an anticipatory hush when Mark Lazarus, a staunch opponent of the Greyshirts, entered the dock. The British-born Labour Party activist and chairman of the Marxian Football Club in Port Elizabeth was far removed from formal Jewish life in the city. Yet he had been implicated by name in the document, no doubt because he owned the Mercantile Press, responsible for printing anti-Greyshirt pamphlets. This had drawn the ire of Inch and Von Moltke, but throughout their cross-examination of Lazarus they were unable to link the publisher to the Western Road Synagogue. 'I have never been inside it in my life,' Lazarus told Inch with a sense of secular pride. Furthermore, he had a watertight alibi for the date on which he was alleged to have been involved in the so-called plot.

Of particular interest in the proceedings was the clear nexus of international antisemitism and the input of Nazi ideas with a conspiratorial anti-Jewish worldview that included notions about Jewish machinations in South Africa. Von Moltke was demonstrably inspired by Hamilton H Beamish, a well-known Irish-born antisemite, whom he called upon as an expert witness.[74] The son of an admiral who had served as naval aide-de-camp to Queen Victoria,[75] Beamish had found his way to the Cape Colony via Alaska and Ceylon as a member of the Ceylon Mounted Infantry during the Anglo-Boer War. Rising to the rank of captain, he remained in South Africa after the war, and then went to Rhodesia before returning to the Transvaal. During the Great War he had distinguished himself as a jingo-istic anti-German, ultimately fighting on the Western Front with the South African Infantry Brigade. Thereafter he returned to England and entered the world of far-right British politics, where he founded the Britons, a society whose aim was to spread antisemitic propaganda.[76]

Shortly after the formation of the Britons, Beamish attracted publicity in a 1919 libel case brought against him by Sir Alfred Moritz Mond, the First Commissioner of Works in the British cabinet. Beamish had called Mond (who was Jewish) a traitor, and had used that occasion to impugn Jews, who he argued could not be real Englishmen, asserting that a 'person can't be by race both English and Jew'.[77] Beamish was found guilty and, following a failed appeal, returned to South Africa without paying the fine. During his active years with the Britons, Beamish had founded the Judaic Publishing Company (renamed the Britons Publishing Company in 1922), noted for its antisemitic propaganda. In 1920 he published *The Jews' Who's Who*, allegedly exposing Jewish financial and political interests. Perhaps most importantly, the Britons kept the *Protocols* in circulation, having purchased the plates of a British edition from the publishing firm Eyre and Spottiswoode in 1920. In 1923 it published a new edition by Victor Marsden, based on a translation Marsden had done for the *Morning Post*, entitled *The Protocols of the Wise Men of Zion*.[78]

As one of the key witnesses for the defence – and much to the court's mirth – the pugnacious Beamish claimed to have taught both Hitler and Henry Ford about the Jewish peril. In his view, the document at the heart of the trial was a 'miniature of the *Protocols* with South African conditions superimposed upon it'. With an air of omniscience, Beamish indicated that he was 'a firm believer in *The Protocols of the Elders of Zion*', and that he was prepared to prove its validity, protocol by protocol. He then went on to air a veritable flood of absurd conspiracies: all the prime ministers of England had been under Jewish influence; Jews had been behind all the revolutions in history, and even the Jameson Raid had been engineered by Lionel Phil-lips and Alfred Beit, both Jews. Predictably, he claimed Jews were involved in illicit trades, including prostitution, liquor and gold, and contended that all governments, including South Africa's, were manipulated by Jews and their money. Even the political parties of Malan and Tielman Roos were under Jewish control, as was Mahatma Gandhi. He claimed that there was not a single newspaper in the country that was not controlled by Jews. In his view, Hitler was the 'bright spot' in Germany, and he approved 'entirely of his policy of clearing his country from Asiatic blood and other corruption and filth'.

The clearly obsessed Beamish claimed to have known about the Jewish plot for forty years. He was sure that it had originated from the Kahal, which, he told the court, 'is a super-Jew Parliament' of 300 that controlled 'all countries throughout the world, particularly European countries. It consists of revolutionary Jews, the ones who are out directly and indirectly to destroy, as I told you, our civilisation.' He also noted that the 'Jew Communists' wished 'to disturb the coloured race' in South Africa and that out of the ensuing chaos the Jew will rule. Beamish added that he had received a solemn Nordic word of honour from Von Moltke and Inch that the document was genuine, and he believed them to be honourable men fighting for a cause he shared.

During cross-examination Beamish deemed it an insult to be called an antisemite; he was, he said, simply anti-Jewish. The Semites included Arabs, Assyrians, Abyssinians, among them 'fine fellows', although he would object to them in South Africa.[79] Other witnesses called on or subpoenaed by the defendants were engaged essentially to establish whether they understood that it was Reverend Levy who had been identified by name in the Aberdeen and Port Elizabeth addresses.

The judges made an inspection of the Western Road Synagogue and followed this with a harsh grilling of Inch, Von Moltke and Olivier. Cross-examination of Inch focused on how he had obtained the document, including his claim that he had originally received two documents from two young boys he had sent to observe a Jewish community meeting held at the Emmanuel Hall in Port Elizabeth. These documents, Inch told the court, had led him to break into the synagogue, where he found the document under discussion.

In their defence, Von Moltke and Inch alleged that they had been the victims of a Jewish plot and that they were not guilty of libelling Levy because they had not mentioned him by name, but had directed their attack 'against the Jewish race as a whole'. They insisted that the document was indeed stolen from the Western Road Synagogue, but their testimony was full of contradictions. The burly Olivier – 'the bewildered tool of the others', as Lewis put it – broke down in the witness box. Under cross-examination he lost his voice, presenting a pitiful figure.

Von Moltke's evidence began with an outline of his life and those who had influenced him, recalling in particular the role of one Bernard Lewis, whom he described as a Jew who had reshaped his life. According to Von Moltke, Lewis had denounced Judaism some forty-seven years earlier: 'From him I learned quite a lot about the hypocrisy of the synagogues and what he called the rank materialism of the Jewish religion.' Von Moltke had named his eldest son after Lewis, who was still his friend, a fact he claimed indicated he could not be described as an antisemite. Indeed, it was only after Hitler came to power that he had gained insight into the power of the Jews and their pervasive influence in Germany which had created such havoc in that country. This realisation drove him to reflect on the role of Jews in South Africa (whom he incorrectly claimed comprised seven per cent of the population)[80] and the possibility that they had been behind the country's travails – especially over the past thirty to forty years – and were responsible for the massive poverty. Indeed, he cast his net wider, holding Jews in England, as represented by Disraeli, liable for imperialist policy in South Africa and for most of South Africa's troubles, including the Jameson Raid and the power of the mining magnates. He identified a long list of Jewish industrialists to demonstrate the hold Jews had on the South African economy; to prove his point, he described that already when working for *Die Vaderland*, he had realised that even that newspaper was in the clutches of a prominent Jewish industrialist, Isadore William Schlesinger.

Having met Weichardt, Von Moltke said he knew something had to be done. He left his job with *Die Burger* following what he claimed was an attempted bribe of that newspaper by Adolph Schauder, a prominent Jewish communal leader (who would become mayor of Port Elizabeth in 1940–41), to keep Greyshirt advertisements out of the newspaper, after which he became an activist believing in the *Protocols*. Maintaining that he had always known that merit alone could not explain the Jews' success, the *Protocols* had proved to him that the explanation lay in organised world Jewry. He denied that his movement was intent on persecuting Jews or confiscating their property. The reason they were fighting the Jews was to ensure that Gentiles enjoyed their legitimate birthright 'before they allow an alien race like the Jews to get all the key positions'. And the only way to do that was to 'denationalise them' and exclude them from the economy until 'our own people will get the full share first', leaving the leftovers for 'a race that will not assimilate with us'. Von Moltke went on to praise Beamish's writings for alerting him to the subject of Jewish power, including its octopus-like control over the press, the retail trade, diamonds, gold and international finance. In a rigorous cross-examination, Reynolds ridiculed Von Moltke's capacity for conspiratorial madness built upon a wide-ranging knowledge of classic anti-Jewish tracts.

After nearly two weeks of proceedings, the court found the documents to be false and the defendants to have conspired to promote the interests of the Greyshirt movement. Their evidence was riddled with fabrications and contradictions and the story surrounding it was labelled pure invention. In an extremely detailed and careful judgment of more than 30 000 words, which took two and a half hours to deliver, Graham and Gutsche awarded damages in favour of the plaintiff against each of the defendants: Inch, £1 000 for 'concocting or assisting in the concoction of the defamatory document and thereafter foisting it upon the plaintiff'; Von Moltke, £750 for playing 'a leading part in the plot, and in the dissemination of the document'; and Olivier, £25 for acting 'improperly in publishing the document'.[81]

In the assessment of the judges, the document emanated from the Greyshirt movement and was portrayed through the prism of its worldview. Summing up the question of the 'World Plot' and the 'Protocols', the judges unanimously endorsed the testimony of Nahum Sokolow, who they believed had conclusively demonstrated that 'the Protocols are an impudent forgery, obviously published for the purpose of anti-Jewish propaganda'. The defendants had 'failed to produce a vestige of proof to establish the existence of this plot. They rely on a long series of opinions of persons who are admittedly hostile to the Jewish religion, and whose opinions are based upon the assertions of previous writers, who give no authority of any value in support of their conclusions.'[82]

Beamish, the key spokesman for the defence, was described by the judges as an obsessed and intolerant man with an exaggerated idea of his importance:

> He regards himself as a modern crusader whose mission is to reveal to the world the existence of a world plot organised by the Jews since the beginning of their history to overthrow Christianity and to destroy civilisation. He has greedily swallowed every anti-Jewish publication that he has discovered and accepted as facts every anti-Jewish statement they contained, and upon this question he is a fanatic; he has been unable to produce a vestige of relevant evidence in support of his charge.

Beamish had, moreover, made no attempt to assess the accuracy of the story told by Inch and Von Moltke, the latter described by the judges as a man 'replete with mean and contemptible pettiness – deliberate perjurer and a man destitute of all principle'.

Citing American and South African legal precedent, the judges refuted the defendants' claim that they were referring to the Jewish race as a whole and not specifically to the Reverend Levy: it could only be inferred from the document's wording that the 'Rabbi' mentioned in the plot was the Reverend Levy, as in the public mind he was the rabbi of the Western Road Synagogue. Von Moltke had failed to show that he did not act recklessly in publishing the document, and as for Inch's story, it was patently false. Von Moltke knew this and had 'acted *mala fide* in publishing the document and did so to benefit the Grey Shirt movement in general and himself in particular. In these circumstances it becomes absurd to speak of a moral and social duty which impelled him to publish the document. There was no such duty and therefore there was no privilege.'[83]

The *Zionist Record* predictably welcomed the outcome of the trial, praising the judgment for revealing the unsavoury nature and methods of the defendants and their aping of Hitler and his odious prejudices.[84] An editorial in the *SAJC* was less sanguine:

If judgment in the Grahamstown case will help to mould public opinion in this country to an adequate appreciation of the infamies of which
the Jew-baiter is capable it will have done a single service to the non-
Jewish as well as the Jewish population of South Africa. If, on the other
hand, public opinion fails to take a definite stand on the matter, the
judgment, severe as it is upon the particular individuals concerned, will
serve as no deterrent against others of similar mentality.[85]

Some mainstream newspapers also commented positively on the outcome of the case. The *Friend*, for example, suggested that the time had
come to extend legislation that would outlaw all interracial agitation. More
importantly, the newspaper wondered why the 'shirt nuisance' was not
being dealt with by the authorities.[86] In similar fashion, the *Natal Witness*
appreciated the outcome, noting that 'even in liberty-loving South Africa
there are tens of thousands of people who are prepared to believe the most
monstrous things of their political opponents'. Such accusations, the newspaper contended, had little traction in the larger centres, but warned that
there could be serious repercussions should the Greyshirts be given free rein
to spread propaganda in the countryside.[87]

THE RADICAL RIGHT GATHERS PACE

Despite the crushing court judgment, the *Protocols* continued to be used in
radical right circles.[88] *Die Waarheid/The Truth* was certainly far from chastened. As an observer writing in the *Zionist Record* nearly three months after
the trial noted:

> *Die Waarheid* consisted almost exclusively of articles intended to incite
> hatred against the Jews. Its spirit is that of some of the worst Nazi
> products of present-day Germany; its main theme, the domination of
> the Jews over the affairs of the country; its chief policy, the boycott of
> the Jews in every branch of the country's life. It has brazenly avowed
> its belief in the authenticity of the 'Protocols of the Elders of Zion,'
> and quoted long extracts therefrom. There can be little doubt that the

readers of this paper (though what the number is, is conjectural) must
be deeply impregnated with anti-Jewish poison.[89]

That poison manifested itself beyond the SANP. A number of radical
right groups were now operating: in addition to the SANP's headquarters
in Cape Town under Weichardt,[90] there was a branch in Pietermaritzburg
(Natal) under RK Rudman;[91] the *Suid-Afrikaanse Nasionale Demokratiese
Beweging* (South African National Democratic Movement, known as the
Blackshirts), under Manie Wessels, with headquarters in Johannesburg;[92] the
Volksbeweging (People's Movement) in Cape Town, also known as the South
African Gentile Organisation, under HS Terblanche; a *Bond van Nasionale
Werkers* (National Workers' Union, known as the Brownshirts), which was
established in Pretoria in September 1934 under Dr AJ Bruwer; and the
Oranjehemde (Orangeshirts), under François Erasmus, Secretary to the Fed-
eral Council of the National Party and MP for Moorreesburg.[93]

In Natal, the SANP resonated particularly well with the large German
settler community of Vryheid, known for its antisemitic activities, which
sometimes even penetrated the school playground. Under the guidance of
Dr Theunis Stoffberg, anti-Jewish and anti-Asiatic meetings were regularly
held and pamphlets widely circulated.[94] The Volksbeweging distributed its
newspaper *Terre-Blanche* (with swastikas on the masthead) mainly among
the poor, as well as leaflets alerting readers to the Jewish menace, while the
Bond van Nasionale Werkers employed Nazi salutes and expressed its goal
as ridding South Africa of exploiters – 'those living on the sweat and blood
of South Africans'.[95] Rather than focusing specifically on the Jewish threat,
the Oranjehemde targeted the ills of capitalism in general.[96] On the whole,
the radical right was quite explicit in employing blatant anti-Jewish language, which had great potential resonance at a time of political uncertainty,
massive rural poverty, drought and heightened Afrikaner nationalism.[97]
Politicising Jew-hatred and inventing conspiracies aroused passions in a way
that reasoned argument would fail to do.

SANP meetings, which often turned violent, were held in both rural and
urban centres, and if town halls were difficult to secure, in private homes.[98]
Obviously concerned about the spread of these gatherings, some newspapers

chose not to publicise such events.[99] But this did little to deter anti-Jewish activities, which were being closely monitored by the Board. Expanding audiences, which included railway workers as well as intellectuals and civil servants, were of particular concern. Meetings in Natal – and Vryheid in particular – attracted increasing support, much to the consternation of the Natal Council of the Board.[100] In Cape Town, swastika-waving Greyshirts brazenly paraded in Adderley Street, the city's main shopping precinct – an ominous portent of things to come.[101]

It is difficult to ascertain with any precision the extent to which the wider community supported the antisemitism of the radical right. When 'Bitterly Perplexed' wrote to the *Cape Argus* insisting that hostility towards Jews had grown massively but was ignored in the press because of Jewish pressure,[102] the newspaper responded that the letter writer, a university professor, was bent on propagandising: 'Of course we all know that anti-Semitism exists. It has probably been increased by the activities of the Grey Shirts. But does he expect a responsible newspaper to manufacture news out of irresponsible chatter, mostly behind closed doors, or, alternatively, to publish obediently the sort of "news" sent out from 166 Longmarket Street? The thing is too childish for words.'[103]

The *SAJC*, too, advised the Jewish community not to overreact, despite rumours that some firms were donating large sums to antisemitic movements. A panic reaction, it suggested, could only exacerbate relationships between Jews and their neighbours. Nonetheless, the *SAJC* did recognise the threat, and was at pains not to minimise anti-Jewish sentiment, which, it acknowledged, was appealing to both urban and rural audiences.[104] Indeed, in a carefully calibrated survey, conducted nine years later, Jewish students at the University of the Witwatersrand recalled anti-Jewish taunts and discrimination from childhood. Those from small towns recalled that they 'grew up in it' and were inclined to regard it as almost natural and inevitable.[105]

The Board was certainly concerned: the 'Jewish Question' was becoming a political issue. This hostile mood was attested to in a fulsome report in the *Zionist Record*, whose correspondent, after an extensive national tour, had confirmed that the spread of an anti-Jewish movement was now quite visible and carried with it the potential for serious consequences. The writer maintained that government warnings were ineffective, as were the scathing comments of the court in the Greyshirt trial, which had palpably failed to curb enthusiasm for extremist views: 'There is little doubt that there is a good deal of money behind these movements and organisations. They have official headquarters, with fully equipped offices and staffs, and they carry out extensive propaganda.'[106]

The proceedings of a typical Greyshirt meeting in the small northern Natal town of Newcastle capture the tenor of hatred and the character of radical right discourse. Chaired by Rudman, the meeting's focus was on both the Jewish and Asiatic problem, the latter group well represented in the town. As was so often the case, the meeting opened with a savage attack on the press by Stoffberg, coupled with an appeal for English- and Afrikaans-speakers to cooperate against Jews and Asiatics, who were likened to a cancer eating away at the nation's very existence. Weichardt, who was the main speaker, began his address by discussing the coalition between the South African Party and the National Party, which he maintained would plunge South Africa into darkness. More importantly, he emphasised how the Jew, or 'hoek nose', would milk divisions in South Africa while getting hold of the diamonds and gold, despite these minerals being dug out of the ground by the 'Boer and Briton'. Weichardt denied that the Greyshirts wanted 'to militarise South Africa', arguing that this was a figment of the 'Jew controlled press'. The Jew was being fought 'because of his moral code, not because he is a Jew. Let gold be discovered in China and at once you will find him leaving his South African nationality behind him and rushing off to China where he will become Mr Hong Kong if necessary.' Weichardt also scoffed at the idea of Jews as the Chosen People: 'They are not and even if they had been, they forfeited that right 2000 years ago. Did they crucify Christ or did we?' There were roars of laughter when he said, 'You English can very well sing "Rule, Britannia, Britannia rules the waves", but what does the Jew sing? He sings "We rule Britannia!"'[107]

The influx of approximately 700 German Jews in the two years following Hitler's ascent to power imparted a sense of urgency to Weichardt's message.[108] These newcomers were widely regarded as an unwelcome addition to the country's racial composition and an added source of economic competition. The SANP's JHH de Waal (Jnr) made this quite clear to a Dr Hillel Schulgasser of Wesselsbron in the Orange Free State, from whom he was soliciting funds for the party to fight the exclusion of South African Gentiles from professional and business life by Jews. Obviously doing his best to terrify the doctor, De Waal warned Schulgasser that hundreds of Jewish doctors were entering the country from Germany, threatening the livelihood of many Gentiles: 'The Jewish system of setting up Jews in business, by loans or guarantees, provides aliens who have been deemed undesirable elsewhere with an immediate footing here, and they soon become established, mainly through strong support from the Jewish community in the first instance. This support, given regardless of cost, is putting many Gentiles out of business.'[109]

Even though De Waal was exaggerating wildly, few could doubt the inroads made by the radical right and the penetration of its message. Jan Hofmeyr, now serving as Minister of the Interior, certainly recognised this. In a speech to the Witwatersrand South African College Schools (SACS) Alumni Association in late 1934, he warned against the dangers of antisemitism, and cautioned those present not to close their eyes to this propaganda, which threatened the best traditions of both British and Dutch South Africa:

> There is an open, organised attempt to stimulate hatred against a section of the South African nation. To that end public meetings have been held, and publications issued, some of them appealing to the least worthy instincts of humanity. The attempt has been made to incite racial animosity and religious intolerance, and tendencies have been set in motion which can only tend towards social disruption. We are already plucking some of the bitter fruits. The wells of good feeling have been poisoned, passions have been aroused, there have been actual physical clashes.

Hofmeyr expressed regret that, despite Smuts' appeal almost two years earlier, anti-Jewish agitation had persisted, and the government now found itself facing a grave situation that would have to be dealt with to safeguard the interests of the country — even if that meant introducing specific legislation.[110]

THE SPLINTERING OF THE RADICAL RIGHT

It was a strange anomaly that, despite the proliferation of radical right meetings, and in a time of hardship, alienation and marginalisation of many whites, the SANP had trouble attracting committed members. While meetings were well attended, a paltry 30 delegates (among them a few women) participated in its first national congress, held at the CJV Hall in Observatory, Cape Town, from 18 to 20 December 1934. Welcomed by Frikkie du Toit, the gathering was told that they were assembled in the interests of Christianity and would be guided by 'the Almighty'.[111] Somewhat defensively, he referred to the small number of delegates, but reminded those present that quantity was not important: 'If we had wanted quantity we would have to resort to the methods of corruption and money distribution — money freely distributed by those we are fighting. If we had adopted these methods we would need the Jew-controlled City Hall to accommodate all delegates.'[112]

This set the tone for Weichardt's keynote address, in which the SANP leader reminded delegates of the party's origins and expounded upon its principles: strong leadership, which did not mean dictatorship but rather strong guidance, and non-tolerance of democracy. It was the task of the SANP congress to elect such an all-powerful leader. As if to illustrate his decisive leadership, Weichardt referred to 'the traitor' Von Moltke, who had misbehaved and was now no longer a member of the SANP.[113] Thereafter he dealt primarily with the party's vision, its programme of principles and the 'Jewish Menace'. But a subtext ran throughout his address that related, obliquely, to feuds and divisions within the party and, to a lesser extent, to the weighting of antisemitism in its programme.[114] Weichardt blamed the poor attendance at the conference on the fact that many party supporters held government positions that prevented them supporting the movement in public, as doing so would jeopardise their positions due to the 'power of Judah in South Africa'. Clearly aware that some delegates objected to the overemphasis of the SANP's anti-Jewish message, Weichardt made his position clear: dissenters would have to voice their concerns and decide whether they would or would not 'join the Cause against the mighty Judaism in South Africa'. He reminded all present that the SANP had never hidden the fact that it was an anti-Jewish movement. There were a dozen anti-Jewish movements in the country, he told the congress, but only the SANP possessed the added advantage of being National Socialist as well.[115]

After Weichardt had spoken, he was nominated by Izak Zuidmeer (leader of the SANP in the western Cape Province) and seconded by Rudman to continue as leader of the SANP.[116] With unanimous support, Weichardt proceeded to make his acceptance speech and once again outlined the party's programme of principles, which were underpinned by the wish to save and unite Christianity as 'a blow to Judah who has only one religion for one people and are trying to smash up all other religions'. Speaking bluntly, Weichardt told the meeting that Jews were not welcome in South Africa and that he would put an end to their exploitation and domination of the country, including their control of the media. They could have their own schools but would be unable to go beyond standard six, and those who came to South Africa after 1918 would be considered guests in the country. Those not worthy of their professions would have their licences revoked.[117]

Despite the poor attendance, the SANP congress attracted substantial press coverage. In an editorial, the *Cape Argus* even commented on the resignation shortly before the conference of JHH de Waal, suggesting that he had left the movement because he had lost confidence in Weichardt and was opposed to a dictatorship.

> The 'South African National Party' is merely a bowdlerised version of the National Socialist Party in Germany. It has never seriously pretended to be anything else. And the essence of Hitlerism is dictatorship. If Mr de Waal thought that Hitlerism could be combined with democracy he was making a fundamental error. But perhaps the real truth is that the more he saw of Mr Weichardt the less he fancied that hero in the role of a South African Hitler.[118]

The *Cape Argus* was wrong to regard De Waal's departure as a matter of ideological differences: the SANP generally was unhappy with his administrative style. Within weeks, De Waal had started a new anti-Jewish organisation, 'Die Christenvolk-Beskermingsbond – The Gentile Protection League', with its headquarters in Bethlehem in the Orange Free State.[119] At its launch in Cape Town, at the Koffiehuis, De Waal announced that those in attendance were gathered to establish a national movement to specialise in anti-Jewish measures. The sole aim of the movement was to fight 'the Jewish menace in South Africa',[120] an aim embodied in its programme of principles, which identified the removal of Jews from their alleged control over South Africa. The policies were clearly defined:

a) To prohibit the further immigration of Jews into the Union.

b) To cancel certificates of Union granted to Jews as and from 1918.

c) Henceforth no right of citizenship to be granted to a Jew.

d) No Jew to be employed in the Civil Service or the administration.

e) Protective measures to be taken against the supplanting of Christians in Commerce, Trades and Professions.

f) To make the exploitation of the nation, or of any class or person a punishable offence.

g) To prohibit the present cruel method of slaughtering animals.

h) The Government will be empowered to deport any Jew who misconducts himself in whatsoever manner.[121]

The bespectacled and dapper De Waal now became a serious player on the radical right, but, unlike Weichardt, he had a substantial pedigree. His father, JHH de Waal (Snr), was a prominent Afrikaans writer, Cape politician and one-time Speaker of the House of Assembly. De Waal himself had practised as a lawyer in Hopefield and Vredendal, north of Cape Town. Although by then based in the Orange Free State, his political focus was the western Cape Province, a region well known to him, but he too had difficulty obtaining permission to hold meetings: in the wake of the formation of his organisation, he was refused the use of venues in Somerset West, Strand, Oudtshoorn and Riversdale, among others.[122]

Nonetheless, several open-air meetings were held during an upcountry tour from late April through May of 1935,[123] with good attendances in Porterville, Prince Alfred Hamlet, Ceres, Wolseley, Riebeek Kasteel and Riebeek West. Religious leaders joined some proceedings, no doubt encouraged by the main message – the protection of Christians in South Africa from unwanted Jewish immigrants.[124] The movement also advocated a boycott of Jewish stores in Dewetsdorp and Zastron in the southern Orange Free State, where depressed conditions made the region 'ripe for anti-Jewish agitation of a more serious kind', as the Zionist Record had explained a few months earlier.[125] By June 1935, De Waal claimed his movement had a membership of over 5 000.[126]

While such figures are not substantiated, it is beyond doubt that De Waal gained notoriety with a 61-page booklet entitled My Ontwaking (My Awakening). In this memoir he discussed the evolution of his insights into the Jewish question and how he had been alerted to the Jewish menace. One chapter, lifted directly from the Protocols of the Elders of Zion, crudely drew inspiration from an international web of antisemitic literature in which Jews were described as exploiters, followers of Satan, ritual murderers and Bolsheviks, and likened to an international octopus bent on dominating the world. One of De Waal's cartoons, 'Rituele Moord' (Ritual Murder) was taken directly from the 'Blood Libel' issue of the infamous Nazi publication Der Stürmer, as indeed were other pictures. Age-old canards about the Talmud were also included, all grafted onto De Waal's warped beliefs about Jews in South Africa, including their corruption of Christian women and their alleged manipulation of insurance agencies through the setting of fires in order to make fraudulent claims. A Jewish verborge hand (hidden hand) guided all affairs, with Jews in 'al die landsrade' (all the land's councils). Jews even changed their names in order to gain access to business and professional positions that might otherwise be denied them. He also reminded readers of Jewish objections, five years earlier, to attempts to transform Potchefstroom College into a Christian institution.[127]

In terms of 'scurrility', noted the Zionist Record, My Ontwaking exceeded anything previously published in South Africa and required government action. Laws had to be amended to prevent such 'mediaeval barbarism' being disseminated with impunity. South Africa, continued the weekly, was being 'flooded with literature designating a large and law-abiding element as thieves and murderers, practising every open and secret vice, battening upon their fellow-citizens, and worthy of extermination'.[128]

In addition to De Waal's newly established organisation, other radical right movements also attached themselves to the anti-Jewish bandwagon: soon after his break from Weichardt in late 1934 over accusations of improper behaviour, Von Moltke established the South African Fascists, whose uniform consisted of blue trousers and grey shirts.[129] Active primarily in the Orange Free State and eastern Cape Province and aimed more at English-speakers, the movement's headquarters were in Aberdeen and its official organ was *Die Swastika*. Manie Wessels' Suid-Afrikaanse Nasionale Demokratiese Beweging also splintered when Chris Havemann, a virtual unknown, broke away to form his own Blackshirt organisation, the Suid-Afrikaanse Nasionale Volksbeweging, which operated from Johannesburg. In addition to pursuing an anti-Jewish campaign, Havemann's Blackshirts advanced the idea of group representation – obviously drawn from European fascism – instead of popularly elected representatives. By October 1937, the Blackshirts had 265 branches in the Transvaal and several in the other provinces.[130]

All these groups shared conspiratorial views about Jews captured in a speech by Wessels to farmers in Davel, a hamlet in the eastern Transvaal. South Africans, he claimed, were under the stranglehold of the 'international capitalist Jew' and his 'demoniacal plans' to destroy Afrikaner livelihoods by taking control of banking institutions, fixing prices and fabricating so-called depressions. Jews were living in luxury at the expense of the true descendants of 'those who sacrificed their lives for this country' and, with their money, controlled the country's political life. In fact, they constituted a threat to the fabric of society and indeed to the very existence of genuine South Africans. To compound the situation, Jews were also responsible for the communist menace and for currently 'organising ten thousand Kaffirs on the Rand and elsewhere'. To round off this litany of accusations, Wessels also accused Jews of cowardice, maintaining they would be sure to run away if the position became untenable, leaving others to fight the battle.[131]

Despite sharing antisemitic views, none of the breakaway movements attracted the levels of attention enjoyed by the SANP, which, by early 1935, was concentrating its activities in the Transvaal. Weichardt visited Maquassi, where he met with local farmers, and a branch was established at Zwartruggens. Anti-Jewish propaganda was disseminated among teachers and schoolchildren, and speakers regularly made disparaging statements about Jews.[132] In May, Weichardt and Zuidmeer undertook a national tour. In addition to meetings in small towns, one was also held in the basement of the Durban Town Hall at which (much to the consternation of the Natal Council of the Board) ten Active Citizen Force members were present. Rudman was a key speaker on that occasion, railing once again against the press and the Jewish 'menace' and, interestingly, describing Weichardt as a 'German South African'.[133]

The tour was not without its problems. Some meetings were violently disrupted and venues were on occasion hard to come by.[134] Nonetheless, Weichardt persisted with his antisemitic message. When speaking in Smuts' parliamentary seat, Standerton, he focused on the supposed close ties between the Jews and the government.[135] Of course Smuts had for some time been described as a lackey of the Jews. Standerton was also chosen as a venue to attack Jews by the leader of the Volksbeweging, Terblanche. Declaring that his eyes had been opened to the power of the Jews after spending seventeen years in Europe, he went on to claim that all South Africa's problems could be laid at their feet:

> Ours is the richest land in the world and yet we are the poorest people. This is because our products here are in the hands of Jews ... You fought for your freedom and your country and yet you allow yourselves to be ruled by a people who never fired a shot in their lives ...
>
> If we solved the economic conditions in South Africa and can get rid of the Jews, we will improve by 50 per cent our standard of living ... If they put me in parliament I would have all Jews out of South Africa within a month.

When a member of the audience remonstrated with Terblanche that the

Jew was 'descended from God', he answered that he is 'descended from the devil'. Moreover, he contended, the Jew was not a European but an Asiatic.[136]

The danger posed by radical right activists such as Weichardt, Terblanche, Von Moltke and De Waal was fully recognised by the Board. At its Eleventh Biennial Conference in May 1935, the issue was uppermost in the minds of delegates, and the Board resolved through the establishment of a 'Propaganda Committee' to educate public opinion about the unfounded and slanderous nature of the anti-Jewish propaganda being disseminated throughout South Africa. The conference also agreed to convey to the government the serious nature of the hatred and the need for legislation to make the defamation of Jews a criminal offence.[137] Delegates garnered some satisfaction from Smuts' message to the conference in which he acknowledged that the government recognised the gravity of the problem, but implored everyone 'to remove causes of friction and misunderstanding' – a probable reference to those Jews involved in skirmishes with the radical right at public meetings, as well as to those allegedly advocating a boycott of German goods. Smuts, however, remained firm on the question of law and order, expressing regret that despite previous admonitions, the various movements were persisting with their activities. He issued a strongly worded warning to those wishing to stir up trouble between the various sections of South Africa's population: the police and law enforcement officers would be watching the situation carefully and would take strong action against those who disseminated antisemitic propaganda.[138]

Reflecting upon the proceedings of the conference, the *Zionist Record* lamented that Jew-hatred, formerly a thing 'of holes and corners', had 'come out into the open' and had taken on 'the garb not merely of an organised and stable movement but of a social and economic philosophy and a political programme'.[139]

A COMBUSTIBLE MIX

The proliferation of radical right movements was largely related to white poverty – the furnace that fired extremism. To be sure, three months before the 'Purified' National Party had been formally established, the 'poor white' question had been the subject of a major *Volkskongres* (People's Congress) convened in Kimberley under the auspices of the Dutch Reformed Church. The plight of the unskilled and ill-equipped Afrikaner monopolised addresses and discussions.[140]

The Volkskongres was based on the 1932 Carnegie Commission report into poverty, and a range of speakers, including government representatives, spelt out the magnitude of Afrikaner poverty to the 500 delegates. 'In the life of our people,' said Daniel Petrus van Huyssteen in his opening remarks, 'walls are torn apart and are in ruins; they call out to be rebuilt. Thousands live in poverty, in misery, in pitiful conditions, and there is degeneration in all areas of life, social, moral and spiritual.'[141] The respected Reverend William Nicol added his sombre assessment, pointing out that when the problem had first attracted public attention, seventeen years earlier, there had been 80 000 poor whites, a number that had risen to 250 000 despite all the measures taken.[142]

The opening addresses by Van Huyssteen and Nicol set the tone for a workmanlike, wide-ranging and well-reported conference in which all dimensions of the crisis were covered, as well as possible ways to ameliorate the situation. In an address that received wide coverage, DF Malan spoke of the failure of the capitalist system, which he characterised as doomed.[143] Here he reaffirmed the sentiments he had expressed some months earlier at the National Party's Cape provincial congress in Somerset West, on the eve of his breakaway. Always wary of the power and meddling of financiers, Malan had on that occasion lambasted the Hertzog government for acting at the behest of Hoggenheimer.[144] Now he warned that it was unacceptable that so much poverty was surrounded by so much wealth. The *volk*, he maintained, had to be rescued.

This call to action was reinforced by the Dutch-born Hendrik Frensch Verwoerd, one of the key organisers of the conference. Scholarly and didactic, the young Stellenbosch academic, who had been appointed to the Chair of Applied Psychology at the age of twenty-six and who was to become the master-builder of apartheid, spelled out the magnitude of the problem: the Carnegie study had classified one in four Afrikaners as 'poor whites', but,

A young HF Verwoerd is shown seated at right in this photograph.
(courtesy JS Gericke Library, University of Stellenbosch)

if the categories of 'very poor' and 'poor' were combined, that number, he explained, would jump to 56 per cent.[145]

A rising star in Afrikaner intellectual circles, the thirty-three-year-old Verwoerd, a graduate of Stellenbosch (with postgraduate studies at the psychological institutes of universities in Leipzig, Hamburg and Berlin), was imbued with a gravitas beyond his years and spoke with a ponderous but mesmerising authority.[146] Fully cognisant that English-speakers were also among the impoverished, Verwoerd nevertheless chose to focus only on Afrikaners, as he believed that 'a people must be uplifted by its own folk'.[147] As one of his earliest biographers put it, Verwoerd's address was a call to join the 'crusade of Afrikaner nationalism'; the distress of the 'poor white' required a state-driven ethnic solution, a cast of mind that Verwoerd three years later would translate into the advocacy of limitations and quotas on Jewish economic and professional activity. At the Kimberley Volkskongres, however, his emphasis was simply on rescuing Afrikanerdom.[148]

Although there were signs of economic recovery by mid-1935, the aggrieved Afrikaner underclass remained a political time bomb and a potential source for ethnic mobilisation. Seeking a scapegoat to account for their plight was always politically useful. As an observer writing in the *Zionist Record* put it, the spread of antisemitism was built upon deep social tensions in South Africa linked to 'rabid and uninformed nationalism'. In the writer's estimation, domestic conditions were not unlike those in Germany, although in South Africa the government was stable and the antisemites had few resources. On the other hand, warned the writer, amid a sea of poverty the highly concentrated presence of Jews in certain areas of the economy – especially mining – was hugely problematic. Farmers on the platteland were also struggling, and antisemitic organisations would 'not be slow to seize upon the obvious poverty of the farming community as compared to the Rand'. Although antisemitism was 'not an indigenous plant in this country', the writer maintained that 'once it has taken hold it is apt to spread with horrible rapidity and it is almost impossible to eradicate this racial "khaki-weed" once it has taken root'.[149]

This was well understood by Malan's 'Purified' National Party – rapidly consolidating itself as the voice of exclusivist Afrikaner nationalism – as well as by Afrikaner ethnic entrepreneurs. Behind the scenes, the Broederbond continued to act as the coordinating agency of the *volk*. Leading intellectuals appealed in ethnic terms to Afrikaners across the spectrum,[150] while religious and cultural institutions, infused by Broederbonders, strove to foster a sense of ethnic exclusivism to ensure a proud future. By now, the FAK – the Broederbond's literary and cultural arm – had moved squarely into the Malan camp following his breakaway, as had the Dutch Reformed Church, albeit in a less vocal way.[151] The goal of the 'Purified' National Party was to capture the cultural, economic, and political levers of state to ensure the ascendancy of the *volk*. Afrikaners could not expect help from Hertzog's United Party, depicted in Malanite circles as the handmaiden of British imperialism and firmly ensconced in the pocket of Hoggenheimer.[152] As Malan told an audience in Stellenbosch, Hertzog had abandoned the cause of nationalism when he returned to the old South African Party.[153]

Malanites were also concerned about trade union and left-wing activism – increasingly personified by Solly Sachs, the general secretary of the Garment Workers' Union, who was Jewish – and by the dangers associated with the militancy of African workers.[154] Particularly troubling for hardline Afrikaner nationalists was the advance of Afrikaner men and women into leadership positions in the union movement. Some had even visited the Soviet Union and returned with great enthusiasm for what they had seen.[155] The Communist Party of South Africa had also begun publishing an Afrikaans monthly, *Die Arbeiter en Arme Boer* (Worker and Peasant), in January 1935, in an effort to attract Afrikaner members.[156]

These initiatives were not looked upon kindly by Broederbonders, who perceived unions as divisive and distracting, turning Afrikaner workers away from Afrikanerdom's national project. Class struggle ran counter to the interests of *völkisch* ideologues and their vision of Afrikaner cohesion. Particularly disturbing was the wooing away of the Afrikaner working woman, who, according to Moodie, had been 'lionised' in Nationalist mythology as the mother who gave comfort to her husband in times of crisis, ensured the preservation of racial purity within Afrikanerdom, and inculcated the 'true civil faith' in her children.[157]

Young Afrikaners, especially students, joined the battle for ethnic solidarity. As we saw in the previous chapter, the ANS under Piet Meyer had already broken away from NUSAS over the issue of black membership. Two years later, the movement – now with branches at all Afrikaans universities – published a manifesto in which it declared its intention 'to inspire students to national service and cooperation on the basis of the Protestant-Christian and Cultural-National principles of our nation'.[158] The new mood was lucidly captured by Nico Diederichs, an upcoming voice in Afrikaner intellectual circles, in his booklet '*Nasionalisme as Lewensbeskowing en sy Verhouding tot Internasionalisme*' (Nationalism as Worldview and its Relation to Internationalism). The German- and Dutch-educated lecturer in Political Studies and Philosophy at the University of the Orange Free State contrasted the arid 'materialism of internationalism' with the richness of nationalism and its emphasis upon the *geestilike* (spiritual) nature of man and attacked 'Bolshevist and International cosmopolitanism'.[159] Appointed to the university teaching staff at the age of twenty-five, Diederichs drew his inspiration from German Romantic thought in general, and in particular from the ideas of Johann Fichte, with their stress on the centrality of the *volk*. For Diederichs the individual did not exist; one belonged to a national community.[160]

Sympathetic but not fully aligned to the Nazis, Diederichs' worldview – no doubt informed by his studies in Germany and a doctorate at the University of Leiden on 'Suffering and Patience' – resonated among an Afrikaner nationalist intelligentsia deeply imbued with the spirit of the Voortrekkers and nurtured by a deep-seated anti-British hostility that had been fuelled by two freedom struggles. Theorists such as Diederichs placed great emphasis upon an exclusivist and culturally pure nationalism that would manifest itself in republicanism, a belief in the organic state, and a profound disillusionment with Fusion. Many others shared this disillusionment.[161] Malan's 'Purified' National Party, writes Giliomee, hoped to mobilise these Afrikaners 'by staking group claims based on the notion that Afrikaners occupied a special place in the South African society'.[162]

The 'Purified' Nationalist principles reflected these aspirations. Indians would be segregated or sent back to India, while Coloureds would lose the vote insofar as they exercised this option in the Cape Province.[163] In the context of protecting European civilisation at the tip of Africa, 'white' immigration had a place, but it had to be limited 'to elements which can be assimilated by South African people and will not, by their presence, lower either the material standard of living or the moral standards of the white population'.[164] Here the party's constitution spoke directly to racialised notions of Jewish morality and the contentious issue of ongoing Jewish immigration, identified by many as a source of yet another racial problem.

For all its exclusivism, however, the National Party did maintain a belief in, and respect for, parliamentarianism. Broadly speaking, this was not the case with the radical right and certainly did not apply to the SANP. In addition to making it clear that he had no respect for effete Western constitutionalism, at every opportunity Weichardt projected what the European right described as a 'third way', namely, fascism, as an alternative to capitalism and communism. Neither was his the politics of ethnic mobilisation. English-speakers were encouraged to join with Afrikaners in the revolutionary project whose outcome anticipated no place for Jews.[165]

In this regard, the SANP was aware that some members of the government and many 'Purified' Nationalists were of the same mind.[166] Indeed, at every opportunity they taunted Malanites as well as Pirow, the Minister of Railways, Harbours and Defence, on this question. When questioned by Zuidmeer at the hustings about Jewish dominance in the economy, the United Party's Pirow carefully staked out a position in line with his government. He was opposed to blaming poverty on Jews and would not countenance judging citizens according to their religion. 'If a man is a good citizen he must be treated as such, or, if he is a bad citizen, be his name Moses or Reitz or Pirow he must be treated as such,' said Pirow.[167] Malan responded similarly when challenged by the radical right: 'If a Jew does wrong, deal with him; if a Jew is a parasite, deal with him, but if an Afrikaner who is not a Jew does wrong or is a parasite, deal with him in precisely the same way … If a Jew did wrong he must be punished according to the laws of the country but he could not be punished simply for being a Jew.'[168] Malan went even further, claiming that if Jews subscribed to the 'Purified' National Party's principles they were welcome to become members[169] – a hollow claim, of course, as the party's constitution included an opening clause emphasising the envisaged Christian character of the state.[170]

Such responses satisfied the Jewish press but of course failed to assuage the radical right, for whom Jews were the personification of the evils of both capitalism and communism.[171] Meetings and propaganda ensured a continuing focus on the 'Jewish Question' and what was alleged to be the inordinate and malevolent power of Jews. In one of his many tirades, Rudman accused the 'Judah Press' of owning every newspaper and deliberately misleading the people. The SANP 'was not fighting the Jew because he was a Jew, but because he was regarded as a menace in their midst'.[172] Conspiratorial thought had not subsided, reported Morris Alexander after a fact-finding tour of the country. Indeed, it appeared as though 'every Predikant had a copy of the *Protocols* and did not know it was refuted.'[173]

Speaking in Newcastle, Weichardt made it clear that if he came to power he would scrap the Act of Union, which was 'Jew made', and in its place institute a group system in parliament with representatives from the various sectors, such as farmers, workers and professionals.[174] Such a framework, purely fascist in conception, was no doubt informed by European currents of thought, as well as by Weichardt's sympathy for Hitler and his connections with pro-Nazis in South West Africa. These ties had been exposed in evidence presented to a special commission (chaired by Justice Hendrik Stephanus van Zyl) on Nazi activities and agitation in the mandated territory.[175] Material seized by the Union government in July 1934 from Nazi offices in South West Africa had uncovered subversive documents, as well as incriminating references to secret financial aid to the Greyshirts, considered a sister movement by the South West African Nazis.[176] Major Heinrich Weigel, referred to as the 'Territorial Fuhrer' for South West Africa, had made this link quite clear in a communication to the Auslands-Organisation in Hamburg:

> Perhaps it would be possible to make provision for a nominal amount, say several hundred pounds, out of some political fund which one could then place in some suitable form at the disposal of the Greyshirt movement along devious ways. It is obvious that I must avoid any open

fraternisation with the South African sister movement. The support of the movement can take place only through intermediaries without any direct connection with us.[177]

While Weichardt strongly denied ties between his movement and the Nazis in South West Africa,[178] it was widely understood that the SANP did in fact enjoy financial support from Weigel's outfit.[179] Seized letters certainly suggest that the Nazis perceived Weichardt's movement as the 'National Socialists in the Union', worthy of aid and a useful means of splitting Afrikaners in South Africa, whom they believed were on the whole recognised as unsympathetic to Nazism.[180] 'Naturally party (i.e. Nazi Party) members must only support the movement anonymously,' wrote Weigel in another communication with the Auslands-Organisation, adding that, in the interests of the Greyshirt movement, it should not be made known that it was receiving financial support from Germany.[181]

The evidence of ties between Weichardt and German Nazis is substantial. Actual contact was documented some years later in a 1942 South African Military Intelligence report noting that Weichardt had open access to German consulates in South Africa.[182] Certainly the SANP and other radicals also benefited from the Nazi propaganda emanating from the Deutscher Fichte Bund, a nationalist, antisemitic organisation based in Hamburg, and the Welt-Dienst, a news agency and publisher of antisemitic literature in Erfurt. Innumerable leaflets were also being sent from Germany, many of them in perfect Afrikaans.[183] With good reason, the Nazi regime knew it had fellow travellers in place.[184]

Correspondence between Weigel and Professor Hermann Bohle (who resigned from the University of Cape Town in 1936 and returned to Germany) was yet another indication of subversion emanating from South West Africa:[185]

It may be possible for us to establish with the Grey Shirts a united front based upon similar world views ... Perhaps it is possible for you to interview Weichardt in this connection and to arrange that he sends sufficient propaganda material to South West ... I have sent 58 copies of 'Die Waarheid' along with Mr Mohl, who I have reason to know is a highly reliable person, as the latter is travelling straight to Windhoek.[186]

SEEKING POLITICAL POWER

Despite Nazi propaganda and support from South West Africa, the radical right did not operate in an easy environment. Venues for meetings remained a problem and audiences were not always enthusiastic. In some cases it was curious onlookers, among them Africans, who constituted the majority of the audience.[187] Financial difficulties were also apparent: the Eendrag Printing Press of Ermelo, the printers of *Ons Reg/Our Right* (organ of the Suid-Afrikaanse Demokratiese Beweging), ran into financial trouble and was successfully prosecuted for not paying its employees, as was the printing press at Aberdeen and other printers of anti-Jewish pamphlets.[188]

More importantly, electoral support proved elusive. Radical right political efforts at the local level were not successful. Voters unhappy with the status quo obviously believed their best hope lay with the National Party. In a municipal contest in Aliwal North, the candidate favoured by the SANP fared the worst, and even antisemitic pamphleteering by Von Moltke's South African Fascists could not prevent the election of a Jewish candidate, A Marcow. Another Jewish candidate, HM Jaffe, was elected in Somerset West, despite his religious affiliation being raised at the hustings.[189] However, in Paarl, the SANP candidate, Zuidmeer, came close to defeating the town's former deputy mayor, David Nelson (who was Jewish), in a hotly contested municipal election. With a turnout of 65 per cent of the ratepayers, Zuidmeer lost by a mere 26 votes.[190]

Although these municipal results were mixed insofar as the fortunes of the radical right were concerned, a parliamentary by-election in Senekal in 1935, which saw the United Party scrape home by 179 votes against the 'Purified' Nationalists in an 86.4 per cent poll, was of national significance. As a bellwether contest on the state of Fusion and the pull of ethno-nationalism, heavyweights such as Pirow and Hofmeyr for the United Party and Malan for the 'Purifieds' were brought into the battle. The focus at the hustings was on republicanism, but the question of the Coloured and Afri-

Prime Minister JBM Hertzog (far left) addresses a public meeting, with Oswald Pirow at right in the foreground. (courtesy Museum Africa)

can franchise also loomed large. Apart from Malan invoking the power of Hoggenheimer, the 'Jewish Question' hardly featured, and ultimately the 'Purified' National Party leader failed to swing the result.[191] Nevertheless, Senekal was a major setback for Hertzog's United Party. As Malan put it, Senekal was 'the writing on the wall'.[192]

Notwithstanding poor performances at the polls, radical right anti-Jewish agitation and incidents, as well as calls to boycott Jewish businesses, persisted. A particularly vitriolic speech by Von Moltke in the small eastern Cape Province town of Molteno resulted in ill-feeling and bitterness between Jews and Gentiles, with Jewish merchants subsequently feeling the pinch of a boycott.[193] For its part, the Board passed a resolution at its Orange Free State congress in August 1935 urging 'the Executive Council to carry out more vigorously the resolution adopted by the last Congress and to pursue a policy of counter-propaganda in print by disseminating in both official languages leaflets, pamphlets, etc. showing the harm done to the religious, political and economic life of South Africa by the Grey Shirt movement and all other anti-Semitic movements.'[194]

By early December 1935, the Board was reporting increased Blackshirt activity. Of particular concern was the fact that civil servants and railway officials were joining the movement. The Board was also alerted to a planned meeting of Wessels' Suid-Afrikaanse Nasionale Demokratiese Beweging in Potchefstroom, on 18 and 19 December, to fight the threat of 'total destruction in the Christian, National and Economic domain'. In a lengthy appeal to the public to attend the meeting, its proposals were riddled from beginning to end with Jew-hatred that presented the 'poor white' as a victim of the international Jewish capitalist who dominated South Africa. The pamphlet also maintained that South African farmers faced a boycott of their products by Germany in retaliation for the Jewish boycott of German goods.[195]

Yet, despite the loss of some lustre, it was the SANP that continued to define – at least in part – the terms of political debate. By persistently raising the 'Jewish Question' in general, and the influx of Jews in particular, they kept both the government and the 'Purified' National Party on the back foot. Letters to the press, moreover, indicated a persistent and widespread concern with these matters. With Weichardt continuing to hold regular meetings,[196] and *Die Republikein* displaying a venom and hatred that was the equal of publications of the radical right, Jewish leaders had every reason to remain alarmed and vigilant.[197]

On 28 November 1935, the incoming executive of the Board, under Cecil Lyons, had a very satisfactory meeting with Hertzog. Ostensibly convened as an opportunity for the newcomers on the Board's executive to meet the Prime Minister, members took the opportunity to update him on the state of anti-Jewish agitation in the country. Discrimination against Jews in the civil service and the ties between the Nazi Party and the Greyshirts, as outlined by the South West Africa Commission, were also discussed, while Hertzog encouraged the Board to place before him any information in its possession.[198]

On the surface, at least, the government remained concerned. But Hertzog and his cabinet had matters of greater import to address. A long struggle to remove Africans from the common voters' roll in the Cape Province had generated grassroots opposition. On 16 December 1935, an All Africa Convention – a non-racial and progressive umbrella body of trade unionists, communists, liberals and intellectuals – met to reject the government's plans for political and social segregation. Participants sought common cause in the defence of democratic values, the rejection of political and territorial segregation, and improved wages for workers.[199] The convention, however, posed no real threat to Hertzog since most of the participating organisations were in a state of disarray, deeply compromised by the financial legacy of the depression.[200] To be sure, African resistance was episodic in the 1930s and certainly far less threatening than in the preceding decade. For Weichardt, on the other hand, it was precisely economic hardship that provided the leaven for optimism. The Greyshirts depended on the disillusioned; those who were newly urbanised and marginalised were inclined to believe in conspiratorial theories and as willing as their rural cousins to identify a Jewish scapegoat.

The SANP was presented with an opportunity to test its political support with the death of Charles Frederick Kayser, the sitting United Party MP for Port Elizabeth North. A by-election was scheduled for 22 January 1936, and it was believed that many struggling workers would look to options other than the United Party. On 13 December 1935, *Die Waarheid/ The Truth* announced that Weichardt would stand for the vacant seat. Here was a man who, with his simple explanations for life's deprivations, could potentially attract both English- and Afrikaans-speaking voters.

The tone of Weichardt's planned campaign was apparent from the outset. 'The Jews, we are informed, have already started a special fund for the purpose of preventing by hook or by crook, Mr Weichardt's return to Parliament,' stated *Die Waarheid/The Truth*.[201] Confident that he could take advantage of an electorate that had seen hard times, and armed with positive memories of well-attended Greyshirt meetings in the Feather Market Hall, Weichardt no doubt believed he would be warmly received in 'Die Baai' (the Bay), his old stomping ground. After all, members of the ravaged underclass, only just beginning to emerge from the depression, would surely want an alternative voice in parliament.

CHAPTER THREE

THE JEWISH QUESTION MOVES TO THE CENTRE

'Unless in very exceptional cases the "decent" Jew is pure sham. He is a wolf in sheep's clothing, and is much more dangerous than the "bad" Jew who makes no attempt to disguise his inherent vileness.'
– Die Waarheid / The Truth, 9 April 1936

'The debate which took place in the House of Assembly on Thursday a week ago in regard to the banning of certain Greyshirt meetings in various centres has come as a rude shock. It has revealed the extent of a certain frame of mind in certain political circles which, if it should persist and spread, is fraught with ominous potentialities …'
– Zionist Record, 15 May 1936

'If you read the history of the Jews throughout the Middle Ages and in modern times, you see the same facts always repeating themselves. The Jews are received into a country, kindly treated, allowed to accumulate wealth, etc. Then they invariably overreach themselves.'
– Professor JK Wylie to Sir Carruthers Beattie, 7 May 1936

'We have a Grey Shirt movement here of young men who go about in a semi-uniform dress in imitation of the Fascists and Nazis but their objects do not seem to go beyond baiting the Jews. They have a good deal of support in the country and small towns and they have almost captured the Malan party.'
– Patrick Duncan to Lady Maud Selborne, 28 October 1936

FAILURE IN PORT ELIZABETH

Electioneering for the Port Elizabeth North by-election in January 1936 began to gain momentum in the wake of the Christmas and New Year festivities. By the end of the first week in January, the *Eastern Province Herald* was reporting that as many as three meetings a day were taking place.[1] Weichardt, however, received very little press coverage. According to *Die Burger*, he was an outsider with little chance of garnering more than two or three hundred votes.[2] More attention was devoted to the independent Labour candidate, CA Retief, a man believed to have had Greyshirt sympathies at one time,[3] but now rumoured to be secretly in cahoots with Malan's National Party which had chosen not to field a candidate.[4] Because of his appeal to the poorer voter, it could be anticipated that Retief would undercut much SANP support.

Predictably, Weichardt focused on the Jews as the source of all misfortune. His campaign targeted both English- and Afrikaans-speaking voters, many of whom were still suffering the ravages of the economic downturn: Port Elizabeth had indeed been badly hit during the depression and was only beginning to recover. Five days before the by-election, the SANP mouthpiece published 'A Short Biography of a Great Leader & Patriot, Louis Theodore Weichardt', and made the case for their candidate. Its essential message to the voters was simple and crude. Wildly exaggerating the significance of the contest, it contended that:

> ... for the first time a Greyshirt champion of Christian Civilisation against Jewish oppression, exploitation, corruption and injustice is standing as a candidate for the South African parliament.
>
> The issue is between Christendom and Jewry. If Mr Weichardt is defeated, no matter by whom, the result will be hailed by the Jew throughout the world as another Jewish triumph over the hated enemies, the Christian. Mr Weichardt's victory will make the craven heart of international Jewry quail with terror.
>
> The Jews regard South Africa as one of their chief strangleholds. They openly speak of it as a Jewish possession. It is the main source of their gold supplies – at the lowest estimate 70% of the shares in our gold

mines are held by Jews. They are going to fight to the last ditch for the retention of their hold on OUR Country, OUR People, OUR wealth!

Stand firm and united. The Jews are trying their hardest to divide you, to deceive you, to bribe you, to intimidate you. Show them that you are worthy of your great forefathers and render their dastardly efforts futile. The ballot is secret. You are safe from victimization. The Jew can never discover how you vote.[5]

Scaremongering tactics, albeit aimed at a different target, were also used by Willem Steenkamp – Malan's old adversary – who came to Port Elizabeth to speak on behalf of the United Party candidate, Henry Johnson. Identifying SANP connections with the Nazis and focusing on their racism and hatred, which he deemed a clear threat to South Africa, Steenkamp explained that a forthcoming book based on documents recovered by the South African government in Windhoek would expose the Nazis as the real power behind the SANP, providing the party with financial support in order to foster divisions within Afrikanerdom. That in turn would result in parliamentary pressure to convince the League of Nations that South West Africa should be handed back to Germany. If that should happen, he warned, every 'Dutchman and Englishman' would be expelled from South West Africa, which would then become a perilously close enemy base.[6]

Judging by the extent of campaign coverage, the outcome of the by-election was of considerable importance. To be sure, the turnout on election day, 22 January 1936, was high despite the cancellation of electioneering on the night before the poll – due to the death of King George V – as well as the inclement weather on the morning of the election. Retief put up a good showing, losing to the United Party's Johnson by a mere 90 votes. Weichardt, on the other hand, performed poorly, losing his deposit with only 498 votes out of a total of 5 868.[7] Voters in Port Elizabeth had forcefully demonstrated that they had no real appetite for vulgar antisemitism and conspiratorial fantasies.

Trying its best to put on a brave face, an editorial in *Die Waarheid/ The Truth* claimed that Jews had been behind the anti-Weichardt campaign and had invented the idea that the SANP were the agents of Nazi Germany, but fighting the election had been worthwhile: 'The conspiracy of silence against us on the part of the infamous Jew–controlled press is an obstacle of the most serious nature which we have to surmount, and it is only by putting forward candidates that we can force ourselves on the notice of the public in spite of the press.'[8]

SETTING THE AGENDA

Despite Weichardt's unsuccessful foray into parliamentary politics, the SANP remained a powerful voice on the radical right and *Die Waarheid / The Truth* continued its attacks on Jews and the way in which Labour parties were tools of 'Jew–Capitalists and Jew Communists'. In line with this conspiratorial mindset, the League of Nations was described as 'Jew controlled'[9] and Jews continued to be accused of involvement in nefarious global activities, including Bolshevism, white slave trafficking[10] and the sexual exploitation of young Gentile girls.[11] Well-worn labels such as 'parasites', 'bloodsuckers', 'human vermin', 'refuse' and 'Peruvians of the lowest and worst kind' peppered its propaganda assault, as did claims that the 'poor white' problem would only be solved by the elimination of Jews and Asians. Noticeably, English-speakers continued to be identified alongside Afrikaners as South Africans.[12]

Less than six weeks after the Greyshirt leader's electoral drubbing in Port Elizabeth, the Board's Press and Propaganda Committee presented a detailed assessment of the state of anti-Jewish agitation. Speaking as a member of the Board, the youthful, learned and energetic Gustav Saron (who would become secretary of the Board in July 1936) pointed out that Terblanche's Volksbeweging had been very active, particularly among railway workers in De Aar and Kimberley, and that a considerable amount of anti-Jewish propaganda had been spread in Tzaneen in the northern Transvaal.[13] Uitenhage, a railway town close to Port Elizabeth, had also seen some activity. Importantly, Saron noted that while there had been a decrease in anti-Jewish agitation in some towns and a slight lull in radical right activism, there was now a change of tactics, with meetings switching from local halls to private homes.[14] This was also noted by the *Zionist Record*, which reported much underground activity and personal canvassing, as well as a great number of public and private meetings in the Cape Province.[15]

Certainly Terblanche did his utmost to appeal to the poor and the alienated. On his return from a visit to Germany, he held meetings in Kimberley, Warrenton, Potchefstroom and Germiston. Copies of his propaganda sheet, *Terre-Blanche*, were distributed,[16] its columns filled with fabrications of Jewish conspiracies modelled on the movement's Nazi mentors.[17] But Terblanche's meetings were not always successful and, despite support from the Blackshirts, the leader of the Volksbeweging soon made his way to the more promising voter terrain of Natal.[18]

Terre-Blanche was another addition to an array of publications spewing anti-Jewish propaganda. These included *Die Waarheid/The Truth*, *Die Rapport*, *Patria*, *Die Leier/The Leader*, *Thingbod* and *Ons Reg-Our Right*, as well as thousands of leaflets and propaganda sheets that, as one commentator recalled some years later, were directed mainly at the economically depressed classes in urban and especially rural districts 'where ignorance and human hardships and misfortunes were unscrupulously exploited for a vicious end'.[19] Wessels' Blackshirts, too, were making some headway in the Transvaal where they held meetings on the Witwatersrand and in country towns,[20] while there were reports of 'diminished business in Jewish shops' in Ermelo and Standerton.[21]

Printed antisemitic material was flooding the country, either through the post or by personal distribution, targeting primarily the urban and rural poor, but also 'the native and coloured peoples'. The message faithfully imitated that of the Nazis and was aimed at arousing hostility and hatred against Jews. Even the slanderous 'blood libel' charge reappeared in *Die Waarheid/The Truth*, in an article entitled 'Was the Lindbergh baby a victim of the Jews?':

> Now, in spite of all the Jewish denials, there is certainly authority for the assertion that the Jews, when they can, employ Christian blood for ritual purposes on the occasion of the feast of Purim. Numerous cases of so-called 'Jewish Ritual Murders' are recorded in history, and it is somewhat difficult to dismiss all these stories as mere malicious fabrications.

> Furthermore, though it may be a mere coincidence, there are said to occur in different countries an abnormal number of mysterious disappearances of Christians during the weeks preceding the feast of Purim.

The article questioned whether the timing of the Lindbergh baby's kidnapping, twelve days before the Jewish festival of Purim, could not in fact be regarded as proof of Jewish involvement, particularly in the light of the fact that the baby's corpse had been discovered with its throat cut in a manner reminiscent of the 'barbarous ceremony of Schechitah', whereby Jews drain off the blood of animals before they are finally killed.[22]

By mid-1936 six anti-Jewish organisations were operating: the SANP, better known as the Greyshirts, under Louis Weichardt, with headquarters in Cape Town and branches in all four provinces; *Die Volksbeweging* (People's Movement), under HS Terblanche, based in Cape Town; the *Suid-Afrikaanse Nasionale Demokratiese Beweging* (South African National Democratic Movement, known as the Blackshirts), under Manie Wessels; *Die Suid-Afrikaanse Nasionale Volksbeweging* (also known as the Blackshirts), operating in the Orange Free State and the Transvaal, with an offshoot in Johannesburg, under Chris Havemann; the South African Fascists under Johannes von Strauss von Moltke, mainly active in the Eastern Province and Orange Free State, with headquarters in Aberdeen and its own journal *Patria – An Organ for Racial Fascism*, and 'Die Christenvolk-Beskermingsbond – The Gentile Protection League', under JHH de Waal (Jnr), dealing exclusively with the 'Jewish Menace', and aiming above all to remove Jews from their alleged control over South Africa.

According to the Board, the leaders of these organisations had little social standing and used 'the anti-Jewish cry to achieve personal aggrandizement and political power', while some of them nursed the ambition of becoming South Africa's future dictator. Despite some differences, the Board correctly argued that these organisations were substantially similar. Propaganda originating from their headquarters was systematic and distributed through a network of local branches, cells and individuals. The Board had little doubt that the funding behind these movements went beyond mere subscriptions.[23]

Despite the array of anti-Jewish organisations, it was Weichardt, with his

Antisemitic propaganda leaflet, 'Life and Life in South Africa', highlighting the gap between the conditions of poor Afrikaners and Jewish plutocrats.
(JBM Hertzog Collection, courtesy Archives for Contemporary Affairs, University of the Free State, Bloemfontein)

indefatigable Jew-bashing at venue after venue, who set the agenda. After addressing a meeting at the Koffiehuis in early March 1936, the SANP leader proceeded to arouse the disaffected in Malmesbury and Moorreesburg. His sidekick, Zuidmeer, who had recently returned from a visit to Germany, also conducted private meetings in Paarl and Moorreesburg, where he spread pro-German and anti-British propaganda. In addition to targeting the southwestern Cape Province, the SANP was also active in the eastern Cape Province, still a favourite hunting ground, notwithstanding its humiliating defeat in Port Elizabeth.[24]

One highly publicised Greyshirt meeting on the Grand Parade in Cape Town turned violent when the platform party descended to attack a rival anti-fascist meeting. On this occasion Weichardt was the chief speaker, hurling his usual invective against Jews, identifying prominent Jewish politicians by name, and accusing Jews of financing the opponents of fascism. The government was attacked for failing to suppress 'revolutionary and seditious Jewish organisations' which masqueraded under false names such as 'anti-fascists', but in reality aimed to destabilise South Africa and encourage foreign interference.[25] Here Weichardt was harping on the now commonplace association of Jews with communism. This connection was also apparent in a pamphlet entitled 'Communism with the Mask off' that circulated among the African population in the Warmbaths area north of Pretoria.[26]

Shortly thereafter, the Board met with Hertzog to discuss once again the introduction of anti-defamation legislation. The Prime Minister admitted that things had deteriorated: freedom of speech and liberty were now developing into licence and something would have to be done. He gave the Board his assurance that the government was investigating the possibility of introducing anti-defamation legislation, but cautioned that such legislation was not without difficulties.[27] For its part, the Board informed Hertzog that the activities of the various anti-Jewish movements had increased, and presented examples of anti-Jewish leaflets that had been circulated across the country. After the meeting, the chairman of the Board reported that, despite its energetic endeavours to counter the present wave of activity, a much greater effort was needed to educate the public about the true facts behind the agitation.[28]

The Board's rather pessimistic assessment of the situation was not simply a negotiating gambit; anti-Jewish activism had in fact increased. Weichardt, in particular, was on the warpath, addressing meetings in the Orange Free State, visiting farms and presiding over gatherings that often spiralled out of control. At one meeting in Gezina, he was prevented from speaking amid chaos in the hall. Weichardt told his colleague Frikkie du Toit that over 500 Johannesburg anti-fascists had come over 'fully armed with batons, revolvers, knuckle dusters'. The Greyshirts, although outnumbered, had put up a spirited defence, and were determined to meet 'Terror with Terror'.[29] The Board reported that about 30 people were injured, with many having to receive medical treatment.[30]

Chaos of this kind did not deter the SANP; on the contrary, it courted publicity. Between 8 April and 8 May 1936, the party held 27 meetings, mainly in small Transvaal and Free State towns.[31] The message remained as it had always been: Jewish 'money-power' and influence, and the need for Christians, both English and Afrikaans, to stand together to defeat it. The name of Schlesinger was regularly invoked as the personification of Jewish financial power,[32] while left-wing Jewish activists – invariably identified by name – were simultaneously labelled subversive. At a time of increasing trade union activity, this charge had some resonance, at least in the larger cities. On the whole, however, the radical right continued to devote more attention to poor rural towns and farming communities. But their task was not easy, as the plight of many Afrikaners had eased somewhat. White farmers were supported by the state and many unskilled white workers found relatively secure employment on the railways. Employment opportunities generally were widening. On the other hand, many whites, including those who had found employment in the new South African Iron and Steel Industrial Corporation (Iscor), faced competition from cheaper African labour.[33]

Generally, SANP meetings attracted audiences from the lower economic strata who sought simple explanations for their plight. But a worried Board reported that a more intellectual type of person was increasingly being seduced.[34] Also disturbing for the Board was a report that the Lichtenburg Town Council had tabled a motion to restrict the granting of business licences to Jews (and Asiatics) until such time as the Afrikaner had obtained his rightful share of approximately 85 per cent of these licences.[35] Of even greater concern was a report in *Die Burger* that Stoffberg, the northern Natal SANP leader, was planning to contest Vryheid as an independent in the Provincial Council elections, and that SANP candidates would possibly also run in Volksrust, Bothaville and Cradock.[36]

The *Zionist Record* also reported an intensive radical-right campaign in the country districts of the Transvaal and the Orange Free State, while Terblanche's Volksbeweging too was disseminating abusive anti-Jewish literature in the larger centres, including those in Natal.[37] The Suid-Afrikaanse Nasionale Beweging, or Blackshirts, under Havemann, had renewed its activities, concentrating its efforts in the eastern Transvaal and on the Witwatersrand.[38] At one meeting in Germiston, outside Johannesburg, a crowd of 600 gave the movement a sympathetic hearing.[39] Reports received from a number of country towns, noted the *Zionist Record*, 'show that the farmers are associating themselves with the dissemination of anti-Jewish propaganda'.[40]

It was, however, not only the 'poor whites' or disaffected urban Afrikaners who were susceptible to radical right propaganda. From the very beginning, English-speakers were also among SANP supporters, including – as we saw earlier – the one-time editor of *Die Waarheid / The Truth*, Professor Kerr Wylie. As noted, the University of Cape Town academic had been the subject of Jewish concern for some time. In January 1935 the Board had alerted the principal of the university, Sir Carruthers (Jock) Beattie, to Wylie's open association with the Greyshirts, which, as the Board asserted, 'did not befit a gentleman holding a responsible educational position in the University'.[41] But the matter did not end with that communication. A year after Wylie (in response to the Board's complaint) had assured Beattie that he did not discriminate against Jewish students, Morris Alexander forwarded a letter from Advocate Michael Comay to Beattie that included an accusatory affidavit from Russel Kilgour Hallack, a former university student, who related how he had overheard Wylie make defamatory anti-Jewish remarks at a political meeting in Claremont.[42]

In his astonishing reply to the principal, which bears reproducing almost in full, Wylie betrayed a bravado that suggested antisemitism, if not comfortably ensconced within the polite halls of academe was at least legitimate discourse. Students 'of the Communist type', Wylie told the principal, had had an altercation with him after he told a 'coloured' man during Weichardt's meeting in Claremont that the Greyshirts were against Jews and not Coloureds. The Board had then taken up the matter and he anticipated that they would want him to 'apologise for having made a remark detrimental to the "Chosen Race" and to promise never to say or do anything against that race again'. Wylie denied harbouring ill feelings against individual Jews, but, as far as the Jewish race was concerned, he was prepared to assert that he did not have sufficient words to describe 'the enormity of their crimes against humanity and the misery and suffering they everywhere leave in their train'. The truth had only dawned on him when he became aware of the havoc Jews were creating in South Africa:

Now, however, I feel as certain as one can be of anything that the Jews are at the bottom of all the evils which at present afflict South Africa. Furthermore, if you study any political question, whether national or international, in almost any part of the world, and try to penetrate beneath the surface of all the mass of lies, pretence, hypocrisy, deceit etc, in which such problem is involved, it is remarkable how in nearly every case you come upon the Jew at work, and always working mischief. In fact, it seems no exaggeration to say that, using theological language, organised Jewry is the leading agent of the Devil on earth ...[43]

That a Professor of Law at the University of Cape Town could so brazenly display his anti-Jewish prejudices suggests a certain confidence that antisemitic comments were quite acceptable, even at the highest level. At the same time, a letter from one John Neville to *South African Retailing* reminds us of the need to maintain some perspective when trying to assess the extent and potency of antisemitism at the time. Neville reported on the activities of several antisemitic organisations that were appealing for donations from firms in country towns to finance their work – regrettably, he added, with some measure of success: 'The bait, or lure, laid down by these agitators is that if support is forthcoming, they will start a boycott of Jewish shops in the particular districts in which the supporters carry on business.' But, added Neville, the public 'are beginning to look with extreme disgust upon them, as the introduction of something entirely foreign and un-South African, to our shores'.[44]

It was the Board's view, however, that abusive and violent anti-Jewish propaganda was on the ascendant. Morris Alexander and other members of the executive had received anonymous letters containing death threats, while the radical right continued to attract members of the more educated sections of the population, a fact borne out by *Die Waarheid/The Truth*'s adoption of a less crude and more intelligent editorial line. These developments, asserted the Board, lent credence to the fact that South Africans were becoming 'Jew-conscious'.[45]

MOVING TO THE CENTRE

This consciousness was increasingly penetrating mainstream politics and even parliament itself, where the Malanites exploited and exacerbated the negativity surrounding the 'Jewish Question'.[46] In particular they chose to focus on the immigration question, arguing that the entry of more Jews would have a deleterious impact on the employment prospects of impoverished Afrikaners. Malan had in mind the increasing influx – albeit insignificant in real terms – from Nazi Germany. In 1933, the year Hitler came to power, 204 German Jews had entered South Africa, followed by 452 in 1934 and 388 in 1935.[47] The numbers increased as Arab opposition to German-Jewish settlement in Mandatory Palestine intensified. In the month of April 1936 alone, 98 German Jews entered the country.[48]

While these numbers were tiny, South African diplomats in Europe began to sound alarm bells. To be sure, as early as 1 May 1933 there were indications that the government was concerned about a potential influx of German Jews:[49] on 22 October 1935, the South African ambassador in Berlin, Stefanus Gie, informed South Africa's influential Secretary for External Affairs, Helgard Bodenstein, that his office was being flooded with applications from German Jews wishing to come to South Africa. Gie (a noted Germanophile) did not have a favourable impression of these prospective immigrants, among whom he alleged were a number of communists, and wondered if they could not be denied entry into South Africa on those grounds. Even the better class, he warned, was problematic and would harm South Africans, particularly the latter's chances of finding employment.[50] Eric Louw, then serving as South Africa's Minister Plenipotentiary in Paris, added his voice and, in a direct communication to Malan, urged action to halt Jewish immigration: 'I say in all earnestness that if it goes on at this rate the Union will become the destination of all German Jews.'[51]

On a more formal level, Louw submitted a 'Memorandum on European Emigration to South Africa' to Prime Minister Hertzog in early 1936. Signed by himself in Paris, together with South Africa's representatives in The Hague (Herman van Broekhuizen), Rome (Willem Heymans), London (Charles te Water) and Berlin (Stefanus Gie),[52] the document warned of a potentially huge influx of European (mainly German) Jews, assisted by important international Jewish agencies and prominent Jewish individuals. 'In these circles South Africa is sometimes referred to as a "Jewish country",' noted the signatories. The memorandum expressed particular concern about the nature of the potential European émigrés, who were described as small traders or craftsmen in the main. 'It is not a matter of race,' the signatories defensively maintained, 'but of type and the type in question does not inspire confidence. Can South Africa without detriment and even danger to its national interests continue to allow its commerce and related vocations to be fed by recruits of this type from overseas?' The memorandum went on to express fears that such immigrants would bypass the Quota Act of 1930 (as that applied only to eastern Europeans) and affect 'the future racial, social and economic structures of White South Africa ...' After all, the signatories noted, other Dominion countries had already moved to restrict such immigration.

Clearly influenced by decades of anti-Jewish stereotyping, the signatories recommended that the South African government revise its immigration policy and exclude those entering fields of work 'for which the population of the Union already supplies enough suitable recruits'. Certainly there was already an abundance of 'small traders' of 'foreign origin', and the memorandum recommended that full use be made of Section 4(1)(a) of the Immigration Regulation Act 22 of 1913, which allowed for the exclusion of those unsuited on economic grounds from entering the country:

> Not only should no immigrants be allowed to obtain employment in commercial concerns except possibly to a limited extent and on a temporary basis to bona fide agencies of large overseas firms, but steps should also be taken to render it impossible for an immigrant with sufficient means to support himself and his dependants to become a small trader. This might be achieved by debarring an immigrant from obtaining a trader's licence unless he possesses at least £10 000.[53]

Known as the Te Water Memorandum, the document resonated with the wider anti-Jewish sentiment that was increasingly being driven by Malan's mouthpiece, *Die Burger*. Indeed, shortly after the memorandum found its way into bureaucratic corridors, the Cape voice of Afrikaner nationalism was claiming that the new immigrants would be of no benefit to the country and would not assimilate or enhance the welfare of South Africans. The government had to act on the matter and Hofmeyr, the Minister of the Interior, had to take a stand. The longer the delay, argued *Die Burger*, the more serious the problem for the established inhabitants of South Africa.[54] Four days later, *Die Burger* reported that, although the government was examining the immigration question, it doubted whether Hofmeyr would exclude Jews as an 'unwanted class' or that the courts would support such a policy. The only way to deal with the matter, it suggested, was to prohibit all people who followed specific callings from entering the country.[55] To bolster their case the Nationalists downplayed the persecution of Jews in Germany – much as Hertzog had done three years earlier – by maintaining the fiction that a positive revolution was in progress under Hitler. Dr Karl Bremer, a Nationalist firebrand representing the farming region of Graaff-Reinet, went so far as to deny flatly that Jews were being ill-treated in Germany and warned South African Jews that a boycott would ricochet on the community itself.[56]

Such voices, as well as *Die Burger*'s sabre-rattling, provoked the *SAJC* to accuse the Nationalist daily of 'terrifying the Platteland with threats of a foreign invasion, and a clamouring for the Government to do something about it'. The newspaper's message was that hordes of German Jews were flooding into South Africa, refusing to integrate with the rest of the population, and taking jobs away from Afrikaners. Whereas arguments in favour of the Quota Act of 1930 had been cloaked largely in the discourse of culture, standards of living and business ethics, these had now been replaced by more blatant anti-Jewish prejudice, concluded the *SAJC*.[57]

Alongside the vociferous opposition to Jewish immigration went a concurrent parliamentary battering of the South African Jewish community that focused on two main issues: the supposed Jewish-led boycott of German goods and the contentious issue of the banning of radical right meetings. Bremer, for one, expressed great concern about 'a certain section of the population' which was pushing for a boycott of German goods. The aim of these people, he claimed, was 'to stir up our people against the country with which we are doing good and proper business'.[58] Three weeks later, an irate Roelof van der Merwe, the Nationalist MP for Bethlehem, also warned against boycotting 'a good friend'. The Jews, he crudely asserted, were disturbing the good relations between the Nordic races, and were doing so for their own gain: 'They are exploiting our people, and are nothing else but parasites. Are we going to permit it? I say no. If they go with it, then I am going to stir up Britons and Afrikaners in South Africa to boycott them. I want to tell them, "be careful, be warned." If they try this kind of weapon, called boycott, then they will just have to take up their packs and go elsewhere.' The Nationalist MP for Victoria West, Pieter Luttig, a cattle farmer, added his voice, accusing the Board of injuring farmers by organising a boycott of German goods just because 'Germany is not well-disposed towards their race'. Jan Haywood, the National Party MP for Bloemfontein South, also urged the necessity of action against those organising the boycott,[59] as did Stephanus Bekker, National Party MP for Wodehouse, an important wool-farming region. Blackie Swart, the youthful republican-inclined deputy leader of the National Party in the Orange Free State, also cautioned Jews that their actions could be counter-productive.[60]

It made little difference that Jewish leaders had consistently denied any formal initiation of a boycott. Nor was any sympathy forthcoming when Alexander and Joseph Verster, the United Party MP for Swartruggens, delineated in great detail the appalling abuse heaped upon Jews at radical right meetings, and shared with the House the calumny contained in JHH de Waal's memoir, *My Ontwaking*. In a display of fatherly devotion, De Waal *père* defended his controversial son and blamed Jews themselves for the abuse hurled at them. *Inter alia*, he accused them of using their power to keep the municipal halls closed for meetings they objected to and held them responsible for the many instances where Christian South African descendants of families who had been in the country for hundreds of years were chased 'like dogs' by the police in areas where meetings had been forbidden by a magistrate acting on the instructions of Smuts, the 'King of the Jews'.[61]

For Jews, the tenor of debate was extremely disturbing. 'It has revealed the extent of a certain frame of mind in certain political circles which, if it should persist and spread, is fraught with ominous potentialities, not only for the Jewish citizens but for the political life of the whole South African nation,' noted the *Zionist Record*. The newspaper reserved its greatest concern for Malan's followers, some of whom it suspected of using Jew-baiting as a political tool, and warned them to avoid following the road Hitler had taken. The persecution of Jews in South Africa would spell the moral collapse of the nation and threaten the very basis of Christianity and civilisation, it warned: 'Let South Africa realise that anti-Semitism has become bound with movements which aim at the destruction of the constitutional liberties so laboriously won, and that it paves the way to a new paganism. The values at stake are too sacred to be used as mere instruments in a bid for political power.'[62] Some weeks later the *Zionist Record* devoted an editorial to the 'Boycott Business', condemning the veiled threats against Jews, as well as Malan's appropriation of antisemitism, and advising him to think hard and long before encouraging his followers to exacerbate race relations. Even more unfortunate, added the *Zionist Record*, was the possibility of government actions being construed as an endorsement of the Nationalist accusation that Jews were organising the boycott of German goods:

> There is no organised Jewish boycott. The leaders of South African Jewry have had nothing to do with the boycott of German goods. Where Jews have abstained from purchasing German goods, they have been actuated by the dictates of their own conscience and need make no apologies therefore. When organised labour, for reasons of its own, has chosen to declare an open boycott of Germany, surely that is its own affair. Moreover, it is known that Catholics and Freemasons in this country have also had reason to abstain from purchasing German goods.[63]

Nationalist rhetoric that increasingly echoed SANP propaganda provoked the *Cape Argus* to ask, 'Is the Malanite party to be an anti-Semitic Party?' Hitherto, the newspaper asserted, 'Dr Malan has managed to keep the temptation in check without actually condemning it. His favourite answer to the question whether the party will take a stand against the Jew is that the party is against all parasites, whether Jewish or Gentile – a characteristic shuffle which enables his followers to make the best of both worlds.'[64]

HOFMEYR UNDER PRESSURE

Hofmeyr, who was hostile to any discrimination against Jews, attempted to defuse the agitation by informing the House (in response to a question from Frans Erasmus) that the actual immigration figures from Germany could not be regarded as extraordinary when compared to the figures in respect of other non-restricted countries.[65] The government, he insisted, had no plans to differentiate against immigration from Germany;[66] but his efforts fell on deaf ears. Even the *Cape Argus*, a pro-government newspaper, advocated keeping an eye on the situation.[67]

Pressure was indeed mounting on Hofmeyr, not least from within his own party. Only one week after downplaying the extent of Jewish immigration came the announcement that an Immigration Amendment Bill would in fact be introduced. Among other requisites, the new legislation would require immigrants to present a passport from their country of origin, allowing them right of return.[68] When the Board told Hofmeyr that this would have severe implications for German Jews – who did not enjoy a right of return – and that the suggested provision would exclude even Albert Einstein, the minister's private secretary replied that they were misinterpreting the Bill's intentions. Rather disingenuously, he maintained that the proposed legislation did not 'discriminate against any particular section or race, religion, or cultural ideal'. In fact, very few immigrants would be affected as, according to the principles underlying South African immigration policy, the government already reserved the right to deport anyone entering the country. The aim of the new legislation (which never saw the light of day) was merely intended to render this option legally possible.[69]

Hofmeyr was clearly struggling to find a formula that would not discriminate against Jews but would nevertheless address the mounting clamour against Jewish immigration. The issue stubbornly refused to disappear, and at the twilight of the parliamentary session both Roelof van der Merwe and Malan took advantage of an appropriation debate to raise the question yet again. Speaking in an evening session, Van der Merwe warned the House of a stream of immigrants flowing into South Africa that would have huge implications for South African workers, making the introduction of a vocational quota a necessity. Malan in turn spoke insensitively of the need to stop 'so-called refugees' streaming into the country from Germany, but, on the other hand, he went out of his way to tell the House that his views were not informed by animus towards Jews, and indeed any discrimination towards them would be wrong. Quoting from Chaim Weizmann (the international Zionist leader) and other Jewish sources that spoke of an increase of antisemitism when Jewish numbers exceeded a certain percentage, Malan – in a remarkable display of hypocritical double-speak – claimed that South Africa faced a potentially huge influx of German Jews which would provoke great hatred, as evidenced by the Greyshirt phenomenon. Steps had to be taken to stop this influx 'not because we are anti-Jewish, but because we are pro-South African, and also, in conclusion, in the interests of the Jewish population itself that is in South Africa'.[70]

On the last day of the parliamentary session, Erasmus taunted Hofmeyr for permitting the alleged Jewish boycott of German goods and for dropping the planned Immigration Amendment Bill that had been tabled in May.[71] The absence of such legislation, suggested Bremer, would mean German Jews swamping the country, with the help of enormous funding from American and English Jewish leaders. He predicted that, within ten years, between 30 000 and 50 000 Jews would enter South Africa. These people, he reminded the House, were unassimilable.[72]

In the meantime, senior bureaucrats had been toying with the notion of 'assimilability' as a criterion for entry. Hertzog had set up a special committee, under Helgard Bodenstein, to identify possible modalities for exclusion in the wake of the Te Water Memorandum's warning of the prospect of a looming Jewish immigration problem.[73] The committee's recommendations were essentially the curtailment of the influx of undesirable or unwanted persons into the Union to obviate the effects of unrestricted admission, which would affect all aspects of South Africa's national life. Alien Jews brought with them foreign doctrines, such as communism, that undermined South Africa's political and economic structure and threatened to destabilise the existing interracial order. They also rigidly retained their identity as a separate community, were prepared to subordinate the interests of South Africa to those of its group, and encouraged the assistance of Jewish immigration. Another negative factor arising out of the arrival of aliens was the denial of employment opportunities for South African citizens. Bodenstein, a learned jurist who had at one time held a chair in Law at the University of Amsterdam and then at Stellenbosch, expressed concern at what he alleged were attempts to bribe civil servants by 'an unassimilable and alien group' whose standards of public morality were at odds with South African practices. Building on these premises, the special committee recommended admitting into the Union only those persons who:

a) are of good health and character;
b) are likely to become readily assimilated with the inhabitants of the Union and to become desirable citizens of the Union within a reasonable period after their entry into the Union;
c) are not likely to be harmful to the economic or industrial welfare of the Union; and
d) are not likely to pursue a profession, occupation, trade or calling in which a sufficient number of persons is already engaged in the Union to meet the requirements of the inhabitants of the Union.

Bodenstein believed that existing laws could meet the case with minor amendments, but one potential loophole – the power of the Minister of the Interior to allow for exceptions – should be closed. In addition, language provisions, financial demands and visa arrangements could be tightened. The following final recommendations were offered by the committee:

1) That the fullest use be made of paragraph (a) of Section 4(1) of the Immigration Regulation Act of 1913.[74]
2) That, in consultation with the Departments of Labour and of Commerce and Industries and any other Department which may be concerned, a list be drawn up of occupations and professions for which there are sufficient recruits in the Union, such list to be

revised from time to time, according as the economic and industrial circumstances of the Union may alter.

3) That the Minister issue confidential instructions to the Commissioner for Immigration and Asiatic Affairs, that every person who on account of his habits of life is not readily assimilable or who follows one or other of the occupations referred to in S2 should be prohibited under Section 4(1)(a).

4) That a copy of the list be supplied to the Union's representatives abroad.

5) That press notices be published in England, America and on the Continent to the effect that the provisions of the Union immigration laws are being strictly enforced and advising all intending immigrants to approach the Union's representatives to ascertain whether they are likely to be admitted to the Union without previous permission.

6) That the Union's representatives abroad be authorised summarily to reject any obviously unsuitable or undesirable immigrant, either because he belongs to a class mentioned in the list supplied, or for some other reason, and provisionally to select suitable immigrants *not* falling within any of these classes who should be admitted because of exceptional circumstances.

7) That all cases of provisional selection be referred for consideration to the Department of Immigration which would, if necessary, consult the Department of Labour or other Department concerned, before issuing permission for the intending immigrant to proceed to the Union, for examination at the port of arrival. Every case referred to the Immigration Department should be accompanied by a full report on the intending immigrant by the Union's representative abroad who has dealt with the case.

8) That in cases where passport visas are necessary, visas be withheld from intending immigrants who have been rejected either summarily or after their cases have been referred to the authorities in the Union, and that in cases where passport visas are not necessary, intending immigrants, who have been rejected, should be warned that if they proceed to the Union they will be prohibited on arrival.[75]

Bodenstein's memorandum betrayed a demonstrable hostility to Jews, particularly when it addressed the term 'assimilability'. Here it was made clear that the newcomer would have to be incorporated into the substance of the assimilating body. Habits of life, customs and conduct were all relevant, as was behaviour. Homogeneity, it contended, was necessary for a country and, although different ideas could exist between individuals, it was problematic to have fundamental differences between 'classes' or 'groups'. Religious, moral, cultural, political and economic differences were problematic, and those individuals not willing to marry outside their cultural group were also considered unassimilable.[76]

Hofmeyr was greatly angered by the Bodenstein document. In a strongly worded response, he noted that Hertzog had appointed the committee without reference to him and that he was therefore unable to accept any responsibility for its report. More than that, while ostensibly targeting 'Communists, German Nazis and Jews', the tightening of section 4(1) (b) and (c) would affect only Jews: 'I am driven to the conclusion that the Committee is not really serious in its proposals as far as the exclusion of German Nazis or Communists is concerned. What it is concerned about is the exclusion of Jews. It should have been better if it had said so frankly at the outset.'

To enhance his case, Hofmeyr presented a list of illustrious Jews who had made invaluable contributions the world over, and also identified legal contradictions as well as impracticalities in the proposals. He questioned the use of paragraph (a) of section 4(1) of the Immigration Regulation Act 22 of 1913 to exclude Jews on the grounds of unassimilability and stated that, while he was not questioning the legality of the clause, parliament had not contemplated using it for this purpose when the legislation was first enacted. Hofmeyr also took exception to the memorandum's use of various examples of unassimilability, such as deep-seated differences in religious beliefs and opposition to marriage between members of different groups, and questioned whether Roman Catholics would also be regarded as unassimilable.[77]

STEPPING UP THE PRESSURE

Although Malan's fears of an uncontrolled influx of 'unassimilable' Jews might have been genuine, his intervention in the closing stages of the parliamentary session, when the immigration question was not on the agenda, was in reality a political response to the threat from the radical right. The prospect of the National Party being undercut at the polls by extremists appeared very real and Malan was well aware of this possibility. Certainly *Die Waarheid/The Truth* and its vituperative anti-Jewish message appealed to many voters sought by the National Party in their quest for increased Afrikaner support.

Yet, on the whole, the Nationalists never stooped to the level of the radical right who, besides empathising with European fascists, employed gross conspiratorial fantasies about Jews at every opportunity. In addition to alleging that they manipulated South African affairs,[78] the extremists (in the wake of the report of the South West Africa Commission into Nazi activities) even suggested that Jews were being encouraged by the South African government to exploit and oppress locals in the former German colony in order to undermine relations with Germany. Windhoek, commented *Die Waarheid/The Truth*, was no better than a vast synagogue:

> The Germans are our near kinsmen, and with them we must knit ties
> of the most intimate and enduring nature. But until the Jewish tyranny
> over South Africa and the South African people is broken, all our efforts
> in this direction must prove futile. Germany has put the foul Asiatic
> exploiter and oppressor in his place. Let South Africa follow suit and
> that without further delay![79]

The SANP's unceasing focus on the alleged Jewish-led boycott of German goods and the ongoing issue of Jewish refugees entering the country ensured that the 'Jewish Question' remained a national issue. Even mainstream newspapers voiced concern: the Transvaal-based *Die Republikein*, for instance, though initially supportive of Malan, now competed with *Die Waarheid/The Truth* on matters Jewish. The government had little room to maneouvre, and some of its own members were distinctly uncomfortable with these two issues. Yet apart from some important clerics and politicians who showed empathy for the plight of European Jewry,[80] few public figures spoke out unequivocally against the anti-Jewish rhetoric.

Within this context, a very concerned Board reminded Hertzog in a lengthy communication of the meetings held with him on 29 November 1934 and 22 April 1935, at which it had expressed concerns about the activities of certain organisations and movements and had urged the introduction of legislation making it a criminal offence to publish defamatory statements harmful to a group or section of the population of South Africa. Since then the situation had deteriorated considerably:

> The activities of the anti-Jewish organisations are manifest in the increased number of their meetings and in the intensified propaganda conducted by them through the press, pamphlets and leaflets, and by means of an elaborate system of personal canvass. Grossly defamatory statements continue to be made and cannot be dealt with under the existing laws.
>
> The antagonistic feeling against the Jew has been greatly increased by the fact that during the last session, Members of the House of Assembly – for the first time in the Parliamentary history of this country – voiced outspoken anti-Semitic views.
>
> The Greyshirts and other anti-Jewish organisations, in their written and spoken propaganda, are openly misconstruing the silence of the Government as a tacit condonation of their activities.

To support this claim, the Board cited an article in *Die Waarheid / The Truth* which had indicated that even Smuts – invariably depicted as a lackey of the Jews – had been silent during the debate on the banning of the Greyshirts. As two years had elapsed since Hertzog had last made a statement about radical activism, the Board felt it was now necessary for him to issue another to curb the growth of a movement that threatened South Africa's peace and stability.[81]

Responding on behalf of the Prime Minister, Bodenstein asserted that the government was conscious of the dangers presented by the radicals and would always protect South African Jewry – as it would any other section of the population – but did not anticipate 'any serious interference with the rights and liberties of the Jewish Community in the near future ...' Having given this assurance, Bodenstein went on to acknowledge that anti-Jewish feeling did in fact exist, but, in a somewhat chilling assertion, described it as emanating from the community's own conduct:

> There is a fast-growing conviction that members of the Jewish community in the Union in order to promote the interests of the Jewish race, whether in South Africa or elsewhere, do not hesitate to avail themselves of measures and means in direct conflict with the interests of the rest of the population and of the state. This source of grievance with the non-Jewish section of the population, has on more than one occasion been pointed out to the leaders of the Jewish people by the Prime Minister, and the warning expressed that if persisted it must inevitably alienate the good feeling of the rest of the community towards the Jewish section, and could not be approved of by the Government.

Bodenstein was referring here to what he called the indiscriminate immigration of foreign Jews and the boycott of German goods – two issues that encapsulated the resentment felt by the rest of the community when they were called upon to make sacrifices for people who were not South Africans. It was thus in the interest of the Jewish community itself to realise the grave implications for South African Jewry occasioned by unfettered immigration and actions that went against the national interest.[82]

In essence, Bodenstein was blaming 'provocative' conduct by Jews for the hostility directed towards them. With the government expressing such views, and with the radical right gearing up to participate in the Provincial Council elections, the Jewish community had every reason to feel uneasy. In fact the tenor of debate was already apparent in the Pretoria Central contest, where a pamphlet issued by Louis Bergen, an independent candidate with blatant SANP sympathies, called for the building of a 'Christian nation' by restricting 'the number of traders' licences granted to aliens, who are incapable of assimilation within the South African Nation, and whose code of business morality is found to be harmful to the country'.[83]

Weichardt now held a frenetic series of meetings in Cape Town and its environs. At the Koffiehuis in Cape Town, he referred to German-Jewish immigrants as 'the scum of the land' and warned that once the newcomers were apprenticed to 'Jewish shops' they learnt to 'cheat the Afrikaner'.[84] He went on to speak at Wellington (17 August), Cape Town (18 August), Claremont (20 August), Malmesbury (21 August), Woodstock (2 September) and Paarl (8 September). Attendances everywhere were good and, significantly, all municipalities permitted the use of their halls.[85] In general the SANP leader focused on Jewish immigration, the boycott of German goods and Jewish power, but, contrary to expectations, the SANP did not put up official candidates in the Provincial Council elections. Instead they assisted certain independents such as Bergen. The Blackshirts, on the other hand, put up candidates in Carolina (JW Vorster), Bethal (FE Olivier), Ermelo (JJ Smit), Witbank (SJ Grobler) and Wakkerstroom (MC Pretorius). According to the Board, all these candidates had little social standing or influence in their districts.

Nonetheless, the Board feared the continued penetration of antisemitism into political debate. It certainly was being used by a number of candidates in their campaigns. In Oudtshoorn, for example, the Hoggenheimer motif loomed large,[86] as did the German boycott issue. In addition, resolutions were submitted to the annual congress of the Cape Agricultural Association and the conference of the Orange Free State Agricultural Union threatening a counter-boycott of Jews in response to their alleged boycott of German goods. At the Orange Free State Agricultural Union conference, no less than 15 resolutions were submitted on this subject,[87] and at a meeting in Worcester the Cape National Party resolved to compile a list of traders who stocked German goods, to be sent to all branches of the party with the request that such traders be supported.[88] In the meantime, agricultural societies were asked to tell their members not to buy goods from stores that boycotted German goods.[89] It was also reported that moves were afoot to organise objections to applications for business licences made by Jews. Malan was undoubtedly aware of these initiatives. Having hitherto been reasonably measured in his utterances, he now changed direction, going as far as to tell a political meeting in Lichtenburg that he shared the Greyshirt view when it came to immigration and parasitism. 'I am not a Greyshirt,' he said, 'but I can support them to a large extent.'[90]

On the eve of the elections, a *Zionist Record* editorial entitled '"Shirts" and the Provincial Elections' noted that avowed antisemitic candidates had come into the open. Although the newspaper did not anticipate much electoral success for them, it was nevertheless concerned about the appearance of these candidates, which demonstrated that 'anti-Semitism can be made, at least to some, an appealing electioneering cry'. It was most concerned that certain 'Purified' Nationalists had also jumped on the anti-Jewish bandwagon. Since its break with Malan, noted the *Zionist Record*, *Die Republikein* had taken on the tone of *Die Waarheid / The Truth*, 'spicing its columns with references to "British Jewish Imperialism and Capitalism"'. Fortunately, the newspaper opined, most South Africans were not enamoured of the country's 'little Hitlers', and it urged liberal South Africans 'to assert themselves and prove to these political upstarts of many hued shirts that our national life can well do without the additional "colour" which they lend to it'.[91]

During the campaign, those 'little Hitlers' were in fact attracting impressive attendances. Conduct at meetings was orderly and protection well organised. Weichardt continued to speak in small towns in the interior, where farmers turned up in substantial numbers. He was particularly well received in Reitz, a town in the Orange Free State with a historic German settlement, which, according to one observer, was being turned into a Greyshirt nest.[92] Dr Henry Sonnabend, director of research and publicity for the Board, captured this in a report which noted that numerous free copies of *Die Waarheid / The Truth* had been distributed some days before the meeting and a number of well-attended meetings had been held.[93]

Despite good attendances on the hustings, radical right performances in these provincial elections were unimpressive, with the exception of a few constituencies such as Vryheid, where Dr Theunis Stoffberg did fairly well, as did Johan Adendorff in Newcastle. 'It is significant that so large a number of votes was given to the two men who, though they stood as Independents, did not disguise their affiliation with the Greyshirts,' reported the Board.[94]

It was, however, of some relevance that Adendorff had told his audience at his first election meeting that, although he was a Greyshirt, he was standing as an independent because the SANP had never intended to be a political party and did not believe in Provincial Council party politics.⁹⁵ Although this was a somewhat disingenuous justification, it suggests that the SANP was not entirely confident of its own brand. Yet the electoral results did illustrate at least some limited support for extremism.⁹⁶

Things quietened down in the immediate wake of the election campaign, only to liven up soon thereafter with more Blackshirt activity. A meeting in Booysens, a poor working-class Johannesburg suburb, attracted a substantial crowd, signalling that the radical right remained a factor in South African politics.⁹⁷ The propaganda campaign also resumed. One SANP pamphlet, with an introduction by Weichardt, detailed the party's principles, which again revealed the centrality of the 'Jewish Question'. The Grey Workers Bond, an organisation apparently allied to the Greyshirts, issued bulletins in Afrikaans and English, and *Terre Blanche* resumed distribution after a lengthy absence. Especially ominous was the founding of a 'National Socialist Students Association' at Stellenbosch University.⁹⁸

Reporting to the Board on these developments, Sonnabend observed that, in an effort to establish contact with a more educated electorate, the Greyshirts were attempting to camouflage some of their activities by creating what they called 'Political Science Associations'.⁹⁹ These had been established in Pretoria, Durban and Cape Town and were being addressed by Weichardt. With the SANP moving closer to mainstream politics, *Die Waarheid/ The Truth* now rather optimistically called upon the movement to use more restrained language as 'befits a political party, which will soon be called upon to undertake the responsibility of governing the country'.¹⁰⁰

Weichardt certainly continued to feel confident that his party could mobilise around the immigration issue and take advantage of the 'Jewish Question', which he considered the central issue of the country's political discourse. He believed that the SANP was poised to make rapid gains; the party's newly published edition of its 'Constitution and Programme of Principles' had been favourably received and its meetings were well attended. Despite the efforts of the 'Jew-controlled press' to ban its publicity, he claimed that the SANP's message was being received enthusiastically:

> Large numbers of professional men, university professors, lecturers and
> students, civil servants, school teachers, etc., belong to the Party, if not
> as open, at any rate as secret members. The workers, too, despite all
> attempts of the Jews to catch them with the poisoned bait of Commu-
> nism and Bolshevism, are everywhere getting their eyes opened. Largely
> through the efforts of our members and supporters, the Jew-controlled
> and Communist-infested South African Labour Party is being rapidly
> disintegrated, and I have strong hopes that before long the workers as a
> body will have rallied to our banner.

Weichardt boasted that future electoral victory was in sight, as people had
become sick of the degeneracy, empty promises, hypocrisy and corruption
of South African politics. His accusations that political parties were 'tools
in the hands of Jewish money power', and that the majority of their representatives were only concerned with 'feathering their own nests' would
resonate with the electorate, and so support for the SANP would grow.[101]

A NEW INITIATIVE

The government fully appreciated the mounting pressures and challenges it faced from the radical right arising out of the festering issue of
German-Jewish immigration. Patrick Duncan (once again inflating immigrant numbers) went so far as to write of a political time bomb in the
making: 'We are going to be faced with immigration problems before long,'
he told Lady Selborne. 'The Jewish immigration is the most serious – the
only really serious one. They are coming at present at the rate of 2 000 a year
… The Jews have done much for SA but we are getting too many of them
in comparison with the non-Jewish immigrant.'[102]

If an English-speaking and relatively liberal member of the United
Party could hold such views,[103] it is easy to appreciate the levels of anger
in Weichardt's camp and among others on the radical right. The German-
Jewish influx had to be dealt with, and the government knew it. The Bill

that Hofmeyr had planned to introduce in May 1936 clearly illustrated this. Although it did not mention Jews by name, it was quite apparent that the intention of the proposed legislation was to limit, if not block, their entry. But the Bill had been hastily abandoned, possibly due to the Board's intervention. What we do know is that on 19 August Hofmeyr met with representatives of the Board in Pretoria, where he indicated that the cabinet had been engaging seriously with the matter. Because of the impact of German-Jewish immigration, the government believed it might be compelled to introduce restrictive legislation. If the number of immigrants could be curtailed, he hoped this would not be necessary and expressed appreciation for the Board's assistance in encouraging alternative destinations for German Jews.[104] The cabinet had, however, not yet come to any definite decision, and he would strongly endeavour to avoid any legislation that would savour, directly or indirectly, of racial discrimination.[105]

Hofmeyr was operating within a difficult context. As a liberal deeply opposed to discrimination against Jews, he was, as in many other instances, seemingly out of step with his government's policy-making mandarins. This was made quite evident in an angry 12-page memorandum circulated by the constitutional and legal advisor to the Prime Minister, Albertonie Broeksma, on 19 August 1936, directly challenging Hofmeyr's earlier response to Bodenstein's memorandum, in which he had accused the committee of concerning itself only with Jews. Broeksma once again sounded alarm bells, claiming that the huge influx of immigrants (now mentioning Portuguese agricultural labourers as well) threatened South Africa's national interests. 'We're faced with a potential "invasion" not only by Jews from Germany, but by large numbers of other persons,' he wrote. 'It may mean, comparatively speaking, depopulation of certain European countries and swamping of our own country.' Broeksma also challenged Hofmeyr's observations on the legalities and practicalities of the Bodenstein memorandum. On the assimilability issue, Broeksma noted that, in his personal view, it was obvious that on the whole Jews were unassimilable. In his estimation, the illustrious Jewish names Hofmeyr had mentioned to make his case were exceptions to the rule.[106]

Broeksma's retort suggests that Hofmeyr had managed to hold at bay only temporarily those who were calling for an amendment to the immigration legislation. Not to act would probably mean loss of political support to the National Party and radical right.[107] Changes were in the pipeline: in early September the Acting Secretary for the Interior, AB Smit, informed the Board that, while no amendments to the regulations issued under the Immigration Regulation Act 22 of 1913, were being contemplated, it had been decided that the practice of accepting guarantees in respect of the maintenance and employment of prospective immigrants would cease as from 1 November 1936. Even guarantees that had already been accepted would be regarded as lapsed if the individual did not arrive in the Union before that date. Smit went on to explain that immigrants would on arrival have to satisfy the immigration officer that they complied with the provisions of section 4(1)(c) of the Act, which stipulated that any person who was likely to become a public charge would be declared a prohibited immigrant.[108] This was the government's response to the anti-immigration clamour that had intensified as numbers crept steadily upwards: from a mere 17 who entered in September 1935, the total number of immigrants had jumped to 224 in August 1936.

Die Burger and other opposition newspapers, including those on the radical right, shared Broeksma's pessimism: a further influx of Jews was a recipe for disaster. *Die Kerkbode*, too, warned that if Jewish professionals and others were allowed to enter South Africa unchecked, schools might as well be closed, since there would be no reason for South African citizens to receive higher education or be trained in the professions.[109] Headlines expressing concerns about Jewish immigration[110] and a flood of angry letters to the press demonstrated the mounting pressure, which would be used by the opposition to mobilise support.[111] One correspondent accused the ruling United Party of having no desire to tackle the Jewish problem in South Africa,[112] while *Die Republikein* went so far as to quote approvingly the arch-Nazi propagandist, Joseph Goebbels, who had lambasted the Jewish communist press and Jewish Bolshevism for trying to destroy European civilisation and replacing it with international Jewish capitalism.[113]

Weichardt capitalised on the mood and undertook an extensive speaking tour of the Natal Midlands, where the SANP had enjoyed some electoral support, albeit under the guise of Independent candidates. At venue after venue he berated the government's limp-wristed policies and the power of Jews.[114] In Ladysmith he threatened to 'create a revolution' and challenged the government to a 'war to the finish'. The true government of the country, he asserted, was the Jewish Board of Deputies.[115] In Durban Weichardt addressed a closed meeting of the local 'Political Science Association' where he outlined to the 'more intellectually-inclined' (mainly an Afrikaans audience numbering approximately 350) his conspiratorial worldview, which included a Jew-driven world communism and offered a solution to South Africa's problems based on the principles of National Socialism.[116]

Weichardt was merely reiterating the favourable comments on Nazism expressed by the University of Cape Town's Professor Hermann Bohle when he had lectured on Nazism even before Hitler's accession to power in 1933. As noted earlier, Bohle had been a founder member of the Landesgruppe Südafrika,[117] and his efforts were then part of an extended set of Nazi propaganda operations in Johannesburg, Pretoria, Durban, Port Elizabeth, East London and Bloemfontein, as well as in some smaller towns such as Tzaneen. Support was provided by diplomatic and consular representatives of the Reich, particularly H Wedemann in Port Elizabeth and Bruno Stiller, the German consul based initially in Cape Town. Nazi sympathisers were especially active in towns with historically substantial German communities such as Tzaneen, where a branch of the German Labour Front (*Arbeitsdienst*) had erected the 'Wilhelm Gustloff Halle', named in memory of the Nazi activist murdered in Switzerland by a Jewish assassin in February 1936. Many guests from Pretoria and Johannesburg attended the event and heard P Schneider in his opening address refer to the 'Jewish murderer' of Gustloff, who he claimed had died for the great ideals of the Führer. Bruno Stiller, at the time the acting South African territorial leader of the Nazi Party, in place of Professor Bohle (then in Germany), also spoke on behalf of the German Reich.[118]

Despite the impact of Nazi propaganda, it is apparent that both the radical right and the Malanites were driven essentially by domestic concerns informed by nativist notions of 'racial stock'. Policy-makers built upon this, but they went further, blaming the South African Jewish community for harming ties with Germany. This was illustrated in a communication to the Board from Bodenstein, the man who two years earlier had warned of the importance of South Africa's economic ties with Germany and expressed regret that the Jews had turned the German issue into an international matter. World Jewry, he now wrote, was provocatively following a course of conduct inimical to Germany and German interests, and he blamed the Jewish community for the strong feeling of antipathy it was experiencing because the community had not hesitated to engage in acts that were in direct conflict with the interests of the rest of the population. Its actions generally were injuring the country's economy and this had led to understandable resentment.[119]

The President of the Board, Siegfried Raphaely, who was once again at the helm, repudiated in the strongest terms the idea of Jews acting against the interests of the country by boycotting German goods and encouraging immigration. His missive had no impact. In a strongly worded reply, Bodenstein – speaking specifically on behalf of Hertzog – informed Raphaely that he retracted nothing of his earlier statement 'beyond taking the strongest exception to the manner in which the mere mention of the existence of a certain state of feeling with the non-Jewish public concerning the conduct of individual members of the Jewish Race is construed by you into a general charge against the Jewish community as a whole'.[120]

Only three weeks before Bodenstein penned his letter, reports had emerged of the new restrictive immigration regulations referred to earlier by AB Smit.[121] From the beginning of November 1936, immigrants would have to make a £100 cash deposit, as a bond, rather than have in their possession a signed guarantee, as was previously the case. This was clearly impossible for refugees who had been stripped of their possessions.[122] In addition, a departmental committee of not less than three people, appointed by the Minister of the Interior, would consider applications under the quota. In effect, the use of influence (or bribery, as Jewish detractors put it) to ensure entry would now be prevented.[123]

These harsh new measures to curtail German-Jewish immigration did not dampen anti-immigrant voices. Hofmeyr was accused of playing with the figures to make it seem as though there was no problem, while the government was accused of acting in the interest of Empire and the mining magnates.[124] Columns and letters in *Die Waarheid/The Truth*, opposing what were considered inadequate measures, were particularly virulent, often raising questions about the very presence of Jews in South Africa.[125] Impoverished Afrikaners, the newspaper suggested, were threatened by the 'scum of Europe', while 'thousands of our own flesh and blood are unemployed and must loaf about on the streets'.[126] Although *Die Burger* was somewhat less inflammatory, it nevertheless accused the government of playing a dangerous game that would ultimately harm Jews already in South Africa.

With provincial elections due to take place in the Cape Province, focusing on the immigration issue was a useful (and ultimately fairly successful) means of mobilising support. At one meeting in Stellenbosch, Malan expressed regret that the government had dropped its earlier plans to deal with immigration, and accused the organised Jewish *geldmag* (money power) of orchestrating affairs. Apart from his usual objections, Malan claimed that the influx of Jews would add to South Africa's vexed racial question,[127] effectively repeating the sentiments he had expressed at the time he introduced the Quota Act in 1930. On another occasion, speaking at Porterville, he denied being antisemitic, arguing yet again that inevitable hostility would ensue once Jews exceeded a certain proportion of the population.[128]

THE *STUTTGART* AFFAIR

Anti-immigrant anger reached boiling point when word got out that Jewish organisations were planning to help as many Jews as possible to enter the country before the new immigration regulations came into effect. To beat the 1 November 1936 deadline, Jewish organisations abroad had hurriedly chartered the German liner *Stuttgart*, which sailed from Bremerhaven with 537 German-Jewish refugees on board. This took place despite the reservations of the Board, which had good reason to fear domestic repercussions.[129]

Angry letters protesting the ship's arrival filled the pages of the press and meetings were organised across the country.[130] Unless Jewish immigration slackened off, there 'will be anti-Semitic trouble here', Patrick Duncan told Maud Selborne. 'It is growing fast in this country as it is and it could easily get quite out of hand.'[131] Significantly, the anti-Jewish-immigration cudgels were now taken up by young academics, especially at the University of Stellenbosch.[132] Driven by a *völkisch* agenda, and deeply concerned about the economic plight of the Afrikaner, these intellectuals added a dose of gravitas to the anti-immigrant hullabaloo. In the 'Mecca of Afrikanerdom' – as the *Cape Argus* put it – professors Hendrik Verwoerd, Christian (Krissie) Schumann, Johannes Basson and Dr Theophilus Ebenhaezer (Eben) Dönges led the charge against the *Stuttgart*, adding academic ballast to the cries of the hoi polloi.[133]

These formidable young Afrikaner intellectuals (all, apart from Basson, still in their thirties) had enjoyed distinguished academic success. The fifty-year-old Basson, armed with a doctorate from the University of Berlin, held the Chair in Classics. Besides his academic field of expertise, he was greatly concerned with the plight of the Afrikaner and had even established a youth employment bureau. Schumann too was engaged with the 'poor white' question. He had been appointed the first Professor of Business Economics at Stellenbosch and Dean of the Faculty of Commerce at the tender age of thirty-four. Holding a Stellenbosch degree in Mathematics and a doctorate in Economics from the Economische Hoogeschool in Rotterdam, this cultured man, who had a great interest in fine art and music, would play a significant role as a champion of Afrikaner mobility. Dönges too had enjoyed a meteoric academic career. At the age of twenty-seven he was awarded a doctorate in Law from the University of London, adding it to his MA in Philosophy from Stellenbosch University. Dönges was admitted to the Bar in both the Transvaal and the Cape Province and lectured part-time at Stellenbosch. Verwoerd, it will be recalled, had played a prominent role in the Volkskongres of 1934 that had examined the 'poor white' question, arguing the case for *völkisch* mobilisation.

All four of these men were determined to help the Afrikaner. Schumann explored the rescue of Afrikaners through entrepreneurship,[134] arguing that only ethnic mobilisation, combined with what Dan O'Meara has termed *volkskapitalisme* (capital mobilisation in the interest of the *volk*), could solve the 'poor white' problem.[135] Dönges and Basson also beat the ethnic drum. In their eyes, the Jewish influx stood in the way of the rehabilitation of the Afrikaner. Verwoerd, too, was passionately concerned about Afrikaner poverty and believed it imperative that the Afrikaners be uplifted by their own folk. But their advance was contingent on limiting the domination of Jews in the economy.[136]

The imminent arrival of the *Stuttgart* galvanised these academics into action. An audience of over 1 500 heard Basson, Dönges and Schumann address a meeting billed as 'The Jewish Danger', held under the auspices of the ANS (by then decidedly pro-Nazi) at the Recreation Hall in Stellenbosch on 27 October.[137] Although the chairman opened the meeting with a claim that the gathering would not descend into an attack on Jews, each speaker alluded directly or indirectly to the alien quality of the newcomers. Should immigration persist, warned Basson, there would be serious consequences for South Africa's social fabric, since Jews were unassimilable. Dönges had the crowd roaring with laughter when he said that if food did not digest, indigestion followed. With an unresolved national diet, he added, you get national indigestion.[138] Schumann was struck by the 'strength of feeling in South Africa against the present Jewish immigration' and was convinced that, if a referendum were held, 90 per cent of the white population would vote for the cessation of Jewish immigration. The essence of the whole problem, he said, was that 'the Jew always remained a stranger – even in Jerusalem', with no real patriotism or love for the country that was his new home. Moreover, by standing together, Jews had made profitable use of the capitalist system and thus had no right to object when Gentiles made a united stand to secure their own interests. 'We are at the beginning not of a normal migration,' warned Dönges, 'but an organised and deliberate colonisation on a big scale' that was backed by important Jewish figures.[139]

It was not only the Stellenbosch intellectuals who spoke out against Jewish immigration. An audience of 600 attended a meeting in Potchefstroom, where a senior lecturer at Potchefstroom University College, Frans Jacob Labuschagne, secured a resolution that protested against the influx of Jews: they were 'undesirable' on account of their religion, and 'blood mingling' and 'cultural cooperation' with them was impossible. In addition, they would 'not be an asset to South African Commerce'.[140] It was in the southwestern Cape Province, however, that the impending arrival of the *Stuttgart* generated the most hostility, with meetings organised in Malmesbury, Caledon and Paarl, the latter a town singled out by the *SAJC* as a hotbed of antisemitism. An antisemitic German propaganda film was screened at Stellenbosch University,[141] and the immigration issue was raised in the Provincial Council election in the Cape Province only a few days before the liner was scheduled to dock.[142]

On the eve of its arrival, the Greyshirts held a 3 000-strong protest meeting at Cape Town's Koffiehuis. Crowds spilled into the adjacent Church Square, and shortly after ten o'clock a rumour that the *Stuttgart* was due at one o'clock in the morning provoked hundreds in the audience – 'drunk with beer and with savage frenzy', reported a *South African Jewish Times* correspondent – to march on the docks. Within half an hour about 400 Greyshirt supporters had gathered at the quayside, but their plans came to naught when the ship dropped anchor outside the entrance to Table Bay. By the time the liner (with swastika flags flying) eventually docked, at six o'clock the next morning, the crowd had largely dispersed, leaving only a small group of protesters on the quayside shouting antisemitic slogans and giving the Nazi salute.[143] The refugees were horrified. Melanie Schnitzer recalled the shock at knowing that a section of the population did not want them because they were Jews. 'It was an indescribable blow to us,' she explained. 'Some women were in tears and begged to be allowed to go back. Nobody knew what to do.' At the age of ninety, Claire Lampel remembered telling her family that it would have been preferable to have stayed in Germany. 'Why are we here?' she had asked.[144]

AFTER THE *STUTTGART*

The reactionary forces sweeping across many European countries, endangering civilisation and democracy, had obviously not left South Africa untouched, explained Morris Kentridge at the time antisemitic hostility was reaching its peak shortly before the arrival of the *Stuttgart*.[145] That students and professors were at the helm of the agitation to launch a campaign emulating the organised antisemitism of Germany was particulary worrisome for the *SAJC*.[146] 'Clouds of anti-Semitic vapour have arisen from Stellenbosch and Potchefstroom during the last few days,' asserted the weekly shortly after the arrival of the *Stuttgart*. It accused the professors of having forgotten their own history as descendants of the persecuted Huguenots who had found a welcoming home in South Africa, and of allowing themselves to be blinded by racial prejudice and fear of economic rivalry. Aping the uncultured and uneducated language and philosophy of the Greyshirts and Blackshirts, they were ignoring the fact that only those who were stupid and incompetent feared competition from the Jews.[147]

Obviously alarmed at the outpouring of hate, the Board sent three representatives to meet with Smuts and Hofmeyr. Somewhat surprisingly, Hofmeyr appeared unperturbed by the events surrounding the *Stuttgart*. While empathising with Jewish fears, he believed that the agitation would eventually simmer down and suggested that the Jewish community simply suffer in silence, as, in his view, little could be done. When the Board reminded him that it had been two years since a member of the cabinet had publicly commented on the subject of anti-Jewish agitation, Hofmeyr expressed surprise and read out an extract of a speech he planned to make the following day at the Armistice Day memorial service in Pretoria, where he would appeal for racial harmony.[148]

Unlike Hofmeyr, Smuts had been taken aback by the intensity of the agitation surrounding the *Stuttgart*. He told the Jewish representatives that he had never been in agreement with the principle of the 1930 Quota Act because it had been too blatantly anti-Jewish. So long as he was in the cabinet there would be no legislation that discriminated directly or indirectly on racial lines.[149] But he also made it clear that, in light of the *Stuttgart* affair, something would have to be done about immigration, and he anticipated some revision to existing legislation. The gravity of the situation and the depth of anger, he noted, had already been evident in questions posed to United Party candidates during the recent Cape Provincial Council elections. The mass of people in South Africa, he claimed, were genuinely alarmed at the prospect of an enormous influx of Jews from Germany.[150]

Smuts' instincts were soon confirmed. Within days of the *Stuttgart's* arrival, a series of meetings took place across the country where the rhetoric went well beyond immigration issues only. In Bloemfontein, the Orange Free

State congress of the National Party lashed out at 'Hoggenheimer' who 'grows ever richer while the rest of the population sinks deeper every day into the morass of ever increasing poverty'. Predictably, Hertzog was condemned as a puppet in the hands of Jews. Most importantly, the congress expressed a bellicose and exclusivist nationalism that had hitherto been the preserve of the radical right.[151] At the Transvaal congress, Johannes Gerhardus (Hans) Strijdom, the Transvaal leader of the National Party, succinctly articulated this newfound chauvinism when he claimed: 'We have the right to say that we do not want to become a Jewish or Italian nation or whatever, but want to remain an Afrikaner nation.' The National Party's task was to ensure that and to keep the white race white, while another duty was to ensure the economic salvation of the *volk*.[152]

In such terms did Strijdom effectively capture the essence of the National Party's agenda: uniting the *volk*, uplifting the 'poor white' and extricating the Afrikaner from what it saw as British and Jewish economic domination. As a young man, Strijdom had farmed in the Willowmore district of the eastern Cape Province, an anti-Jewish stronghold. After the collapse of the ostrich feather market on the eve of the Great War, he joined the civil service before studying Law and then establishing a legal practice in the eastern Transvaal town of Nylstroom, where, in addition to legal work, he was also a successful farmer. The 'Lion of the North' – as he would subsequently be known – probably imbibed his anti-Jewish feelings in an environment where Jews had played a prominent role in the ostrich feather industry.[153] Until the Transvaal National Party congress, little had been heard from him in parliament, where he had represented the Waterberg constituency for the party since 1929, but he had spoken out against eastern European Jews at the time of the Quota Act and had also raised the communist bogey.[154] As leader of the breakaway Nationalists in the Transvaal, he became more vociferous.

At the Orange Free State congress in Bloemfontein, the National Party had resolved that no Jew, Asiatic or Coloured could be a member of the party.[155] These sentiments reflected a widely shared segregationist ethos that had reached partial fruition under Hertzog in 1936, when Africans were removed from the common voters' roll in the Cape Province, the last bastion (albeit watered-down) of non-racialism. While Strijdom did not anticipate removing Jews' citizenship rights, he was convinced that the United Party had not adequately addressed the 'Jewish Question'. There remained a sense – in certain circles, at least – that Jews were 'not white like us', to borrow Peberdy's phrase. As she explains, South Africa understood itself as 'a white nation constructed on the basis of only two kinds of founding immigrant and "racial stock": the British and the Afrikaner, the "two great European races" of the Union'.[156]

It is within this framework that miscegenation between black and white generated great anxieties. Although Jews were not the issue in this connection, eugenic obsessions and floating anxiety around 'racial stock' perpetuated fears of pollution and the erosion of the healthy white population[157] which impacted, perhaps sometimes subliminally, on the Jewish immigration debate. Racial purists were extremely concerned. One correspondent to *Die Burger* even suggested that Jews were no longer God's people because – as Madison Grant had shown in *The Conquest of a Continent* – they had mingled with the Khazars and Mongols.[158] A worldview continued to be presented in which Jews were a people apart, alien to the white 'Nordic' South African stock.[159]

Such thinking reflected a cultural essentialism or cast of mind that considered the Jew an additional racial problem (like Africans, Coloureds and Indians) in a country already grappling with racial divisions and in its search for a national identity.[160] Resolutions approved at the Transvaal National Party congress reflected this obsession and would in due course translate into theories of separate development, invested over time with scholarly rationales. As far as Jews were concerned, however, the great task was to stop further immigration and limit occupational options. This was spelled out at the Orange Free State congress, with Malan warning that, unless the government took the necessary restrictive steps in regard to legislation, he would introduce a Bill that would be built upon the following principles:

1) That only people who could be assimilated by the nation should be allowed to enter the country.

2) That Yiddish be not recognised as a European language as far as

    immigration laws are concerned.

3) That Union citizenship may not be granted to any person that belongs to a class which is described by the laws as 'a class which cannot be assimilated'.

4) That no one who is not a Union citizen should be allowed to follow a profession or an occupation or have any interest in property, either as owner or as tenant, without special permission from the Government and under special licence.

5) That the Government should have the power to indicate certain occupations in which only Union nationals should be employed.

6) That no one should be allowed to use a name in business which had not been his before he came to South Africa or which he did not have at a period prescribed by law.[161]

The Board noted that only the first two of the six points in Malan's threatened Bill referred to immigration, while the remaining resolutions were a direct threat to Jews in the country and not simply hostility to German-Jewish immigration.[162] While the principles were clearly predicated upon the notion of 'unassimilability' and the idea that Jews challenged notions of 'South Africanness' and threatened to subvert the social order, at the root of these sentiments were fears of putative Jewish power and domination – notwithstanding the fact that Jews comprised less than five per cent of the 'white' population.

Weeks after the arrival of the *Stuttgart*, the 'Jewish Question' still loomed large in the press and at public meetings. Jews were vilified at raucous meetings in Paarl, Worcester and Potchefstroom. An audience of 600 in Caledon heard a number of professors call on the government to halt Jewish immigration. 'If the Government refuses to act in relation to this question then it is the duty of each citizen of the country and not least the professors to make their voices heard,' exhorted Basson. Professor Cornelis (Con) de Villiers – a Stellenbosch zoologist who had completed postgraduate studies in Zurich and taught in Rome – in particular expressed Nazi-like sentiments.[163]

Hostility had clearly gone beyond the masses; it had entered the halls of the academy and was part and parcel of the mainstream Afrikaner right. As the Board concluded, the period immediately before and after the arrival of the *Stuttgart* had witnessed an unprecedented wave of antisemitism driven by the National Party.[164] This escalating anger included the fear of a growing communist threat, with which Jews in particular were associated. They were also seen as responsible for inciting African workers,[165] who were increasingly perceived as likely converts to labour activism as they flocked to the cities. At the same time, *Die Burger* continued to publish vitriolic letters about the power of 'Hoggenheimer' and Jewish domination of the professions that had such a deleterious effect on the Afrikaner's self-confidence and wellbeing.[166] An ugly tone had entered the discourse, clearly articulated by Professor Geoff Cronjé, a Pretoria University criminologist and Afrikaner intellectual:

> If the 'anti-Jewish' movement in our country now becomes stronger by the day and is destined to play a large role in the political life of South Africa, nobody ought to be surprised, least of all the Jews themselves. They were simply looking for trouble by loading off on our shoulders that element which Germany no longer wanted ... flotsam from the national life of anther country.[167]

The SANP rhetoric was even more venomous than that of the Nationalists. Successful meetings were held in Malmesbury and Paarl, where Willem Laubscher, the leader of the Nationalist Socialist Students Movement in Stellenbosch, joined other colleagues in accusing Malan of stealing Greyshirt thunder. In addition to issuing a warning about the threat of Jewish communist agitation, Laubscher appealed to those present not to be misled by the half-hearted antisemitism of the National Party.[168] After Weichardt had been denied the use of the Pretoria Town Hall, an audience of 2 000 heard him address a meeting in Church Square.[169] At a National Party meeting in Paarl, some speakers threatened to organise a mass march on parliament if the government failed to take action against Jewish immigration. But this did not mollify the Greyshirts in the audience, who appeared to control the meeting. They even compelled the organisers to withdraw a clause in a resolution which stated that if immigration were stopped, antisemitism would cease.[170] Von Moltke, as leader of the South African Fascists, also joined an anti-Jewish chorus in Stellenbosch. The Jew was 'the hidden hand behind the Government', he told a cheering crowd of 500.[171]

Reflecting on developments, the Board observed that the economic issue appeared to be displacing the issue of assimilability, but what was becoming more significant was the potential capital to be gained by employing the 'Jewish Question' for political mobilisation:

> The Jews are accused of being 'unassimilable', of constituting a for-
> eign element in the population, of not identifying themselves with
> the culture of the Afrikaner: but more and more the economic motive
> is asserting itself: the Jews are regarded as threatening the economic
> independence of the Afrikaner people and a call is being made for Afri-
> kaners to keep together. When the cue has just been given by a large
> political party, it is to be expected that Greyshirts and other organisa-
> tions would follow it up. They are obviously small fry at this stage and
> important, only insofar as they may help to swell the voting power of
> the Malanites in the country.[172]

The Malanites were clearly cognisant of the political gain to be derived from Jew-baiting. Malan in fact told Eric Louw that the 'Jewish Question' presented new opportunities: 'We are advancing particularly well with our volk cause. What has helped us a great deal are Hertzog with his bitterness, Hofmeyr with his liberalism, the Jews with their storming of our land and the King with his antics.'[173] Hofmeyr's condemnation of the Stellenbosch professors, for allowing themselves to be used to fan flames of hatred and intolerance, was clearly ineffective.[174]

While there were some important voices who spoke up against the pre-vailing bigotry,[175] it was apparent that the United Party government shared, at least to some extent, the racial assumptions of the right. Hofmeyr may have deplored the attacks made on the Jewish community and he may indeed have been keeping a close watch on the situation,[176] but it was clear that the government had to take more decisive action to deal with the immigration issue if it wished to stay in power. This was spelled out by

Hertzog in a speech to the party faithful at Smithfield, his home constituency, where he promised that legislation would be forthcoming in the next parliamentary session. Persons admitted into South Africa should be an asset and not a burden to the country, he said, but nobody could be an asset unless they were prepared to associate themselves fully with the national community – obviously a veiled reference to the 'unassimilable' Jew.[177]

Significantly, both the English and Afrikaans press broadly shared Hertzog's nativism. 'The Jewish community in this country', explained the *Cape Times*, 'realises, we are sure, that in a relatively small white community of 2 million people, it is not unnatural that the character of immigration from overseas should be examined with very special attention. A relatively small immigration of a particular type, if continued persistently for several years, might easily change fundamentally the characteristics of the South African people of the future.'[178] In similar fashion, the *Cape Argus* noted that 'with the best will in the world, the Union cannot accept all the victims, whether Jewish or "Aryan" of Dr Goebbels' frenzy, and must introduce some form of discrimination to keep the numbers down to reasonable limits'.[179]

Clearly the United Party had no desire to maltreat Jews in South Africa, but it did harbour strong feelings about Jewish immigration. All South Africans should be treated equally, maintained Richard Stuttaford, but added that he did not think South Africa was bound to receive any other nation's unwanted citizens: 'Today a large percentage of Germany is trying to exclude Jews. Tomorrow Spain may want to exclude communists.'[180] Other commentators, while not necessarily identifying with Hertzog's nativist views, recognised and feared the tensions surrounding the 'Jewish Question'.[181]

In early December 1936, the *Times* of London accurately pinpointed a Nationalist anti-Jewish militancy 'more fanatical than it has known since 1914'.[182] Smuts, too, acknowledged the spread of antisemitism, but tried to downplay its extent in a letter to an anxious Sarah Gertrude Millin (a leading South African writer who was herself Jewish), assuring her that the situation was not as bad as she feared. 'For the moment things have become worse owing to the fear of a German-Jewish influx. This minor panic has led to serious political developments, especially at the Cape, where good seats were lost at the Provincial elections because voters thought they were going to be swamped by the Jewish influx from Germany ... Tactful handling and an avoidance of noise and retaliatory measures and speeches may go far to allay feeling and allow the important storm to pass.'[183]

Weichardt certainly had no intention of allowing the storm to pass. He smelt blood. In his Christmas message he called for vigilance against the 'Jewish enemy' who, he asserted, was 'constantly devising fresh means of attack'.[184]

CHAPTER FOUR

FELLOW TRAVELLERS ALONG THE NAZI DIRT TRACK

'I never thought that I would live to see the time when a political party in this country, a party which looks forward to becoming the government of this country ... should ever have so far forgotten themselves and forgotten the true interests of South Africa, as to take up this unsavoury and discreditable cause.'
– Jan Smuts, parliamentary debate on immigration, 14 January 1937

'The South African people have been hoodwinked long enough under the system of party politics which has involved the downfall of our nation. By virtue of this system our public enemy No. 1 – the Jew – gained the control, when we were hopelessly divided by senseless party squabbles.'
– Beaufort West correspondent to *Die Waarheid/The Truth,* 5 March 1937

'Everywhere throughout the Union the doctrines of National Socialism as proclaimed by the South African National Party (Greyshirts) are spreading like wildfire. The English-speaking section of our population must not stand aside. We must have a united South African nation.'
– *Die Waarheid/The Truth,* 14 May 1937

'The tyranny of this Jewish money-power must and shall be destroyed, and my whole strength of mind and body shall henceforth be devoted to achieving this end.'
– Harry Inch, on his release from prison, *Die Waarheid/The Truth,* 14 May 1937

THE ALIENS ACT

Even before the government could fulfil Hertzog's promised immigration legislation, Malan introduced an Immigration and Naturalisation Bill based on the principles outlined almost three months earlier in his keynote address to the 1936 National Party congress in Bloemfontein.[1] No longer would Yiddish be accepted as a European language in terms of the 1913 Immigration Regulation Act (thus terminating a long-standing agreement dating back to the old Cape Colony), but a range of restrictions would also apply to aliens with regard to occupations and property.[2] Name-changing, too, would be prohibited and the disclosure of altered business names – to disguise Jewish ownership – would be made mandatory. Assimilability as a criterion for entry was uppermost in Malan's Bill.

Commenting only days later, the British High Commissioner, William Henry Clark, noted the Bill's 'very high level of intolerance' and its vagueness with regard to assimilability. 'Vagueness, of course, cuts both ways in legislation of this kind,' he added. 'One is tempted to think that it was beyond Dr Malan's ingenuity to devise a specific restriction which would not savour too much of the Hitlerian manner; the Nationalist leader has hitherto, of course, been a staunch protagonist of democratic method of government.' Clark obviously fully understood the motivation behind the Bill:

> Such legislation should be anathema to anyone of a reasonably liberal mind; but in view of the overcrowding of the professions in the Union, and the success in them attained by Jews, it may meet with a certain amount of, one hopes, shamefaced sympathy. Dr Malan is doubtless aware of this, and while he probably does not regret that there is no chance of his Bill passing into law, he is in the happy position that meanwhile its early publication gives his party excellent material for political propaganda.[3]

Twelve days later, Malan's Bill was forestalled by the government, which, on the day parliament resumed, gave notice of its intention to move for leave to introduce its own Immigration Bill. But the astute Malan, keenly aware of parliamentary rules, rose from the floor to give notice of his own

motion in which, with sincere anger, he castigated the ruling party for failing both 'to prevent the further influx of Jewish immigrants and especially
the so-called German refugees' and 'to impose certain restrictions upon
aliens'.[4] At issue were the well-worn accusations of the 'unassimilability'
of Jews, their domination of the economy at the expense of Afrikaners
and English-speakers, and their hold on commerce, which hindered the
amelioration of the 'poor white' problem. Their international connections,
too, had been apparent to all at the time of the *Stuttgart* affair: Jews were
'an *imperium in imperio* in all countries', said Malan. He was now advocating
documentary proof of nationality for all immigrants, as well as an unrestricted right of return to their home country.[5]

While in the past Malan had been more circumspect about attacking
Jews as Jews, he was now quite happy to target them publicly. 'I have been
reproached that I am now discriminating against the Jews as Jews,' he told
the House. 'Now let me say frankly that I admit that it is so, but let me
add that if you want effectively to protect South Africa against the special
influx from outside, it must inevitably be done ... South Africa has a Jewish
problem and that being so we cannot deal with it in an effective way unless
we name it.'[6]

Malan's forthright critique generated much discussion, with Jan Hofmeyr,
Richard Stuttaford, Charles Coulter, Walter Madeley and Morris Alexander lashing out at the National Party leader. Hofmeyr accused him of
blatant antisemitism and of replicating ideas that had seen the destruction
of democracy in some European countries; Madeley admonished Malan
for placing himself effectively at the head of the Greyshirts, while Coulter
asserted that Malan had pandered to Greyshirt extremism in his desperation
to capture support. In similar vein, Alexander accused Malan of simply trying to win votes by 'competing with the Greyshirts and the Blackshirts and
all the other gentlemen who display their political underclothing.'[7]

Despite this criticism, it was soon apparent that the United Party's
own Aliens Bill (introduced shortly after the defeat of Malan's motion
by Stuttaford, Hofmeyr's successor as Minister of the Interior) had similar underpinnings. Although the Bill did not explicitly mention Jews, and
would thus not draw the ire of the Board and Jewish parliamentarians, it

proposed that aliens would be subjected to an Immigrant Selection Board.[8] The notion of 'unassimilability' within the Bill's guidelines also avoided mentioning Jews by name; its target, however, was palpably obvious. Smuts was merely playing politics when, in defence of the Bill, he suggested it was merely a case of excluding 'undesirables'.[9]

That Jews were the target was obvious to the Nationalists, who revelled in the discomfiture of their opponents across the floor as the government spokesmen squeamishly did their best to justify their contention that Jews per se were not the target. Once again the Nationalists trotted out the old stereotypes, including the notion of Jewish usurpation of the country's resources and their exploitation of English-speakers and Afrikaners. 'My objection is not against immigrants who would be a gain to our country', said the Nationalist MP for Stellenbosch, Bruckner de Villiers, but 'against immigrants who come here to take the bread out of the mouths of our people:

> I am thinking of occupations which were formerly in the hands of Afrikaners in our country, and when I speak of Afrikaners I include English-speaking people. Many of those businesses are now in the hands of immigrants ... Some of our noblest people in the country are today working with pick and shovel while they deserve something better ... As long as that is the position, there is no room for immigrants.[10]

Hans Strijdom went even further, claiming Jews had taken the retail trade out of English hands by methods that would not be used by Christians. That, he explained, was why he objected to the admission of any more 'members of that race' to South Africa.

Nationalist MPs Roelof van der Merwe, the Reverend Charl du Toit (Colesburg) and Nico van der Merwe (a fierce republican and Orange Free State leader) each spoke to the notion of Jews as aliens, with the two Van der Merwes rehashing issues of business probity, international Jewish financial manipulation and Jewish power. 'Even in South Africa the Jews rule the government of the country and prescribe what laws and what policy the government must carry out,' said Roelof van der Merwe. At the heart of the 'Jewish Question' today, claimed Nico van der Merwe, was 'Jewish nationalism' which accounted for the 'unassimilability' of Jews and 'the economic power which Jewry has acquired in our country'. These issues, he pointed out, were not unique to South Africa.[11]

Such accusations captured the essence of the Nationalist argument, buttressed also by the idea that South Africa should not absorb more than 'a certain percentage of Jews' if it was to avoid adding to the already fragmented groups – defined by Strijdom as the natives, the Indians, the Coloured people and the Europeans.[12]

Importantly (and predictably) Hertzog, too, acknowledged concerns about Jewish assimilability and, in defence of the Bill, argued that South Africa simply could not absorb too many Jews. But in his view this did not make the Bill antisemitic, as it was an appropriate response to Europe's problems and a growing bitterness against Jews in South Africa. However, it was the socialist Duncan Burnside who got to the nub of the matter when he identified those really responsible for the Aliens Bill: 'The real rulers of the country today are not the Prime Minister and the Minister of Justice but … the Purified Nationalist Party. The Purified Nationalist Party only need to say that there are too many Jews coming into this country and the Government promptly brings in a Bill to prevent Jews from coming into the country.'[13]

The Board knew this too. But recognising the widespread hostility to further Jewish immigration, it prudently concluded that employing the term 'assimilability' rather than mentioning Jews by name left Jews relatively untarnished.[14] Alexander went along with the compromise, going so far as to say there was nothing antisemitic in the Bill since it was 'dealing with aliens' in general.[15] But everyone knew the real target. The Labour Party's Madeley put it succinctly:

> I being a blunt man, perhaps dull of comprehension, cannot understand how this legislation is not anti-Jewish, when they, the progenitors of the legislation, confess that the practical result is going to be a diminution of Jewish immigration. And I want to ask them to cut out the cackle and stop all this verbiage surrounding their real intentions and say frankly and outspokenly that they are anxious to prevent Jewish immigration.

Madeley was quite right. Malan's initial request that the word 'alien' in the legislation include 'a person of the Jewish race' had been turned down, but in reality the legislation ensured that it would be very difficult for Jews to enter South Africa.[16] Among the new requirements (all subject to an Immigrant Selection Board) were:

i) a certificate showing competency in trade or occupation
ii) a certificate of character
iii) details and proof of financial circumstances
iv) specification of 'race'. The form read: European, Hebrew, Asiatic, or African.
v) Reasons for desiring to enter the Union.[17]

Yet despite these stringent requirements, the Nationalists opposed the Bill on the grounds that it did not go far enough. In reality, however, Malan himself could take some credit for the legislation.[18] Indeed he correctly maintained that it was pressure from his party that had led to the drafting of the Aliens Bill;[19] but in his view the proposed legislation was inadequate as it did not deal sufficiently with the dominance of Jews already in South Africa and the threat they posed to all:

> The question arises with us, as a people, not only how we are going to keep them out in the future, but how are we going to protect ourselves against those who are here ... An agitation will arise among the people ... that they should be protected in the country, and that we should eventually have a quota system to give the old population, English and Afrikaans-speaking, back again what they are entitled to and which they have been deprived of in the course of years.

Malan reminded the House that, when he introduced the Quota Act in 1930, he had warned Jews that if they did not want to cooperate in moves to halt unrestricted immigration it would be impossible to stop discrimination against them. But the Jews had ignored his warning and now they alone were to blame for the present state of affairs.[20]

In the final vote, on 27 January 1937, the Aliens Bill received 87 votes for and 26 against. Among the latter were Dominion Party and Labour Party MPs. The real motivation underpinning the legislation was fully understood by the *Zionist Record*: both Hertzog and Malan were in agreement that the number of Jews in South Africa had reached 'saturation' point and that further Jewish immigration had to be stopped if the Jewish problem was to be resolved.[21]

Fortified by the radical right, Malan had done his job. In the process he had been engaged in what the British High Commissioner referred to as 'excellent party politics'. Clark reported to his principal in London, Malcolm MacDonald, that this had been confirmed by Stuttaford in a frank private talk. Clark also noted a growing antisemitism in South Africa that he believed was embarrassing to the government, which had no truck with such hatred; but it too wished to control the influx of German Jews. Clark described speeches from the government benches as 'disingenuous', as 'neither the Minister nor the Prime Minister himself would deny that there was a Jewish problem and that one of the reasons for introducing the bill was the existence of that problem'. On the other hand, Clark reported that Malan felt no qualms about being openly antisemitic, realising that attacking Jews made him something of a hero to all Jew-baiters.[22]

As we have seen, the question of restricting Jewish immigration had confronted policy-makers for some time. When Hofmeyr was Minister of the Interior, he had avoided dealing with the issue and even now refuted accusations that the Bill introduced by his successor, Stuttaford, was antisemitic; it was simply meeting the widespread demand to put an end to all Jewish immigration.[23] Predictably *Die Waarheid/The Truth* went much further, warning that action would also have to be taken against Jews already living in South Africa, whom it described as a more deadly menace than any future immigrants. The only way to free South Africa from the domination of Jewish money power was to do away with what it characterised as the present antiquated and corrupt system of parliamentary government.[24]

With the passing of the Aliens Act, the question now was whether the radical right would inform the Nationalists or the Nationalists tame the extremists. Malan's rhetoric during the debate certainly suggested the former. In his speech at the third reading of the Bill, he revealed the same concern as *Die Waarheid/The Truth* when he raised the issue of how South Africa could protect itself against Jews already in the country. 'How are we going to find a living for our children?' he asked. 'How are the people going to regain their lost ground?'[25]

A NORDIC FRONT

The Aliens Act did not curtail anti-immigrant rhetoric. Within weeks of its passage, the Nationalist press denounced it as a 'bargain' between the government and the Jews; replacing the Quota Act with the Aliens Act, opined *Die Volksblad*, was in fact a great victory for the Jews.[26] Speeches by Nationalists at various by-elections shortly after the Act was passed continued to accuse Jews of usurping opportunities for young Afrikaners and urged a complete end to Jewish immigration.[27] Johannes Brill, who won the by-election in Vrededorp for the National Party, described the United Party as pro-Jewish (presumably the kiss of death in this tough working-class neighbourhood) and Smuts as a lackey of the Jews, and he accused Jews of trying to crush everthing Afrikaans.[28] Boisterous meetings characterised Brill's campaign, with an angry crowd on one occasion asking the Labour Party candidate, Dr Venter Odendaal, to 'Tell us about the Jews', and then drowning out the candidate by singing patriotic Afrikaans songs such as 'Sarie Marais' and 'Perdeby'.[29] Taking another tack, Hans Strijdom, speaking on behalf of Brill, urged Afrikaners to stand together against the false creed of Fusion that united Unionists, Imperialists, Jews and Coloureds.[30] According to the Board, Brill had expressed himself all too frequently in an antisemitic manner, and his eventual victory, it noted, had been ascribed by *Die Vaderland* to the backing of the Blackshirts and Greyshirts.[31]

Malan had good reason to sense a growing wave of support. In the Waterberg by-election, the National Party comfortably increased its majority. Demography, moreover, was on his party's side, as was the electoral system, which favoured the predominantly Afrikaner rural constituencies over urban constituencies.[32] Malan's game plan, writes the historian Lindie Koorts, was to consolidate this support by drawing into the fold the smaller radical right parties established during the Fusion crisis.[33] In so doing, Malan was quite prepared to play the Jewish card. In addition, he knew that focusing on Jewish immigration was a way in which the National Party could prise open the United Party. As the historian Keith Hancock argues, Malan did his best to say 'the things which many of Hertzog's followers wished in their hearts to hear their own leader say'.[34]

Malan's language now became increasingly shrill and his comments bordered on the extreme. Indeed, his rhetoric went beyond the simple manipulation of the 'Jewish Question' for party political gain. He now genuinely appeared to see the Jew as an additional racial problem, as politically subversive and as an obstacle to Afrikaner advancement. At a meeting in Paarl he accused Hofmeyr (whom Nationalists commonly identified as a dangerous liberal because of his public opposition to Hertzog's Representation of Natives Act of 1936) of championing the Jews and non-Europeans. 'Jews have the vote, and in the Cape, Coloureds have the vote,' Malan explained in an hour-long harangue, and because of this Hofmeyr would never be removed from the cabinet, as the result would be too costly for the party. Responding to those who accused him of 'racialism', Malan was quite explicit: 'If we shut the doors to the indiscriminate influx of Chinamen, Indians and others, why not Jews, if we consider that too large a number of them will be detrimental to the interest of the South African people?' South Africa, he added, should not be made a dumping ground for people who were not wanted by their own countries. Ominously, Malan called for a 'Nordic front' to win back for the English- and Afrikaans-speakers the ground they had lost.[35]

Here Malan illustrated the interconnectedness of regnant European currents of thought and South African intellectual traditions. His *völkisch* attitudes were well known, and his call for a 'Nordic front' echoed South African nativist thinking of the 1920s, with its eugenic obsessions and fears of racial mixing, that was shared by English- and Afrikaans-speakers alike.[36] Most importantly, he had crossed the antisemitic Rubicon, moving far beyond the more guarded comments he had made during the debate on the Aliens Act only one month earlier.[37]

Malan's journey into the heart of Jew-baiting was succinctly captured in an insightful and lengthy editorial published in the *SAJC*. Headed 'The

Nordic Front', it confirmed the journal's long-standing belief that Malan would eventually become an adherent of the 'Nordic theory', as the trajectory of his thinking followed a set and easily recognisable pattern. Beginning as mild animosity emerging from an economic basis, it appealed to less enlightened members of society and transformed itself into concern for the 'ethnological' composition of the country's population. From there it soon mutated to violent opposition to Jewish immigration, while at the same time professing the greatest goodwill towards Jews already in the country. Then, appreciating the political benefits of antisemitism, 'he begins to repent of his generosity towards even the local Jewish population and, generally, begins to advocate a policy of differentiation towards them as well. Finally, having indulged his bigotry to a stage where even he becomes somewhat ashamed of it he looks around for some ideal concept with which to whitewash his own blackened conscience and finds ... the Nordic theory.' If in power, the *SAJC* maintained that the National Party would find a pseudo-scientific justification for a racial doctrine, such as the theory of Aryan superiority used by Hitler. In the meantime, the idea of the 'Nordic Front' was being used as a 'shoddy political trap' to identify a dangerous Jewish question that had no basis in reality. The Aliens Bill, stated the *SAJC*, had set up an Immigrant Selection Board that to date had already turned down something like 90 per cent of applications, most of them Jewish. The contentious issue of Jewish immigration, it maintained, should therefore have ceased to exist, but a new fantasy was being posited: the overwhelming danger to Malan's Nordics of a tiny 4.75 per cent Jewish population.[38]

The *SAJC* was not alone in its condemnation. Mainstream English newspapers also castigated Malan's idea of a 'Nordic Front' and considered his speech a clear indication that Jews were not welcome in South Africa. Malan had gone over to the reactionaries, concluded the *Cape Argus*,[39] while the *Natal Advertiser* refused to believe that 'any Englishman of average intelligence will be caught by the new net drawn out by Malan'.[40] Malan had learnt lessons from Hitler, wrote Sarah Gertrude Millin in a letter to the *Star*. 'If you want to attract people you must give them something to hate: the Jews are handy and helpless ... And alas, not only has Dr Malan learnt from Hitler, but his opponents have also learnt from Dr Malan. They have all learnt that anti-Semitism pays, and there is consequently in South Africa now a competition in anti-Semitism.'[41]

SUBVERSIVE COMMUNISTS AND OTHER CANARDS

Malan was riding the crest of a wave of Afrikaner nationalism built upon Christian-National and republican ideals. Cultural unity was conceived in terms of national roots and opposition to the foreigner, notably the Jew. Calls to mobilise along *völkisch* lines – driven largely by the Broederbond in the interest of a frustrated Afrikaner petit bourgeoisie – were proliferating. Hertzog's acceptance of class politics and incorporation of English-speakers within his definition of 'Afrikaner', a notion deeply rooted in his two-stream policy that dated back decades, was being challenged by Broederbonders who increasingly expressed an organic sense of preordained Afrikaner destiny.[42]

Leading Afrikaner intellectuals had joined the Broederbond, among them Dr Albert Hertzog, a Stellenbosch- and Oxford-educated lawyer and son of the Prime Minister. Deeply concerned about the seduction of Afrikaner workers by subversive trade unionists (50 per cent of Afrikaners now lived in the cities), he had founded the *Nasionale Raad van Trustees* (National Council of Trustees) in October 1936,[43] tasked primarily with reforming trade unions by either voting its own members into leadership positions, or by establishing rival unions to bring Afrikaner workers into the *volk*.[44] Afrikaner railway employees had already formed the *Spoorbond* (Railway Union) in 1934 and now, three years later, Hertzog established the *Afrikaner Bond van Mynwerkers* (Afrikaner League of Mineworkers, or ABM) to oppose the well-established Mine Workers Union (MWU).[45] But the new organisation struggled within what Malan and other nationalist intellectuals believed to be an anti-Afrikaner environment.[46] The Chamber of Mines, reinforcing the worst of Malan's fears, soon introduced a 'closed shop' agreement with the MWU that effectively crushed the ABM.

Predictably, Malan believed that the Chamber of Mines was under Jewish influence.[47] Some observers even went so far as to link the MWU to a huge Jewish conspiracy seeking to undermine the white population.[48]

Blackie Swart told the House that the MWU was controlled by a strong 'communistic' element, while a range of Nationalist speakers highlighted the dominance of Jews in the union movement.[49] Despite Afrikaners comprising the majority of the MWU executive, Hans Strijdom maintained they were all dupes of a small number of 'Bolshevistic Jews'.[50] 'We have no quarrel with the Afrikaans workers, or the English-speaking workers,' said Brill, 'but we are fighting the communist Jews who attack us in our language, and our Afrikaans movements, and suppress everything that is Afrikaans in order to suppress us.'[51] Lodewicus (Wicus) Johannes du Plessis, a leading Broederbonder and Professor of Constitutional Law at Potchefstroom University College, similarly expressed concern at the direction of labour activism in South Africa, believing it to be driven by British and Jewish unionists who were informed by Bolshevist principles. The MWU, he claimed, was colour-blind, affiliated with non-white unions and connected to the international communist movement which was exclusively under 'British-Jewish' control. Among its other sins were sympathy for the Spanish Republicans, the boycott of Germany and support of the Soviet system.[52]

These sentiments reflected the concern of Nationalists who, writes O'Meara, saw the mobilisation of all Afrikaner workers as 'the *sine qua non* of Nationalist political power'. It was, he notes, imperative that these workers 'be weaned away from the ideological and organisational hold of class groupings'.[53] If this had to be done by focusing on the Jew, so be it.[54] The colour bar was being eroded and workers increasingly organised.[55] There was a sense of urgency, and the Jew was an ideal scapegoat. Patrick Duncan clearly understood this: 'The anti-Semitic movement, the attempt to keep the Afrikaans mine workers on the Rand away from the corrupting influences of non-racial trade unions, are ripples of the same movement which is setting up the cult of an Aryan race in Germany. It will probably show itself still more forcibly here before long.'[56]

Duncan's prediction proved to be correct. As more and more Afrikaners were attracted to the industrial unions – with a significant number achieving leading positions, some even visiting Moscow and returning with glowing reports plus a determination to tackle the dangers of fascism – the threat to *völkisch* ambitions was apparent.[57] Afrikaner nationalists

Antisemitic propaganda leaflet, 'Communism the Danger', suggesting the reach of the alleged communist-Jewish world conspiracy.
(JBM Hertzog Collection, courtesy Archives for Contemporary Affairs, University of the Free State, Bloemfontein)

had to build an Afrikaner working class and could not afford to lose the support of this growing sector to English-led unions often perceived as Jew-dominated. Communism, or denationalising internationalism, writes the historian André van Deventer, 'was identified as one of those measures employed by Jewry to subjugate Gentile states and perpetuate existing patterns of domination'.[58]

Fear of communism had deep roots. It went back at least to the Rand

Rebellion of 1922 and underpinned Pirow's Riotous Assemblies Act of 1930, which was aimed at labour unrest. Significantly, that Act allowed for the deportation of foreign-born nationals if convicted of engendering feelings of hostility between whites and other sections of the community – a direct response to growing African radicalism from the 1920s.[59] From the mid-1930s, unionist activism among blacks was on the rise. Coloured, African and white workers were increasingly well organised on the shop floor, in some cases joining hands with activists (often Jewish) who were mounting a non-racial struggle against what they termed 'domestic fascism'. The dividing lines were in place: alien and internationalist cosmopolitans on the one hand, *völkisch* entrepreneurs on the other.[60] As Van Deventer explains, in addition to being widely regarded as 'unassimilable' – an 'Oosters Semitiese ras' (eastern Semitic race) in SANP parlance – Jews were now increasingly characterised as radicals and a menace to the Afrikaner *volk*.[61]

The fear of communist inroads further undermining Afrikaner unity, as well as eroding 'Christian dogma', as the Reverend Charl du Toit told the House, was obviously also a concern of the SANP.[62] An editorial in *Die Waarheid / The Truth* entitled 'Pasop vir Camouflage' (Beware of Camouflage) pointed out that communism did not announce itself with trumpets, but came 'like a wolf in sheep's clothing' – necessitating constant vigilance. The 'Jew-Capitalist', by undermining the *volk*, forced it into the clutches of the 'Jewish Communist' and at the same time weakened the small independent businessmen who were the backbone of commerce.[63]

The SANP regarded the Labour Party as communist, and identified the ties between the Fusion government and Labour as nothing less than evidence of a 'Jewish International Front' bent on establishing an international world state in which Jews would hold all the reins of power.[64] Such conspiratorial fantasy was a staple of radical right demagoguery. Newspapers were filled with articles that would have been acceptable fare in the Nazi state. Indeed, *Die Republikein* had become 'almost entirely devoted to anti-Jewish propaganda' and was 'openly glorifying everything in Nazi Germany', reported the *South African Jewish Times* (hereafter the *SAJT*).[65] Adding to local anti-Jewish commentary was a flood of antisemitic leaflets pouring into the country from abroad,[66] while Louis Weichardt and Johannes von

Strauss von Moltke persisted with their anti-Jewish invective on the campaign trail.[67] Weichardt (grossly exaggerating the numbers) told an audience of 400 in Bethlehem that, despite the efforts of parliament to curb undesirable immigration, 11 000 Jews – 'the scum of the earth and international wolves and thieves' – had entered the country in the past three and a quarter years.[68]

Importantly, Weichardt also continued to woo English-speakers (thus running counter to his *völkisch* opponents), using *Die Waarheid/The Truth* to publish his speeches in English because the English press gave him no coverage.[69] The message was always the same: to deny rumours of an SANP amalgamation with the National Party, on the grounds that the latter upheld 'the present corrupt and antiquated system of party politics and professional parliamentarianism'. The SANP, on the other hand, stood for an *eenheidsvolkstaat* (unitary state for the *volk*) that included English-speakers as equals, all with an undivided loyalty to the People's State governed according to 'Group representation' under 'Responsible Leadership'.[70] The National Party was invariably attacked for its hypocrisy in attempting to steal the SANP's thunder on the 'Jewish Question', while at the same time claiming that they were not truly anti-Jewish. 'In point of fact, by their present attitude they are simply making themselves ridiculous and so playing into the Jews' hands,' noted *Die Waarheid/The Truth*. 'They have no practical scheme whatever whereby the control of the Jewish money-power over South Africa may be broken and the South African people saved from social and economic disaster and ruin.'[71] Jews also came under fire for supposedly dominating party politics, with 'Jew-king Smuts and his secretary, the Jewess Sally Richardson' singled out for attack.[72] *Die Waarheid/The Truth* even objected to Jews serving on juries and indeed anywhere 'in the administration of Justice in OUR Fatherland'.[73] Correspondents to the newspaper expressed similar ideas, while its columns continued to take the *Protocols* seriously and to accuse Jews of stalking Christian women.[74]

Besides *Die Waarheid/The Truth*, other publications such as Von Moltke's *Patria* (the organ of the South African Fascists) and HS Terblanche's *Terre Blanche*, were in circulation.[75] *Patria* in particular appeared to be well funded, with articles in English and Afrikaans seemingly culled from the

Welt-Dienst press agency in Germany.[76] Local writers, including academics, demonstrated the same hostility towards Jews as their European mentors. By way of example, when Professor Johannes Andreas Wiid, a young Stellenbosch University historian with a doctorate from the University of Munich, reviewed Louis Herrman's *The Jews in South Africa* (which detailed the early history and contributions of South African Jewry), he pointed out that Jews had arrived in the wake of the discovery of diamonds and gold that had turned South Africa into a 'Jewish paradise'. Far from contributing to the country, Jews were speculators rather than producers. Wiid also claimed that 'Randlords', supported by the banker Alfred Rothschild, had been responsible for the Anglo-Boer War.[77]

The publishers of *Patria* claimed that 20 000 free copies had already been distributed, with another 10 000 waiting to be sent to South African homes, the ultimate aim being to supply a copy to every South African household.[78] The newspaper gained much publicity when the Board accused Von Moltke of stealing documents from its Cape offices and planning to publish them in *Patria*.[79] After being made aware of plans for the publication of a book based on the documents, the Board initiated a court action and the publication was ultimately blocked in early 1938.[80] In the meantime, publication of *Patria* was suspended due to financial difficulties, as Von Moltke was in a precarious financial situation, which eventually resulted in an insolvency case.[81]

GROWING CONCERN

It was patently obvious that the Aliens Act had had no effect on defusing escalating anti-Jewish agitation. A Board member who visited the eastern and western Transvaal soon after the passing of the Act observed that hostility towards Jews was in fact gaining ground, especially in smaller centres such as Ermelo, Wolmaransstad and Davel,[82] while the Greyshirts were operating a serious boycott of Jewish shops in various Orange Free State towns.[83] In a detailed letter, Gustav Saron informed the Acting Minister of the Interior, Hofmeyr, about the proliferation of propaganda material imported from abroad aimed solely at inciting animosity against Jews.[84]

Smuts, now Minister of Justice, assured the Board that the activities of the radical right were being closely monitored by the police and that the situation was not serious.[85]

What was of concern to the government was growing Nazi activity in South West Africa and its potential spillover into South Africa. In April 1937, a government proclamation on South West Africa granted it sweeping powers to combat Nazi activities in the mandated territory.[86] The German government took great exception to this action, as it did to the South West Africa Commission report of 1936 which it felt was in conflict with South Africa's obligations under the mandate. The proclamation was described by the Nazi Party newspaper, the *Völkischer Beobachter*, as 'a declaration of war on Germanism, designed to make the work of the "Deutsche Bund" in South Africa impossible'.[87] Even *Die Burger* sympathised with German concerns, as did *Die Waarheid / The Truth*, which characterised the South African government as 'the tool of the anti-German Jewish Money Power', arguing that friendly relations with Germany were absolutely essential:

> A large proportion of our population have German blood in their veins, and the cultural intercourse between the two countries has always been of the closest and most intimate nature. Germany is the home of new ideas in the political sphere and is the most forceful champion of Aryan civilisation. She has solved within her own territory some of the very problems with which South Africa is faced, and we may therefore look to her for guidance and assistance in our future struggle.[88]

Undeterred by such adverse comment, Hertzog told parliament that some German elements in South West Africa had seriously undermined the government's ability to govern the territory and that action was imperative.[89] He regretted upsetting the German government, but had no option but to act. In similar vein, Charles te Water, the South African High Commissioner in London, informed the German ambassador to Britain (and its future foreign minister), Joachim von Ribbentrop, that 'Government in South West Africa had become practically impossible during the last few years owing to Nazi activities'.[90]

The government's strong response was welcomed by the *SAJC*, but the tide of Nazi propaganda that was entering South Africa remained a serious concern:

> Masses of propaganda literature originating from Germany have been in circulation throughout South Africa for a number of years. Also, it is impossible to read any of the numerous anti-Semitic publications of South Africa, e.g. 'Patria,' 'Die Republikein,' 'Die Waarheid,' without being struck by the fact that most of the anti-Jewish material contained in them is taken from 'Welt Dienst,' a news service published in Erfurt in six languages, for use by anti-Semites in countries outside Germany. Similarly, the German paper 'Der Blitz' the official organ of the Deutsche Aktion, has regular correspondents in South Africa reporting upon the activities of local anti-Semitic organisations and carries propaganda material designed for use by anti-Jewish organizations in Ausland.[91]

Also of concern was the activity of Nazis within South Africa. Aided by diplomatic and consular representatives of the Reich, Nazis had extended their Cape Town operations to other centres all over South Africa: Johannesburg, Pretoria, Durban, East London, Port Elizabeth and Bloemfontein, and even to the small towns of Tzaneen in the northern Transvaal and Philippi in the Cape Province. Meetings were held in private houses or other safe venues. The German consul, Bruno Stiller, was particularly active, first in Cape Town and then Pretoria.[92] Supported by Ernst Wilhelm Bohle, Stiller's task was to transform South Africa into a German protectorate after working it out of the British Commonwealth.[93]

The Nazis saw opportunities inherent in the divisions between English- and Afrikaans-speaking whites and hoped eventually to separate the Union from the rest of the Commonwealth, using South West Africa as the key to that strategy. They therefore encouraged, by all possible means, the growth of Malan's party. A South African-German Society had been formed to facilitate contact between the two countries, and Nazi agents were regularly dispatched to South Africa. With its sizable German population, Natal was seen as a particularly fertile field for the spread of Nazi propaganda. Northern Natal was especially receptive, and Otto von Strahl – a German consular official and a leading informant on Nazi activities in South Africa before and during the war – reported that 'many of the farm gates bore the swastika badge and visitors were welcomed with the words "Heil South Africa!"' According to him, the strongest Nazi following was in the Wartburg area, while specific German days attended by Greyshirts were held in small Natal farming towns. A school at Hermannsburg flew the Nazi flag on special occasions and the children of German farmers sang the 'Horst Wessel Song' and gave the 'Heil Hitler' salute. Next to Cape Town, Durban was the most popular place for Nazi propaganda, and crews off German ships were welcomed and entertained at Twine's Hotel, noted Von Strahl.[94]

A COMPETITION IN ANTISEMITISM

Such activism, coupled with persistent public debate about the 'Jewish Question,' elicited some concern from the clergy. Two months before Hertzog's proclamation giving his government sweeping powers in South West Africa, the Witwatersrand Church Council, representing Protestant denominations (including the Dutch Reformed Church), had passed a resolution that condemned all 'attitudes and actions based on race prejudice' as 'contrary to the spirit of Christ'. The council deprecated in the strongest terms the antisemitic propaganda that was being disseminated through certain channels in South Africa and believed that the Christian churches of South Africa should exercise a restraining influence on its spread.[95]

These views were shared by the Roman Catholic Church whose newspaper, the *Southern Cross*, noted that it was as 'wrong and sinful for a Christian to hate a Jew as it is for a Christian to hate a Christian'. It was hoped that no Catholics would forget the lessons of their religion and identify themselves with any movement inspired by hatred or fear of any race or creed.[96] On the other hand, a Dutch Reformed Church Synod meeting in Pretoria adopted a rather confusing and ambiguous resolution on antisemitism. 'The persecution of any section of the community,' it declared, 'is not countenanced by the Synod. Where anti-Jewish movements are started

for economic or other reasons the Synod will leave it to the Christian conscience of its members to judge the extent to which these movements are
justified in the general public interest.'[97] This was regretted by the *SAJC*,
which pointed out that the church was equivocating by refusing to decide
whether or not these movements were justified. In the strongest terms the
Jewish weekly called on all churches to totally reject the 'filthy racial crusade' carried on against Jews.[98]

Malan certainly abandoned any reservations about attacking Jews for
political gain. In early April 1937, he delivered a most vitriolic attack in a
speech in Stellenbosch, where he linked Jews to a range of evils, particularly
communism, and accused them of using the help of international financial
organisations for personal gain. He accused Jews of being 'disintegrative'
because they objected to the united power of the nation and were antago-
nistic to all national movements. Malan went on to blame 'Coalition and
Fusion' on Jews, accusing them of doing everything in their power to keep
Afrikaners from uniting, resulting in 'their lowly and insignificant position'
in South African society. Furthermore, their opposition to discrimination
would lead to miscegenation with all of its attendant 'evils'.[99]

The speech attracted widespread criticism in the English press, with the
Cape Argus suggesting that Malan's 'astounding farrago' proved that 'the
Party has gone over lock, stock and barrel to Anti-Semitism'.[100] The speech
was also condemned by the *SAJC*, which (much as it had done six weeks
earlier) traced the historical trajectory of Malan's views as a means of illustrating how the Nationalist leader had 'travelled along the Nazi dirt track'.
At the time of the Quota Act in 1930, it noted, Malan had denied any hostility towards Jews, and in 1932 had welcomed a suggestion to have a history
of South Africa published in Yiddish.[101] After Fusion, Malan had done his
best to avoid singling out Jews, but now, a mere three years later, his condemnation was unqualified:

> All of a sudden there are trotted out the sickeningly familiar stalking-
> horses of the International Jewish Communist, the International Jewish
> Banker, and so forth – the dark and secret creators of everything which
> the Nationalist Party might dislike. Not only are the dastardly Jews

behind the Trade Union of the miners (one Jewish secretary corrupting 11 000 Afrikaners!), but they have suddenly and belatedly become responsible for Fusion! The motto seems to have become: 'When in doubt, play Jews.' What does it matter if the same set of plotters seem to be Moscow-communists, Hoggenheimer-capitalists, Imperialist, Internationalists and peaceful South African citizens, all at one and the same time? That only shows how clever they are![102]

A short while after Malan's diatribe, JFJ (Hans) van Rensburg, the Administrator of the Orange Free State, took the opportunity to praise Hitler and Nazism during an address in Stellenbosch to the ANS, of which he was President. Just under forty years of age, the able Van Rensburg (a future leader of the paramilitary pro-Nazi Ossewa-Brandwag) had enjoyed a meteoric career in the civil service. Holder of a doctorate in Law from the University of Pretoria, he was legal advisor to the Ministry of Justice at the age of thirty-one and Administrator of the Orange Free State at thirty-eight.[103] Van Rensburg had visited Germany at the time of the 1936 Olympic Games and had been greatly impressed by the pageantry on display at the Nazi Party congress at Nuremberg. He was proud to have met Hitler and other leading Nazis, and willingly accepted an invitation from the Nazi Party to become the representative of the 'Anti-Comintern' for Africa. His acceptance, according to the historian Christoph Marx, was not just to please his hosts; it was out of conviction.[104]

Clearly seduced by the Führer and impressed with what he had seen in Germany, Van Rensburg told the students that National Socialism was the only salvation for South Africa and the only answer 'to the subversive doctrines of Marx the communist, a man who never did a stroke of hard work in his life'. Hitler himself was 'the Saviour of the Fatherland against the danger of International Communism'.[105] Filled with *völkisch* and sometimes mystical allusions, Van Rensburg's speech described the synthesis of nationalism and socialism as the perfect fusion: the submission of the individual to the *volk*. 'My tour in Germany showed me clearly that unless some form of National-Socialism be adopted in South Africa, we cannot hope to keep pace with the progress of the world.'[106]

Bruno Stiller was among those who attended the Stellenbosch meeting, and in a communication to his superiors waxed eloquently about the content of Van Rensburg's speech:

> The Administrator particularly emphasised that National Socialism meant a synthesis of nationalism and socialism, and that through this synthesis Germany was being saved from the great danger of communism. The fact that van Rensburg has frankly and freely upheld national socialism as an example to the Afrikaners, not only to the German-Afrikaans Cultural Union, but also before the student body of Stellenbosch, from which the future leaders of Afrikanerdom will be drawn, shows how lasting are the impressions which he gained on his visit to Germany.[107]

Die Waarheid/The Truth was equally enthusiastic about Van Rensburg's speech, which it saw as a harbinger of the SANP's political success: 'When the chief executive officer of a Jew-infested province like the Free State openly expresses views like these, we may be certain that victory is not far off.'[108] Five weeks later, in Pretoria, and obviously cognisant of the public appetite for radical politics, Malan gave yet another rousing address in which he once again questioned the Jewish presence in South Africa and the role played by Jews in blocking the advancement of the Afrikaner.[109] He also espoused the principles of the SANP, but not the political system they advocated, as he valued multiparty democracy and was opposed to the one-party fascist politics of Weichardt's organisation.[110] In its response, *Die Waarheid/The Truth* agreed that a wide gap remained between the SANP and the National Party, but castigated Malan for claiming some SANP principles as his own. Can we believe, asked the newspaper, that he is anti-Jewish or was he simply trying to gain votes?[111]

There was indeed a chasm between Malan's opportunistic antisemitism – albeit sometimes expressed with disturbing conviction – and the chimerical fantasies of the SANP, with its radical vision of a National Socialist state threatened by international Jewry, both capitalist and communist. Weichardt had spelt this out in a speech at Salt River in Cape Town some weeks earlier. A largely working-class audience heard him berate 'the Jew-Capitalist and the Jew-Bolsheviks [who] are everywhere working hand in hand for the workers destruction' and inciting class hatred, in contradistinction to National Socialism, which rejected artificial class distinctions.[112]

Weichardt brought these ideas to the SANP congress in Pretoria where, in a keynote address delivered in Afrikaans, he reported the party's positive growth despite press hostility and attempts to destroy the party from within.[113] He announced that the SANP would participate in the upcoming elections where it was strongest, and, where it did not compete, would work to ensure victory for the National Party against the United Party.[114] There would, however, be no merger, as the SANP considered multiparty democracy to be bad for South Africa. In addition, unlike the National Party, asserted Weichardt, the SANP was not fighting the British, and neither was it fighting for a republic.[115]

Here Weichardt delineated the core difference between the SANP and the National Party: Malan spoke essentially as the leader of an Afrikaner nationalist movement, republican in orientation, corporative in leaning, but democratic in inclination. The SANP, on the other hand, courted English-speakers in pursuit of a vague Christian-Aryan ideal in the mould of European fascism. In fact one of its advocates, Captain Charles Cherry, toured Natal precisely to garner English support. Audiences were told specifically that the SANP was not anti-British and, although greatly respecting the Nazis, was not a German party, nor was it supported from Germany as Jewish and communist propaganda claimed. Bonds with Germany were however welcomed, and Hitler was praised for 'the wonderful work he has performed in regenerating his country and people'. The aim of the SANP, according to Cherry, was 'to build up a united South African nation and to amalgamate into one all the various Christian Aryan-European elements of which our white population is composed'.[116]

The SANP was clearly defining its own space. As a manifestation of its independence it established Grey House in Cape Town, an obvious imitation of the Nazi Party's Brown House in Munich.[117] Political meetings were rough, with heated exchanges. SANP hecklers took great pleasure in taunting Nationalist speakers by asking if the National Party would allow

Jews to be members of parliament.[118] Havemann's Blackshirts, too, were on the move. Now known as the *Suid-Afrikaanse Volksbeweging* (South African People's Movement, still commonly known as the Blackshirts, but formally the Patriotte), they published their own fortnightly, *The Leader*.[119] In August a vicious fight broke out between anti-fascists and Blackshirts at the Johannesburg City Hall during an anti-fascist meeting. Two hundred policemen with batons charged a large crowd of Blackshirts who had tried to stage a demonstration on the City Hall steps.[120] Not surprisingly, the *SAJC* painted a picture of a Jewish community facing a growing threat:

> The 'Shirt' movements under various names continue to spread their filth by every means in their power, and have of late been trying to break into political life, by contesting elections. Thus 'Shirt' candidates have stood at a Parliamentary by-election at Port Elizabeth, municipal elections in the Cape, and Provincial Council elections in the Transvaal and Natal. The fact that every one of these gentry was soundly defeated is a tribute to the good sense of South African public opinion, but that a certain amount of harm is done cannot be doubted.[121]

In addition to so-called Shirtist activities, a worrying development for the *SAJC* was the now overt anti-Jewish position of the National Party. It had moved beyond an 'unfriendly' attitude, as expressed in the boycott issue, and adopted a much more aggressive stance. Frequent mass meetings continued to target Jewish immigration – despite the very significant decline in numbers since the 1937 legislation – and Malan and his party launched bitter attacks against Jews during parliamentary debates. It was clear that the more reactionary elements in the party were in the ascendant.[122] With a senior public servant like Van Rensburg praising Nazism, with Weichardt, Von Moltke and other radical rightists on the stump, and with the leader of the parliamentary opposition aping the Greyshirts, the *SAJC* had every reason to show concern.[123]

Especially disturbing was the narrowing of the erstwhile gap between the National Party and the radical right. Some Nationalist intellectuals even looked to the Nazi state for inspiration. Both Nico Diederichs and Piet

Meyer, respectively the organiser of the FAK and founder of the ANS, had studied in Germany, while Hendrik Gerhardus Stoker, Wicus du Plessis and (Broederbond head) Joon van Rooy at Potchefstroom University College, as well as Albert Hertzog – a group described by Giliomee as 'the northern intelligentsia' – were to a greater or lesser extent sympathetic to Germany's 'revolution'.[124] There were also many other young Afrikaner intellectuals who had been attracted to a neo-Fichtean idealism.[125] With notions of a common culture – 'a community of feeling', in Moodie's words – and a national calling at the behest of God,[126] the conflation of *volk* and nation was manifest. And even though Afrikaner nationalism differed from Nazi notions of biological descent of *Blut und Boden* (blood and soil), a burgeoning exclusivism did not bode well for the Jews.[127]

MALANITES ON THE OFFENSIVE

With a general election anticipated in the first half of 1938, the National Party's congress, held in August 1937 in Uitenhage, set the tone for the coming campaign. Numerous hostile speeches revealed that fear of both Jewish communist agitation and Jewish commercial domination lay at the heart of delegate concerns. A number of resolutions once again echoed the demand for trade and other licences to be granted on a proportional basis and for the names of Jews engaged in business to be publicly disclosed. Eric Louw drove a resolution requesting that the government put a complete stop to Jewish immigration in order to loosen the Jewish grip on business which was denying opportunities to both English-speakers and Afrikaners.[128] Although he claimed that identifying the Jew as an economic impediment to Afrikaner advancement was not driven by a deep-seated racial view, it certainly did serve to essentialise the Jew and reinforce assumptions of Jews as an unassimilable and alien race.[129]

Even before the Uitenhage conference, Malan's attacks on Jews had been gathering momentum during speaking engagements in the Orange Free State. At Boshof he claimed there were already enough Jews in the country and expressed a determination to stop the influx of more, warning that failure to do so would incite more antisemitism.[130] In a speech lasting over three hours in Kroonstad, he attacked Hofmeyr as the champion of the Jews and once again expressed his fears of Jews dominating South African commerce. Singling out for special mention the diamond magnate Ernest Oppenheimer and the industrialist Isadore Schlesinger, Malan repeated the oft-used argument that business quotas would have to be considered, as Jews were depriving both English-speakers and Afrikaners of a livelihood.[131] A few days later, in Parys, he even expressed his admiration for Mussolini and Hitler, and once again voiced concern about the overrepresentation of Jews in trade and the legal profession.[132] In addition, he made much of the 'communist menace' in South Africa, claiming that unions were being converted to communism and that the 'pro-Jewish' Labour Party was 'nothing but a kind of Jewish organisation'. Little wonder that the *Rand Daily Mail* believed the National Party was moving into a fascist phase.[133]

As a political opportunist *par excellence*, Malan could not avoid playing the Jewish card, but as one who essentially felt uneasy with unadulterated antisemitism, there must have been moments when he felt twinges of discomfort. For example, in a speech at Garies shortly after the Uitenhage conference, he asserted that he had no intention of 'kindling hatred' against Jews, but, in defence of his actions, reminded the gathering that he had warned the Jewish community against encouraging unfettered immigration and that they had fought his request tooth and nail.[134] When he spoke at Springbok, Malan quoted Chaim Weizmann to bolster his case against Jewish immigration, asserting that even the world Zionist leader had acknowledged that a country could absorb only a certain number of Jews.[135] In Vredendal, he returned to the old accusation that after the Quota Act Jews had made up their minds to wreck him and the National Party.[136]

Malan's speeches continued to be closely monitored by the British High Commissioner, William Clark, as they were seen as preparing the ground for the general election and thus represented a window into National Party thinking. Clark believed that Malan's major political concerns were South Africa's relations with the Crown, its prospects as a 'white man's country', and, as a means of wooing potential support, blaming Jews for the existence of dire poverty amid great wealth. In a communication to Malcolm MacDonald at the Dominion Office, Clark summed up Malan's tactics, accusing him of playing on the notion that overrepresentation of Jews in South Africa posed an economic danger to certain sections of the population. The steps Malan was suggesting to deal with that threat included, primarily, a ban on further Jewish immigration and limitations on Jewish participation in certain professions. 'His party stood for Christian nationalist principles,' reported Clark, and 'if Jews were prepared to become Christian and lead a Christian life, they would be allowed to join the Nationalist Party; it was for them to decide.' Clark maintained that Malan was cagey about revealing his policy as regards Jews or communists, and as a result one was left with the impression that 'his stirring up of prejudice, White against Black, Christian against Jew, Fascist against Communist, is merely a device to embarrass the Government by playing upon divisions of opinion which naturally exist'. Clark also stressed Malan's 'sneaking regard for the political methods of modern dictators' – something the National Party leader had himself claimed – and reported that, in recent months, Malan's thinking had been developing along fascist lines.[137] Clark's communication also expressed fear of Afrikaner nationalism's ties with Germany, illustrating that Jewish concerns about the direction taken by the National Party were not parochial or paranoid. In fact, Malan's growing obsession with Jews was being reported in many sections of the press.

But it was not only Malan who was targeting Jews. Other high-placed Nationalists also harped on the 'Jewish Question', focusing as always on the threat posed by further immigration. This had the desired effect of both garnering support among the disaffected and, equally important, dealing with the SANP challenge. For example, in Oudtshoorn – once dubbed 'the Jerusalem of South Africa' because of its substantial Jewish community – the Nationalists were able to neutralise an SANP challenge by repeatedly criticising Jewish immigration, and by demonstrating their desire to limit Jewish commercial power, which they claimed dated from the ostrich feather boom at the turn of the century, when eastern European newcomers dominated the trade. With changing fashions, the industry had collapsed and by 1914 relations between Jews and Afrikaners (always ambivalent) had deteriorated. Credit squeezes and rising prices took their toll, mainly on Afrikaner farmers, during the First World War. In the 1920s, Jews, who were not an inconsequential voting group, were being courted by both the National Party and the South African Party, but increasing references to 'Hoggenheimer' made by Stephanus le Roux – a farmer and National Party MP for Oudtshoorn – resulted in Jewish constituents consolidating around the South African Party. Afrikaner farmers began to develop cooperatives to avoid the Jewish 'middleman', and verbal attacks, as well as arson in the late 1920s, gathered momentum against the backdrop of rising poverty.[138]

Tensions escalated, and in 1933 Le Roux comfortably defeated the United Party candidate in Oudtshoorn. Building on the 'Hoggenheimer' bogey, the Nationalists also won an Oudtshoorn provincial seat in October 1936. Increasingly, Le Roux spoke out against Jewish immigration, and even after the passing of the Aliens Act warned of the 'danger of a third race in South Africa' if the influx from Germany was not stopped. Indeed, he went so far as to threaten Jews who thought that they could 'create a land for themselves within our country'.[139] Here Le Roux's animus was directed at the conflict between the Afrikaner-driven cooperative movement and the Jewish commercial sector (particularly the tobacco business) in Oudtshoorn. Importantly, Le Roux's extreme rabble-rousing succeeded in undermining Afrikaner support for the SANP in Oudtshoorn: the Nationalist strategy of embracing the antisemitism of the radical right had succeeded.[140]

This, however, did not mean a slowing-down of radical right activity. The Board, always a keen observer of events, noted an increase in SANP activities in Cape Town, where the party's headquarters served as a distributing centre for various Nazi journals imported into the Union from abroad. The Board also commented on the fact that *Die Waarheid / The Truth* had changed from a fortnightly to a weekly, while Von Moltke's *Patria* – which had been suspended for some time – was now appearing monthly. Harry Inch was also active again on the Witwatersrand, and despite National Party denials an electoral agreement with the SANP appeared to be on the cards.[141]

In its wish to incorporate all Afrikaners into an organic ethnic unit, the National Party was determined to fuse cultural and political activities, thereby giving 'a political tinge to culture', as the Board explained. This intended fusion had effectively been declared at the Bloemfontein congress of the FAK, a body purporting to be purely cultural and not political.[142] But in July 1937, the FAK announced that it would enter the political realm and support the AMU as well as Albert Hertzog's efforts to organise Afrikaner workers in a range of industries into Christian-National unions akin to the Spoorbond.[143] It also pledged to fight communism. Nico van der Merwe, chairman of the FAK, lamented that while most Afrikaners observed 'Culture Day', there were others who were in the hands of 'Harris and Sachs' celebrating Labour Day on 1 May.[144]

All Afrikaner institutions were now focused on ethnic mobilisation. As the *SAJC* commented, 'the simplest way to be pro-Afrikaner is to be anti-British, anti-Jewish, anti-Asiatic, anti-coloured, anti-native, anti-Fusion, anti-Imperialist, anti-Labour, and … anti-Communist'. Instead of combating hatred and fear, continued the *SAJC*, Malan had taken the lead in exploiting these sentiments and proclaimed 'a Holy War in which traditions, the religion, the culture and the racial pride of the Afrikaner are inspanned in a drive to political domination'. Accusing the Nationalists of 'stealing the Jewish World Pest from the Greyshirts', the *SAJC* commented that the 'usefulness of anti-Semitism in race politics was too good a discovery of the Nazis to let slip'. The paradox inherent in the association of the Jew with both communism and capitalism did not seem to register, and the twin bogeys of Judaism and communism continued to be used as scare tactics for political gain.[145] Meanwhile, during a tour of the Orange Free State, Malan once again expressed opposition to Jewish immigration (despite its drastic reduction), as well as concern at the 'vast and growing activities of the Jews and their ascendancy in commerce'.[146] He also increasingly identified liberalism and communism − both closely associated with Jews − as twin threats to South Africa.[147] At a meeting in Tulbagh, in the Cape Province, he claimed that the first task of his party, once in power, would be 'to crush the existing elements of Liberalism and Communism in the Union'. These movements were so powerful, remarked Malan, that they were 'making South African industries black and the road gangs white'.[148]

What the Board found particularly worrying at this time was the National Party's increasing use of the 'Jewish Question' in South African politics. Jews were being linked to liberalism, a term associated in Nationalist circles with cosmopolitanism which led inevitably to communism and miscegenation – both associated with forces seeking to undermine Hertzog's grand segregationist designs. Liberals and communists in fact had a high profile in elections for the Natives' Representative Council in June 1937, which followed in the wake of the All African Convention and the passage of the Representation of Natives Act 12 of 1936. The latter Act terminated the common voters' roll in the Cape Province and established indirect African representation in the Senate as well as a Native Representative Council.[149]

FLIRTATION: THE NATIONAL PARTY AND THE SANP

It remains difficult to gauge the extent to which Malan sincerely held anti-Jewish views or whether he was merely employing them for party political gain. As we have seen, the *SAJC* was convinced that the Nationalist leader had evolved into a dyed-in-the-wool antisemite; yet one of South Africa's leading rabbis, the Galician-born Judah Leo Landau, disagreed, claiming that Malan was not 'at heart' an antisemite but was merely posturing to strengthen support for his party.[150]

At the time, Landau's comments were reported with approbation in *Die Waarheid/The Truth*: any move by the Malanites into SANP territory was to be resisted, and the Jewish card was jealously guarded.[151] In the struggle for the support of the disaffected and alienated, the SANP wished to play down the antisemitism of the National Party for fear of losing potential voters, particularly in the smaller rural towns. But in reality Malan had regularly employed the language and discourse of the radical right, albeit not informed by the visceral hatred and conspiratorial mindset of Weichardt or Von Moltke. Many Afrikaner nationalists certainly were Nazi fellow travellers: Van Rensburg's eulogy to National Socialism at the ANS meeting in Stellenbosch was only one example of many, reported the Board. Indeed, much to the Board's consternation, a number of Afrikaner professors, among them the prominent writer DF Malherbe, had been to Germany and had returned full of praise for National Socialism.[152]

Given Malan's proclivity for political opportunism, it is possible that Rabbi Landau's assessment was correct and that the National Party leader's turn to anti-Jewish extremism was only a ploy to attract votes and was designed to explore potential ties with the SANP with an eye on the forthcoming general election.[153] In fact, this appears to be corroborated by the approach of the secretary of the National Party in the Cape Province, Frans Erasmus (who was no doubt acting with Malan's approval, according to Koorts), to Willem Laubscher, the secretary of the SANP, indicating that the National Party might be amenable to an electoral agreement with the SANP to enhance its chances of defeating the United Party at the upcoming 1938 election.[154] Laubscher replied that the SANP would seriously consider this if the two parties could collaborate on a 'no compromise' basis.[155]

In his reply, Erasmus welcomed the possibility on condition that the principles of agreement and disagreement were made quite clear, in particular specifying those issues on which the SANP was not prepared to compromise.[156] Laubscher was unhappy with what he perceived as a half-hearted response and delayed his reply for three weeks, eventually agreeing to send Erasmus the SANP principles in order to illuminate the differences between the parties. But he also asked for clarification of some offensive anti-Greyshirt accusations recently made by two National Party members, which did not bode well for cooperation between the parties.[157]

Erasmus responded by reassuring Laubscher that the difference between the parties revolved around policies rather than beliefs, but talks could not continue unless the 'no compromise' issues were clarified. In addition, the precise relationship between the Greyshirts and the SANP needed to be spelt out, including the control exercised by the SANP over the Greyshirts. A further concern centred on similarities between the SANP and anti-democratic German National Socialists. Despite the SANP's assurances of continued support for democratic ideals, Erasmus maintained that he experienced difficulty in separating the SANP from the Nazis, and stressed that the National Party had to have a pure South African character and not be too closely allied to parties from foreign countries.[158]

Laubscher's response came a month later. He pointed out the difference between the SANP and the Greyshirts, the former being a political party working within the framework of a unitary *volk* state while the latter was not a political party but more of a cultural organisation acting as propagandists for the SANP. As far as National Socialism and Nazi links were concerned, he accused the National Party of a lack of understanding. The SANP was not in any way affiliated to Germany, and the swastika was used only because it was an international symbol employed by nationalists in Europe as the banner under which 'international Jewish-Communism' was fought on behalf of the 'Christian Idea and Western Civilisation'. Despite some differences in ideology, Laubscher claimed that the principles of both parties were the same: both were against the 'Fusionists' and 'Bolshevists' and both believed that the Fusionists were prepared to work with the 'Communist' Labour Party and 'Jewish-Liberalism'. Differences in ideology would remain, but neither party would need to compromise its values in order to find common cause.[159]

Erasmus was not convinced by Laubscher's explanations and penned a rather brusque reply noting, *inter alia*, that while thousands of South Africans were concerned about the Jewish and communist danger and not hostile to Nazism in Germany or Fascism in Italy, they were opposed to the transplantation of those movements to South African soil. Solutions to South African problems had to be approached 'from a South African point of view' and the dictatorship principle was at odds with South Africa's character and traditions.[160]

Laubscher then blamed the National Party for ending the possibility of electoral ties, and thereby the chance of defeating the United Party's liberalism and Labour's communism. It labelled as 'Jewish lies' the claim that the SANP was a German party that sought a dictatorship. However, he was grateful for one thing – the National Party's acknowledgement that the Greyshirts were responsible for awakening South Africa to an awareness of its Jewish problem.[161]

It is apparent from the communications between Laubscher and Erasmus that Malan did indeed value parliamentary democracy and that he had a distinct distaste for totalitarian ideologies.[162] But even though negotiations with the SANP fell through, Malan must have known that he had sufficiently valorised the 'Jewish Question' so as to undermine Weichardt in the general election scheduled to take place within months. As an 'SA Liberty Press' pamphlet noted, Malan had taken 'over the only plank in the Nazi-Greyshirt platform'.[163] He now had to prepare for the polls. Playing the ethnic card and building on Afrikaner exclusivism appeared to be his best hopes for success. Employing the 'Jewish Question' was always helpful, particularly among marginalised Afrikaners and the urban petit bourgeoisie who resented the Jewish commercial presence. But much work remained to be done to ensure electoral success for the National Party. Some months earlier, in a provincial by-election in Fordsburg, the Nationalist candidate, ERP Vermeulen, had been defeated – despite the working-class character of the constituency and National Party propaganda around the question of Jewish immigration.[164]

Malan apparently faced a most challenging situation: Hertzog's United Party had paved the way for Afrikaans- and English-speakers to put their differences behind them, and the improving economic outlook was certainly propitious for a United Party electoral victory. The rising gold price was fuelling an economic recovery, with increased state revenue aiding major projects.[165] White farmers were beneficiaries of Land Bank loans, and price stability had been ensured by the Marketing Act of April 1937, while the introduction of control boards had increased financial security for farmers. Tarred roads had been widely extended, the airways improved, Cape Town's harbour modernised and the South African Broadcasting Corporation, founded in 1936, was a success. The manufacturing sector, too, was expanding through a policy of local production, aided by the needs of agricultural development. Clothing, textile and food processing had expanded rapidly, and segregationist policies had been fulfilled in the Native Trust and Land Act and the Representation of Natives Act. Sovereign independence from Great Britain had also moved further along the road with the Statute of Westminster of 1931 and the Status of Union Act of 1934.[166]

Yet despite the political challenges and hurdles facing Malan, he knew that Afrikaners outnumbered English-speakers by about 45 to 55 per cent. This meant that non-Nationalist parties needed at least 25 per cent of the Afrikaner vote to maintain power. More importantly, there was almost double the number of Afrikaans- as opposed to English-speakers in the age group seven to twenty-one.[167] Culture and politics were now being conflated by the Broederbond, an increasingly powerful body that envisaged a triumphalist National Party in the not too distant future. The Board of

Deputies remained fearful: Afrikaner nationalism had little place for the Jew, who was considered hostile to its political agenda. In a national statement, the Board adamantly rejected the notion. Far from being unfriendly to one section of the population, the Board believed South African history had furnished abundant evidence of friendly cooperation between Jews and Afrikaners. 'Without the slightest cause or justification a "Jewish question" has been artificially created and suddenly forced into the political arena,' declared the Board.[168] The political landscape had indeed witnessed a shift towards a more vigorous anti-Jewish invective aimed at winning the hearts and minds of voters in the general election of 1938.

CHAPTER FIVE

ANNUS HORRIBILIS: A BARRAGE OF ANTISEMITISM

'The Nationalist Party still entertained for the Jew as an individual exactly the same feelings as always, but regarded the threatening Jewish domination, especially in the business world, as a danger to South Africa, not only to all the other national groups, but also to the Jews themselves, because it promoted anti-Semitism.'
– PJ Hugo, *Die Burger*, 30 March 1938

'In spite of local setbacks in certain countries, the Jews are, at the present moment, looking forward with high hopes to an early realisation of their "Plan for World Domination." This "Plan" holds the foremost place in Jewish literature starting with the "Talmud," and throughout the ages it has ever formed the highest goals of Jewish ambitions and aspirations. These are fact recognised and admitted by every-one who has studied the Jewish problem, particularly in the light of modern events.'
– *Die Waarheid/The Truth*, 1 April 1938

'If the Jew conducts himself as the enemy of South Africa then he must expect to be treated as an enemy. South Africa is not prepared to accept more Jews.'
– AJ Werth, *Die Burger*, 28 March 1938

'For the first time in the history of South Africa the Jews find their rights of citizenship challenged.'
– Henry Gluckman, *Rand Daily Mail*, 30 April 1938

ENTER *DIE TRANSVALER*

While the SANP spewed out its crude anti-Jewish propaganda, filled with fantasies and conspiracies, the National Party maintained that its antagonism towards Jews was based on rational criteria. This was best illustrated in the first issue of *Die Transvaler*, the Transvaal-based National Party mouthpiece launched in October 1937 under the editorship of Hendrik Verwoerd.[1] Established as a weapon in the struggle for the soul of Afrikanerdom and to garner support in the north, the daily's first op-ed (written by Verwoerd) was entitled, 'The Jewish Question from the Nationalist Point of View'. In it Verwoerd went out of his way to deny that National Party policies were driven by race hatred, contending that they were aimed rather at securing a place in the sun for Afrikaners.

At the root of the conflict between Afrikaners and Jews, maintained Verwoerd, were material interests. The Nationalist did not hate the Jew, just as he did not hate the Englishman, Russian or German; but Jews posed a threat to the *volk*. Although the original Jewish *smous* had been warmly welcomed by the Afrikaner, the relatively recent arrival of the Afrikaner in the cities meant that, for the first time, he came into contact with the wealthy English foreigner and now the wealthy Jew. Without skills, the Afrikaner had to engage with owners and managers, initially English-speakers, but more recently Jews whose business methods and ethics differed from those of Christians. Verwoerd also accused Jewish businesses of employing only fellow Jews, thereby hindering opportunities for Afrikaners. In addition, Afrikaners in the workplace were being exposed to 'a communist spirit among certain Jewish leaders'. These areas of conflict had been exacerbated by Jews moving into the professions, thus further blocking Afrikaner advancement. 'Is it any wonder then,' he asked, 'that young Afrikaner professionals had joined the protests against German-Jewish immigration because of their awareness that Jews would find positions for their own compatriots at the expense of Afrikaner opportunities.' The majority of the Jewish community, continued Verwoerd, kept themselves apart and was indifferent, if not hostile, to the national aspirations of the Afrikaners. Backed by capital accumulated from the exploitation of the country's resources, the Jewish community had become involved in the political struggle with an eye to personal advantage, and was using the English press and political parties to exert influence on governments of the day. No Afrikaner dared underestimate their political activities, which were aimed at hindering the cause of Afrikaner nationalism and, in so doing, sharpening a 'clash of interests' (*botsing van belange*).

Verwoerd claimed that the only solution to these problems was to remove the source of friction, namely, the disproportionate domination of the economy by Jews, by ensuring that Afrikaners received a share of commerce and industry 'proportional to its percentage of the white population'. This in turn could only be achieved by gradually adopting a quota system for Jews in certain areas of economic life. As far as the professions were concerned, Jews would require licences to pursue their profession, the granting of which would once again be proportionate to their percentage of the population. Legislation would be needed to ensure that those currently disadvantaged (and here Verwoerd cleverly included English- as well as Afrikaans-speakers) would be able to enjoy a proportionate share of each of the major occupations:

> This situation is called balanced distribution [*ewewigtige verspreiding*], but it has also been called a 'quota system'. As Jews presently enjoy a disproportionate share of the wholesale and retail trade, such a balanced distribution can be achieved only by refusing them further trading licences, until such a time as the other main population groups, such as English- and Afrikaans-speakers, have gained a proportion which (as far as practicable) corresponds to their percentage of the white population. When trading licences held by Jews lapse due to special circumstances, they may not be allocated to compatriots, until all other population groups have achieved the above-mentioned equal privileges [*gelyke bevoorregting*] in this regard.

Within this framework of socio-economic engineering, Verwoerd proposed the creation of an industrial bank to help Afrikaners who lacked capital, just as had been the case in Germany in the 1870s and Japan at the turn of the century. 'In the allocation of capital and top management posts, the banking institution would discriminate against the Jew, until a stage is reached where the Jew, and the English- and Afrikaans-speakers, enjoyed a share of industry, proportional to their percentage of the population.' Verwoerd was convinced that a large number of English-speakers also felt threatened by Jewish economic competition but were not prepared to express their opinion in public. Instead they were leaving it to the National Party 'to pull their chestnuts from the fire', possibly because they feared economic retribution by Jews, or else because they chose 'to side with their Jewish brothers-in-arms to oppose the Republican ideal'.[2]

Verwoerd's brazen advocacy and the implicit centrality of the 'Jewish Question' in the National Party agenda stunned the Board of Deputies.[3] Representing the official voice of the opposition, Verwoerd's editorial demanded a response.[4] But more was to follow. Six weeks after *Die Transvaler* was launched, Jews were accused by Hans Strijdom of seeking to ruin the new daily by withholding advertising. In 'A Warning to the Jewish Population', the Transvaal leader of the National Party accused Jews of fighting his party by instituting or advocating an advertising boycott:

> ... now we find that the Jews are perhaps also taking the dangerous step of wishing to fight us in the economic field. One need merely look at the advertisement columns of the 'Transvaler.' Advertisements are the life-blood of a paper, but if we look at the advertisement columns of the 'Transvaler' we shall see that the Jew, who has made himself master of the economic field, is to a certain extent fighting us by means of a boycott. I warn them that if they proceed with this they will make the position infinitely more difficult.[5]

Strijdom's assault – and it was nothing less – led to high-level exchanges between the Board and A van Zyl, the manager of Voortrekker Pers Beperk, publishers of *Die Transvaler*.[6] Van Zyl told the Board that whereas Verwoerd had intended to take the emotion out of the 'Jewish Question' and to resolve the present clash of interests without direct conflict, the *SAJT* had instead chosen to incite a boycott.[7] To avoid excessive repercussions on the part of aggrieved Afrikaners, an immediate disclaimer from the Board, as well as the resumption of Jewish advertising, was necessary.[8]

Writing on behalf of the Board, Gustav Saron told Van Zyl that he had no control over the *SAJT*. Moreover, while the Board itself opposed any advertising boycott, it could not tell businesses where they should or should not advertise. For its part, *Die Transvaler* had given initial assurances to advertisers that it had 'no plans to be inimical to Jews', but this had not turned out to be the case. Saron's firm rebuttal concluded with an assurance that Jews wished to live 'in amity and goodwill'. The matter, however, did not end there. In reply, Van Zyl denied that *Die Transvaler* had misled Jewish advertisers, and, while he was pleased to hear that the Board was not organising a boycott, he warned the Jewish community that if individual Jews were involved, it was possible that Afrikaners might well retaliate by boycotting Jewish firms.[9]

A LOOMING CONFRONTATION

Although something of a modus vivendi had been reached, the exchange reflected a strongly confrontational tone in Afrikaner-Jewish relations.[10] Added to that was the decision of the Transvaal National Party congress to debar Jews formally from membership and their recommendation to the party's federal council that all provinces should follow suit. The motion was based on the view that, because of their religion and international character, Jews formed a state within a state in opposition to the Christian–National character of the National Party. One delegate told the congress that Jews would only join the National Party when it was within striking distance of forming a government and when they saw an opportunity to amass the 'usual plunder' from the party. Nico van der Merwe warned that if Jews wished to join they would have to subscribe to a Christian-National basis, while another delegate who urged caution was almost shouted down.[11]

According to press reports, the recommendation that all provinces debar Jews from membership went against the wishes of the National Party leadership, and, although this did little to reassure Jews, Malan was reported to have said that the resolutions of individual provinces were not binding on the federal council of the party.[12] In effect, Article One of the party's Programme of Principles identified Christian values at the core of the party and thus effectively precluded Jews from membership.[13] Yet it is fair to say that in refusing to bind the federal council of the party, Malan had once again demonstrated unease with outright antisemitism. On the other hand, there was still talk of the National Party and the SANP forming an electoral pact; the radical right generally appeared to be doing well and continued to attract substantial interest in a number of cities and smaller towns. Indeed, the SANP even spoke of fielding parliamentary candidates in Gordonia, Malmesbury, Bellville, Newcastle, Weenen, Klipriver, Vryheid, Wakkerstroom, Harrismith and Umvoti. Meanwhile, Von Moltke – touring the Orange Free State and eastern Cape Province – was threatening to produce 500 advance copies (of a promised print run of 2 000) of his virulently antisemitic book.[14]

Obviously aware of the growing strength of the radical right, Malan and his more extremist colleagues continued to pursue an anti-Jewish line. In a speech at Loeriesfontein, the National Party leader claimed that Jews were behind Willem Steenkamp's proposed candidature for the United Party in Calvinia in the forthcoming elections, and reminded his audience of the alleged ties between Steenkamp and the Jews going back to 1931.[15] Malan repeated the stock accusations against Jews while simultaneously continuing to assert that he was not against Jews as individuals but against the 'Jewish system'. And yet, contrarily, when asked whether people should discriminate against Jews as Jews, his reply was now unequivocally in the affirmative.[16] A few days later, Karl Bremer launched a scathing attack on the Board, accusing it of 'creating antipathy and strife between the sections of the settled population of South Africa', and claiming that the reason no action was taken by the authorities was because the Board governed the United Party.[17] Nico van der Merwe lashed out as well, repeating the allegation that Jews were boycotting the Nationalist press and warning that this would result in a retaliatory Afrikaner boycott of Jewish businesses.[18]

It was obvious that, one year after the Stuttgart affair, and nine months after the passing of the restrictive Aliens Act, the 'Jewish Question' remained very much alive. Indeed, the tone within mainstream politics had become even more aggressive and the rhetoric of the National Party more extreme. This toxic anti-Jewish mood was confirmed by the British High Commissioner's office, which took seriously an accusation (although acknowledging it could not be corroborated) that the Nazis were providing financial aid to Malan. For the High Commissioner, it seemed suspicious that the party's previous shortage of campaign funds had been resolved, and that enough money was suddenly available to fund a newspaper.[19]

Even without concrete evidence of ties between the National Party and the Nazis, Nationalist sympathies with Germany and with what they termed the 'German revolution' remained unequivocal. And when it came to the question of Jews, it was clear that the National Party – by its own admission – shared much with the SANP.[20] To be sure, this relationship was keenly noted by an anonymous German agent in a report to Berlin. Detailing preparations for the upcoming election, the agent conceded that while the fundamentals of both parties differed radically, they shared enough to anticipate an eventual alliance: 'Both stand in open and honest opposition to the government, both retain the Jewish Question and Bolshevism as an essentially crucial element in their programmes, and both want to secure the independence of South African money markets from international Jewry by establishing a purely South African National Bank.'[21]

It is not surprising that the *SAJC* struggled to understand why the talks between the National Party and the SANP had failed to reach a successful conclusion, given the fact that the two parties shared so much – in particular their awareness of the value of antisemitism in attracting voters. While initially this had been appreciated by the radical right only, antisemitism was now included in the Nationalist political arsenal, and it appeared to be in the interests of both parties to form an alliance.[22] *Die Transvaler* arrived at a more accurate conclusion, suggesting that a merger had failed because the SANP advocated a fascist model of government, with emphasis on the 'Great Leader', as opposed to a parliamentary system which was respected by the National Party.[23] Meanwhile the Board reported that Nazi propaganda continued to pour into the country and was being sent to ministers of religion, editors of newspapers and others with a view to their cooperation in further distribution.[24] Most worrying was *Die Waarheid/The Truth's* revival of the infamous 'ritual murder' charge against Jews.[25]

At the beginning of November, the Board met with a sympathetic

Hertzog to discuss a number of issues: the antisemitism of Malan and the National Party, the Blackshirt and Greyshirt menace, and the Board's correspondence with *Die Transvaler* over the alleged advertising boycott. In a cordial exchange, the Prime Minister expressed his deep sympathy with the position in which the Jews of South Africa found themselves and empathised with the resentment they felt at the unfounded attacks directed at them. Hertzog emphasised that eighteen months earlier he had issued instructions for the Department of Justice to consult European legislation dealing with group defamation. Its assessment was that such legislation would probably exacerbate the South African situation, but Hertzog was by no means satisfied that this was the case. He had again taken up the issue and was gratified to hear from Helgard Bodenstein that he had reviewed all the European legislation and was busy drafting legislation to combat group defamation in South Africa, to be introduced in the foreseeable future. Turning to the Board's correspondence with *Die Transvaler*, Hertzog claimed that the initial letter from the Nationalist mouthpiece accusing the Board of complicity in the boycott issue approximated blackmail. But he approved of the dignified way in which the Board had responded to attacks made on Jews, which, he believed, were actuated by political considerations.[26] Finally, Hertzog emphasised that Jews should bear in mind that they had the sympathy of the great majority of the population, and that elements like the Greyshirts were not to be taken too seriously, as they were rapidly 'becoming a jest in the countryside'.[27]

Presumably not entirely reassured, the Board called on Jan Hofmeyr a fortnight later to share its concerns about the increasingly serious public attacks on Jewry and to seek his guidance on the matter. Hofmeyr suggested that the Board meet with Malan (whom he believed did not have a closed mind but was 'purely dishonest' on the 'Jewish Question') to complain about the wild charges being made against Jews. It was clear to him that antisemitism was playing into the hands of the extremists, a situation that undermined the interests of the whole country. The upcoming general election was also discussed, with Hofmeyr expressing the opinion that if the National Party did not make headway at the polls it would realise the futility of using antisemitism for political gain.[28]

Hofmeyr did not need the Board to remind him of the extent of Jew hatred. He was fully aware of it, and only a few days before their meeting had addressed the annual meeting of the Society of Christians and Jews, in Johannesburg, where he castigated Malan for promoting hatred imported from Germany that was quite foreign to South Africa.[29] Hostility towards Jews, he warned, was a precursor to dictatorship. He did acknowledge, though, that world circumstances necessitated a selective policy as regards immigration, but stressed that 'it is a Christian policy to give equal treatment to all who have lawfully entered into our land'. According to Hofmeyr, antisemitism in South Africa had two causes: the 'otherness' of the Jew, which led to accusations of unassimilability, and the success of Jews, which bred envy.[30]

In the wake of Hofmeyr's speech, the *SAJC* wondered who in fact represented the authentic voice of Afrikanerdom. There was, after all, evidence that the best elements among the Afrikaners were 'recoiling from this dangerous and cynical propaganda ... and realised how detrimental to its own people the ultra-Nationalist policy is'.[31] Presumably believing that there was mounting opposition among Afrikaners to antisemitism, the Jewish weekly clearly wished to avoid generalising and treating them as a monolith. Certainly there were many English-speakers and Afrikaners who held no truck with offensive antisemitism. The government-supporting *Independent*, for example, referred to domestic politics as 'going back to the Middle Ages' and criticised the government for not having 'the courage and humanity to put a stop to this mass libel of a section of the South African population'.[32] Even the Dutch Reformed Church's Commission for the Jewish Mission (which served to convert Jews) condemned antisemitism, which it believed harmed the Church's proselytising work: 'The un-Christian spirit which manifests in the Jewish problem is not content to leave it at that, but goes further to reject the fundamental truths of Christianity as Jewish and thus to undermine religion in general.'[33] These sentiments were reinforced by a resolution of the Dutch Reformed Church Synod of the Cape Province that decried attacks on Jews as un-Christian.[34] On the other hand, after a lengthy theological investigation by a team of experts, the Church's Orange Free State Synod had some months earlier 'ousted' Jews from their appelation as the 'Chosen People'.[35] These varying positions reflected a theological ambivalence on the part of the Dutch Reformed Church that should not be minimised. Theology, after all, meant a great deal to the National Party. With neo-Kuyperianism and its organic rationales merging into *völkisch* thought, divisions could only be sharpened.

Ambivalence towards Jews was again evident at the National Party's Cape Province congress held in Ladismith, where the focus was on economic matters, as well as on legislation to prevent mixed marriages and halt the spread of communism. Even though Jews were commonly associated with the latter, Frans Erasmus chose rather to focus his address on the foreign nature of Greyshirt ideology, and accused the SANP of playing the game of Hoggenheimer, which emphasised Jewish power, with the intention of causing a split in Afrikanerdom. 'We shall combat the imported Swastika exactly as we do the Hammer and Sickle and the Union Jack,' said Erasmus.[36]

Notwithstanding their public differences, the National Party and the SANP appear to have continued discussing electoral strategies. The *Sunday Express* reported the possibility of an 'underground pact' between the two parties on the Witwatersrand, despite internal dissension within the National Party on that score.[37] Certainly, National Party spokesmen (particularly outside the Cape Province) kept hammering away at the 'Jewish Question', the favourite target of the SANP. The Orange Free State leader, Nico van der Merwe, was particularly hard-hitting during a speech in Vrede in which he accused 'organised Jewry' of planning 'to break the Nationalist Party'. He resuscitated the alleged Jewish boycott of advertisements in Nationalist newspapers and warned that, if it were so, the National Party would be compelled to declare open warfare. 'We shall not allow ourselves to be trampled upon by the Jewish trading power,' he said.[38]

Responding to Van der Merwe's speech, Gustav Saron noted that his reference to 'organised Jewry' embodied a sinister meaning, something that was becoming all too common in Nationalist circles. For more than a year, asserted Saron, the National Party had carried on a bitter attack against the Jewish community, and while the passing of the Aliens Act had deflected the party's attention away from the immigration question, it had not halted the party's provocative tirades, in which grave charges devoid of any factual basis were repeatedly made. Now threats were being made to discriminate against Jews in the economic field and to deprive them of the elementary rights of citizenship.[39]

As the year – an *annus horribilis* for South African Jewry – drew to a close, it should be noted that occasional Nationalist voices were now being heard in defence of the Jews.[40] In fact, the secretary of the Waterberg branch of the National Party, FH Odendaal, actually resigned in protest against Jew-baiting.[41] Significantly, the *Sunday Times* claimed that many Afrikaners were uneasy with Malan's expedient use of antisemitism for political gain.[42] Outside formal politics, important voices such as the University of the Witwatersrand's Professor Theo Haarhoff were also being heard calling for tolerance of other cultures,[43] while the United Party's Henry Fagan warned that attacks on Jews in other countries had been the harbinger of attacks on democracy itself.[44]

For all that, speakers at public meetings persisted with scurrilous and violent attacks on South Africa's Jewish community, so much so that the United Party congress in Bloemfontein in December 1937 passed a strongly worded resolution condemning the attempts of the National Party and SANP to divide the country on racial lines.[45] Instigated by Smuts and Klasie Havenga, the resolution had no effect on the actions of the two parties or indeed on the radical right as a whole. Blackshirts, according to the Board, were now cooperating closely with the National Party, and two of their members had even been nominated as National Party candidates on the Witwatersrand.[46] At meetings on the Witwatersrand and on the platteland, Jews were constantly blamed for the 'poor white' problem, and their expulsion from South Africa was advocated.[47] The Blackshirt broadsheet, *The Leader* (published in both English and Afrikaans), contained the usual charges against Jews and even quotations from the *Protocols*. In early January 1938, articles on 'Capitalism, Bolshevism and Judaism' purported to reveal an orchestrated plot by Jews for world domination as described in the *Protocols*.[48]

Von Moltke, too, was throwing his weight behind the National Party, addressing meetings in the Orange Free State, where resolutions were passed condemning the Board. The SANP also continued its attacks on the Board, and *Die Waarheid/The Truth* – back on the streets of Johannesburg after an absence of some months – persisted in its focus on Jews.[49]

WEICHARDT TRIES AGAIN

The buoyant optimism of the radical right was further evident in Weichardt's decision to stand in a parliamentary by-election in Piquetberg (now Piketberg), a quaint town some 120 kilometres northeast of Cape Town. Dominated largely by Afrikaner wheat farmers, Piquetberg was a place where the 'Jewish Question' had attracted attention from the time the SANP had raised its objections to Jewish immigration.[50] Indeed, the party had been campaigning in the southwestern Cape Province for years, and Weichardt was certainly well known among the locals.

Having his roots in nearby Paarl and a well-oiled organisational capacity in the region, he must surely have fancied his chances. But he was also aware that Piquetberg was close to Calvinia, Malan's home constituency, and any attempt to establish a serious SANP presence in the area would not be looked upon kindly by Doktor.[51] With Malan planning to represent the constituency in the forthcoming general election, it was probably to test his own party's strength that Weichardt decided to enter the by-election.

From the time of Weichardt's announcement, Malan led a powerful campaign in support of his party's candidate, Albert van Zyl, a local businessman. In an important opening salvo, the National Party leader, seemingly wanting to stamp his authority on the 'Jewish Question', drew attention to his own impeccable anti-Jewish credentials, stressing his role in curtailing the influx of Jews through the Quota Act of 1930, as well as his role in the Aliens Act of 1937. Yet for all that, Malan again reiterated his oft-used mantra that he was not fighting the Jew as an individual but was 'against Jewry as a system'. His party, he shouted, wanted 'to break that system'. On the other hand – and perhaps goaded by a phalanx of SANP supporters in the audience – Malan was quite prepared to tell the meeting that he accepted Weichardt's blatant antisemitism, but objected to the SANP's fascism and their desire to 'destroy all other parties'. He accused Jews of being a tightly knit group

manipulating things behind the scenes at national and inte[
His allusions to a sinister web of international Jewry no d[
some of the locals, although Piquetberg's Jewish inhabitant[
enjoyed harmonious relations with their neighbours.[53]

Malan had spoken earlier at the nearby hamlet of Graafwater, where he was even more explicit about his record on the Jewish question. On that occasion he told his audience that he was now in a position to tell Weichardt 'that the Nationalist Party has a policy in regard to the Jewish problem and that it intended to submit legislation to parliament'.[54] Here Malan was presumably alluding to the policies advocated by Verwoerd in his infamous op-ed in *Die Transvaler* dealing with Jewish economic domination of South Africa.

Any lingering doubts about Malan's intentions were dispelled when he spelt out his party's legislative vision vis-à-vis the Jews in another speech at Piquetberg:

> We have proposed that the Jews who come here and have not yet received citizenship shall not receive it. The Jews must be regarded as unassimilable. They may also, according to our Bill, not follow any occupation here without a special permit from the nation. We laid down that firms must place the names of their owners on their signboards; if the name is changed, then the previous name must also be mentioned … These are things we have proposed; it is our intention to supplement these with other measures which will admit the Jews to the vocations according to their numerical strength. We wish to give our Afrikaans sons and daughters an education in commerce on a large scale in order that they can take over the places of the Jews who have vacated the vocations.[55]

There was little more that Weichardt could add to this explicitly anti-Jewish message, but he did gain substantial publicity, albeit mostly hostile, in the wake of a luncheon address he gave to the Sons of England Society in Cape Town, at which immigration issues and the Board of Deputies (which he described as a sinister 'state within a state') topped his concerns.

n particular he represented as a grave threat his outrageously inflated and invented claim that 180 000 Jews were about to be naturalised in England before coming to South Africa.[56]

Back in Piquetberg, Weichardt told a 600-strong audience that the voters had a choice between communism and Bolshevism on the one hand, and National Socialism on the other.[57] But his scaremongering tactics were to no avail.[58] The SANP leader was resoundingly thumped in a 61 per cent poll. Van Zyl won the seat for the National Party with 3 357 votes, against Weichardt's paltry 452, which amounted to even less than that obtained by the independent candidate. The SANP leader's second attempt to enter parliament had ended in ignominy.[59] Malan had obviously satisfied those voters obsessed with Jews that he himself was sufficiently determined to deal with the 'Jewish Question'. This was noted by political columnist George Heard, who warned that although the SANP had been shown to be a negligible force, their votes 'would go to other Jew haters in the National Party'.[60]

The SANP, however, viewed defeat differently. Malan had only posed as 'the great champion of anti-Jewism in South Africa! What a mockery,' claimed *Die Waarheid/The Truth*. He had simply borrowed from the Greyshirts' Programme of Principles and tried 'to go one better! This is the sort of tactics that any fool can adopt, provided he is devoid of all conscience and scruples.'[61] For the SANP, the Piquetberg by-election had demonstrated that it stood alone in its 'fight for Country and People'. As far as it was concerned, the United Party and the Malanites were identical: 'Both are striving for the continuance of the present unsound political system under which the Jews and their allies are able to exploit and plunder the South African people and live on the fat of the land, while thousands of our fellow-countrymen are starving.' *Die Waarheid/The Truth* predicted a 'Fusionist' victory in the upcoming general election, while 'the alien Jew, who finances the whole affair, sits behind the scenes rubbing his greasy hands and grinning!'[62] Weichardt, on the other hand, was more upbeat in his response to his dismal performance. 'Defeated but not conquered,' he exhorted. 'We Greyshirts have been beaten many times, but we never have and never will be subdued.'[63]

NAZI SCARES

Only a few days before the Piquetberg by-election, the *Cape Argus* had published a series of exposés of a network of organised Nazi activities in South Africa. This could not have helped Weichardt's campaign, but to what extent this was the case is impossible to assess.[64] What we do know is that alarm bells sounded once again as the South African government and the British Foreign Office confronted reports of subversive German activity in South Africa.

According to the *Cape Argus* investigations, 'large numbers of Germans throughout the Union were members of organisations and bodies styled on those operating in Germany: the Reich National Socialist Party, the Young Hitler Movement, the Labour Front, the Strength-through-Joy Movement, and the charity organization, Winter Help.' These Nazi organisations made their presence felt in Johannesburg, Cape Town, Bloemfontein, Durban, Port Elizabeth, East London, Tzaneen and Stutterheim. Occasional Nazi demonstrations had also taken place in other centres, including Ermelo, Paarl, Kroondal, Cape Flats, Springs, Middelburg (Transvaal) and Stellenbosch. There had also been extensive dissemination of propaganda, as well as lectures delivered by high-ranking German officials at private meetings, and German ships visiting South African ports were said to contain Nazi cells. The *Cape Argus* reported that South Africa was recognised as *Landsgruppe Südafrika* (Country Grouping South Africa), falling under the control of Gauleiter Ernst Wilhelm Bohle, son of Professor Hermann Bohle who had founded Landsgruppe Südafrika in 1932, four years prior to his return to Germany. Although Bruno Stiller had replaced him as the official leader of the Nazi movement in South Africa, it was reported that Bohle exercised control from Berlin.[65]

The *Cape Argus* exposé even named leaders of Nazi groups in South Africa,[66] as well as a number of extremely active centres such as Tzaneen, the Westphalia Estates (belonging to Dr Hans Merensky, a German-born geologist)[67] and the farm Asta, belonging to LA Brinckmann, allegedly the regional Nazi leader. Nazi activities directed at young people were also taking place on an extensive scale under the *Deutsche Jugend Suid Afrika* (German Youth South Africa, also known as *Jungvolkjungen* and *Jung-*

volkmaedel), founded in 1933 by a schoolteacher, Heinrich Mueller. His wife, Maria Mueller, was *Bundesführer* (Federal Leader) of the allied *Bund Deutscher Maedel* (League of German Girls). Special youth singsongs were held as well as charity drives for Germany. The *Cape Argus* noted that in an interview conducted a year earlier, Ernst Wilhelm Bohle had stated that Germany's National Socialist Party had the 'incontestable right' to operate in South Africa.[68] It also reported that Stiller, in an article in *Wir Deutsche in der Welt*, had claimed that Nazism in South Africa had been fuelled by Jewish immigration from Germany and by the widespread falsification of events in Germany: 'The daily false reports in the Press, the unrestrained attacks on everything that stands under the Swastika, the deliberate denial or distortion of clear facts, have contributed more to win the South African Germans to National Socialism than Party propaganda.'[69]

The revelations initiated widespread comment in the English press,[70] with an editorial in the *Cape Argus* calling for the situation to be monitored.[71] The *SAJC* also weighed in, challenging those who would compare these Nazi groups to 'the Cambrian or Caledonian or Nederlands Society, or to the Sons of England, or the Jewish Board of Deputies'. The reality, it maintained, was that 'a state within a state' loyal to Nazi Germany was operating domestically. All South Africans, it warned, had to be alive to the danger of the growth and spread in their own country of the virus Hitler was trying to inject all over the world.[72]

It was not long before Smuts faced a question in parliament about domestic Nazi propaganda and espionage. Asked what steps the government was taking to safeguard civic and political security, Smuts chose to interpret the question as a reference to the Greyshirts and other radical right movements.[73] Commenting on the response, the British High Commissioner, Clark, accused Smuts of deliberately skirting the real issue, maintaining that he clearly understood the question related to Nazi activities in South Africa and was in fact already considering steps to limit the influx of Germans and to closely monitor the activities of Germans already in the country. Indeed, Colonel Isaac de Villiers, the Commissioner of Police, had already been warned that arms were being smuggled into South Africa from Germany in crates meant for the importation of DKW motorcars.[74]

It was quite apparent that Clark took the *Cape Argus* exposé seriously. He included the articles in a secret communiqué to Sir Harry Batterbee, the Assistant Permanent Undersecretary of State for Dominion Affairs, noting 'that here, as in other parts of the world, the German colony is highly organised, and, despite the denials of German authorities, there is I think, no doubt that many Union nationals of German extraction have been incorporated into the various Nazi organisations'.[75] Batterbee, in a covering letter to Foreign Office senior civil servant Sir Orme Sargent, noted that the *Cape Argus* articles would have served to open the eyes of the general public to the Nazi threat.[76]

In the meantime, the Board reported that the Greyshirts and Blackshirts had established a serious presence on the Witwatersrand and in Witpoort, southeast of Pretoria.[77] A further report described *Die Transvaler*'s coverage of the largest anti-Jewish demonstration ever seen in the Union, when uniformed Blackshirts marched with swastikas and banners through the centre of Johannesburg while another crowd, comprised mainly of Jews and communists, staged a counter-demonstration.[78] In Benoni, blood flowed at a Blackshirt meeting after about 200 anti-fascist youths alighted from motorcars and attacked the crowd.[79]

The anti-Jewish temperature remained elevated. Although publication of *Die Waarheid/The Truth* was now erratic, whenever it did appear it was riddled with the usual anti-Jewish canards and fantasies – accusations of Jews controlling 'International Capitalism and International Communism', and planning a world war 'designed to overthrow Christian European civilisation and to introduce the universal reign of the Jew':

> This 'Plan' holds the foremost place in Jewish literature starting with the 'Talmud', and throughout the ages it has ever formed the highest goals of Jewish ambitions and aspirations. These are facts recognised and admitted by everyone who has studied the Jewish problem, particularly in the light of modern events. Anyone who denies these facts is either an ignorant simpleton who fails to see what is happening under his very eyes, or else a rogue and a traitor who has allied himself with the Jews in their warfare against humanity.[80]

Die Burger, too, continued to harp on matters Jewish, going so far as to acknowledge the important job the SANP had done in alerting the nation to Jewish issues.[81] In early February it published figures on applications for business licences in the Cape Province to illustrate the disproportionately high number requested by Jews.[82] *Die Burger* even endorsed Von Moltke's decision to abandon his movement and join the National Party. Seemingly unconcerned about his track record, including his conviction in the Greyshirt trial almost three years earlier, the National Party mouthpiece enthusiastically welcomed Von Moltke into the fold and urged his supporters to cast their votes for the National Party.[83]

In truth, Von Moltke was facing bankruptcy. The Centlivres judgment in the Cape Supreme Court had proscribed the publication of his book, *The Jew of South Africa*, which contained extracts from documents stolen from the Board. Unprincipled and driven by expediency, he had jumped ship as he was desperately in need of a new political home.[84] But, according to *Die Burger*, Von Moltke's pro-Nationalist sympathies had long been apparent to those who perused *Patria*. Reminding readers of the National Party's differences with the SANP, it pointed out that, in contradistinction to Weichardt's party, Von Moltke had declared his willingness to avoid making his approval of fascism a point of issue with the Nationalists. As far as the 'Jewish Question' was concerned, Von Moltke was satisfied that the National Party, unlike the United Party, was prepared to safeguard the interests of Afrikanerdom, and he was therefore happy to leave his anti-Jewish policy safely in its hands.[85] Malan also expressed his approval of Von Moltke's decision, as long as he and his followers remained bound by the National Party constitution and did not abuse the privileges of membership.[86]

APPROACHING THE GENERAL ELECTION

The fact that Von Moltke was welcomed into the Nationalist fold showed just how far along the anti-Jewish road the party had travelled. While some Nationalists opposed the incessant Jew-baiting,[87] the party in general continued to harp on the immigration issue and the disproportionate role of Jews in the economy. Verwoerd attempted to eschew naked antisemitism by describing the problem as a simple clash of interests, arguing that Jews and Afrikaners clashed in their desire to attain power. It is for this reason, maintained Verwoerd, 'that the Nationalist talks of his positive pro-Afrikaner policy in the commercial field'.[88] Two weeks later, *Die Transvaler* accused Jews of threatening to engineer an economic depression if support for the United Party was not forthcoming. The newspaper claimed that Jews were purposefully damaging the garment industry, which was largely under their control, while Jewish residents of Pretoria and Johannesburg, fearing a National Party victory, were accused of selling property to enable them to send money out of the country.[89] At regular intervals, audiences at political meetings were also called upon to support fellow Afrikaners in business.[90]

In parliament, Erasmus gave notice that, in the interest of all, he would move that the immigration laws should be amended without delay so as to prevent any further immigration of Jews into South Africa.[91] Meanwhile, Eric Louw continued to focus on the Jewish-communist bogey and the prominence of Jews in the professions and universities, as well as what he claimed was the ongoing flood of Jewish immigrants. But he insisted that the National Party was targeting recent arrivals and not Jews who had been in South Africa for years.[92]

Although spokesmen for the National Party similarly went out of their way to explain that they were not against Jews per se but against the 'Jewish system' or 'the spirit of the foreigner', the party clearly recognised the usefulness of the Jew as a stick with which to beat the United Party and what it considered British imperial machinations. 'If we interfere with the Jews then we interfere with the British Empire,' Wicus du Plessis told an election meeting in Vereeniging. To defeat the machinations of the British Empire, the National Party would stop Jews from entering the country, and Jews who had entered recently would be sent home.[93]

This was tough talk, and not all that far from the rhetoric of the radical right. Not surprisingly, rumours still circulated about a possible electoral arrangement between the National Party and the SANP, or between the National Party and the Blackshirts. The latter's leader, Chris Havemann, made it quite clear that he would consider an arrangement with other parties, but both he and Weichardt advised their supporters not to vote for the

Labour Party, which was considered to be under communist influence.[94] At a meeting in Goodwood, Weichardt made the surprise announcement that the SANP would contest the election after all, but only in four constituencies: Cape Flats, Vryheid, Weenen and Newcastle – a move welcomed by Malan.[95] Addressing the small fishing community of Rooiverlorenvlei soon after Weichardt's announcement, Malan once again acknowledged that his party and the SANP shared a common approach to the 'Jewish Question'.[96]

This limited engagement was seen by several newspapers as a sign that the National Party and SANP had resolved their differences.[97] However, Malan still appeared wary of wholesale endorsement of the SANP as a political force. In fact, the possibility of an alliance would have been a miscalculation on his part, as the radical right was already beginning to experience problems. A meeting of Blackshirts in Benoni had failed to attract an audience, and the Board had reason to believe that they had similarly failed in Newcastle. In Brakpan too the town council had resolved to deny Greyshirts the use of the town hall.[98]

Malan remained prudent. On the one hand he appreciated the threat posed by marginalised urban Afrikaners, angry that Jews were disproportionately dominant in business and commerce, but on the other hand he was fully cognisant that white standards of living had actually improved under the United Party and that many Afrikaners had been saved from the worst ravages of the depression. English- and Afrikaans-speakers now appeared to be working together to put the past behind them, and there were some signs that the United Party would tackle the 'Native Question' and move positively on the nagging issue of sovereign independence. The National Party's task would not be easy.

By contrast, the SANP (and other radical right movements) simply continued to appeal to voters at the level of crude fantasy, telling them that they were the victims of a vast and faceless Jewish conspiracy. *Die Waarheid/ The Truth* had done this for years, and with the election date set for 18 May 1938 it moved into top gear. The 'International Jewish Money-power' in South Africa had to be broken, it contended. It was part of 'an organised world-wide force for evil which is endeavouring, by every diabolical means, to destroy the Christian religion and Christian culture and to bring the entire nations of the earth under the dominion of an atheistic and materialistic Jewish super-State'.[99]

In addition to its Nazi-like propaganda, the SANP also placed on record its wish to reform the democratic system and 'to introduce a purified system of honest democracy, based on the principles of Responsible Leadership and Group Representation under which the will of the people shall truly prevail and all power shall be used to promote the public good'. The party also claimed that it would destroy 'the barbarities' of the present economic system under which comparatively few enjoyed comfort and luxury, while most were condemned to a life of hardship and privation. Finally, it wished to avoid the politics of white ethnicity by eliminating any distinctions between English- and Afrikaans-speaking whites – excluding Jews, of course.[100]

While not sharing the SANP's overall agenda or its crude propaganda and rhetoric, the National Party's election manifesto made the party's anti-Jewish intentions patently clear. Only 'assimilable' whites would be welcomed as immigrants, and because of South Africa's specific problems, the party would halt Jewish immigration, forbid name changing, strengthen naturalisation procedures and introduce an occupational permit system for unnaturalised aliens along the lines of other European countries. The party also promised to take steps to prepare Afrikaans- and English-speakers for employment in all fields and to protect them against unfair competition.[101] Another paragraph in the manifesto, under the heading 'General Economic Reform', was identified by the Board as also possibly detrimental to the Jews. It spoke of safeguarding 'the legitimate interests of the producers, distributors, employees and consumers' and protecting 'all classes from exploitation of any nature'. In this regard, a central economic council would be established to deal with price-fixing as well as with retailers and distributors.[102]

Yet, for all this, the real political focus of the National Party was elsewhere: on segregation, constitutional anomalies, the representation of Africans in parliament, African land issues and South Africa's attitude to the gathering storm clouds in Europe.[103] Jews were not facing 'impending doom', noted the *SAJC*. Nevertheless, the reality was that the National Party had adopted an attitude of undisguised hostility towards them[104] and a justifiable wave of concern swept over the Jewish community. For the first time, noted the Board, a 'Jewish Question' had assumed prominence in a general election.

Certainly the seven weeks prior to the election saw a spike in the anti-Jewish temperature. Weichardt set the tone, railing against the Jewish presence, ongoing Jewish immigration, the effrontery of Jews for 'seeking racial equality', and their alliance with 'non-whites'.[105] 'Jews and Kaffirs' were running the unions, he told an exuberant crowd at Newcastle. When asked if his objective was a united country under Hitler, he replied that the Jews were already sufficiently afraid of him and that there was no need for a Hitler.[106] Willem Laubscher, too, attacked the Jews during a speech in Cape Town, complaining that the *volk* were slaves to Jewish international capitalism. It was not that he hated Jews, he maintained, but that he loved his people more.[107]

The National Party added its voice, hoping to position itself as the only party that could safeguard Afrikaner interests. Indeed, speaking in Citrusdal shortly before the official launch of the party's campaign, Malan accused Jews of having their 'thumbs on the throat' of the government, which appeared incapable of stopping the influx. The Aliens Act, he said, 'was about as useful in keeping the Jews out as a sieve was in stopping the east wind'. A vote for the National Party was the only way to prevent South Africa being overrun by Jews.[108] In Porterville, he went further, speaking of the need to get rid of 'parasitic exploiters' who were robbing the poor.[109]

This was classic Malan: by using a thinly disguised metaphor for Jews, he could avoid being labelled an antisemite, while at the same time blaming Afrikaner misfortune on the presence of Jews in the economy. It was quite obvious that the 'Jewish Question' was being utilised for political ends. As *Die Vaderland* concluded, Malan and his lieutenants had over the past year pursued a vigorous and relentless campaign against Jews, giving the impression that they were 100 per cent anti-Jewish.[110] Extremists like Von Moltke and Maritz – who had defected to the National Party – would now compete with the radical right during the election campaign, thereby narrowing distinctions between the National Party and the SANP.[111]

Accusations against Jews continued unabated. They were charged with

sending money out of the country;[112] of interfering with a radio broadcast because of their objections to a programme on German culture;[113] of
financially backing the United Party – called the 'Jew-nited Party'[114] – and
of continuing to arrive in South Africa by the boatload.[115] As always, Smuts
was labelled a praise singer for the Jews.[116] Speaking on behalf of Petrus
Hugo, Nationalist candidate for the Paarl constituency, Albertus Werth – a
Stellenbosch graduate and former Administrator of South West Africa –
warned South African Jews that they 'were playing with fire' by fighting
the National Party, as forces would be unleashed that not even Malan could
control. Dangerous liberal ideas were gaining ground, he contended, and
the natives, urged on by the communists, 'were becoming restive'.[117] Hugo
enlarged on Werth's address, maintaining that as far as Jews were concerned,
South Africa had reached saturation point. A good deal of the press, he
declared, was directly or indirectly under Jewish control and Jews had too
great a portion of trade and also dominated the entertainment industry.[118]
In another speech, Werth accused Jews of disloyalty, maintaining that in
the event of Jewish interests clashing with South African interests, the Jews
would 'sacrifice those of the country for their own'.[119]

It was quite apparent that the issue of Jewish immigration and the prominence of Jews in certain professions and the economy constituted the
Achilles heel of the ruling United Party. Speaker after Nationalist speaker
dealt with the harmful impact of further Jewish immigration and accused
the government of opening its doors to these newcomers.[120] Opposition
was primarily based on the notion of Jews being unassimilable, as well as on
their dominance (often allegedly dishonest) in the economic sphere. Paul
Sauer (MP for Humansdorp) captured all this in an address in Lydenburg:

> In connection with the Jews the Nationalist Party is opposed to further
> immigration because there are already too many Jews in the country.
> Another reason is that the Jew is unassimilable and always remains a Jew.
> He never becomes a true citizen of the country like members of other
> nations. A further reason is that when a Jew comes to South Africa,
> within a short time he enters commerce or one of the professions and
> the ethical standard of commerce or of the profession is lowered or

undermined. The Jews take work out of the hands of our own people and bread from their mouths. Our duty calls us in the first place to our own people.[121]

Yet despite these ongoing attacks, a mere five weeks before the poll the Board downplayed anti-Jewish sentiment by penning a measured and surprisingly not too negative assessment of the electoral mood. To the extent that hostility was being expressed, claimed the Board, it centered mainly on Jewish immigration and, in some cases, the preponderance of Jews in commerce and industry. The Board was pleased to note that Smuts had described as 'mischievous party politics'[122] an accusation that Jews were threatening a slump in trade as a weapon to fight the National Party.

As the election drew nearer, however, the anti-Jewish voices grew louder, some more guarded, others unabashedly vulgar. The Jewish-communist bogey predictably surfaced, as did allegations of Jews funding the United Party.[123] Another bogey bandied about by the National Party concerned Jewish dominance of the professions, especially law and medicine,[124] which led Malan to advocate the limitation of occupations for Jews.[125] The presence of too many Jews in the country was the root cause of antisemitism in South Africa, he asserted.[126] As *Die Vaderland* commented, Malan was attempting to show that his shirt was as grey as Stoffberg's.[127]

For all that, when addressing a largely Jewish audience at the Jewish Guild in Johannesburg, Maurice Franks, President of the Board, did his best to put a reassuring perspective on events by emphasising the failure of the 'Shirt' movements to attract individuals of consequence to their ranks. Franks was, however, forced to acknowledge that anti-Jewish prejudice had in fact escalated within the National Party. Of particular significance in this regard was the fact that Malan seemed to have abandoned his oft-avowed principle of not discriminating against Jews as Jews. Fortunately, noted Franks, the South African press – with the exception of certain party organs – had spoken out forcibly against the introduction of foreign hatreds into South Africa, and there were many Nationalists who were unhappy with the turn to antisemitism. In a somewhat fanciful observation, he even managed to suggest that the National Party's election manifesto was 'soft-pedalling' on the issue.[128]

For its part, the United Party's pre-election meetings concentrated on accusations that the Nationalists were a local variant of the Nazis. When campaigning in Frankfort, Havenga claimed that Malan was doing his best to steal the Greyshirts' 'anti-Semitic thunder',[129] but reassured his audience that Jews had no need to fear the fulminations against them, as 'the anti-Jewish bark was not serious'.[130] Smuts, on the other hand, was much more condemnatory. At a meeting in Johannesburg he denounced the 'poisonous plant' that had been transported from Europe into South Africa by Malan.[131] In Cape Town he went even further, warning of the erosion of democracy and the threat posed by the Nationalists and the radical right to all South Africans. 'Today it may be the Jew whose rights are attacked; tomorrow it may be your own rights. You never know when it will stop.' Speaking on the same night at another venue, Smuts dealt specifically with antisemitism, which he claimed had only entered public life in the last few years: 'But now a spirit of bitterness, of racial pride, of hatred of the other man's opinion was apparent, and we would have to be careful to keep our house in South Africa clean. The microbe was in the air and the winds were wafting across; there were signs of disease being disseminated here.'[132]

THE LAST PUSH

As the election date drew nearer, and notwithstanding the reassurance offered at the Jewish Guild meeting, the Board had to concede that 'almost all political speeches now contain the Jewish Question'. While it expressed relief that most anti-Jewish attacks came from 'extremists' rather than mainstream Nationalists, the Board nevertheless pointed to the latter's continuing vocal and written commitment to the protection of Afrikaans- and English-speakers from unfair (meaning Jewish) competition. From the Nationalist camp came the denial that the party was anti-Jewish, and Malan continued to claim that his party would not readily discriminate against the Jew as long as no more Jews entered the country.

Faced with these ambivalent messages, the Board once again tried to reassure the Jewish community by claiming that, even though the Nationalists evidently found it necessary to keep the Jewish issue alive, their concrete proposals (apart from the prohibition of immigration) were of a very vague nature. Nevertheless, the Board did acknowledge that the antisemitic cry remained a political weapon that would not be dropped too readily.[133] Less sanguine, and perhaps more realistic, was the *SAJT*. In an editorial headed 'Afrikanerdom and Anti-Semitism', it reflected on a disturbing trend that revealed changing attitudes of the National Party towards the Jew:

> For years the Jews of this country lived in peace and harmony with their Dutch neighbours. The descendants of the Huguenots have indeed much in common with the Jews in this country. Both fled from religious persecution; both cherished a deep love for the Bible and its ideals, and both prized liberty above all earthly possessions ... This state of affairs continued till a few years ago, when Hitler showed demagogues throughout the world how to ride to power upon the back of the Jew. A Purified Nationalist Party was formed, and presented itself to the world with an anti-Jewish programme ...[134]

The United Party's Henry Gluckman, a prominent Johannesburg Jewish doctor, also sounded a pessimistic note. In his maiden speech as a candidate for the Yeoville constituency, he criticised the use of antisemitism as a plank in Malan's election platform and sounded a warning that, for the first time, South African Jews found their rights as citizens under threat. This was especially repugnant, as it was being used 'almost entirely as an act of political expediency, a sort of business proposition pure and simple; it lacks even the passion and hatred of the rabid anti-Semite'.[135]

While Malan might avoid being labelled a rabid antisemite, he utilised the 'Jewish Question' forcefully in his appeals to the electorate. In reply to a question posed during a speech in Heilbron, he demanded that Jewish immigration cease, that a limit be placed on name changing, that all businessmen reveal their true names on business premises, and that aliens not be allowed to follow any occupations that disadvantaged the established population. Citizenship should also be refused to 'unassimilable aliens'. Yet Malan continued to insist that he had nothing against the Jew as a Jew and denied accusations that the National Party was anti-Jewish, maintaining that the

'Jewish Question' was an international and not a uniquely South African issue.[136] 'If the Nationalist Party is stamped as anti-Semitic on the ground that it wishes to put a stop to Jewish immigration, then America, Holland, England and Australia are also anti-Jewish.' But in a follow-up question as to whether his party was prepared to discriminate against Jews, he brazenly replied: 'Yes, I am discriminating now. Jews from Eastern Europe can be kept out without discrimination.'[137]

The National Party's attack dogs took an even harsher position. Manie Maritz, for example, displayed a blatant hatred of Jews when he defended Malan and poured scorn on Willem Steenkamp, Malan's old adversary, accusing him of being too close to the Jews who did not respect him but simply used him to defeat the Afrikaner. Smuts, he claimed, had no time for Afrikaners and was encouraging voters to support Morris Kentridge (who was Jewish) and threatening his fellow Afrikaners with the 'hunger-revolver' to vote for the United Party.[138] Von Moltke also vilified the Jews for 'sucking' the Afrikaner dry in almost every sphere and abusing the hospitality extended to them: 'Today they owned ninety-seven per cent of the country, while the Afrikaner remained with only three per cent.'[139]

Insofar as Jews were concerned, Maritz and Von Moltke were the hard men of the National Party's campaign. Their rhetoric hardly differed from that of the radical right, which continued to employ vicious propaganda,[140] with Weichardt and Havemann, in particular, keeping the fires of extremism burning. Speaking in his old high school town, New Hanover, Weichardt claimed that the type of Jews they objected to were 'the ones who preach sedition among the natives' and these should be thrown out of the country by the scruff of their necks.[141] Another veteran antisemite, Hamilton Beamish, joined the fray. Reportedly just back from the United States and on his way to Rhodesia – and not heard of since his cameo appearance at the Greyshirt trial in Grahamstown – Beamish addressed a Blackshirt meeting in Mayfair, boasting that the National Party was the only political party that had named 'the Jew' as the enemy.[142]

Nationalist attacks on Jews became more frequent and more vicious as the election drew nearer. No empathy was shown for the Jews of Germany,[143] while local Jews were accused of being in league with international Jewry and of colluding with the United Party as a means of taking control of the economy.[144] It was even suggested that Hertzog had a secret agreement with Jews to protect the Jewish minority as soon as parliament assembled, thereby allowing Jews to continue their domination of South African society.[145]

Shortly before the poll, a storm broke over a National Party poster, or *Basterplakaat* (produced by Voortrekker Pers), that condemned mixed marriages and suggested that a United Party victory would result in support for miscegenation, an ever-present *völkisch* fear.[146] The poster's dominant figure was that of a Voortrekker woman, with a mixed couple occupying the bottom left section. To the right of the woman was a representation of *Samesmelting* (Fusion) by way of four well-dressed men, identified by labels on their trousers: 'Capitalist, Communist, Imperialist, Jew – the threat of "Fusion with Foreign Elements"'.[147] Here was the essence of National Party fears: the alliance of forces pitted against it, each represented in the Hertzog-Smuts merger.

The Basterplakaat received wide coverage, with each party doing its best to extract political capital. The poster was degrading to Afrikaner women, argued the United Party,[148] while the National Party blamed the Jewish-controlled United Party press for launching a bitter campaign insulting to Afrikaners. 'What do these people, however, care for the honour of the South African woman?' asked *Die Transvaler*. 'It is in the money-making interests of their protectors to keep the Nationalist Party out of the government and the honour of the woman is used as an election trick.'[149] *Die Transvaler* upbraided the United Party for accusing the Nationalist poster of denigrating the dignity of white women 'in the eyes of the native'. It claimed that far more pernicious and 'morally shocking' were the overseas publications that natives obtained from Jewish-owned stores.[150] A special motion on the matter – passed during a National Party meeting in Pretoria – provided a good measure of the political temperature:

> This meeting strongly protests against the defamatory manner in which the Jewish and capitalist press misrepresents the poster on mixed marriages ... We warn the Jewish capitalistic press that the honour of the

Afrikaner women is safe in the hands of the Afrikaner himself and that we will no longer tolerate the criminal and contemptible efforts of this parasitic press to exploit the honour of the Afrikaner women for their own low political benefit.[151]

Speakers on the hustings continued their savage attacks on Jews. 'We have become slaves and squatters in our own country, because Boer children must beg for work from Jews,' said the National Party's Muller van der Ahee, and concluded that the 'greater the influx of Jews the greater the poverty in our country'.[152] *Die Volksblad* was similarly unabashed with regard to the National Party's policy towards the Jews. 'What is our policy in regard to the Jew?', the newspaper asked. 'Simply that he cannot be allowed to dominate even more seriously the economic life of South Africa and to stream into the country still more. There are Jews who today use their mighty economic power to attempt to suppress the national aspirations of Afrikanerdom.'[153] The Reverend Jan Hendrik Boneschans, the Nationalist candidate for Germiston-South, was even more forthright. 'I shall use all the might which God has given me to bring the factories, especially the garment factories, in the country under state control. Our daughters and the future mothers of our people are being exploited by the Jew; they work together with the native, live on starvation wages, and are used by the Jewish communists to make our people ripe for communism.'[154] Louw, too, weighed in, accusing the United Party of duplicity and of misleading the electorate. One of their pamphlets, 'The Fruit of Fusion', he noted, omitted any reference to Jewish immigration. On the other hand, the Afrikaans version, 'Die Vrug van Volkseenheid' (The Fruit of Unity), which aimed at a different market, placed substantial emphasis on Jewish immigration and the government's concerns surrounding it.[155]

In attempting to utilise the 'Jewish Question' as a political tool, *Die Transvaler* regularly published insulting letters about Jews. A pamphlet entitled 'Domination of Foreigners in our trade', included with the newspaper two days before the poll, captured the very essence of its stance: the necessity of breaking the hold of the unassimilable Jew on the South African economy and of ensuring opportunities for the Afrikaner in trade and the professions.[156] The newspaper also contained a two-column article on the misfortunes of an Afrikaner who, as a result of drought, had been forced to bond his farm to a Jew. When no interest was paid, the Jew foreclosed the debt and settled his own sons on the farm. The article attempted to give the impression that the Jew had trapped the Afrikaner farmer and was now mercilessly ejecting him from his own farm. The article also made reference to an Afrikaner girl who had been seduced by the son of a Jewish factory owner who subsequently managed to evade responsibility for his actions.[157] These accusations – by now deeply embedded in South African consciousness – were the hallmarks of classic antisemitism, and were no doubt supported by Verwoerd as editor.[158]

As election day approached, some meetings turned violent. Besides a chaotic Blackshirt meeting in Benoni, advertised as 'anti-Jew' in the Afrikaans press,[159] a fracas followed the conclusion of a National Party meeting in Vrededorp, when the crowds moved off to a United Party meeting that was being held nearby with shouts of 'We want the Jews'. The Jews fled, reported Die Transvaler, only to regroup and throw stones at the Nationalists, who in turn retaliated by stoning cars owned by Jews.[160] Recriminations followed, with the Malanite press placing the blame for the trouble on a group of Jews,[161] whereas, according to the Star, there was 'an orgy of Jew-baiting' with the presence of a large body of police having little effect.[162]

THE POLL AND THE AFTERMATH

On the eve of the election, Die Transvaler published a letter urging Afrikaners not to allow this 'God-given country' to fall into the hands of foreigners, to remain true to their Christian National principles and not become the slaves of foreigners.[163] Yet, overall, the National Party's election campaign seemed to be moving away from its focus on the 'Jewish Question'. Growing Nationalist ambivalence towards the constant beating of the antisemitic drum was in fact identified by the SAJC in its final pre-election editorial. While 'Greyshirtism' had infected certain sections of Malan's supporters, and Malan and his party had certainly adopted 'naked ugly anti-Semitism', the Jewish weekly claimed that there were signs that more moderate and liberal Nationalists were uncomfortable with this development. They had perhaps seen 'the dangers of working up yet another brand of racial hatred in this race-torn country', it surmised; a reason perhaps for the party's manifesto to have avoided a full-blooded anti-Jewish programme.[164]

Whether or not the 'Jewish Question' helped the National Party at the polls is arguable, but what is apparent is the key role played by growing Afrikaner nationalism. To be sure, the election results revealed some interesting trends. Notwithstanding its energetic campaign, the National Party obtained only 27 seats as against the ruling United Party's 111,[165] but, despite its relatively few seats, the National Party received more than half the number of United Party votes, with its vote in the Transvaal increasing from 30 000 in the 1936 provincial elections to 70 000 in the general election.[166] Malan had evidently succeeded in harnessing Afrikaner nationalism, revealing that his ethnic-oriented political message undoubtedly appealed to the poor and marginalised – a clear sign that mobilising the Afrikaner vote might in time ensure the political kingdom. 'This is the turning point,' wrote *Die Transvaler.* 'Nationalism cannot die, cannot bend. We accept the task which lies ahead with fresh courage, and next time our opponents will not find us so poorly armed financially and organisationally.'[167]

Reflecting on what it described as a tough and hurtful campaign, a clearly worried *SAJC* looked to the United Party to remove obstacles in the way of 'racial' harmony. 'It is not sufficient that candidates advocating policies of Jewish suppression have been soundly beaten at the polls,' noted the weekly. 'Democracy, unless it takes care to protect itself, unfortunately allows activities subversive to itself to continue after election day.' Malan and his party were urged 'to help eradicate the weeds of anti-Jewish discrimination' and to rein in the more irresponsible elements in the National Party.[168]

This was not to be. Ten days after the poll, the *SAJC* observed that post-election Nationalist comment seemed to focus on Jewish responsibility for its election defeat.[169] Predictably, *Die Transvaler* led the charge, but it was by no means a lone voice. Describing the election outcome as 'a Jewish victory', the National Party mouthpiece noted that in many constituencies the party had begun with an 'arrear of 1 500 votes – those of the Coloureds and the Jews'. United Party success, it maintained, was built upon 'the colossal sources of help' placed at its disposal by 'its Jewish allies', and the government 'would now have to dance to the tune of the Jews, whom they had to thank for their victory'.[170] Cartoonist DC Boonzaier confirmed these sentiments by depicting Hoggenheimer carried aloft by a rather smug Hertzog and a visibly contented Smuts.[171]

Writing of the Reverend Charl du Toit's defeat in Johannesburg West, *Die Transvaler* expressed disappointment but revealed what it considered to be the reality: he was defeated by 'the money of organised Jewry'.[172] And in Caledon, a youthful PW Botha described organised Jewry as 'an enemy of Afrikaner nationalism'.[173] Letters to the editor took up the refrain of the 'organised money power of Jewry' being responsible for the victory of the United Party.[174] In thanking those Nationalists who had 'kept their Afrikaner soul' by voting for him in Gezina, Dr Theo Wassenaar said they did so in spite of the huge Jewish financial power. He urged fellow Nationalists to boycott their 'enemies whoever they may be, and organise, organise, organise. The next battle must be won.'[175] A report from Pietersburg, deep in the northern Transvaal, pointed to a powerful, post-election anti-Jewish backlash: 'Everyone now speaks of general steps to be taken against Jews who with their money power opposed the Nationalist Party ... There are many reports current as regards the sum of money which the Pietersburg Jews put into the chest of the local United Party. Many people say that the poorest Jew gave £5.'[176] For some observers, Jews were tied to British imperialism, the great bugbear of Afrikaner nationalism. Columnist Sylva Moerdijk, the sister of Oswald Pirow, contended that the contest had not been between Afrikaner and Afrikaner, but a contest between Afrikaner and imperialism, in which the United Party had revealed itself as 'a tool for English-Imperialism and Jewish capitalism'.[177]

Reflecting on the election, the *SAJC* lamented the penetration of antisemitism into the body politic:

> One of the most unpleasant and ominous aspects of the recent political
> years of South Africa has been the rapid growth of anti-Semitism and
> the adoption of it as an avowed plank in the platforms of certain parties.

The caricature figure of Hoggenheimer is carried on the shoulders of JBM Hertzog and Jan Smuts, following the United Party's victory in the general election of 1938. Cartoon by DC Boonzaier from *Die Burger*, 23 May 1938. (courtesy *Die Burger*)

Where in former years the words 'Jew' and 'Jewish' were scarcely heard in the addresses of aspiring election candidates, the recent contest for seats in the House of Assembly was smirched by a nation-wide exploitation of the so-called 'Jewish problem' and an appeal to crude racialism and the baser human sentiments.[178]

Yet the Board rather inexplicably held to the view that there had in fact been less outright antisemitic propaganda during the National Party's campaign than had been feared initially.[179]

Such cautious optimism is difficult to fathom, especially given Malan's post-election message to National Party supporters, in which he claimed the 'organised power of money' had once again triumphed: 'Never before in our whole political history have the monied powers spent so much on an election and made so much use of methods of bribery, intimidation and even compulsion … For this Hoggenheimer victory the Afrikaner nation must unhappily pay the price with its national ideals, its future and its honour, but it will rise and emerge from its humiliation. It will not and cannot take very long.'[180]

Even more menacing tones are evident in the minutes of a Broederbond meeting held a month after the general election. These clearly reveal an organisation (considered the intellectual boiler room of Afrikaner nationalism) that saw the Jew as a menace and threat to South Africa and as the root of all the Afrikaners' problems dating back to the nineteenth century. The British Prime Minister Benjamin Disraeli (a Jew) had overseen the annexation of the Transvaal soon after gold had been discovered in Barberton, while Lionel Phillips and Alfred Beit (both Jews) had used Leander Starr Jameson and Cecil John Rhodes for their nefarious purposes. The minutes also noted that Jewish financiers were the only ones to have benefited from the Anglo-Boer War, and Jews were even blamed for the discord between English-speakers and Afrikaners. Commenting on the 'Chosen People' issue, the Broederbond concluded that it was in fact the Church of the Kingdom of Jesus Christ that was the Chosen. Yet, in agreement with the Dutch Reformed Church Synod of the Orange Free State, the Broederbond was opposed to harming Jews – with the caveat that one could not go against God's prediction that Jews would in time be persecuted. Speculating on ways to deal with the 'Jewish Question' in South Africa, the Broederbond concluded that blind hate and persecution would be inappropriate, as would warfare between Jews and Christians. The Afrikaners were too weak economically, did not constitute a political unit, and generally were too disorganised and uninformed. Warfare, moreover, would be in conflict with Christian principles. Thus the 'Jewish Question' had to be understood essentially in economic terms. The number of Afrikaners in trade had to be increased through the development of corporations and businesses, both large and small. While the removal of all Jews from business was impracticable, a quota system that was set fairly high at the start and then gradually lowered was sensible. Jews, moreover, had no right – on account of their unassimilability – to object to the state treating them as a separate group. The Broederbond also raised the question of communist propaganda, which it believed emanated largely from Jews. Current legislation, it asserted, gave both the Jew and the communist an opportunity for malpractices (*wanpraktyke*). Most vital was the wooing of English-speakers to the cause; Afrikaners alone were unable to fight the Jews.[181]

CHAPTER SIX

IN THE CROSSFIRE OF AFRIKANERDOM'S BATTLES

'*Mr Pirow is a South African patriot: this fact no one will dispute. And, as a South African patriot it is impossible for him to be anything but anti-Jewish at heart.*'
– Die Waarheid/The Truth, 7 February 1936

'*Behind Communism and Liberalism there was a power which had grown tremendously of late – a power that made itself felt during the last elections. That power was Jewry.*'
– DF Malan, speech at National Party conference, 11 November 1938

'*I remember the Soviet delegation to the League of Nations. In that delegation there were seven Jews and one Russian. We find that in most countries where communism has taken root, the leaders of Communism are Jews. That is also the case in South Africa.*'
– Eric Louw, speech to parliament, 24 February 1939

'*If there is one point on which most Nationalists are united today it is anti-Jewish discrimination to a greater or lesser extent.*'
– South African Jewish Board of Deputies, 'General Review', *South African Jewish Chronicle*, 30 May 1941

EEUFEES AND THE OSSEWATREK

Not much time had elapsed before Malan's post-election message of an ascendant Afrikaner nationalism found expression in the celebrations surrounding the centenary of the Great Trek, a pivotal event in the maturing of Afrikaner nationalism.[1] Known as the *Eeufees* (centenary festival), a symbolic trek of ox-wagons started out from Cape Town on 8 August 1938, diverging at Vegkop in the Orange Free State, where the Voortrekkers had defeated the Ndebele in 1836. One group continued to Pretoria, the other to Blood River, where Andries Pretorius had vanquished the Zulu in 1838. The two groups finally met in Pretoria on 16 December, the Day of the Vow, to lay the foundation stone of the Voortrekker Monument. According to *Die Burger*, about 100 000 Afrikaners – that is, one in ten – attended the commemoration festivities.[2]

The Ossewatrek, as the symbolic journey was known, passed through small and large towns where mounted commandos and adoring onlookers greeted the ox-wagons. A theatrical and intense sense of identification saw thousands upon thousands of Afrikaner enthusiasts participating in the festivities that included the traditional *braaivleis* (barbecue), *volksliedjies* (folk songs) and *jukskei* (a Voortrekker sport), while traditional forms of address such as *oom* (uncle) and *tante* (aunt) were commonly employed. Some even sported beards like their forebears, and women wore Voortrekker dress. In a remarkable display of *volkseenheid* (people's unity), wreaths were laid on the graves of Afrikaner heroes and streets were renamed after Voortrekker leaders.[3] The memory of this 'oxwagon unity', writes Moodie, 'would constitute a potent political force during the next decade'.[4]

Although the celebrations were government-sponsored, the *Afrikaanse Taal en Kultuurvereniging* (Afrikaans Language and Cultural Union, a subsidiary of the FAK) effectively managed the Eeufees arrangements, pushing Hertzog and Smuts to the periphery and turning the limelight on Malan instead.[5] Recognising the importance of harnessing a *völkisch* mood, Malan grasped the opportunity, and it was he who addressed the Day of the Vow crowd in Pretoria beneath a giant *vierkleur* (Transvaal republican flag), while the audience sang 'Dat's Heeren Zegen op U Daal' (May God's blessing descend upon you).[6]

For the alienated and unskilled Afrikaner, the Ossewatrek bridged a halcyon, albeit mythical, rural past with a powerless present, providing hope that by strengthening ties to the organic roots of an ascendant *volk*, the disruptive and corrupting challenges of urban life – including the threat of equality with blacks – would be countered.[7] This was, writes the historian Joanne Duffy, 'the ultimate reclamation of Afrikaner culture – not only was it to be taken back from the English-speaking Afrikaner, but also from Smuts and Hertzog who, in the eyes of the Broederbond were not "ware Afrikaners" (true Afrikaners).'[8] Little place was left for high-profile Fusionists, let alone English-speakers.[9] There was certainly no place for the Jew, a symbol of the city, and for many the personification of modernity and the reason for hard times. Foreign elements had proved disastrous for the rural culture of the Afrikaners' ancestors, the Reverend Christiaan Rudolph Kotzé told a Dutch Reformed Church service in Cape Town. The discovery of gold and diamonds had precipitated the first cataclysm, soon to be followed by the arrival of the English, Greeks, Indians and Jews in such numbers that they could not be assimilated. The exodus of rural Afrikaners to the towns, and their contact with these foreigners, he maintained, had degraded them to such an extent that 'in some cases they sank lower than swine'.[10]

For Afrikaner ethno-national entrepreneurs, the Eeufees was a step along the road to economic revival. It 'provided an opportunity to engage in an "Act of Rescue": to collect hundreds of thousands of pounds to save fellow Afrikaners from poverty and ruin', explains Norval.[11] As Nico Diederichs and Geoff Cronjé told the crowd at an enthusiastic trek celebration in Bloemfontein, the *volk* had to be saved and the Afrikaner had to take his legitimate place in professional and commercial life. Diederichs went so far as to advocate that Afrikaners use their spending power 'for the benefit of their own people' and not allow their funds 'to stream into the pockets of aliens'.[12] Similarly, Wicus du Plessis told a gathering at Ottoshoop that it was time for the Afrikaners to retake the towns from the 'aliens'. The Afrikaners, he said, had to 'conquer commerce'.[13] In much the same vein, Marthinus Cornelius van Schoor (Oom Tienie) called on the Afrikaner to claim what was their due and to bring an end to their exploitation by foreigners.[14]

This heightened nationalist mood, described by the Board as 'the intensification of Afrikaans sentiment', was recognised by Jewish leaders for its exclusivism.[15] The speeches and propaganda aimed at consolidating the Afrikaners into a compact racial group left no place for English-speakers and Jews (dubbed 'foreigners'), the Board reported.[16] This sentiment was best exemplified in the Benoni celebrations, where the Eeufees organisers prevented the town's Jewish mayor, Morris Nestadt, from partaking in the festivities because of the 'Christian religious nature' of the event.[17]

Despite this snub, the Board extended its good wishes to the chairman of the Voortrekker Centenary Committee, Dr Ernest Jansen.[18] The *SAJC* similarly wished the Eeufees success, although its editorial on the subject, published shortly before the culmination of the trek, carried a carefully crafted and pointed message. While praising the 'courage, endurance and other spiritual qualities' of the Voortrekkers, it compared the values of these hardy pioneers to what it referred to as the 'narrowness, reaction and bigotry' that presently infected a 'certain section' of the country and which threatened to negate the heroic ideology of the Great Trek. Heroes of the Great Trek, suggested the *SAJC*, would have been profoundly perturbed if they had heard 'the defamatory tirades that have been levelled against the "people of the Book"'.[19]

REKINDLING THE 'JEWISH QUESTION'

Although the embers of anti-Jewish hatred had cooled somewhat in the wake of the 1938 general election, the Board had presciently warned that these could be easily reignited, a warning that proved accurate, as the heightened *völkisch* sensibilities aroused by the Eeufees did indeed result in a resurgence of the 'Jewish Question'. Added to that, the Board reported the presence of Nazi agents in many districts, as well as escalating Nazi activity in South West Africa.[20] Here it was referring to a series of syndicated articles (originating from the earlier investigation by the *Cape Argus*) that had exposed Nazi activities in South West Africa, where the Nazi Party remained as influential and strong as it had been four years earlier when the movement had effectively been banned. The German consul in Windhoek had glorified Hitler in a speech, and it was clear that propaganda was being widely distributed from the consulate.[21] The investigation revealed that at the Obrealschule in Windhoek the day began with pupils giving the Hitler salute, while the German-medium high school at Swakopmund followed a Nazi-oriented curriculum. In Windhoek, one business firm had even sent a circular to all shareholders extolling its purely Aryan character, which rendered it safe from the undermining influence of Jews, Freemasons or Jesuits. According to the *Cape Times*, the German-language press in South West Africa was almost entirely pro-Hitler. The public was being bombarded with Nazi pamphlets,[22] swastika flags were flown from cars in Windhoek, and cinemas screened Nazi propaganda. Behind the scenes, 'local Fuehrers' advanced Nazi plans, and initiated commercial boycotts against non-compliant Germans and non-Germans. Few Germans held out against the Nazi movement, and those who did risked social isolation.[23]

As noted earlier, the South African government viewed these developments in a serious light.[24] South West Africa's contiguity to South Africa and the putative ties between Nazis in the territory and the radical right in South Africa were of serious concern. However, at the same time, the SANP – the most important group among the radical right – was experiencing difficulties. Its mouthpiece, *Die Waarheid / The Truth*, faced closure because of straitened financial circumstances, and serious infighting within the SANP ranks had led to the expulsion of Willem Laubscher and a few colleagues who had expressed a loss of confidence in Louis Weichardt.[25] At a fiery SANP congress in Pretoria in August 1938, it was agreed that the SANP would revert to its original status as a movement, as opposed to a political party, and that this would be confirmed at its next congress.[26]

After his expulsion from the SANP, Laubscher, who had done reasonably well as the party's candidate for the Cape Flats constituency in the May 1938 election, announced that he would be joining the National Party, as he believed the Greyshirts had outlived their usefulness. In a letter to *Die Burger*, he pointed out that the Greyshirts had performed a useful service in calling attention to the Jewish threat in South Africa; but, because the National Party had now taken up the cudgels and was in a position to act, the SANP had become superfluous. According to Laubscher, at least three-quarters of Greyshirt members in the Western Province were dissatisfied with Weichardt's leadership and had joined the Nationalists, where they felt they would be able to fulfil their ideals.[27]

Laubscher was correct to note that the National Party had now taken on board the 'Jewish Question'. Foreigners, immigration, communism and Jewish economic power, as well as calls for a 'Christian country', were regularly identified as matters of concern by Nationalists at public meetings. Speaking in Kuils River, Eric Louw – perhaps more sophisticated but no less hostile to Jews than Weichardt – said it was time that the English and especially the Afrikaners gained control of the economy, currently under alien control.[28] Malan similarly inveighed against 'foreign exploiters' during a speech in Porterville, where he warned against the country being made into a 'plaything for these people'. Sharing the platform with Malan, Louw railed against the mining magnates and the capitalists. South Africa 'had been exploited by strangers from abroad' for too long, he said.[29]

A short while later, Louw took a swipe at the alleged Jewish boycott of German goods and what he believed were its ruinous implications for South Africa's wool industry. In parliament he went further, accusing South African Jews of playing with fire when they threatened to use their undoubted commercial ability as a weapon, and he warned of inevitable retaliation by the South African public. Interestingly, and probably with a degree of truth, Louw added that many United Party MPs supported his views.[30] A few days later he pointedly asked Richard Stuttaford, the Minister of the Interior, if he was satisfied with the work of the Immigration Selection Board, which, in his view, was still allowing too many Jewish immigrants to enter South Africa. Louw maintained the newcomers would not qualify as suitable immigrants, as they could never identify with the 'white race' in South Africa's national or economic life. Mossel Bay MP Dr Petrus van Nierop, always Louw's equal when it came to lashing out at Jews, also entered the debate, insinuating that the Board was helping to find jobs for Jewish immigrants.[31]

These calls for further immigration restrictions attracted much support. Anti-Jewish letters peppered the pages of the Malanite press, with one correspondent objecting to Jewish 'free thinkers' at universities and another to Jewish support for racial integration.[32] *Die Burger* and *Die Transvaler*, the southern and northern mouthpieces, respectively, of the National Party, came out in full support of restricting Jewish immigration. South Africans remained concerned about the Jewish influx, noted *Die Burger*, while the government appeared powerless and was ignoring the will of the people as expressed in the protests of 1936.[33] Sylva Moerdijk was similarly critical, referring to the Aliens Act of 1937 as mere 'eyewash'.[34] A report appearing in both the *Sunday Tribune* and *Sunday Express* claimed that Malan had even been planning to introduce a 'Closed Professions Bill', but that it had subsequently been dropped for an indefinite period. The objective of that Bill, explained the newspaper, was to defeat 'the alleged monopoly held by Jews in various South African professions' – a measure that had been one of the main antisemitic planks in the Nationalist election programme.[35]

The fact that Malan's draft Bill never saw the light of day is probably indicative of the fact that there were some Nationalists who did not feel comfortable with the incessant clamour against Jewish immigration and calls to limit the rights of Jews living in South Africa. The *Sunday Tribune* even speculated about a likely split within the party over the issue. According to its sources, a well-known South African antisemite, E Montgomery, had been proposed as a candidate for the National Party, but Malan and Karl Bremer had refused to countenance this. Were Malan to be replaced as leader, the *Sunday Tribune* warned, the National Party would pursue a much more virulent antisemitic policy.[36]

Certainly, heavyweights like Eric Louw, Hans Strijdom and Hendrik Verwoerd persisted in playing the Jewish card, while Malan increasingly began to show disturbing signs of appeasing his fanatical anti-Jewish wing. During a speech in Southfield on the Cape Flats, the National Party leader bluntly stated that the country had too many Jews, and that, as far as trade and commerce were concerned, these areas of activity were passing into their hands.[37] He also fulminated against Jewish immigration in a speech at a Nationalist rally in Heidelberg, in the Transvaal. Denying the charge that he was racist or antisemitic, he noted that similar policies were being carried out by many countries. South Africa had no option but to pursue the same treatment meted out to the Jews in Germany and Austria, although in a less extreme form, and added that France and England – supposedly with no trace of racial hatred – had both discriminated against Jews; in England, for example, if a Jew changed his name, he had to display his original name and changed name at his place of business so that people would know with whom they were dealing. 'If they [South Africans] regard England as a dear, good, human-loving nation, then we want to become like them as soon as possible,' Malan sarcastically exhorted. The position as regards Jewish immigration was becoming more acute, continued Malan, and even Switzerland was prohibiting the entry of Jews. The South African government's present immigration law, however, was ineffectual – 'like a sieve hung out to stop the east wind from blowing'.[38]

Malan no doubt sensed the political mileage to be gained by highlighting the 'Jewish Question', and the embers of antisemitic hatred were now glowing brightly. On the Witwatersrand the radical right clashed regularly with anti-fascists,[39] swastikas were daubed on buildings,[40] and a synagogue in Benoni was bombed.[41] Anti-Jewish tropes that had been maturing for years were now articulated on a regular basis, often at the highest level. Malan, for one, employed many of these in an address to the National Party's Free State congress in Bloemfontein in late 1938:

> Behind Communism and Liberalism there was a power which had grown tremendously of late – a power that made itself felt during the last elections. That power was Jewry. The Jews were in the minority in all countries, but they understood the art of attracting to themselves a great deal more than was due to them in proportion to their numbers. The means they employed were not only their economic power, but, directly or indirectly, they always preached the doctrine of Liberalism, or, where it suited their purposes better, the doctrine of Communism. They disseminated and propagated these doctrines of equality because they wanted no race or colour discriminations. Jews did not always support Communism or Liberalism on the political merits of these creeds, but because they were a means of protecting Jews.[42]

These ideas had widespread resonance, nourished as they were by the influx of African workers into the cities and the competition these newcomers posed for unskilled Afrikaners. The twin threats of 'communism' and 'liberalism', each of which was associated primarily with Jews, threatened an organic Afrikaner nationalism that was increasingly informed by neo-Calvinist (and Kuyperian) intellectuals.[43] Kuyperianism, with its hostility towards cosmopolitanism and its preference for cultural homogenisation, in fact sharpened and complemented an essentialist mindset that immutably tied culture to a sense of biological descent. This potent brew was augmented and underpinned by material fears and hopes, driven by an emergent Afrikaner bourgeoisie that sought to minimise competition and establish a firm foothold in the economy. Such considerations ensured the unanimous adoption of the following resolution at the Orange Free State National Party congress:

> While generally, the Party welcomes the immigration of suitable white elements, it will take measures in the light of South Africa's specific problems to terminate any further immigration of Jews, to prevent the changing of names, to exercise stricter control of naturalisation and to create a vocational permit system for unnaturalised foreigners on the lines of the systems in England, France and other countries. The Party, moreover, will take all possible steps to qualify in all directions original Afrikaans and English-speaking national elements for making a livelihood and to protect these elements from unfair competition.[44]

Prior to this congress, Nationalists at Lindley, Parys and Heilbron had passed resolutions urging more effective control of Jewish immigration and protection of the public from the threat posed by Jewish commerce. The oft-repeated recommendation that licences be issued to Jews only on the basis of their percentage of the (white) population was also on the agenda of Nationalist speakers.[45]

The Cape Province National Party congress also raised the 'Jewish Question', with the Port Elizabeth branch calling for a quota system for professionals, for a ban on Jewish doctors attending to Afrikaner patients, and for Jews and other 'unassimilable strangers' to be deprived of the vote. Calls were also made to follow the Transvaal and Orange Free State examples and exclude Jews from membership of the National Party.[46] Prior to the conference it was reported that the Oudtshoorn branch wanted a clear policy on Jews, and that Vredendal would move that 'as a result of the anti-Christianity and the internationalism of the Jews it be decided not to allow any Jew in the Nationalist Party and not to receive any donations from Jews or Jewish bodies and to endeavour to put a stop to the increasing control exercised by Jews over the lives of Afrikaners'.[47]

Predictably, these sentiments were shared by *Die Burger*, which explained that the National Party was aware of attempts by organised Jewry to subvert national and Christian convictions and institutions, and to spread ultra-liberal ideas and communism while also undermining Afrikaans businesses and industries. Jews, the newspaper asserted, did not serve the *volk*, and it was up to the National Party to resolve the situation.[48] Yet the National Party unabashedly continued to deny any hostility towards Jews as individuals, claiming instead that it was organised Jewry to whom they objected.[49]

Parliamentary by-elections in Pretoria City, Lichtenburg, Bethal and Paarl in early 1939 further highlighted concern about the 'Jewish Question'. This was particularly the case in Pretoria, where the United Party's Adolf Davis competed against the Nationalist candidate, Dr DJG van den Heever. Playing on the fact that Davis was Jewish, Van den Heever focused on Jewish hegemony in South Africa, which he said informed a Bill that Louw would in due course table in parliament. In conspiratorial mode, Van den Heever also accused international Jewry of using communism as an instrument to repress the working class.[50] The South African government, he warned, had to be in the hands of Gentiles to prevent Afrikaners becoming the 'hewers of wood and drawers of water'.[51] As part of Van den Heever's arsenal, an English and Afrikaans propaganda flyer was sent to all constituents. Entitled 'Keep the Jews out of Parliament', it proclaimed that no Jew should take part in governing South Africa, as South African life was based on the Christian faith.[52]

While the Jewish question might have featured less prominently in other by-elections, the matter continued to be raised.[53] Louw told a meeting in Paarl that the 'colour question' and the 'Jewish problem' were the primary issues facing the country.[54] Malan, too, continued to beat the 'unassimilable' drum, arguing that the Jew could not continue to live off the fat of the land while the rest of the population became impoverished. Jews would not be allowed to dominate the country, insisted Pieter Hugo, the Nationalist candidate for Paarl.[55] At Bethal, Strijdom also insisted that the Afrikaner 'must come first', but magnanimously proclaimed that his party wanted to be just to all, 'even to the Jewish section'. Strijdom criticised the British capitalist press for dubbing the National Party a 'Nazi party' and 'un-Christian', claiming that this was a tactic to draw South Africa into the looming war.[56] A month after Strijdom made this accusation, German troops – ignoring the Munich Agreement signed in September 1938 – invaded Czechoslovakia.

Only a week before the invasion, Van den Heever's failure to defeat Davis in the Pretoria City by-election led to an ugly antisemitic demonstration.[57] Following the announcement of results, an angry crowd at the City Hall began shouting anti-Jewish slogans. A fight broke out.[58] Clearly European tensions were reverberating at the foot of Africa. Some hot-heads even saw Smuts operating at the behest of Jews who wanted to drag South Africa into war. As Hitler's aggression unfolded, it was quite evident that National-ists failed to empathise with Britain, or indeed with the plight of German Jewry. Writing in a Dutch daily after a two-month visit to South Africa, a Dutch academic from Utrecht University, Professor Victor Jacob Kon-ingsberger, perceptively noted a 'growing veneration of modern German culture and the new German Reich' that was accompanied by a burgeon-ing anti-Jewish feeling.[59]

WHITHER THE NATIONALISTS?

In early January 1939, Eric Louw notified the House of Assembly that he would introduce an Aliens (Amendment) and Immigration Bill. The objectives were wide-ranging and constituted an undeniable assault on the Jewish community:

a) To prevent people of Jewish parentage being given permits to reside permanently in the Union.

b) To cancel the permits of aliens found to be without visible means of subsistence or to have engaged in Communistic or other subversive activities.

c) To compel aliens to obtain registration cards to be shown on demand to Police.

d) To forbid aliens to change their names.

e) To compel business firms to reveal fully the names of their owners, partners and directors.

f) To compel employers of aliens to obtain permits for this purpose from the Minister of the Interior.

In addition, Louw's Bill proposed to remove the classification of Yiddish as a European language – hitherto accepted for immigration purposes – and contained a clause stating that 'no applicant for permission to enter the Union who is of Jewish parentage shall be deemed to be readily "assimilable"'. Notably, this clause applied also to British-born persons. With regard to the business restrictions of aliens, the Bill provided for the Governor General to designate by proclamation businesses that no alien should be allowed to own or be employed by, as well as to specify the number of aliens who might own or be employed in any business. Louw planned to make these provisions retrospective, to include immigrants who had entered South Africa after 1930. These individuals would have to reapply for permission to reside in South Africa. Moreover, any alien who had entered South Africa after 1 January 1933 would not be permitted to remain in the service of any South African employer unless the Minister of the Interior had issued a written permit for continued service.[60]

A flurry of hostile comment followed the Bill's publication in the *Government Gazette*. 'Let us hope that wiser counsels may prevail and that Dr Malan will induce his exuberant lieutenant to withdraw a Bill which might almost have been drafted by Herr Streicher himself,' noted the *Star*.[61] 'Eric Louw beats the Fascist Drum', was the response of the *Independent*,[62] while the *Cape Argus* referred to the Bill as 'Contemptible'.[63] It was 'an example of naked Jew-hatred', concluded *Die Suiderstem*, a government-supporting newspaper.[64] 'Has there yet been a closer approximation in this

country to the barbaric, reactionary doctrines of the Nuremberg legislation?' asked the *SAJC*. 'Is there a clearer indication that Mr Louw's ultimate
intention is to adopt the whole paraphernalia of German and Italian racialism?'[65] The Board was obviously concerned, noting that the Bill went
beyond the simple restriction of Jews entering the country: 'It also seeks to
deprive aliens, Jews and others, who are lawfully resident in the Union, of
many of their acquired rights. It is a Bill which apes foreign models, chiefly
Nazi, and if it were adopted it would surely disturb the stability of the social,
economic and political life in the Union.'[66]

But Louw, by now dubbed the 'Julius Streicher of his party', was unrepentant.[67] Speaking at Strand, outside Cape Town, he pointed out that he
had the full approval of Malan (whose 1936 Immigration Bill was not dis-
similar) and stressed – quite unabashedly and seemingly oblivious to (or
perhaps in agreement with) Hitler's Nuremberg Laws of 1935 – that no
'person whose father and mother are or were either wholly or partly Jewish, whether or not they profess the Jewish religion' would 'be deemed to
be readily assimilable'.[68] Letters to *Die Burger* illustrated vigorous support
for Louw's proposals.[69]

For Weichardt, Louw's Bill was a decisive and positive turning point for
the National Party, removing any doubt that it was lukewarm about finding
a solution to the Jewish problem.[70] Within days of the Bill's introduction, he
announced that the SANP would be disbanding and that he would be joining the National Party, and he urged his followers to do the same. Seemingly
content for the party to have a self-proclaimed fascist on board, *Die Burger*
welcomed Weichardt's move and, asserting that there was no place for small
parties in the South African political arena, urged his supporters to follow their
leader. The real issue in South Africa, it maintained, revolved around what sort
of nation should be created: 'It is a struggle between two directly opposing ideals: on the one hand the ideals of nationalism and on the other hand the ideals
of a triple alliance: imperialism, money power, liberalism.'[71] The allusions to the
Jewish threat were obvious. Nico van der Merwe, at a meeting in his Brandfort
constituency, was more direct. He accused Jews of financially supporting the
United Party and questioned the right of this racially unassimilable bloc to
complain if Afrikaners too formed their own laager.[72]

Die Vaderland, on the other hand, took advantage of Weichardt's move to accuse the Nationalists of turning towards fascism of the German variety.[73] Its comments followed a major speech by Smuts at a United Party congress in De Aar, where he accused the National Party of drifting towards Nazism.[74] 'Whither the Nationalists?' asked an *SAJC* editorial that reminded readers of the breakdown in negotiations between the National Party and Weichardt's SANP fourteen months earlier. The reason given then was that the National Party was ostensibly wedded to the principle of democracy and would not tolerate fascism.[75] Hitting back at this negative comment, *Die Burger* and *Die Transvaler* defended the defection of Weichardt to the National Party, and denied the charge that the party was undemocratic, because Weichardt would be obliged to abide by its constitution. In fact, asserted *Die Burger*, democracy stood to be strengthened by the dissolution of the hitherto non-democratic SANP.[76]

A month later Louw introduced his promised Aliens (Amendment) and Immigration Bill. This was the moment he had long been waiting for: an opportunity to translate his animus towards Jews into concrete action. His strident tone, incorporating the worst of oft-used and by now commonplace anti-Jewish stereotypes, bears careful examination. It certainly reached a high level of anti-Jewish invective, and the fact that Malan listened impassively to the presentation suggests Louw was speaking with his leader's support. This was confirmed by the National Party's publication of the lengthy speech – no doubt for propaganda purposes.[77]

Louw raised all the old bogeys: world Jewish power; the pressure Jews brought on the media; Jews as an additional 'race problem' and their threatened domination of business, industry and the professions. To support his argument he quoted Abe Bailey, a leading English-speaking industrialist, who had also expressed concern about the disproportionate Jewish presence in business. But Louw went further, accusing Jews like Solly Sachs and Eli Weinberg of fomenting communism, which, he said, was international in the same way that the Jew was international. To bolster his argument, Louw referred to *The Cause of World Unrest*, by Howell Arthur Keir Gwynne, a notorious antisemite who was editor of the London *Morning Post* from 1911 to 1937. Once again Louw asserted that there was much support for his views among the government benches, adding that the same people who attacked him in the English press would not allow Jews in their clubs. Triumphantly, he noted, his Bill was at last confronting the 'Jewish problem' in South Africa.

Like Malan on previous occasions, Louw used the argument that when Jews exceeded a certain proportion of the population they generated a problem. He accused them of a host of nefarious activities, including working behind the scenes during conflicts, creating monopolies and controlling the wholesale, retail and liquor trades, as well as the legal profession. They also dominated the medical profession and brought pressure to bear on newspapers, and it was the Jewish Board of Deputies that had driven the anti-German boycott, which the people of South Africa would not tolerate. Their actions, he alleged, were guided by the Talmud, which accounted for Jews being able to compete so successfully with Gentiles.[78] Here he was echoing medieval charges resurrected by modern antisemites in Europe.

Quite remarkably, and disingenuously, Louw denied being antisemitic. The crux of his concern, he asserted, was the unassimilability of the Jew:

> He has maintained his racial identity and his Jewish customs, he has remained true to the faith of his forefathers, he has maintained the purity of his Jewish blood, and above all he has remained a separate nation. Now sir, in spite of my being accused of being an anti-Semite, let me say in all sincerity that I think that it is very wonderful that the Jews over a period of two thousand years, often living under unfavourable conditions, have retained the integrity of their race. But that very fact proves that they are, and will remain, a separate nation; in other words, that they are, and will remain unassimilable.

How Louw could square his characterisation of Jews with his denial of the charge of antisemitism is difficult to fathom. His diatribe certainly angered Jan Hofmeyr who took a very different view. Believing that Jews were not unassimilable and that the Nationalist campaign was abhorrent to the tradition of religious freedom and kindliness of the Afrikaner, he declared antisemitism to be 'irreconcilable with the best traditions of the

South African people'. Both English- and Afrikaans-speakers in fact owed a great deal to the Jews. 'We dare not forget', he told the House, 'that the literature of the Bible was in the main Jewish literature; that the founder of our religion was a Jewish Messiah.'[79]

The government-supporting press followed the debate closely and excoriated Louw for his blatant antisemitism. 'The National Party's policy of race discrimination has never been more blatantly advanced than in Mr Louw's Aliens' Act (Amendment) and Immigration Bill,' noted the *Rand Daily Mail*.[80] Similarly, the *Natal Daily News* condemned what it called Louw's 'nonsense', pointing to 'the old contradictions of the Jews being the great financiers of the world and at the same time the complete Bolsheviks'.[81] *Die Burger*, on the other hand, praised Louw's sobriety of judgement and dispassionate approach to a problem that it considered one of the most burning issues in South Africa.[82] Sylva Moerdijk, too, applauded Louw's initiative in her weekly column in *Die Transvaler*. Recalling a time when there had been no friction between the Jew and Afrikaner, she now greatly exaggerated the immigration figures and claimed that it was the inordinate number of Jews entering South Africa over the past few years that had unsettled things. Afrikaners needed protection against this influx, as indeed did all South Africans.[83]

When the debate resumed a month later, Malan explained why he supported Louw's Bill. Hitherto, he contended, the government had adopted half measures when dealing with Jewish immigration, but, because Jews had continued to enter the country in great numbers, South Africa was now facing a major problem that could not have been foreseen when he introduced the Quota Act in 1930.[84] This Act had welcomed immigrants from Nordic countries and excluded those from countries that did not have a Western Christian tradition. He now adamantly stated that Jews from Germany were also not welcome, as they were not racially appropriate. Moreover, it was not, as Hofmeyr had suggested, 'un-Christian' to exclude them. If that were indeed the case, practically all countries in the world would have to stand accused:

> You must remember that the Semitic question is not specifically a South
> African question, it is a world question, and there is hardly a country

in the world where there is not, if I may call it, an anti-Semitic feeling, and where no steps of an anti-Semitic nature have been taken. We can for that purpose leave out Germany, because the steps that have been taken in Germany, irrespective of how they originally commenced, are the result of a war which exists between Germany and the Jewish race.[85]

Die Suiderstem, edited by the philosemitic Abraham Jonker, espoused an entirely different view, claiming that the debate illustrated that the reactionary elements in the National Party had gained the upper hand. 'With the lining up of the Blackshirts of General Maritz, the Fascists of Von Moltke and the Greyshirts of Weichardt,' it explained, 'it is clear that the Nationalist Party is now going to pursue a Nazi policy that is foreign, unnatural, un-Afrikaans and un-Christian.'[86]

Within days of the parliamentary debate, Weichardt had reiterated his fascist beliefs in an interview with the Daily Express,[87] and again at the SANP congress in Pretoria, assembled to discuss formal ties with the National Party. Fascism, he told the congress, was a constitutional question that ought not to divide the people. He continued to call on English-speakers to join in his struggle and support the National Party, which stood for limiting Jewish immigration and opposing communism and what he termed 'Hofmeyr Liberalism'.[88] The congress duly dissolved the SANP as a political party and agreed that the Greyshirts, with Weichardt remaining as their leader, would continue as a movement in support of the National Party.[89] As a consequence of this realignment, Die Waarheid/The Truth would cease publication and would be replaced by a pamphlet, Die Bulletin. In reality, though, the journal had run out of funds.[90]

Nazi propaganda and local antisemitic literature continued to circulate and anti-Jewish incidents were regularly reported.[91] The Board was particularly disturbed by My Volk op die Drumpel van Ondergang (My People on the Brink of Collapse), published by Dries van Schalkwyk in Trompsburg,[92] and by the many politicians who reaffirmed Louw's sentiments. Van Nierop, for instance, told a rowdy meeting in Mossel Bay that Louw had done South Africa an important service by introducing the Aliens Bill. The Jews were 'a potential danger to South Africa as they were busy creating a state within a state and were living on the fat of the country and were occupying positions which rightly belonged to Afrikaners' who 'had to do all the dirty work'. The usual accusations followed: Jews had caused the Anglo–Boer War; as communists they were responsible for the current world unrest that threatened to destroy civilisation; they controlled the mass media, and their dishonesty had led to the demise of many English and Afrikaans businesses in the Cape.[93] In Humansdorp, another Nationalist, Paul Sauer, castigated the government for continuing to disregard the demands of the people in connection with Jewish immigration. Ninety per cent of the people, he claimed, were in favour of Louw's Aliens Bill, but the government refused to act because it was tied to 'Jewish capital'.[94]

There was clearly little to choose between Van Nierop – an old-timer in the National Party – and radical right newcomers like Von Moltke, a proven Jew-baiter, and the obsessed Weichardt, who certainly had no intention of changing his focus. Having warned the closing SANP congress about the dangers of Jewish Bolshevism, economic manipulation and race mixing, and their harmful impact on domestic culture, Weichardt now threw his weight behind the Nationalists at the hustings.[95] In June 1939 he attended an international anti-communist congress in Switzerland[96] and, obviously inspired by that meeting, turned his focus to the Jew/communist threat and the prospect of Jews forcing a European war.[97] In his usual conspiratorial fashion, all the pieces were neatly connected. In considering who stood to benefit from a European conflagration, it was a case of *cui bono* (for whose good).

Weichardt had lost none of his demagoguery, but Smuts had him firmly in his sights. A meeting he was due to address at the Grand Parade in Cape Town in mid-June was banned, and Weichardt was issued with a suspended sentence for instigating public disorder.[98] The judge wished to avoid making a martyr of him, but the *Cape Argus* described him as a criminal and a danger to South Africa. Weichardt then sued the newspaper, thereby gaining valuable publicity when the case was heard in 1941.[99]

Like Weichardt, Manie Maritz traversed the country on behalf of the National Party to alert the public to the 'Jewish Question'. In a harangue to an audience of 200 at a farm near Vryburg, the maverick Anglo–Boer

War hero and 1914 Rebellion leader contended that divisions in South Africa had been caused by Jews, who bore responsibility for all evil, exploiting both sections of the white community and stirring up strife for their own ends.[100] Maritz launched a similar attack in Pietersburg, where he had to speak in the open, having been refused a venue by the town authorities.[101] Some months later, he held a meeting in Aberdeen with a view to establishing a movement of national unity, the Afrikanervolk, that would welcome all except 'Jews and Asiatics'.[102] Subsequently, Maritz founded an anti-parliamentarian Volksparty in the Pietersburg district in July 1940, but was killed in a car accident a few months later.[103]

More menacing than Maritz's peripatetic speeches was the publication in February 1939 of his autobiography, *My Lewe en Strewe* (My Life and Striving).[104] Most of it was a diatribe against Jews, including so-called quotations from the Talmud and other Jewish sources. Twenty-seven pages consisted of extracts from the *Protocols* translated into Afrikaans and given a South African flavour.[105] In addition, Maritz made use of the publication *The Key to the Mystery*, a conspiratorial account of Jewish world domination by Adrien Arcand, a leading Canadian antisemite and a close friend of Hamilton Beamish. Maritz had simply lifted large chunks of Arcand's book, which identified Jews as being at the root of why 'humanity is overwhelmed with wars, revolutions, acute crises, waves of unemployment etc. etc.' Alleged speeches by prominent Jews were also cited, demonstrating conspiratorial actions by Jews across many countries and over many decades.[106] Here one sees the international web and outreach of antisemites and the impact of Nazi ideas in South Africa. The very title of Maritz's book suggests that it was modelled on Hitler's *Mein Kampf.*

Because of its hate-filled contents, attempts were made by the Board to have the book banned, but they were unsuccessful.[107] Eventually, after the book had circulated in South West Africa, Maritz was tried in Windhoek in August 1939 and found guilty of promoting 'a strong feeling of hostility against the Jewish race'. Gustav Saron, who gave expert evidence at the trial, reported that Arcand's *Key to the Mystery* had been translated directly into Afrikaans. According to Maritz's attorney, the book had been brought to his client's attention by Beamish.

During the trial, Maritz – described by the *Star* as 'a man of physical vigour and strong personality with marked intellectual limitations' – explained how the *Kristelike-bond* (Christian Bond) in Johannesburg[108] had shown him the *Protocols* in 1924, the year in which he had first publicly harangued the Jews.[109] Until then he had had no interest in the Jewish problem, but the publication had opened his eyes to the role of the Jew in the Afrikaner's misfortunes and confirmed his understanding of earlier South African conspiracy theories. Among these were the role of Lionel Phillips in the Jameson Raid of 1895-1896, and the nefarious part Jews played in fomenting the Anglo-Boer War, a canard initially popularised by JA Hobson, a prominent British intellectual.[110] Maritz had been a policeman in Paul Kruger's republic, and claimed to have seen at first hand the Jewish underworld of Johannesburg. Accusing Jews of attempting to silence him by offering him bribes, he was now intent on exposing the power of Jews that lay behind the misfortune of Afrikaners.[111] As a citizen of South Africa, he claimed to have been forced to act in defence of the blood of his nation.[112]

Despite losing the case, Maritz continued his attack on Jews and remained a hero in some quarters. He was indeed carried shoulder-high after a speech at the Paardekraal Monument in Krugersdorp.[113] *My Lewe en Strewe*, described by Judge Hoexter as 'filthy, contemptible and venomous racial propaganda', was easily available in the Union.[114] In fact, *Die Volksblad* reported that the Volksblad Boekhandel was receiving many inquiries for the book and other 'historical works'.[115] It was only after the outbreak of the Second World War that the book was banned in South Africa under the Emergency Regulations.[116]

In the build-up to the annual National Party congresses, a range of speakers continued to vilify the Jews. Sauer told a meeting in Messina that South Africa had a 'Kaffir, Indian and Coloured question' and he wanted to prevent a further racial problem by stopping Jewish immigration and denying the vote to aliens, some of whom were unwelcome communists. Unnaturalised aliens would also be deported.[117] Regarding the mounting tensions in Europe, Louw warned that international Jewry – the proven power behind the English press – would want to exact revenge on Germany.[118] Along similar lines, Jan Haywood claimed the Jews wanted war because of their hatred of Hitler, and were planning to get 'us to fight for them'.[119] As war clouds gathered, it would appear that the National Party believed they would gain support by identifying Jews as the driving force behind Smuts' pro-British stance.

A 'BRITISH-JEWISH' WAR

Although the 'Jewish Question' featured quite prominently in discussions at the National Party's Transvaal and Natal congresses in late September 1939,[120] it was South Africa's declaration of war against Germany on 6 September, in support of Britain, that was uppermost in the minds of delegates. For the Malanites, it was unthinkable to fight on the side of their old adversary. Apart from a deep hostility to 'imperial' entanglements, many Afrikaners had substantial sympathy for Germany and certainly were not concerned with what was happening to German Jews. Even the appalling events of *Kristallnacht* (Night of Broken Glass) in November 1938 had left them unconcerned and unmoved.[121] Whereas the *Cape Times* had unreservedly condemned these acts of 'Nazi barbarism',[122] *Die Burger* considered the reports of the carnage in Germany to be one-sided and exaggerated, and even though it acknowledged that Germany wanted to be rid of its Jews, the Nationalist daily deemed this a domestic matter, similar to the mass murders in the Soviet Union. 'It is not for us to pronounce judgement on the manner in which Germany chooses to treat some of its citizens,' ran an editorial.[123]

Such moral insularity, coupled with a long history of antagonism towards Britain, ensured widespread opposition to the idea of joining the Commonwealth war effort. Indeed, the Status of Union Act of 1934 had confirmed the substance of the Statute of Westminster (1931), which recognised the right of the Dominions to determine their own domestic and foreign policy (including war and peace). Hertzog himself had long sought neutrality, and the aging Prime Minister was confident that South Africa could not forcibly be dragged into another European conflagration. Like the Malanites, in the early years he had empathised with the 'Nazi revolution' and perceived the treatment of Jews in Germany to be part of a wider upheaval. Smuts, on the other hand, spoke of Hitler's 'odious internal policy' and viewed German nationalism and the Reich's treatment of Jews with abhorrence.[124] He watched the storm clouds building over Europe with great concern and, although initially inclined towards appeasement, spoke out forcefully against Hitler from the moment Germany occupied Czechoslovakia.[125] From then on, wrote his colleague Leslie Blackwell, he became convinced that Hitler and Nazi Germany threatened the world order and had to be destroyed.[126]

When Britain declared war on Germany, Hertzog turned to his cabinet for a decision as to whether South Africa should support Britain. But, despite his strong defence of South Africa's independence and its duty to remain neutral, Smuts' call to arms was carried by the slim margin of one vote. The matter then went to the House, where Hertzog's impassioned motion of neutrality – which Malan had told him in advance would be supported by the Nationalists – was defeated by 13 votes.[127] The Governor General, Sir Patrick Duncan, rejected Hertzog's call for a general election and, somewhat controversially, invited Smuts to form a government. Hertzog resigned as Prime Minister and, together with 37 of his supporters, formed the *Volksparty* (People's Party). At the age of sixty-nine, 'slim Jannie' (as Smuts was called) was once again at the helm.

Jews were soon being accused of instigating the war and dragging South Africa into the conflict. Indeed, Malan referred to Smuts sarcastically as a 'good Jew'.[128] The 'Jewish Unionist Party', read a National Party resolution passed at George, had plunged South Africa into war.[129] At his party's Orange Free State congress, held in October 1939, Malan spoke of 'organised Jewry backing England' and referred to Smuts as 'Janowitz Smutsowitz'.[130] Cartoonists, too, had a field day, lampooning the Prime Minister as 'the driver of a machine of war, ruthlessly mowing down Afrikaner men, women and children'.[131] A well-attended meeting in Johannesburg heard Strijdom denounce Smuts for entering the war in order to satisfy 'English Jews'.[132] As Malan put it, the 'Jewish Question' hovered 'like a dark cloud over South Africa'.[133]

In the following days, swastikas were painted on several Jewish houses in Standerton,[134] and 'British-Jewish imperialism' in particular came under fire.[135] The National Party's primary concern, however, was to bring about

233

Afrikaner *hereniging* (reunion) with Hertzog's newly founded Volksparty. This was achieved in principle only a few days after war was declared, and was celebrated at a vast and quasi-religious republican demonstration on Monumentkoppie (Monument Hill) outside Pretoria. In fact, secret discussions on *hereniging* had already been conducted; leadership issues had been raised and the Nationalists in Hertzog's camp had promised the Malanites that they were *ad idem* on race policies.[136] Certainly the National Party and the Volksparty had much in common, although the Nationalists were more preoccupied with the 'Jewish Question'.

Little wonder, then, that the Board of Deputies awaited the outcome of these negotiations with some anxiety. Would the policies of *hereniging* be driven by the less extreme and more inclusive ideas of Hertzog or the exclusivist ideas of Malan, and what would this mean for the future of the Jews in South Africa? Always mindful of Hertzog's past commitment to the equality of all European citizens of South Africa, the Board was now afraid of the possibility of the National Party intensifying its opposition to further Jewish immigration and adopting a far more draconian policy towards Jewish residents in South Africa.[137]

On 27 January 1940 Malan and Hertzog announced that they would be amalgamating as the new *Herenigde Nasionale of Volksparty* (Reunited National Party or People's Party, hereafter the HNP). In a compromise formula, it was agreed that the party would oppose the war, soft-peddle on republicanism and demand the liberation of the country from 'un-Afrikaner' influences. However, because of unresolved differences between moderates and extremists, no specific statements were made on the 'Jewish Question'. Nonetheless, the reference to 'un-Afrikaner' was a thinly disguised allusion to the allegedly powerful and alien Jew.[138] But in the immediate aftermath of *hereniging*, issues of greater import dominated Afrikaner debate. Parliamentary democracy itself was subjected to scrutiny, while the subject of republicanism – or at least advocacy for a republic – remained bitterly divisive. Conservatives like Strijdom and Verwoerd in the Transvaal, and Nico van der Merwe and Blackie Swart in the Orange Free State, were determined to ensure agreement on establishing a republic as a precondition for equal rights for white English- and Afrikaans-speakers, while Hertzog was more circumspect. Some Afrikaners even favoured the fascist option, associating liberalism and parliamentarianism with Jews.[139] One such voice was that of General Jan Kemp, who spoke of the need to end 'our present democracy' so as to enable the 'settled section' of the population to rule. This was presumably a veiled call to exlude Jews and those of British descent from participation.[140]

Yet, in the struggle for the soul of Afrikanerdom – in which the stakes were high and the debates bitter and intense – the Jews were not the central concern. Indeed, at the end of October 1939 the Board reported, with a palpable sense of relief, that preoccupation with the implications of war had meant less time to focus on matters Jewish.[141] But this did not mean the disappearance of the 'Jewish Question' in its entirety. Incidents continued to occur, and anti-Jewish propaganda spewed relentlessly from Radio Zeesen, the popular German shortwave station outside Berlin. The chief announcer was the South African-born former Natal schoolteacher, Dr Sidney Erik Holm ('Neef Holm' in the broadcasts), who encouraged opposition to a war he claimed was being fought at the behest of 'British-Jewish capitalism'.[142] The station's broadcasts – initially supportive of Malan, but increasingly geared to the radical right – highlighted alleged British cruelties and depicted Germany as championing the fight against the 'British-Jewish plutocracy'.[143] 'Night by night South Africa listens to my infamies – some distortions of the facts but mostly pure inventions,' wrote Smuts to his friend Margaret Gillet. 'I have not a shred of character left, and the question at the end often is why such a criminal is still allowed to live!'[144]

In this charged atmosphere, with its constant scares of fifth columns, espionage, sabotage and fears of invasion,[145] Smuts was deeply concerned about possible domestic upheaval. Neighbouring Portuguese East Africa (Mozambique) was teeming with intrigue, and intelligence estimates talked of 2000 German residents in the capital, Lourenço Marques.[146] It was not long before those deemed enemy aliens and subversives began to be interned, a situation blamed specifically on Jews by Die Transvaler and Strijdom.[147] The government also published information on surreptitious Nazi activities, including the shadowy role of German consuls, the Nazi Party's

Auslands–Organisation and individuals from Germany camouflaged as missionaries or businessmen.[148]

Jews were obviously perceived by some as manipulating events behind the scene. 'A certain British–Jewish influence, which played an important part in the fashioning of Fusion – a greater part than the people realise – is again at work,' said Nico van der Merwe, addressing a well-attended Orange Free State National Party rally in July 1940.[149] Malan, too, spoke of organised Jewry 'supported by Jews of the entire world'. A pamphlet issued by the Christian Republican movement, entitled 'Our Christian Republic', declared that Afrikaners alone consituted the South African nation and that Jews ought to return to Palestine.[150] Even Hertzog's inclusivity and tepid republicanism was regarded as appeasing the 'British–Jewish elements'.[151] By December 1940, Strijdom, Louw and Lieutenant Colonel Karel Rood (the MP for Vereeniging) were talking about a 'Jewish War' ascribed to 'Jewish capital'.[152] These ideas would persist.[153]

In the meantime, the Board's attention was drawn to other matters of Jewish concern. These included antisemitism in the Union Defence Force,[154] ongoing Nazi propaganda[155] and outrages against Jewish businesses.[156] The recently introduced mandatory use of the appellation 'Jew' in the government's standard legal summons document was also a cause for concern.[157] Hostile anti-Jewish letters were regularly published in the press,[158] allegations circulated that Jews were not volunteering for the army,[159] and a Jewish store was targeted in an explosion in Potchefstroom.[160] In Oudtshoorn, antisemitic graffiti and swastikas were painted across town, and attacks on Jewish-owned businesses ranged from stores being set alight to windows of buildings being shattered and shops pelted with rotten eggs.[161] The Board also reported that some of the large commercial banks and mining institutions offered very limited (if any) opportunities for Jews.[162]

RADICALISATION

South Africa's participation in the war had patently inflamed antisemitism and encouraged the exclusivist turn in Afrikaner nationalism. Underpinning the latter was a republican ideal, already evident at the time Malan broke away from Hertzog in 1934. Always a bone of contention within the National Party, the issue of republicanism was paramount at an *Economiese Volkskongres* (People's Economic Congress) held in Bloemfontein in early October 1939.[163] Fuelled by the Ossewatrek and led by the venerated *Volksvader* (People's father), the Reverend John Daniel Kestell, who had been a chaplain to the Orange Free State troops during the Anglo-Boer War, the congress was organised by the FAK to discuss the creation of a *Volksfond* (People's fund) to rehabilitate the Afrikaner.[164] About 1 000 delegates attended, constituting what Giliomee describes as 'a "Who's Who" of future Afrikaner entrepreneurs', together with politicians and academics.[165]

One of the leading presentations was that of Krissie Schumann, an admirer of Nazi Germany's economic policies, who implored Afrikaners to support one another and not rely on charity.[166] In another address, Wicus du Plessis argued that the Afrikaner had adopted the imported capitalist system with its 'British-Jewish mentality', including 'its cosmopolitan profiteering and cosmopolitan mode of life', which would have to be eradicated.[167] Albert Hertzog spoke with great passion about the evil of existing trade unions and the necessity to move away from the domination of 'harmful alien leaders', an obvious reference to Jewish communists, against whom he had railed for some time.[168] More practically, to further Afrikaner interests, the Economiese Volkskongres founded a *Reddingsdaadbond* (Rescue Act Alliance),[169] which soon played an important role in the upliftment of the Afrikaner, perceived by many to be the victim of an economy dominated by Jews and the English.[170] Afrikaners were urged to support one another and, to this end, an Afrikaner Business Guide was published, with a call to buy only from Afrikaner firms.[171] Three years later, a Military Intelligence report concluded that the Reddingsdaadbond did more 'to develop racialism, anti-Semitism and anti-British feelings' than the Ossewa-Brandwag (OB) could ever hope to do.[172]

The OB referred to was ostensibly a cultural organisation intent on keeping the spirit of Eeufees alive. Founded in early 1939, it claimed to be aloof from party politics, its aim being to unite all Afrikaners by building upon the Voortrekker centenary celebrations. 'People have joined in the thousands even before the official inauguration, and in some districts the whole population has joined as one man,' boasted the OB's first leader, the rather ineffectual Colonel JCC Laas.[173] 'It is good that we now also have an organisation which can safeguard certain interests of the volk,' asserted Bruckner de Villiers, a senior Nationalist and former MP for Stellenbosch. After all, the English had their societies, such as the Sons of England and the Empire League, to watch over their interests.[174]

The English press looked askance at the OB, which was described (with good reason) by the *Cape Argus* as 'exclusive and rather martial' and certainly not conducive to advancing a spirit of unity among white South Africans. The newspaper had no objection to the promotion of the social, cultural and economic welfare of Afrikanerdom, but warned that organisations such as the Broederbond and the OB (fully supported by the former) were aimed not at the cultural or social welfare of Afrikanerdom, but at its racial and political domination, regardless of the feelings or even the rights of minorities.[175] A 'secret military organisation masquerading as a "culture" movement' was the way Smuts described it.[176] Little wonder it became the focus of Union Defence Force and South African Police intelligence.[177] Within months of the OB's formation, both were monitoring its connections with the Blackshirts under Chris Havemann, a man seen to be closely tied to Nazi agents. In a secret communication to his senior, the Deputy Commissioner of Police reported that the OB leader had met regularly with his Blackshirt counterpart and others on the radical right and was seeking support from Nazis abroad. The Blackshirts had also met independently with Nazi officials in Pretoria.[178]

After some months in which the OB and the Blackshirts avoided public engagement, the veil was lifted and in July 1939 the latter was formally incorporated into the OB. With the Blackshirt focus on recruiting 'Christian-minded national Aryans', an element of Nazi-like excess was infused with *völkisch* nationalism that certainly went beyond conventional Afrikaner national or cultural objectives. It was not simply a republic that was being sought, but rather liberation from the 'international money power' – that is to say, liberation 'from all traders, usurers, exploiters and their paid henchmen who were alien to the volk'.[179]

South African Military Intelligence recognised the danger. 'The first essential is to impress upon the peaceful, law-abiding section of the community that the Ossewa-Brandwag is an enemy of the state,' noted a secret communication in June 1941. 'This fact had to be driven home to every section of the community throughout South Africa, white, coloured and native, and at the same time, as an anticipatory announcement it should be made clear that in the circumstances the government is compelled under the Emergency Regulations to take drastic action against the Ossewa-Brandwag and to declare them an unlawful, subversive organisation.'[180]

It was clear that the OB needed little encouragement when it came to marginalising the Jew.[181] Indeed, from the outset Jews were excluded from membership on the grounds that they were unable to identify with the main principles of the movement, notably the preservation of Boer traditions and the Afrikaans language.[182] It fact, it was envisaged that Jews would eventually be stripped of their civil rights.[183] Inspired by neo-Calvinism and National Socialism, and underpinned by a Christian-National *Volkseeneid* (People's unity), an anti-war stance, opposition to parliamentarianism and support for republicanism (all 'girded by anti-capitalist and anti-Semitic rhetoric'), it associated liberal individualism with 'British-Jewish capitalism'.[184] The 'money-power' had to be weakened, parasites made unwelcome, and the natural resources of the country used for the benefit of the *volk*.[185]

By mid-1940 the OB had 45 000 members in the Orange Free State alone, most of them farmers. A special effort had also been made to incorporate those less well-off Afrikaners in country towns and to encourage them to join the rural commandos. Rapid advances were also made in the western Transvaal and in the far north, where the OB could attract some 15 000 people to meetings. But the movement's greatest growth was in the larger centres, especially on the Witwatersrand, where white miners – seduced by *völkisch* allusions – were encouraged to replace class with national struggle. The OB also made inroads in the south, with one critic estimating that 50 per cent of Afrikaners in the western Cape Province had joined within the first year of the OB's existence. Even in Natal, with its dominant English-speaking population, the OB had 12 000 members at that time, concentrated mainly around Vryheid and Utrecht.[186]

Two astute and well-informed contemporary observers, Michael Roberts

and Alfred Trollip, attributed the success of the OB to the fact that the movement offered every member the chance of contributing to the unification
of the Afrikaner nation. Like all fascist movements, it provided a sense of
belonging, a chance to transcend the material world, and an opportunity
to deal with the anomie of failure. The organisation's cultural and recrea-
tional events offered an opportunity for Afrikaners to meet – often in trekker
dress – and develop a sense of shared culture and common heritage.[187] The
rapid growth of the OB was also encouraged by the success of Hitler's blitz-
krieg in the West, which saw Germany take control of Norway, Denmark,
the Low Countries and France by mid-1940. To be sure, many Afrikaners saw
their salvation in a Nazi victory.[188] By the second half of 1940, it is estimated
that the OB had 75 000 members, mostly male and including a number of
academics.[189] The OB also boasted the elite paramilitary *Stormjaers* (storm
troops).[190] With such widespread support, the talk of a Boer armed uprising
against the Smuts government assumed menacing proportions.

Malan was now under heavy pressure, constantly looking over his right
shoulder at the ever-expanding OB, even going so far as to tell a large
meeting in Stellenbosch that the National Party and OB shared the same
national feeling, friendship and wish to discard British democracy, which
was ruled by money. But despite having some empathy with National
Socialism in Germany, Malan was not a slavish follower, believing that
each country had to develop its own unique political system.[191] In fact, he
was deeply concerned about the OB's orientation and fearful that it was
becoming too powerful and would threaten to undermine the HNP. Following rumours in late 1940 that Laas was plotting to head a coup against
the Smuts government, Malan forced the OB leader to withdraw from the
leadership. In discussions with the OB, the so-called Cradock Agreement
was cobbled together in late October 1940 to demarcate the specific spheres
of action of the HNP and the OB. In essence, the HNP pledged to move
constitutionally towards a republic, while the OB agreed to refrain from
violence and to confine itself to non-political activities.[192]

The agreement promised at least some relief for Malan, who, in addition to his problems with the OB, was facing a growing internal challenge
from the *Nuwe Orde* (New Order, or NO). Founded by Oswald Pirow

to act as a National-Socialist pressure group within the HNP, the Nuwe Orde was potentially as threatening as the OB but much more sophisticated. It published a pamphlet, *Nuwe Orde vir Suid-Afrika* (New Order for South Africa), which fundamentally challenged inclusivity and presented plans for a 'South African national socialism'.[193] Issued in December 1940 and reprinted seven times, the pamphlet built on Otto du Plessis' *Die Nuwe Suid-Afrika – Die Rewolusie van die Twintigste Eeu* (The New South Africa – The Revolution of the Twentieth Century), which unashamedly extolled the corporate state and supported totalitarianism, while attacking liberal individualism and 'unnational' elements.[194] The state, stressed Pirow, should be founded on a Christian basis, which meant that 'anti-Christian' and even 'un-Christian elements' would play no part. It had to be national in the sense of unconditional commitment to the 'Fatherland', and those who did not ascribe to that principle would be regarded as foreigners. Actual power would rest with the 'established section' of the population, with the exception of everything 'anti-nation, unnational and unassimilable'.[195] The intent was to exclude Jews in particular from full participation in the envisaged body politic, although it was only a few years later that this was unequivocally spelt out.[196]

EXIT HERTZOG

From the outset, Hertzog had expressed serious concern about the drift towards Afrikaner exclusivism, apparent in the HNP draft constitution of 28 October 1940, which departed from his deeply held desire to unite English- and Afrikaans-speakers.[197] English-speakers, Jews and Coloureds were being driven away, warned Hertzog, while Afrikaners were being led into the 'desert' and to 'destruction'.[198] But Hertzog was outmanoeuvred by his conservative wing, which turned down his recommendations as a basis for discussion. Instead, an alternative 'Programme of Principles' – drawn up by the federal council of the HNP – was tabled and debated. Riddled with anti-Jewish assumptions, these principles spoke of developing 'our national life along Christian-National lines', with the unrealistic caveat that 'no infringement is intended upon the freedom of conscience and religion of the individual'. Membership of the party would be open to all who subscribed to its principles, as long as they understood that South Africa's interests had to be foremost regardless of race and country of origin.[199] The programme also formalised a number of clauses on which there had previously been agreement between the National Party and Hertzog's Volksparty, although the Coloured and Jewish questions remained a source of contention. The draft programme stated:

> That a serious Jewish problem exists in South Africa concerning which a declaration of policy may rightly be demanded is a fact which the Council must not lose sight of. In a more or less concealed form, this has been recognised by the State, namely, by the passing of the Immigration Quota Act of 1930 and of the Aliens Act in 1937. It is also not denied that the Jewish problem is a world problem which, gradually and especially since the outbreak of war, has assumed greater and more serious proportions; and that the inundation which has already occurred has created for South Africa a new and growing problem.

With this in mind, it was recommended that the following measures be adopted to deal with 'Immigration and the Jewish Question':

a) The repatriation of all 'illegal and undesirable' immigrants.
b) The Party favours in general the immigration of suitable and assimilable white European elements.
c) In view of South Africa's specific problems, the Party recommends the immediate cessation of all further immigration of Jews and, further, of all elements which cannot be assimilated by the South African nation or which are a hindrance or danger to society.
d) It further has in view: (i) exercise of stronger control over naturalisation and (ii) introduction of a vocational permit system for unnnaturalised foreigners as exists in many countries.
e) The Party wants to take all possible steps to fit South Africa's own original white population elements for earning a living in every sphere and to protect them against unfair competition.[200]

Besides its patent hostility towards Jewish immigration, sub-clause (e) opened the way for potential discrimination against Jews already living in South Africa and was very much in line with Verwoerd's call for proportional quotas in the professions.

The draft principles were adopted without amendment by the Cape Province and Orange Free State congresses of the HNP. The Transvaal congress, however, went a step further and expressly barred Jews from membership of the party (as had been the case before the merger) and urged the federal council to endeavour to persuade the party in the other provinces to follow suit.[201] Several other resolutions concerning Jews came under discussion, including restriction of their right to possess fixed property and obtain professional licences, as well as exclusion – along with Coloureds and Asiatics – from executive positions in the civil service or state-supported bodies.[202]

By this time Hertzog had moved into the political wilderness. Indeed, after his more inclusive draft recommendations had been rejected, he withdrew from politics, a broken man. His followers, mainly Orange Free Staters under Havenga, then formed the Afrikaner Party.[203] They numbered a mere 10 of the original 37 MPs who had followed Hertzog into opposition at the outbreak of war; the others remained with the HNP. From time to time, Hertzog would emerge to issue a public statement. Bitterly disappointed in the 'democratic system with its capitalist foundations and press influence', he told the head committee of the Afrikaner Party in October 1941 that he was in favour of National Socialism as a possible form of government for South Africa, but, according to his biographer, CM van den Heever, Hertzog had meant by this 'the adaptation of the old Free State model republic to modern conditions, using the best from recent European experiments', and not in alignment with Hitler's experiment.[204] In truth, however, disillusioned with democratic politics, Hertzog had always equivocated on the meaning of Nazism.[205] Two years later, though, a Military Intelligence report noted that the former Prime Minister had been fed Nazi propaganda – 'every word of which he apparently believed' – by his private secretary, Dr Jan Steyn, and by his son, Albert.[206]

This is confirmed by a revealing communication from William Clark. Writing in December 1938 to Sir Edward Harding, Undersecretary of State for Dominion Affairs, the British High Commissioner spoke of a meeting he had had with Hertzog regarding refugees and antisemitism in South Africa. The Prime Minister had candidly attributed worldwide anti-Jewish hostility to the fact that Jews 'do not become full citizens of the country of their adoption'. In South Africa, Hertzog told Clark, Jews always had an eye on the interests of international Jewry, and if its interests clashed with those of the Union, the former would always prevail. In his view, the British and the Dutch were in the process of becoming one Afrikaner people, but the Jews were 'racially of a different breed to either of the European races of South Africa'. Whereas Clark believed that anti-Jewish hostility was rooted in professional competition and related to Jewish 'practices or malpractices' in business, Hertzog simply blamed the hostility on the lack of business acumen among angry indebted Afrikaner farmers, adding that they disliked Jews no less than they had disliked their Scotch and English predecessors. According to Clark, Hertzog's explanation failed to account for urban hostility. More significantly, Hertzog, although shocked at Germany's treatment of Jews, believed that it was justified since Jews had been responsible for the collapse of the German front in 1918 and indeed for all Germany's misfortunes in the fifteen years before Hitler came to power.[207]

FLIRTING WITH FASCISM

In January 1941, less than three months after the signing of the Cradock Agreement, Malan helped secure the appointment of Hans van Rensburg as Commandant-General of the OB. For years, Nationalists had admired the clever and ambitious Orange Free State Administrator who, as we saw earlier, was an admirer of Nazi Germany and praised its *völkisch* brand of nationalism. Malan anticipated that Van Rensburg would be a more pliable leader than his predecessor. He had reason to be encouraged when, in his inaugural speech in Kroonstad, the new Commandant-General expressed concern about the state of Afrikanerdom and denied that he was an agent of any party or individual. Moreover, he made it clear that he wanted to suppress acts of violence. But he also hinted at an anti-democratic agenda in which he characterised democracy as a means to an end – the end being

Hans van Rensburg, Commandant-General of the Ossewa-Brandwag, on horseback.
(courtesy Museum Africa)

the health of the *volk*. 'If I serve my nation better by democratic action, I will do so, but if I have to choose between Afrikanerdom and democracy then there is no choice.'[208]

During this speech, Van Rensburg could not restrain himself from taking aim at a 'Sunday newspaper', edited by 'one Levi' whom he sarcastically referred to as 'a 110 per cent South African, with a grand Huguenot name'. Van Rensburg thought his audience should know what calumny this 'doughty Voortrekker from Lithuania' had written about their decision to join the OB. Following further uncomplimentary references to Nathan Levi, a Jew who edited *Die Volksblad*, Van Rensburg issued a blatant warning to the Jews: 'If I am to give advice, I would advise the Jewish stranger within our gates to control his language and spite towards our country's daughters and sons ... Just like the Government we wish to maintain law and order, but then this sort of vicious provocation of people who have solely a financial interest in the country must cease.' In conclusion, Van Rensburg appealed to Smuts not to attempt to suppress the movement by applying wartime emergency regulations.[209]

Van Rensburg's soft-pedalling on democracy as a value in itself was a harbinger of the OB's direction, and set the scene for the unravelling of the relationship between the HNP and the OB, both of which were being closely monitored by the government. Prominent Nationalists began to be purged from senior OB positions, while the movement's calls for a republic grew more strident in tandem with Hitler's military successes.[210] In May 1941, a Military Intelligence report noted that the OB were spreading 'their tentacles in every possible direction and wherever these tentacles touch they try to exercise a complete stranglehold on every sphere of life'. The report painted a horrific picture of a movement emulating the Nazis in every way:

> They never rest; they are always on duty. They are terrorising those who do not belong to their organisation, they are making people who will have nothing to do with them contribute to their funds by means of their system of economic blackmail, and what, from a psychological point of view, is even more important, they are creating an inferiority

complex and spirit of defeatism among those who wish to be loyal to the Government and whose sympathies are with the Allied armies.

The OB's influence, asserted the report, 'waxes and wanes to the rhythm of Nazi victories and setbacks', and warned that, unless drastic action was taken at the next general election, the organisation might well succeed in overthrowing the government and introducing Nazism to South Africa.[211]

The war proved to be deeply divisive. Soldiers and anti-war civilians clashed outside the Johannesburg City Hall in late January 1941. Police batons and tear gas became common at highly charged political meetings,[212] while the buildings of the anti-war newspapers *Die Transvaler* and *Die Vaderland* were damaged.[213] 'Every Tom, Dick and Harry, or Abe, Moses and Ikey, would not enjoy citizenship in a future republic', said Strijdom.[214] More seriously, in June 1941, Operation Weissdorn – an audacious plot hatched by German military intelligence, the Abwehr – saw Sidney Robey Leibbrandt (a policeman and Springbok boxer who had lived in Germany since 1936) land on the west coast with a plan to energise the OB and help foment a coup d'état. Van Rensburg, however, showed no interest and Leibbrandt, a potential rival to his leadership, was arrested on Christmas Eve 1941 and subsequently found guilty of high treason. All he had managed to do was recruit a few saboteurs who were happy to take a 'blood oath' to bring chaos to South Africa[215] – and neither Pirow nor Van Rensburg, noted an intelligence report, were losing any sleep over the affair.[216]

Following the appointment of Van Rensburg, Malan had successfully reorganised his provincial structures to limit OB power, and at a *Uniale-Kongres* (Congress of Representatives of all the Provinces) held in early June 1941 to promote Afrikaner unity and shape policies, Malan emerged as *volksleier* (leader of the people). Afrikaners were seemingly unanimous in their quest for an independent Christian-national republic, based not on 'British-Jewish' democracy or on totalitarian principles, but on the sound practices of the old republics.[217] A few weeks later, the OB controversially distributed 100000 copies of the Union Omsendbrief 1/41, a draft constitution for the future South Africa, as drawn up by the *Afrikanereenheidskomitee* (Afrikaner Unity Committee), which detailed a proposed republican constitution[218] and demonstrated very clearly the influence of the OB and its racist and anti-Jewish cast of mind. The document identified five racial groups: whites (both English- and Afrikaans-speakers), Jews, Africans, Coloureds and Indians. Citizenship would be restricted to the white group, who would act as state builders. As far as Jews were concerned, the document described them as unassimilable 'non-Europeans' or 'Semites' who constituted an alien minority race that would fall under the control of the white group. This policy was based on notions of blood, with Jews characterised as a pre-Asiatic race not sharing the blood of the English or Afrikaner.[219]

Malan was greatly angered by the distribution of the Union Omsend-brief 1/41, and it effectively scuttled the Cradock Agreement. But there were many individuals in the HNP who supported Van Rensburg: Nico Diederichs and Piet Meyer, chairman and secretary of the Broederbond, respectively, openly shared OB views and were in fact described by Albertus Geyer, the editor of *Die Burger*, as 'Nazis through and through'.[220] The Broederbond did its best to soothe tensions between the HNP and OB, but relations continued to deteriorate. By September 1941, Malan sensed that an armed uprising might be in the offing and he called on all members of the HNP to resign from the OB.[221] Smuts had also taken action against OB members and had prohibited them from holding civil service positions.

Encouraged by the German war effort, however, the OB went on the offensive and launched its own tabloid, *Die OB*, in November 1941. Although palpably sympathetic to European fascism, the publication focused essentially on Afrikaner politics. Unlike *Die Waarheid/The Truth*, it carried no outrageous antisemitic fantasies, but it did consistently advocate National Socialism while condemning 'British-Jewish-democracy' and 'British-Jewish-imperialism'. Only occasionally did it stress the 'Joodse Gevaar' (Jewish danger).[222] Implicitly and explicitly, however, Jews were not welcome citizens and were always negatively associated with capitalism, parliamentarianism and communism, which made them marginal to the national project.[223] Indeed, the first edition of *Die OB* linked Jews to Smuts and the war effort, while a speech by General FD du Toit noted 'organised Jewry' among those dividing the *volk*.[224]

On 13 January 1942, Malan, clearly on the defensive and needing to placate growing Afrikaner republican impulses, moved for the establishment of a free and independent republic in South Africa. A detailed draft republican constitution was released in which, *inter alia*, the 'surplus Jewish population', together with Indians, was defined as a problem.[225] At the same time, Malan told the House details of OB treachery, political assassination efforts and corrupt practices that had been revealed to him in a sworn affidavit by Johannes van der Walt, a well-known wrestler and general in the OB.[226]

Die Transvaler now went into attack mode, challenging in particular the OB's propaganda.[227] But Van Rensburg refused to be cowed and proudly confirmed the movement's fascist credentials. 'It is a movement that had assumed various names in various countries,' he maintained. 'In Italy it was called Fascism, in Germany National Socialism, in Spain Falangism, and in South Africa the Ossewa-Brandwag.'[228] Shortly thereafter, Van Rensburg issued a manifesto in which he declared that the state must be a 'Christian National Republican Authoritarian State' with a government strengthened by 'the elimination of nationally harmful and liberal attitudes and so-called democracy'. Unassimilable immigrants, including Jews, would be banned.[229] According to an intelligence report, Van Rensburg focused on the dangers of capitalism, imperialism and Jews.[230] It is hardly surprising that Geyer described Van Rensburg as a 'Führer' in the making.[231] Indeed, the OB leader even told two American interviewers that the Nationalists were 'wishy washy' on the Jews and that he would 'get rid of the Jews entirely'.[232]

With the war progressing well for Germany, Van Rensburg's OB posed a real problem for the HNP. Of particular concern to Malan was its militarism, built around newly created 'cells', which effectively functioned as a secret army geared to urban sabotage. Van Rensburg himself was the nominal head of the Stormjaers, the movement's 'shock troops',[233] which, according to George Cloete Visser, a senior security officer actively involved in combating the OB, were 'ready to storm forward as their militant action front when the time seemed ripe'.[234] Indeed, Van Rensburg's refusal to participate in the Leibbrandt operation did not mean that he had turned his back on Nazi Germany, as other connections were maintained. Malan, on the other hand, had made it absolutely clear that Nazism was foreign to both the character and traditions of the Afrikaners.[235] Fostering Afrikaner unity was his main goal, and to this end the focus of his enmity was Smuts, widely regarded by the HNP and radical right as the enemy of Afrikanerdom.[236] But the HNP and the OB had things in common; they shared a visceral anti-communism, for example, and, for some in the HNP, a hatred of Jews, as demonstrated by the utterances of Louw and Diederichs, among others. OB office-bearers, writes Marx, 'joined Louw and other anti-Semites in the HNP in insisting that there was a communist-Jewish-African conspiracy'.[237]

Some commentators have downplayed the OB's antisemitism because of the lack of explicit statements in official documents and policies.[238] But anti-Jewish rhetoric pervades the language of its adherents and publications. To the usual anti-Jewish calumny was added the warning that marriage to a Jew should not be condoned, as Jews were a product of the mixing of pre-Asiatic races with Semites, and their outlook could not be considered European, nor their patriotism taken for granted.[239] Van Rensburg himself epitomised the movement's antisemitic tone, identifying communism as a Jewish creation and characterising Jewish South Africans as a fifth column of world communism.[240] His speeches were redolent with anti-Jewish accusations and his rhetoric utilised Nazi-like ideas, among them *bloedsuiwerheid* (blood purity), *die bonde van die bloed* (the bonds of the blood) *and bloed en boden* (blood and soil).[241]

While the OB's rhetoric might have shared much with the language of the so-called Shirt movements of the mid-1930s, the movement was notably more exclusive, with no room for English-speakers. Authoritarian in outlook and structure, it stood for a state, modelled on the old Boer republics, that would embody the will of the Boer people in a classless society. Within that framework, writes Marx, the Jews were not only unassimilable 'but represented a fundamentally destructive element that was then given biological significance'.[242]

Another exponent of anti-Jewish exclusivism was Pirow's Nuwe Orde. Its 17 members, originally elected on a United Party ticket in 1938, now proudly advocated a variant of National Socialism and lauded fascism in Europe.[243] It was time, said the Nuwe Orde, to replace 'imperialist controlled, capitalistic dominated' parliamentary democracy. Republicanism remained at the centre of its policy, alongside hostility towards 'un-Christian' and 'unassimilable' elements. The entry of Jews or other unassimilable persons into the country would be forbidden.[244]

Pirow had finally emerged from the closet, revealing himself – in the words of the historian Gideon Shimoni – as 'a self-avowed anti-Semite'.[245] In fact, even when he was a member of the United Party, he had been ideologically associated with the radical right and had been taunted for years about his equivocal attitude to the 'Jewish Problem'. When dealing with these taunts, Pirow had consistently adumbrated United Party policy, claiming to be opposed to all, and not only Jewish, parasites.[246] But beneath his apparent even-handedness was an increasing admiration for fascism and a hatred of Jews. As Minister of Defence since 1933, he had been extremely dilatory on the subject of rearmament and had even been accused of softening the country up for invasion. On a visit to the 1936 Olympic Games in Berlin, he had expressed ferocious opposition to communism and assured Germans that South Africans did not look upon the Nazi regime as a future enemy.[247] Two years later in Europe, he rubbed shoulders with Hitler, Mussolini, Franco and Salazar, and a year after that – more precisely, three months after Hitler's occupation of Czechoslovakia – his daughter told London's *Daily Express* that 'the family felt more German than South African'.[248]

The fact that the Nuwe Orde was a fascist anti-Jewish movement was patently evident in a series of 'Lecture' documents for the movement's incoming cadres. These dealt in substantial detail with issues of state, governance, law, propaganda, family life, education, health and the economy. 'Jews, non-Europeans and definitely un-Christian elements' would be excluded from citizenship, which would be confined 'to bona fide South African National Socialists'. Governance was built around 'guilds' under an all-powerful president, who would rule over an organic state. A homogeneous 'Afrikaner National Socialist Fraternity' would be dominant and all 'anti-national, un-national and un-assimilable elements' would be excluded. A special 'Lecture' was devoted to 'The Problem of the Jew' where the matter was considered from three angles: citizenship, right of residence and the right to trade or exercise a profession. Regarding citizenship, a Nuwe Orde handbook laid down the requirements that identified Jews who had come to South Africa after the First World War and their children, whether born in South Africa or not, as prohibited immigrants with no citizenship rights. 'Right of residence' was to be granted to Jews who complied with residential or birth requirements, but they were nevertheless to remain aliens subject to good behaviour. As far as the right to trade or exercise a profession was concerned, a 'special court' could grant Jews who had no residential or citizenship rights the right to follow an occupation or trade subject to a quota, if the court was of the opinion that their special qualifications were in the interests of South Africa. Another recommendation focused on name changes that would have to be reversed and further changes forbidden.[249]

Although Pirow's views were taken seriously by the HNP, which did its best to accommodate the Nuwe Orde within its ranks, his ideology failed to establish a firm foothold in the wider Afrikaner political arena. While much of his message held an appeal for the disillusioned, its obvious symmetry with fascism and opposition to democracy did not sit well with many Afrikaners. Malan flatly told a Smithfield audience during a by-election that while seven-eighths of Pirow's Nuwe Orde had been incorporated in the HNP's 'Programme of Action', he did not agree with Pirow's call for an immediate break wth democracy.[250]

Verwoerd, too, identified the Nuwe Orde's opposition to democracy as a key difference between it and the HNP. At an HNP event in Brits, addressed by both Pirow and Verwoerd, Pirow declared his allegiance to the HNP and ascribed any differences between the two organisations to the meaning of 'National Socialism'. For the Nuwe Orde, it meant a distinctly Afrikaner National Socialism, which was an infinitely better political system than democracy. In Pirow's envisaged South African Nationalist Socialist state, all 'unnational or hostile' elements of the population were to be disenfranchised regardless of numbers, and he also gave his approval to an employment quota system, using Jews as an example. While Verwoerd expressed agreement with many of Pirow's ideas, especially his (and Malan's) long-advocated quota system, he objected to Pirow's wholesale rejection of democracy. But he was happy to oppose the 'British-Jewish' variety, although he felt that the term needed to be more closely defined to reconcile what he perceived to be a difference of terminology rather than of substance.[251]

Despite their common ground and the continuance of unity talks, tensions mounted between Malan and the Nuwe Orde. When a group of Afrikaner intellectuals released a statement against totalitarianism, the Pirowite dominee Charl du Toit accused them of siding with the 'mining-Jewish-Jingo-choir' who feared the danger posed to capitalism and alien domination by the Nuwe Orde.[252] Throughout 1941 the relationship deteriorated, with Malan rapidly losing patience with the Nuwe Orde's espousal of National Socialism and its repeated declarations that party politics and elections were outdated.[253] Matters finally reached a head in January 1942, when Pirow pulled his followers out of the HNP caucus, although he maintained they would remain in the party.[254]

It is quite apparent that, in its battles with Van Rensburg and Pirow, the HNP had been forced to adopt a more exclusivist stance, particularly before the tide of war in Europe turned against Hitler. This can be seen in a series of HNP publications, such as *Die Nuwe Suid Afrika – Die Revolusie van die Twintigste Eeu* by Otto du Plessis, the 'Enlightenment Secretary' of the HNP and editor of *Die Oosterlig*. Writing in 1940, Du Plessis made it clear that, under a new order, plutocrats, the disloyal press, unassimilable elements such as the Jews, groups who placed their own interests above those of the country, and organisations like the Freemasons would be targeted. South Africa, the publication noted, needed a 'social revolution', with the niceties of British parliamentarianism replaced by harsh discipline and the likely elimination of political parties.[255] Similarly, *Die Republikeinse Orde* (The Republican Order), published in 1941 by the federal council of the HNP, and with the unwieldy subtitle, *Party se Toekomsbeleid soos deur dr Malan uiteengesit* (Future Policy as Set Out by Dr Malan), condoned dictatorship (but not the German variety) and praised the political system of the old Boer republics.[256]

This was reinforced in Malan's *Draft for a Republic*, which envisaged independence from the British Empire or any other foreign power, and endorsed a political system 'based on the old South African Republics but adapted to modern conditions'.[257] Repeating many of the ideas he had expressed over the years, *Draft for a Republic* sought to protect the people against 'capitalists and parasitic exploitation' and 'hostile and unnational elements'.[258] Extensive powers would be accorded to the head of state, which, in the view of the *Eastern Province Herald*,

> borrowed from Mussolini for his group system, Goebbels on the matter of press and radio control and propaganda generally, Hitler in respect of the arbitrary, all-embracing, overriding powers of the Fuehrer-President, the notorious and blasphemous Rosenberg on the subject of racial seclusion and purity, Mr Pirow's New Order study groups for various odds and ends dictated by an earnest desire to steal their synthetic thunder.[259]

Malan was obviously pandering to the Nuwe Orde and OB constituencies.[260] Significantly, this turn to exclusivism was supported by young Afrikaners. The youth wing of the National Party, the *Nasionale Jeugbond* (National Youth Union), established in 1940, raised the 'Jewish Question', together with other racial issues demanding urgent attention.[261] In turn, the ANS, increasingly dominated by the OB, demonstrated its sympathy for Germany, as well as its anti-English and anti-Jewish attitudes,[262] while the Federation of Calvinist Student Unions expressed an exclusivist Christian-Nationalist ethnic mood when it included Jews with imperialists, Coloureds, natives and Indians as constituting threats to the Afrikaner.[263]

These developments were clearly understood by the Board's Gustav Saron who, in an attempt to gauge more accurately the public mood, toured the eastern Cape Province and Orange Free State from 14 October to 2 November 1942. He spoke to editors and academics, as well as to the Rotary Club in East London and the Sons of England in Port Elizabeth. 'There is no doubt', reported Saron, 'that during the past few years what had been a latent prejudice against Jews had become articulate, and was more noticeable than formerly in the English-speaking community.' He attributed this partly to Nazi and Nationalist antisemitic propaganda. But underlying the tension was economic competition, as well as the tendency in times of war to identify scapegoats.

Saron believed that improved counter-propaganda was necessary, and suggested the usefulness of informal talks with Afrikaners, or what he termed the 'huisbesoek' (house visits). Everybody he had met on his travels was emphatic that the Afrikaner was prepared to listen and to talk, and held no deep-rooted anti-Jewish feelings. But he advised Jews in turn to reflect upon their attitude towards the Afrikaner and to be careful, especially in towns, to avoid anti-Nationalist sentiment crystallising into an anti-Afrikaans feeling. Jewish-Afrikaner relations, he warned, had to be addressed and contact improved, and it was necessary to be aware of the fact that the Nationalists were presently concentrating on the 'Communist bogey' and were talking of 'Jewish Communism'.[264]

Saron was quite correct. The start of Anglo-Soviet cooperation following the German invasion of the Soviet Union in June 1941 had complicated what was an already problematic situation for those opposed to the war effort.[265] With the success of the Red Army in halting the German advance early in 1943, the communist bogey was assured a lively resonance. South Africa, argued the HNP and radical right, was paradoxically assisting Stalin and thus preparing the way for the destruction of white South Africa.[266]

Such propaganda built on a long history of hostility to Bolshevism (now exacerbated by looming labour activism), the arming of 'non-white' soldiers by Smuts and a radicalised and threatening black proletarianisation. The communist bogey was at once real and useful. Pirow had made it the cornerstone of his ideology and Louw never failed to alert the nation to the threat.[267] In a parliamentary motion in January 1943, he moved that the Communist Party of South Africa and all communist organisations be banned, that foreigners who propagated communism be deported and that those known to be communist be denied entry.[268] He followed this with a tirade against communism, highlighting its international Jewish connections, and accused Jews of being the movement's handmaidens. Apart from the subversive nature of communism and its allegiance to Moscow, it had no respect for the colour bar. This was the price South Africa had to pay for the alliance between Smuts and Stalin, he said, and unless action was taken the country would face grave problems.[269] A short while later, Malan went so far as to argue that it would be more acceptable for Britain and the United States to be defeated than to have a victorious Russia.[270]

Importantly, the Afrikaans churches had developed ambivalent feelings about the Jew. In March 1941, 26 out of the 29 delegates to the Federal Council of Churches (all Afrikaner churches) had accepted the recommendations of an earlier report that disclaimed the notion of Jews as the 'Chosen People'.[271] This certainly had theological implications and reflected currents of thought that should not be minimised.[272] Theology meant a great deal to the Afrikaner. With *völkisch* thought merging with neo-Kuyperianism, divisions could only be sharpened. Potchefstroom University's Hendrik Gerhardus Stoker, one of the *volk's* key Calvinist intellectuals, essentialised categories of race and applauded aspects of Nazism, including 'the organic unity of the people', which marginalised Jews. Although denying any charge of antisemitism, Stoker nevertheless identified Jews as *bloedvreemde* (foreigner by blood) and as such unassimilable. They would not enjoy full rights in an Afrikaner republic.[273]

These impulses had reinforced a sense of Afrikaner mission with Malan at the helm, but Van Rensburg's OB and Pirow's Nuwe Orde remained a constant threat. Like the OB and Nuwe Orde, Malan was happy to castigate 'British Imperialism' and similarly sought a Christian-National republic. But Malan harboured a respect for democracy and had no desire to marginalise the English. The changing fortunes of war had allowed him to gain ground at the expense of the OB, which had been further harmed by violence associated with Van Rensburg's storm troopers. Increasingly, Malan assumed the leadership of the *volk*. By early 1943 he had seen off the challenges from both the OB and the Nuwe Orde. Fascism in Europe was on the retreat and Pirow's doctrines had fallen on deaf ears. Malan was able to rebuff requests from Van Rensburg for an election pact in the anticipated general election, and, on 30 March 1943, Pirow announced that members of the Nuwe Orde would not stand as candidates in the upcoming election. Malan was now the undisputed *volksleier*.

CHAPTER SEVEN

ANTISEMITISM: WAXING AND WANING

'What I call the germ cells of Nazism have grown in number and virulence during the war. Wide sections of the community have become infected. The present position in this regard constitutes a grave danger to South Africa's national future.'
– Jan Hofmeyr, Hoernlé Memorial Lecture, 18 January 1945

'Anti-Semitism is only skin deep with the Nats. What they want is power, and as, with the exception of Eric Louw, their feelings are not very strong, they may consider a recantation of their present anti-Semitic policy, which in these days is pianissimo. The Boers argue that there is more anti-Semitism among the British than the Boers. I am not so certain that they are wrong.'
– Arthur Barlow, *Zionist Record*, 6 September 1946

'You must realise that we cannot overload the country with Jews ... It is not a question of politics. It is a question of objective policy. If we overload the country with Jews then we get an anti-Semitic movement ... I have always said that.'
– Jan Smuts, speech to parliament, 14 April 1947

'The outstanding feature of the scores of Nationalist speeches that have been made in the last two months is the complete absence of anti-Jewish utterances; there is a decided playing down of the Jewish issue.'
– 'Karl Lemeer', *Zionist Record*, 18 July 1947

GENERAL ELECTION, 1943

Six weeks prior to the announcement by Jan Smuts that a general election was to be held on 7 July 1943, *Die Transvaler* published a letter from a 'Grandson of Paul Kruger' in which this descendant of the Afrikaner icon blamed Jews for every war and accused them of exercising massive control through their shady connections with the Freemasons. The real purpose of his letter, however, was to gain confirmation of the HNP's commitment to 'destroying the Jewish presence in South Africa'.[1] In reply, and consistent as always, Hendrik Verwoerd, the editor, reiterated his long-standing views, first aired in his October 1937 inaugural op-ed:

> No Jew can become a member of the HNP and thus try to exercise influence on the policy of the state; all illegal and undesirable Jewish immigrants and those who entered the country after the government were warned that the people did not wish to receive them, will be repatriated, all further Jewish immigration must be immediately stopped; no further naturalisation of Jews must take place, and an occupational permit scheme must be introduced; an occupational quota must be instituted for the various population groups, in accordance with their size, so that the control of capital, or of trading, industrial or professional activities by a minority group (such as the Jews who would remain) would not be possible.[2]

Given such sentiments, it is hardly surprising that, at the Board's May congress, much time and effort was devoted to ways of combating antisemitism.[3] Yet curiously, in the build-up to the July poll, relatively little was heard of the 'Jewish Question'. Perhaps this could be partly explained by increasing revelations of Nazi atrocities. Such news had certainly reached South Africa by early 1942, and few could claim to be ignorant of the horrors. Mass meetings addressed by important non-Jewish figures were held at the end of December 1942, and in early January 1943 Christian clergymen collectively denounced Nazi barbarism.[4] Morris Kentridge's explicit reporting of two million Jews who had been 'treacherously murdered in the slaughterhouse of Poland' and a further 'five million in hourly peril of the same fate' served to further open people's eyes to the awful realities of Nazism.[5]

Malan would certainly have been aware of these developments and the mounting outrage, but his focus now was on domestic matters, particularly on ensuring an improved performance for the HNP in the upcoming general election.[6] Even though the Nuwe Orde and the OB had decided not to contest the election, and Klasie Havenga's Afrikaner Party planned to field only 12 Volkseenheid candidates, the HNP still faced an uphill battle.[7] Malan could appeal to Afrikaners by calling for separation from the British Crown and the creation of a Christian-National republic, while at the same time stressing his commitment to safeguarding 'white civilisation'. He could also attack the Smuts government for colluding with Soviet Russia, and blaming it for the economic hardships and rising prices of the war years. But it was difficult to compete with a wartime leader who, by then, was as internationally renowned as Field Marshal Smuts, and whose opening salvo of the campaign had been the claim that the United Party's first task 'was to win the war: next to win the peace'.[8] In essence this was a 'khaki election'.[9] And the war was going well.

By this stage, however, the 'Jewish Question' had lost much of its electoral traction. In fact, Malan made only a couple of references to it during the election campaign: an assertion that his prospects would have been enhanced if he too had 'Jewish money' backing him (a salvo obviously aimed at the United Party);[10] and an accusation that Jewish refugees were buying up the land and property of Afrikaners.[11] Effectively, for the rest of the campaign, the HNP leader was silent.[12] Even the HNP manifesto said little: all it promised was, *inter alia*, that if the *volk* were united behind it, the party would be able to solve South Africa's greatest and most critical issues, which included the colour and Jewish problems.[13]

In the run-up to the election, the HNP leader's quiescence did not stop the usual suspects from taking aim at the Jews. Eric Louw, for instance, warned a gathering that failure to deal with the Jews would push the Afrikaner completely out of trades and the professions.[14] Reinforcing these sentiments, *Die Burger*, by examining the number of trading licences issued to those with 'alien names', reminded readers of the preponderance of

Jews in business.[15] Other HNP candidates also accused Jews of shirking the war effort and of staying at home to fill their pockets while Gentiles shed their blood on the battlefield.[16] A circular issued by DJG van den Heever exhorted voters to 'Keep the Jew out of Parliament' – a reference to his opponent in the Pretoria City constituency, Adolf Davis.[17] According to the *Rand Daily Mail*, numerous anti-Jewish pamphlets were circulating,[18] one of which, issued by Albert van Hees, the HNP candidate for Fordsburg, contained a quotation from a forged anti-Christian speech ostensibly delivered by a fictitious Rabbi Reichhorn of Prague.[19]

Albertus Werth, now the HNP 'shadow' finance minister, warned his Worcester audience that if his party won the election they would settle accounts with Jews, who firstly would have to pay the war debt and then would be thrown out of the country.[20] In East London, Nico Smith, standing as an independent, announced that membership of the group he spoke for (The SA Producers' and Workers' Party) would be open only to Christians.[21] Jewish communists were also targeted at the hustings, with *Die Burger* warning its readers that, in the existing economic system, the communists could well defeat their Afrikaner opponents.[22] Only very occasionally did the immigration question surface. Eben Dönges, for example, claimed that the Jews who had come to the country in the 1920s had never been threatened, but the Jewish community had chosen to ignore warnings to discourage their coreligionists from coming to South Africa in the 1930s.[23]

Yet, in the overall context of the election, these outbursts were few and far between. Moreover, they hardly affected the outcome. Even the relentless antisemitic propaganda emanating from Radio Zeesen, which attached the label 'Jewish' to everybody and everything it disliked, made little difference.[24] The turning tide of war had, in fact, lessened the appeal of Nazism and this ensured an overwhelming election victory for Smuts, with the United Party winning 89 seats, the HNP 43, Labour 9, the Dominion Party 7 and independents 2. But, significantly, the number of Afrikaners voting for the government dropped from 40 to 32 per cent. The HNP's radical right rivals had been eliminated from parliament and, together with the absence of the OB, the election result meant that (in Hancock's words) the

HNP had 'freed themselves from the lunatic fringe of Afrikanerdom'. No one could now accuse them of 'being subservient to foreign ideologies or dependent upon a Hitler victory. They no longer had any rivals to fear in their bid to bring all Afrikaners into a common camp. They possessed a formidable organisation and a near-monopoly of the Afrikaner press. They possessed a future.'[25]

Fully behind Smuts, the Jewish community breathed a sigh of relief. In particular it took solace at the downgrading of the 'Jewish Question'.[26] But the Board's journal, *Jewish Affairs*, remained wary and unconvinced that the problem had disappeared. The HNP, it opined, had given no indication that it had departed one iota from its official programme with regard to Jews. 'In several Rand constituencies where there is a large Afrikaans proletarian population,' the editorial noted, 'Zeesen's anti-Semitic propaganda was obviously exploited for Party purposes. These and many other facts must be carefully weighed before any definite conclusions can be drawn in regard to the attitude of certain sections of the electorate towards anti-Semitism.'[27]

WIDENING THE BASE OF HOSTILITY

Although prominent figures on the radical right had been sidelined in the general election, Smuts remained concerned about residual anti-Jewish extremism and consistently objected to requests from the Board to allow an increase in Jewish immigration to South Africa. He feared this would accelerate hostility towards Jews, add to the pressure on Allied shipping, and exacerbate domestic food shortages.[28] These issues were explicitly spelled out at a meeting with the Board in September 1943, in which Smuts asserted that antisemitism had become a political issue and that to allow an influx of Jewish immigrants would be generous but very unwise, both for the Jews in South Africa and everyone else. 'We must protect our Jewish friends in this country,' added Smuts. 'South African Jewry should not sacrifice the long view for the sake of the present emergency.'[29]

Smuts' assessment was not unfounded. Despite the 'Jewish Question' having receded substantially into the background during the general election campaign, anti-Jewish hostility had not disappeared. Defamatory leaflets continued to be distributed; German-Jewish refugees were still being described as untrustworthy; jobs were sometimes advertised for 'Gentiles only';[30] and the Nationalist press maligned Jews with monotonous regularity, with accusations of shirking war service (despite the available recruitment and casualty figures), of profiteering, of dominating trade and of interfering with the running of the country.[31] Sidney Warren, the National Party MP for Swellendam, told the House that although it wasn't the party's intention to harm the Jews, it remained opposed to further Jewish immigration.[32] Blackie Swart went even further, blaming the Jews for the 'racialism' between Afrikaans- and English-speakers: 'They foster racialism for their own gain, because, while we quarrel, they are making money out of us.'[33] In December 1944, *Die OB* ran a particularly hostile article, 'The Jewish Dilemma', in which it promised that the end of Hitler would not be the end of antisemitism.[34] In other articles *Die OB* depicted Jews as being dishonest in land trading[35] and of profiting from the war.[36] In particular, *Die OB* fulminated against '*Brits-Joodse Kapitalisme*' (British-Jewish Capitalism).[37]

Accusations of Jewish subversion were also included in the report of a Dutch Reformed Church commission set up in 1943 to reflect on the origins and consequences of antisemitism and what attitude the Church should adopt. The tone of the report – apparently the work of a single individual – with its accusations that Jews were associated with secret organisations, communism and domination, embarrassed the federal council of the Dutch Reformed Church, which agreed to accept the outcome '*vir kennisgewing*' (for general information) only and called for another report.[38] But the very idea of holding an inquiry into the origins of antisemitism had raised the ire of Israel Abrahams, the spiritual leader of the Cape Town Hebrew Congregation. In an open letter, the British-born rabbi acknowledged that there were 'black sheep' among the Jews, but believed there should be love and brotherhood between Jew and Christian, both of whom stood together against paganism: 'Will not the Dutch Reformed Church, recalling its own suffering and oppression in bygone days, remembering its great tradition of passionate yearning for justice and freedom, also speak the word of loving-kindness that will help to bring healing to the wounded spirit of the people from whose loins sprang the Christian Saviour, and from whose soul flowed the Bible's divine stream of religious thought and precept?'[39]

Clearly Abrahams recognised the importance of the Dutch Reformed Church and its potential influence in reducing or exacerbating tensions between Jews and Afrikaners. A vivid illustration of these tensions was evident in Oudtshoorn where, a year after two Jewish incumbents had been defeated by Afrikaners in the municipal elections of September 1943,[40] a prominent local Jew, Benny Gillis, saw his tobacco factory razed to the ground. 'The saboteurs,' writes the historian Daniel Coetzee, 'had been so keen to destroy Gillis' business, that they had rendered the only fire engine in the town inoperable beforehand.'[41] A short while later, Oudtshoorn's Jewish cemetery was desecrated with swastikas painted on gravestones.[42] The act, noted the *Cape Times*, was an 'expression of the poisonous racialism so consistently propagated by Dr van Rensburg and other gentlemen of the opposition'.[43]

The *Cape Times* must have had Eric Louw in mind among those 'gentlemen of the opposition'. At every opportunity he raised the 'Jewish Question'. Immigration should be permitted only to persons 'who are not members of the Jewish race', he told parliament in response to a motion advocating the adoption of a policy of large-scale European immigration, submitted in early 1944 by Frank Acutt, the Dominion Party's MP for Durban Musgrave. The Jewish population, Louw asserted, was already too large, and when numbers exceeded a certain proportion of the total population, a 'Jewish Question' ensued. Louw then proceeded to warn the House – quite dishonestly – that the government was planning for a post-war increase in Jewish immigration.[44] More than that, he accused Jews of being loyal to the nation only when things went well. When there were difficulties, he maintained, 'they shake the country's dust off their feet … then make a fresh start in some other country and there they are again just as loyal until things go wrong there'.[45] Although those supporting increased immigration made no specific mention of Jews during the parliamentary debate, it was apparent – through subtle and not so subtle innuendo – that Jews would not be welcome. For example, in supporting Acutt's call for white immigration, Charles Neate, the Dominion Party MP for Natal South Coast, made it clear that the new immigrants would have to be of 'the right type' and not people with 'ideas foreign to our conditions' and certainly not 'traders'.[46]

This coded language echoed calls made in the 1920s, when the English-language press – flushed with nativist impulses – had led a crusade against the influx of eastern European Jewish immigrants.[47] Indeed, Louw soon dropped all pretences when he told the House that the 'Jewish Question' had to be tackled and that Jews had to appreciate that they themselves had created the problem by encouraging Jewish immigration. Unfortunately Jews denied this, he asserted.[48]

The parliamentary debate that revealed widespread hostility towards Jews – or at least opposition to further Jewish immigration – was not restricted to the Afrikaner. To be sure, Louw was not far off the mark when he spoke of a growing anxiety among some United Party English-speaking sup-porters about the 'Jewish Question' and claimed, some months later, when addressing a Durban audience, that the HNP would gain 100 000 votes from English-speakers on its anti-Jewish platform alone.[49] Only two months ear-lier Major Robin Stratford, the United Party MP for Parktown, identified the 'Jewish Question' as threatening to divide his party.[50] Canon Vernon Inman, too, raised the issue of English hostility at a Church of England Synod held at Pietermaritzburg in November 1944, when he introduced a resolution that expressed 'grave disquiet at the apparent increase of racial antagonism and prejudice in the present economic and social life of South Africa', and pledged the support of the Church to 'all Christians and others who seek to combat this evil'. Inman pointed out that historically there had been no hostility towards Jews in Durban, but that had changed, and indeed in the last municipal election one seat was very largely won on the strength of antisemitic propaganda.[51]

Inman's observations were confirmed by Major General Frank Theron, who, following a brief visit to the country from the Mediterranean theatre of war, expressed alarm over the growing intolerance in South Africa towards 'the Jews, Indians, Coloureds and Natives'.[52] Similar disquiet emerged in a report, 'What the Soldier Thinks', based on a May 1944 survey of 7 000 Union Defence Force soldiers conducted by Ernst Gideon Malherbe, Director of Military Intelligence and Army Education. The report noted that both English and Afrikaner soldiers had succumbed to the anti-Jewish virus.[53] As principal of Natal University College after the war, Malherbe elaborated on his findings when he delivered the Hoernlé Memorial Lecture in 1946.[54] Here he attributed the rise in antisemitism to the cumulative impact of powerful anti-Jewish propaganda, which had thrust the Jew to the forefront of people's consciousness. As an examiner in the public service entrance examination, Malherbe had found participants massively overestimated the number of Jews in South Africa. Most frequently, he noted, the figure submitted was around 20 per cent of the total population, when in fact the Jews comprised a little over one per cent.[55]

Further research by Simon Herman, a University of the Witwatersrand social psychologist, confirmed this trend. In an opinion survey of politicians, journalists, trade unionists, academics, clergymen and army officers conducted in late 1944, Herman demonstrated a rising tide of overt antisemitism among English-speaking whites. 'Previously you heard occasional anti-Jewish remarks; now it is a tirade,' explained one of the interviewees. Jews were accused by both Afrikaans- and English-speaking whites of disproportionate economic and professional representation; of seeking 'to control everything'; of being 'loud and ostentatious'; and of shirking military service or taking 'base jobs in the army'. Moreover, statements such as 'most communists are Jews' and 'Jewish communists agitate among natives' were frequently heard. Afrikaans-speaking interviewees felt that Jewish 'friendship for Afrikaners [was] opportunistic' and that they were not at all interested in Afrikaner culture.[56]

No doubt sensing the political implications of this anti-Jewish mood among English-speakers, a group of senators and parliamentarians – including four cabinet ministers – representing Witwatersrand and Pretoria constituencies, signed a widely publicised document in September 1944 that condemned the increase in antisemitism among people who had previously dissociated themselves from the campaign organised by the opposition and its supporters: 'We feel that anti-Semitism is one of the chief weapons of intolerance and racial division in our country and that those who lend themselves to it, however specious their reasons for such attitude may be, are in effect playing the same game of the Nazis and of Nazi-minded elements in the Union.'[57]

English hostility would mount as Zionist extremists – in their struggle for an independent state – targeted British troops in Palestine. To be sure, following the murder of two British soldiers in late July 1947, the *Zionist Record* referred to 'the flames of anti-Semitism blazing high in South Africa'.[58] This specific anger, however, was short-lived and never really developed beyond irate letters to the press.[59]

PERSISTENT HATRED

Although the base of anti-Jewish hostility had widened to include English-speakers, it was the Afrikaners who remained most concerned about the 'Jewish Question'. Newly urbanised, less educated and less skilled than their English counterparts, they remained anxious about further Jewish immigration and the disproportionate presence of Jews in commerce and the professions. In its deliberations of 1944, the federal council of the HNP (self-defined as the voice of Afrikanerdom) specifically addressed the issue and reiterated (with marginal language changes) the draft 'Programme of Principles' outlined four years earlier. Once again Jewish immigration would be halted, naturalisation strictly controlled, occupational permits introduced for unnaturalised aliens, and steps taken 'to equip the original elements of its own European population with the means for making a livelihood and to protect them against unreasonable competition'.[60]

Clearly the HNP remained focused on the Jewish presence, and, as usual, Louw used every opportunity to drive home an anti-Jewish message that stressed supposed Jewish domination of the wholesale and retail trade, commerce and the professions. To bolster his argument, he referred to an article by AR Ravenscroft, an official of the Department of Census and Statistics, that demonstrated the disproportionate number of Jews in the medical profession.[61] This was an ongoing issue: as early as 1939, the *Report of the Commission on Medical Training in South Africa* (chaired by University of Pretoria Principal MC Botha) had revealed a low proportion of Afrikaans students studying medicine compared to the high number of Jewish medical students. This was described as a highly unsatisfactory state of affairs and one that needed to be redressed.[62] Three years later, the Transvaal Provincial

Secretary, Herbert Pentz, published his own report, entitled 'A Scheme of Free Hospitalisation', in which he argued that the disproportionate number of Jews in the medical profession could be offset by the introduction of a scholarship system for Jewish students aimed at diverting them to other professions and occupations. Without such corrective action, said Pentz, there was a possibility that Jewish doctors would dominate the profession, resulting in 'grave trouble' for Jews themselves.[63]

Pentz was articulating the Verwoerdian line expressed unrelentingly in *Die Transvaler* at this time: only by limiting Jewish options in the professions could Afrikaners advance, since Jews were the cause of the Afrikaners' plight.[64] The Pentz report subsequently mutated into the 'Report of the Committee on the Admission of Students to the Medical Schools in South Africa', which advocated new admission criteria.[65] Some time later, MC Botha convened a meeting of major Afrikaner organisations to discuss the worrying trend of Jewish preponderance in medical faculties.[66] *Die Transvaler* warned that the overwhelming presence of Jews in the South African medical profession was already generating a great amount of opposition among English- and Afrikaans-speakers, and recommended the introduction of a quota principle for medical training and state medical service. In addition, the newspaper warned that Jewish and Christian doctors should attend solely to their own coreligionists, as their work demanded 'not only knowledge of the body, but also contact with the soul'.[67] *Die Transvaler* even objected to Jewish protests against the policy of not allowing 'non-whites' to attend white postmortems. 'Isn't it a fact that postmortems for "scientific" purposes are not permitted on Jews?' it asked. 'In other words, those students who belong to a racial group, whose dead are not affected, may not be allowed to determine a policy which will permit non-Europeans to be present when Christian bodies, male as well as female, are placed under the knife.'[68]

It was not only professional quotas that were the focus of anti-Jewish hostility at that time. Louw also accused Jews of involvement in black market activities, and of being responsible for housing shortages and even the pilfering of cement.[69] In February 1945, he told the House that Jews were profiting from the spoils of war – making money out of war contracts, the black market and profiteering. Ignoring evidence to the contrary, he also warned that an alarming number of Jews were still entering the Union on temporary permits.[70]

Louw was enthusiastically supported by the Nationalist press, which routinely lambasted Jews and targeted them for discrimination.[71] An 'unalterably narrow chauvinistic group' was the way *Die Volksblad* described them.[72] Also disturbing was the tone of the revised report of the 1943 Dutch Reformed Church commission on the question of antisemitism. While less virulent than the earlier submission, the commission nevertheless concluded that there had to be reasonable grounds for the worldwide persecution of the Jews and that the fault lay with the victims themselves rather than with the persecutors. The following ambivalent resolutions proposed by the Reverend JJ Muller of Villiersdorp were carried:

- The Council of the Churches feels that the solution of the problem of anti-Semitism (in the national as well as the international sense) is first of all a matter for the authority of the State and the Church.

- In so far as it falls into the sphere of the Church, it must, above all, be seen as a spiritual problem, the solution of which lies in untiring efforts to Christianise the Jewish people and to carry the principles of Christ into the Jewish way of life and world of ideas.

- As regards the attitude of our Christian people and churches towards the Semitic race groups, the Church expects no other attitude from its members than that of love of one's fellowman, justice, truth and *verdraagsaamsheid* [forbearance], in brief, the attitude of Jesus Christ.

- For these reasons the Church disapproves of un-Christian persecution of other racial groups in any form, but at the same time and just as much as it recognises the right of our volk's endeavour to be itself and to protect its interests in every sphere of life.[73]

The Church's disapproval of outright persecution of Jews did not inhibit Hitler's South African supporters from airing their venomous hostility towards Jews. The radical right felt quite at liberty to brazenly trumpet anti-Jewish views. RK Rudman, now head of the Boerenasie movement, had linked up with Pirow's Nuwe Orde,[74] while Louis Weichardt had founded the *SA Nasionale-Sosialistiese Bond* (SA National Socialist Union, or SANSB) soon after he had broken away from the HNP in the wake of the Cradock Agreement of 1940.[75] The Greyshirts were retained as a movement within the SANSB, and citizenship in the envisaged organic corporate nation state would be limited to Aryans, with Afrikaans as the sole official language. The basis of its foreign policy was defined as collaboration with other totalitarian states related to Afrikaners by ties of blood and culture.[76]

Primarily, however, Weichardt wanted to preserve the *volk*. He was now willing to jettison foreign ideologies and engage more directly with Afrikaner politics. Initially he had sought, unsuccessfully, to establish a triumvirate incorporating JBM Hertzog, Oswald Pirow and the SANSB, but when that failed his aim shifted to the unification of all nationalist groups in a bid to confront the 'growing totalitarianism' of the Smuts government. Weichardt, however, was by then very much an outsider – at best a 'useful idiot' for the HNP. Probably sensing this, he renounced party politics in 1942 and with it any electoral support he might have added to the HNP. Two years later, though, the SANSB did lend its support to Malan in the Wakkerstroom by-election, in which the HNP wrested the seat from the United Party. A couple of months later, Weichardt resurfaced with an announcement of a possible merger of the SANSB and the Nuwe Orde. Shortly after this, however, he was interned and languished in confinement – at first with German internees in South West Africa and thereafter in Koffiefontein[77] – until February 1946, leaving his deputy, Theunis Stoffberg, to continue the SANSB struggle from Vryheid in Natal.[78]

In the final stages of the war, it was clear that the anticipated defeat of Hitler had not quenched the fires of the radical right. The battle against fascism on the home front was far from over, warned Gustav Saron. Antisemitism would remain alive in South Africa as long as there were still groups avowing allegiance to National Socialism who could use the 'Jewish Question' to divert attention from the very real social and economic problems facing South Africa.[79] Saron's fears were well founded. The OB proceeded to honour those South Africans interned for pro-Nazi activities during the war and treated the revelations of the horrors of the concentration camps as propagandist lies.[80] Not only the OB, but also *Die Transvaler* and a Stellenbosch University student newspaper, *Die Matie*, refuted the nature and scale of Nazi atrocities and laid the blame instead on those who had failed to exterminate the Russian anti-Christ.[81] In parliament, Louw also relativised the Jewish tragedy by describing Russian atrocities as putting 'Buchenwald in the shade' and equating the suffering of the Anglo-Boer War concentration camp victims with the victims of Nazism.[82]

The trial of Nazi war criminals at Nuremberg shortly after the war was similarly belittled in the Nationalist and radical right press. *Die Vaderland*, for instance, referred to the trial as 'the ugliest caricature which has yet been made in the history of civilisation of the principle of the administration of justice'.[83] *Die OB* called the procedure a mockery of Christian values,[84] and the product of British jealousy driven by Jewish money,[85] while the dropping of the atomic bomb, according to *Die Kerkbode*, had so dirtied the hands of the Allies that they were in no position to judge the misdemeanours of others.[86] Hans van Rensburg likewise complained that it was ironic that those who had dropped the atomic bomb were the same people who had sent such prominent Nazis as Goering, Keitel and Jodl to the gallows and enabled 'Russian Satanism' to find a place in eastern Europe.[87] Oswald Pirow, too, showed no remorse and shortly after the war boasted that he was an antisemite: 'I firmly believe that if every Jew could vanish from the earth, the world as a whole would be a much better place.'[88] Two years later his mouthpiece, *Die Nuwe Orde,* also ridiculed the 'Nuremberg Court' and, under the headline 'In Memory of the Martyrs of Nuremberg', published a full-page spread of the names of the convicted Nazis surrounded by a black border.[89] Other publications, such as *Die Matie* and the *New Era* – the latter a short-lived Nationalist English-language mouthpiece introduced in 1945 specifically to attract English-speaking voters – shared much with the radical right, including attacks on Allied aggression, the use of the atomic bomb and Russian methods of liquidating opposition.[90] In the same vein, during an acrimonious debate on the expulsion of some German internees from South Africa, Karl Bremer told parliament that history would judge South Africa harshly on these actions rather than on 'the ill-treatment of Jews in Germany'.[91]

WANING HOSTILITY AND REALIGNMENTS

As the wartime alliance between the Western Allies and the Soviet Union began to unravel, signalling the advent of the Cold War, the anti-communist crusade became more strident.[92] Signs of this had been evident from the moment Operation Barbarossa – the German invasion of the Soviet Union – was launched in June 1941. At the time, Malan issued a formal statement that rehashed old arguments and claimed that 'Bolshevism has long had its eye on South Africa':

> It wants to initiate a Bolshevist revolution here and therefore seeks its support mostly with the non-white elements. Under the leadership of Communist Jews it has nestled itself into a number of our trade unions. It does not acknowledge the colour bar in any sphere, and where it is legally possible, it agitates tirelessly – with the vehement incitement of the non-whites – to remove it. It does not know any patriotism. It is the sworn enemy of all religion, not least of Christianity. In short, Bolshevism is the negation of everything Afrikanerdom has stood for and fought for, suffered for and died for, for generations.[93]

Particularly disturbing was Malan's association of Jews with Bolshevism, and linking them to the *swart gevaar* (black danger). Such sentiments intensified and dominated radical right and Nationalist rhetoric as the war progressed.[94] As was to be expected, Louw had published an anti-communist booklet in 1943,[95] and *Die OB* regularly targeted the communist threat – characterised as a largely Jewish evil,[96] hell-bent on a proletarian revolution at the behest of the black population.[97] An ANS meeting at Stellenbosch similarly raised concerns about communism as well as Jewish and English trade unionism.[98] In the closing months of the war, Bremer – a long-time anti-communist crusader – issued a warning about the prospect of a 'bloody revolution'. Communism threatened the existence of South Africa and would surpass the 'barbarism of the native'.[99] Shortly after the war ended, Malan called on South Africans to stand together as a 'white bloc against the menace of communism', which threatened the white race and everything South Africans held dear.[100] Playing on these fears, *Die OB* persisted in identifying a nexus between Jews and communism, claiming that with the exception of the Chief Secretary of the Communist Party, who was an African, all the other Bolshevik leaders were Jews.[101] 'Too long have Jewish Communists been allowed a free home in our country,' exclaimed Louw when advocating the closure of communist newspapers soon after the war.[102]

In addition to the communist canard, Jews were also targeted as liberals threatening to undermine South Africa's racial order. Jewish university students in particular were identified as subversive, an accusation built on mounting campaigns against segregation at English-language universities.[103] The Springbok Legion, a liberal pressure group founded during the war to safeguard the interests of discharged servicemen, was another target. According to the HNP and *Die OB*, the movement was riddled with communists.[104] Its members were described by Van Rensburg as 'spiritual fellow travellers' of the Communist Party,[105] and in September 1945 the Legion was the subject of attack at an anti-communist congress organised by the HNP.[106] By now, left and right were clashing regularly at the City Hall in Johannesburg, with the HNP blaming Jews for the disturbances.[107]

Yet despite name-calling and the persistent labelling of Jews as liberal and communist subversives, there were indications that the HNP wanted to reduce the anti-Jewish temperature as part of a broader strategy to attract English-speaking support. Already in late 1944, a Volkskongres organised by the FAK and attended by 200 church and cultural organisations had ignored the 'Jewish Question' and addressed only issues concerning Africans, Coloureds and Indians.[108] In the closing months of the war, Bremer had appealed passionately for white unity and a 'new beginning'. Although Jews were not mentioned in the speech, many interpreted his words as a sign that wartime divisions would be laid to rest and that hostility towards Jews would be relegated to the dustbin of history.[109] In efforts to foster cooperation between Afrikaners and pro-war English-speakers, the *New Era* appeared to lead the way, doing its best to rationalise the HNP's anti-war stance as a product of Afrikaner history and not in any way indicative of support for Nazism or Hitler.[110]

However, Louw dashed any potential for a significant change of policy when he made it absolutely clear that the HNP had no intention whatsoever of modifying its approach to the 'Jewish Question'. As a member of the Cape head committee of the National Party and the party's federal council, he categorically maintained he had not relinquished his belief in the seriousness of the 'Jewish problem' and trotted out his well-used accusations of 'unassimilable Jews' taking control of trade, industries and the professions and extending that control on a daily basis.[111] Only a week later, an editorial in the *New Era* confirmed Louw's stance, but, in an attempt to soften Louw's message, denied it was hatred of the Jews that motivated the HNP's position. After all, Afrikaners had got on very well with Jews historically, and many among them could point to experiencing Jewish kindness and help, while many Jews in turn had been befriended and assisted by Afrikaners. However, because Jews were loyal nationalists only as far as their own people were concerned, the Nationalists in South Africa regarded them as a 'separate nation of unassimilable people'.[112] Malan also weighed in, blaming the 'mighty Jewish-Capitalist Press' for holding 'the English-speaking section in its iron claws' in what he described as 'a spiritual tyranny'.[113] Here was a transparent attempt to capture English-speaking voters.

It was a confusing picture. But Morris Kentridge sensed a new mood among Nationalists and went so far as to suggest that the parliamentary session of 1945 had seen the opposition soft-pedalling on the 'Jewish Question'. The best illustration of this, he pointed out, was when Louw had spoken for half an hour on immigration without once mentioning the word 'Jew'![114] Yet despite what appeared to be fewer anti-Jewish attacks, die-hard antisemites persisted with their crass accusations. Louw, for one, continued to question Jewish loyalty,[115] while Gerhard Bekker, the MP for Cradock, castigated Jews for failing to repay the Afrikaner for his hospitality, and accused them of oppressing others when 'they were masters'.[116] But it was in discussions concerning the long-standing bugbear of Jewish immigration that anti-Jewish hatred was most manifest. Stephanus le Roux, for instance, warned against a new post-war influx of Jews, which he believed would generate both English and Afrikaner hostility.[117] *Die Kerkbode*, too, inveighed against the influx of 'unassimilable immigrants', focusing this time though on Roman Catholics.[118] Even Smuts told parliament that South Africa could not overload the country with Jews.[119]

Wilhelmus Brink, the MP for Christiana, used the immigration debate to rehash old canards; he pursued the association of Jews with communism, even suggesting that Lenin was Jewish, and sarcastically illustrated the preponderance of Jews in South Africa by referring to the Cape Town suburb of Vredehoek as 'Jodehoek', Muizenberg as 'Jewsenberg' and Johannesburg as 'Jewburg'. Moreover, claimed Brink, Jews were 'Orientals' and South Africans wanted immigrants of 'pure Nordic blood' only.[120] Even more outrageous was Malan's reaction to the government's decision to deport a few pro-Nazi Germans from South West Africa, when he blamed local Jews for wishing to exact revenge by engineering their return to a country where mass murder was being committed against the German people. Betraying his theological background, the HNP leader told the House that the Jews had committed 'a crime at Golgotha' more than 1900 years ago 'and to this day it still clings to them, and the prophecy "Thy house shall be desolate", is coming true today. Every nation bears the consequences of its own sins,' he warned, and South Africa would have to bear the consequences of its actions towards these German nationals.[121]

At the more extreme end of the anti-Jewish spectrum, Rudman advertised subscriptions for *The Jewish War of Survival* by British fascist Arnold Leese. Accompanying the advertisement for this notorious anti-Jewish tract (falsely based on Jewish sources) were choice quotations blaming the war on the Jews.[122] Several other antisemitic books were circulated, most of them imported from abroad and some published by the British Fascist organisation. The *Protocols of the Elders of Zion* was also republished and included an Afrikaans version.[123] Yet despite this continuing anti-Jewish focus, the radical right was in reality becoming a spent force. The OB was in the process of imploding and Pirow lurked on the fringes of South African politics. He was now openly associated with Oswald Mosley, the discredited leader of the British Union of Fascists, sharing his dreams of a worldwide fascist revival. But Pirow's star had waned. Van Rensburg, too, was very much out in the cold and looked to Havenga for succour.[124] Increasingly Malan consolidated his position as the undisputed leader of Afrikanerdom.

LOUW VERSUS MALAN

Having moved to solidify his position as *volksleier*, Malan still faced divisions within the HNP with regard to Jewish issues. These came to the surface early in 1947 when Joseph Nossel, a Cape Town Jew sympathetic to the HNP, informed Malan that in his view many Jews would join the HNP if it declared its opposition to antisemitism and opened its membership to Jews.[125] No doubt with the next general election in mind, Malan responded by saying (as he had so often done) that he was 'not against the Jews any more than I am against the members of any race as such'. Thereafter he resurrected the 'saturation' argument and expressed his fear that a further influx of Jews would inflame hostility. The 'Jewish Question', he believed, was an international problem that had to be addressed sympathetically. With regard to Jewish exclusion from party membership in the Transvaal, Malan explained to Nossel that the HNP's federal structure precluded interference with the provinces.[126]

Soon after Nossel chose to publicise his exchange with Malan, an angry Louw – sensing a possible softening of HNP policy towards Jews – went on the offensive, stating in parliament that Jewish immigration would cease when the HNP assumed the reins of government. To bolster his argument, he pointed to widespread English antisemitism, using by way of example restrictions placed on Jewish membership of the Sons of England society.[127] A few days later, Malan affirmed the HNP's opposition to Jewish immigration, but was silent on its policies towards Jews in general.[128] It was potentially a very divisive situation. In a parliamentary intervention, Louw did his best to scoff at any notion that the party was considering a *toenadering* (getting closer) with the Jews. 'Let me give the House the assurance that there has been no modification of their policy in that respect whatsoever.' Louw stated unequivocally that the federal council's 1944 'Programme of Action and Principles' remained the policy of the party. In the event that anyone was unfamiliar with these, Louw spelt out the full details.[129] A short while later he once again assured the House that the HNP would discriminate against Jews. Nossel, he suggested, should speak to the Prime Minister again, as he had publicly admitted to recognising the danger of Jewish immigration.[130]

A few months later, another Jew, Cape Town municipal councillor Isaac Frank, reopened the question of Jewish membership in the HNP. In a letter to Malan, Senator Bruckner de Villiers, Havenga and Bremer, Frank again stated that no Jew would join the HNP until its ban on Jewish membership in all provinces was lifted. Frank requested – and received – clarification from all four on the party's position vis-à-vis Jews: Malan reiterated his desire not to discriminate against Jews as Jews; Havenga indicated that he was opposed to any form of discrimination against those Jews who had become South Africans; De Villiers acknowledged the existence of only a few anti-Jewish extremists in the party; and Bremer, rather lamely, told Frank that 'one can only try to get the Transvaal Party to change its attitude'. But he did condemn antisemitism as being futile.[131]

Clearly the issue remained contentious, especially among the northerners.[132] *Die Transvaler*, however, opposed any change, arguing that the United Party was attempting to undermine the HNP, with its press doing everything possible to create suspicion and sow divisions in the party. The newspaper bluntly refused to believe Malan would change the party's policy towards Jews.[133]

When Frank publicised his correspondence with the four Nationalists, Louw was distinctly uncomfortable and shared his concerns with Blackie Swart. He was worried about the placatory tone of their responses and indicated that he had received letters from members of the Greyshirts and the Boerenasie, as well as from English-speakers, who wanted to know why the HNP was walking away from its Jewish policy (*afstap van hulle Joodse beleid*) and even threatening, as a consequence, to withhold their votes. Some English-speakers, he claimed, had also warned him that any change in policy would be a fatal mistake, as the very reason they were attracted to the HNP was because of its Jewish policy.[134]

Three days later, Louw wrote yet another letter to the *Cape Times* in which he outlined in detail the HNP's official stance towards Jews, together with the various proposals that discriminated against them in respect of immigration, naturalisation and the freedom to engage in business and the professions.[135] In response, the *Cape Times* described Louw as an antisemite who patently classified Jews as undesirable.[136] This provoked a further response from Louw, who indicated that he had simply said Jews were unassimilable and nothing about their desirability or otherwise.[137] Nossel, too, responded to Louw, pointing out that his views differed from those of his party's leader, and that he was sure Malan would in due course clarify the real position.[138]

A week later, Louw told Swart that he had had two conversations with Malan, who indicated that he would be making a declaration to *Die Burger*. Louw believed certain people had influenced Malan, who appeared intent on appeasing the Jews, and he was extremely worried that, despite a two-hour discussion, he had been unable to change Malan's mind.[139] In a last-ditch attempt to pre-empt any changes to Jewish policy, Louw wrote a forceful and somewhat desperate letter to Malan, arguing that any statement that might be interpreted as a change of policy would be perceived as capitulating to the Jews. This would result in disappointment for 'tens of thousands' of Nationalists, all for no gain in Jewish political support. In fact, argued Louw, English-speaking Nationalists who appreciated the party's Jewish policy would also be estranged, while only a couple of liberals in the National Party would be satisfied.[140] Louw urged Malan to stick to the party's principles, which stated unequivocally that further Jewish immigration should cease immediately. Sensing that Malan might also be inclined to oppose any discrimination whatsoever against Jews, including quotas on licences or trading permits, Louw indicated that while these might not yet be official policy, it had been Malan himself who in the past had advocated such policies and therefore would be well advised to avoid contradicting himself. He also reminded Malan that the Transvaal policy of excluding Jews from membership of the National Party was embedded in its constitution, and he could not simply say he disagreed with it in order to gain a few Jewish votes. Finally, he reminded Malan that their differences of opinion regarding HNP principles underlying Jewish policies were in any event of no consequence, as it was up to the federal council, and not the leader of the party, to act in this regard.[141]

The matter was now a public issue, with the Jewish press devoting substantial attention to the divisions. It was 'Louw Versus Malan', according to an editorial in the *SAJT*, and it was up to Malan to render the venomous

Louw politically impotent: 'It is our guess that Eric Louw has bluntly told Dr Malan that he will if necessary split the Party if he goes too far in his appeasement of the Jew. Dr Malan finds himself in a tight corner, for he knows only too well that, in the present alignment of forces, any rift inside the National Party could finally end all hope of victory in the coming General Election. This is Eric Louw's trump card, and it is worrying Dr Malan.'[142]

One week later, during an in-depth interview with *Die Burger*, Malan took the opportunity to clarify his position on the 'Jewish Question'. Clearly unpersuaded by Louw's interventions, the HNP leader admitted at the very outset that some members of his party were hostile to Jews, but maintained that the party itself was no more anti-Jewish than the United Party and, indeed, even less so if what he characterised as 'underground' hostility towards Jews was included. When asked to clarify what he meant by 'anti-Jewish', Malan defined it as being 'opposed to the Jew as a Jew; in other words, against the Jewish race, as such, independent of circumstances'. He also reminded the interviewer that all legislative initiatives involving Jews were politically broad-based: dating back to 1930, these had been supported initially by the South African Party and thereafter by the United Party. Elaborating on what he understood by the 'Jewish Problem', Malan stressed the international dimensions of the issue; the whole world, in fact, was engaged in a similar quest to find a solution. Without a national home of their own, a race problem emerged as soon as Jewish numbers exceeded a certain percentage in any country. South Africa had reached this limit some time back and it certainly did not need to add another racial problem to those already in existence.

No doubt with his eye on the forthcoming election, Malan's responses attempted to rationalise even contradictory HNP policies and actions. He declared his unequivocal opposition to further Jewish immigration and claimed that the United Party policy was full of contradictions: Jan Hofmeyr, who had in 1930 supported the Quota Act, had now changed his tune, while Smuts had agreed that no country could be overloaded with Jews. 'It is not a question of politics. It is a question of objective policy,' Malan said, quoting Smuts. 'If we overload the nation with Jews then we get an anti-Semitic movement. I have always said so.' When asked why he thought the existing laws against Jewish immigration were ineffective, Malan said the measures were too arbitrary and that the government had given in to pressure too easily. What was needed to halt further Jewish immigration was a firm and more restrictive policy that could be adopted without discriminating against Jews already living in South Africa. If nothing was done, he warned of serious repercussions, even violence against Jews, as he had prophesied in 1937. Asked about Louw's 1939 Bill and his own proposal for the introduction of a permit system to control Jewish entry into occupations in the Union, Malan defensively claimed that Louw's Bill contained 'no regulation which aims at discrimination. And the permit system which I advocate did, it is true, aim at discrimination of unnaturalised foreigners and Union citizens, but then it compares exactly with similar legislation in nearly all other civilised countries, including England, France, the United States and others which aims at the protection of their own citizens. It ropes in all foreigners in the same net, and does not discriminate against Jews as Jews.'

Malan's attempt at softening the HNP's Jewish policies provoked *Die Burger* to ask him about the decision of the party's 1939 Paarl congress to demand the introduction of an occupational quota for Jews. Malan responded by pointing out that this demand had been rejected at the Cradock congress the following year. In response to another query about whether special protection was needed against Jews because they were seen to be exploitive, he acknowledged that he could understand the perception, but exploitation was not the sole preserve of Jews: 'It appears also in other places. The Nationalist Party ... wishes to abolish parasitism from our economic life and to protect every section against exploitation of any sort from whatever source it might come.'[143]

Predictably, Malan's interview generated considerable interest. The *Cape Times* warned that his statement had to be read in the context of an upcoming general election,[144] and *Die Suiderstem* accused Malan of cynically changing his tune to capture the Jewish vote;[145] but the *Zionist Record* was content to look on the positive side. Acknowledging that Malan's statement conflicted with some of the practices of the party, the weekly was nevertheless willing 'to look for points of goodwill rather than rake up past expressions of ill-will' and wished to interpret Malan's statement as a step in the right direction.[146] The *SAJT*, on the other hand, chose to be critical, arguing that Malan exhibited a narrow *völkisch* mindset, whose 'perverted racial outlook' might have Afrikaner support but excluded him from those who were not Afrikaans, and also from those Afrikaners who had had enough of narrow racialism.[147] More significantly, *Die Transvaler* remained silent about the interview. For the first time, wrote Willem van Heerden in *Die Dagbreek*, the paper had failed to comment editorially on an important declaration by Malan. The *SAJT* speculated that the reason might lie in *Die Transvaler*'s realisation that the provincial leadership was not at one with the party's leader.[148]

That there were indeed serious differences of opinion on the part of the Transvaal leaders as regards the 'Jewish Question' is illustrated by exchanges between Hans Strijdom and Frans Erasmus. Strijdom took exception to assertions made by Erasmus at a National Party 'Information' meeting that the party did not discriminate against Jews who were already in South Africa, and that Malan's declaration in *Die Burger* was in line with party policy. He bluntly contradicted Erasmus and claimed that the National Party in the Transvaal in fact did discriminate against Jews with regard to membership, and that the only reason Jews had not been debarred from membership in the Orange Free State was because Article One of the National Party's constitution already effectively precluded Jews on religious grounds. Strijdom reminded Erasmus that Malan had also invoked Article One when Jewish membership of the Cape National Party had been raised. But, asserted Strijdom, Malan had no right to declare to the world that the standpoint of the Cape party was the policy of the party as a whole. He was convinced that if Malan's plans were implemented, there would be friction and little gain. Only a few Jews would vote for the HNP at the expense of thousands of Greyshirt, German and English votes.[149]

In his response to Strijdom, Erasmus held his ground, acknowledging only that the exclusion of Jews from membership of the HNP in the Transvaal was indeed discriminatory, but that this had been rejected by the Cape HNP. The party, he asserted, was concerned solely with 'unassimilables' (and not only Jews) and wished to discriminate against '*vreemdelinge as vreemdelinge*' (foreigners as foreigners).[150] Strijdom disagreed and immediately responded by pointing out that the HNP in fact recommended discrimination against Jews, as confirmed in a pamphlet written by Erasmus himself and in a speech made by Malan. He accused Erasmus of selectively choosing one of Malan's speeches to suit his argument while ignoring all the others. Strijdom went much further and suggested it would ultimately become necessary to introduce repatriation as well as a quota system as party policy.[151] Communications between the two ended inconclusively.[152]

GENERAL ELECTION, 1948

Because of the obvious divisions within the party, the HNP agreed to avoid raising the 'Jewish Question' during the general election campaign.[153] Of greater moment was the question of ties with Havenga's Afrikaner Party. Malan favoured an alliance of some sort, while Strijdom, Verwoerd and Louw were fearful that OB members had penetrated the Afrikaner Party, and, before considering ties, wanted Havenga to publicly repudiate the OB. In addition, they were concerned about the prospect of the Afrikaner Party maintaining its own identity. Further arguments raged around the make-up of the HNP's Information Committee, which had hitherto been in the hands of young hot-heads. Much to the chagrin of Strijdom, Malan was now insisting on greater balance.[154] Where there was agreement, it was on the rejection of the idea of bringing the now marginalised Nuwe Orde and OB into a coalition. The opportunity for an alliance of some kind with the Afrikaner Party arose after Smuts spurned overtures from Havenga, and within a short time a coalition agreement was reached between the HNP and the Afrikaner Party.

Differences of opinion notwithstanding, Malan had reason to be optimistic about the party's electoral prospects: a number of United Party MPs had crossed the floor to the HNP, and the party had been victorious in six of the ten by-elections held since the 1943 general election.[155] The United Party's defeat in the Wakkerstroom by-election in 1944 had been especially encouraging. The lessons were obvious: the United Party was vulnerable and a united opposition had the potential to ensure an HNP victory. The HNP was confident of its growing support, and its eye was now firmly focused on the big prize: the defeat of the United Party.

Malan knew he could also rely on Weichardt, who had supported him at Wakkerstroom in 1944 and who, subsequent to his release from confinement in February 1946, had turned his attention away from the Jews and focused instead on what he perceived as the rising African and communist threat.[156] Although still a self-proclaimed fascist, Weichardt was determined to assist in uniting opposition groups in a bid to overthrow the Smuts government. He warned that a United Party government under Hofmeyr (the probable successor to Smuts) would be unable to secure the future of a white South Africa and was happy to have his Greyshirts serve the National Party in an extra-parliamentary capacity.[157] This was indeed confirmed at a Greyshirt congress (the first in eight years), where it was also agreed that a new party would be formed, the *Blanke Werkersparty* (White Workers' Party). Its constitution mirrored that of the SANSB, although it was agreed that the new party could formally participate in politics.[158] While there remained no place for Jews in that party's credo,[159] and while Weichardt continued to abhor party politics and define himself as a National Socialist, he also made it clear that the Blanke Werkersparty was 'prepared to sacrifice everything for white South Africa'.[160] At its congress in early 1948, the new party agreed that the Greyshirts would be its action front, with its own disciplinary code.[161] The party called for white unity and came out formally in support of the HNP. Weichardt was determined to defeat Smuts and prevent workers from being dragged into the 'Jew-inspired' Labour Party.[162] To drum up support for his new party, he toured the country for three months, but managed to establish only nine Blanke Werkersparty branches.[163]

In the build-up to the election it was obvious that the HNP had drawn important lessons from its 1943 defeat. The party's propaganda now veered away from republicanism and secession, and focused instead on other factors: the needs of returning soldiers and their reabsorption into civilian life; housing shortages; welfare programmes for the poor; the cost of living; and, most importantly, South Africa's 'colour' question. It was easy enough to build upon white fears, which were gaining ground as Africans encroached on urban areas, and slums and settlements mushroomed around the larger cities.[164] On the platteland, race relations were also tense, while strikes (often supported by activist whites) had become commonplace. That trade unions had enhanced their capacity during the war was vividly evident in an extensive – albeit ultimately unsuccessful – African mineworkers' strike on the Witwatersrand in August 1946,[165] and again in a white (mainly Afrikaner) mineworkers' strike in 1947.[166] The 'Indian Question' loomed large as well; Smuts' Asiatic Land Tenure Act and Indian Representation Act of 1946 – a classic compromise between the needs of Indians and whites – had made more enemies than friends, alienating the Indian population as well as the international community. Piecemeal change with regard to the colour question was clearly problematic. Another point in the HNP's favour was the warm welcome extended by Smuts to the Royal Family during their visit to South Africa in 1947, something that did not sit well with republican-inclined Afrikaners.

With so many wedge issues, Malan had little cause to mobilise support around the potentially divisive 'Jewish Question'. The destruction of European Jewry and the creation of the State of Israel had in any event ended the prospect of large-scale Jewish immigration. Always the arch-opportunist, Malan sensed other unfolding political opportunities. He accused Smuts of *niksdoen* (doing nothing) about the great issues of the day, and built his campaign on social and economic issues as well as vague promises of territorial separation between the races. South Africa, he told an increasingly colour-conscious electorate, would remain a 'white man's country' and a bulwark against the communist threat linked by Nationalists to the 'Black Peril'.[167] Here they chose as their bogeyman the liberal Hofmeyr, whose franchise policy they predicted would ultimately result in the collapse of 'white civilisation'.[168]

Although the National Party's race policies had yet to be defined, the words 'apartheid' or 'separate development' had a visceral appeal, especially among recently urbanised working-class Afrikaners who saw the growing presence of Africans in the cities as a threat to their livelihoods.[169] Apartheid promised Afrikaner survival; it served as the glue that held together various interest groups.[170] Smuts, on the other hand, called for large-scale white immigration to ensure the continuance of 'Western civilisation', an approach seen by Malan as a ploy to dilute Afrikaner numbers.[171]

Besides some anti-Jewish pamphlets circulating early in the election campaign,[172] and brisk sales for a new edition of the *Protocols of the Elders of Zion*,[173] it was only Louw (in a letter to *Die Burger*) who bothered to reaffirm the National Party's attitude to the Jews.[174] Even Petrus van Nierop now denied he was an antisemite.[175] Other extremists, such as Strijdom, Swart and Verwoerd, were largely silent. 'It remains to be reported that not a single Nationalist paper has given a line of publicity to any anti-Semitic utterances or statements generally unfriendly to Jews,' noted 'Karl Lemeer' in his regular *Zionist Record* column, less than two weeks before the poll. The Jewish question, he asserted, 'is a dead letter'.[176] More than that, many individual Nationalists took pains to reassure the Jewish community that the party had turned its back on its past policy of discrimination.[177] It was clearly far more rewarding for the HNP not to play the Jewish card and rather to concentrate on other issues, including the liberalism of Hofmeyr and the hubris of Smuts and his closest lieutenants.[178]

Shortly before the election, Smuts cobbled together a deal with the remnants of the Labour Party, ensuring a free run for them in eight seats, while Malan's pact with Havenga ensured the Afrikaner Party a possible 11 seats, thus avoiding the 'great schism' among Afrikaners.[179] This also meant a lessening of Afrikaner support for the United Party and attracted the support of a small number of English-speakers, enticed with the promise that a republic would only be decided upon by referendum.

In a weighted constituency system that favoured rural areas, Smuts and his allies won just over 53 per cent of the popular vote but lost the election, despite only a 41 per cent vote for Malan and Havenga. It was apparent that rural Afrikaners in the western Cape Province had turned away from the ruling party in droves, and in the Transvaal the tide truly turned, with Smuts suffering a humiliating defeat in Standerton, his own constituency. In the final tally, Malan obtained 70 seats, Havenga 9, Smuts 65 and his ally, the Labour Party 6. 'My own colleagues have turned against me,' a chastened Smuts told an old friend, who replied, 'How could they turn against you? They are all dead.'[180]

South African Jews were relieved at the scant attention paid to them during the election campaign, although the loss of Smuts as Prime Minister was extremely worrying.[181] However, the Board had held closed-door meetings with Malan prior to the election, and Jewish leaders sensed a change for the better in his attitude. Nevertheless they remained cautious, with Saron warning that the onus was on the new government 'to prove that it had learned the lessons of history' – a direct reminder of the National Party's Nazi sympathies during the war.[182] The *Zionist Record* shared these anxieties: Malan had not sufficiently repudiated Louw and his ideas, and his party still harboured concerns about Jewish immigration.[183]

Six weeks after the election, the Board met with the new Prime Minister, who assured them that the 'Jewish Question' was now behind them: his government stood for a policy of non-discrimination against any section of the European population in South Africa and he looked forward to a time when there would be no further talk regarding the so-called Jewish question in the life and politics of the country.[184] In essence, the National Party had little to fear. The prospect of continuing Jewish immigration was negligible, and, with the political kingdom at hand, Afrikaner economic advancement was just a matter of time.[185] The sense of inferiority that had underpinned so much of the animus towards Jews had been removed.

Apart from intermittent anti-Jewish comments from die-hard antisemites like Louw, Pirow and Van Rensburg, there were greater issues with which the party had to engage. Most importantly, it had to fashion a new race policy, and it was not long before a range of legislative decisions were presented and acted upon. Insofar as Jews were concerned, the Transvaal party continued to exclude them from membership. This restriction was only lifted in 1951, with the fulsome support of both *Die Vaderland* and *Die Transvaler*.[186] Importantly, antisemites like Pirow and Weichardt maintained a low profile; indeed, in May 1951 the Board reported that, with the exception of Rudman and, to a lesser degree, Terblanche, all those who had been associated with large-scale antisemitic propaganda in the 1930s had disappeared from the scene.[187] In 1953 Malan became the first sitting head of government to visit Israel. Two years later he wrote a preface to Chief Rabbi Israel Abrahams' *The Birth of a Community*. Here, in a remarkable and ironic about turn, he praised the Jews of South Africa for managing to maintain a distinctive 'racial' identity while contributing significantly to the society at large. Jews could, he argued, serve as a model for a complex 'multi-racial country' like South Africa.[188]

CONCLUSION

At a party given to celebrate his silver wedding in early 1948, Louis Weichardt was introduced as 'the leader who made our volk Jew- and race-conscious'. To this Weichardt responded that he had fully supported Hitler's policies of racial purity and that it had been a mistake for western European nations to fight one another in a war that had been conducted 'only and always to benefit Jewry'.[1] Clearly unrepentant, the man whose star had waned during and after the war years was obviously proud to be identified as the first South African to endorse publicly the toxic racial fantasies that had led to the death of so many millions in Europe. He had peddled these fabrications from the moment he launched the South African Gentile National

Socialist Movement in October 1933. Building upon decades of anti-Jewish stereotyping dating back to the late nineteenth century, and exploiting the mounting nativism of the 1920s that defined the eastern European Jew as alien and unassimilable, Weichardt unleashed an anger that saw the 'Jewish Question' move rapidly from the margins of public debate in South Africa to its centre. Outrageous accusations, which included the most nefarious ambitions of Jews, were fabricated by a plethora of 'Shirt' or radical right movements. While the United Party (including many English-speakers) shared concerns about the number of Jews entering South Africa and supported calls to halt this influx, the 'Purified' National Party – seemingly pressurised by the radical right – called for programmatic action against Jews, even beyond the Aliens Act of early 1937, which effectively precluded the entry of Jews. These radical right groups shared a vision of South Africa in which Jews would be relegated to the margins of society.

As argued in this study, the injection of the 'Jewish Question' into public life was the product of a host of contingencies, beginning with a 'poor white' crisis in which one in five whites (mainly Afrikaners) lived below the poverty datum line, according to the 1932 Carnegie Commission report.[2] Hapless victims of decades of structural change, these alienated, unskilled and marginalised 'poor whites' constituted a political time bomb, an easily available target for ethnic mobilisation and populist promises. Weichardt and others on the radical right appealed to these malcontents. Aided by a flood of propaganda from Germany (often via South West Africa), the radical right offered simple solutions for complex problems. Although not a major political force, its message resonated widely and was taken seriously by mainstream political parties. The 'Purified' National Party in particular was forced to take up the challenge. Indeed, already in 1931 when interviewed in *Die Burger* in the wake of the Quota Act, DF Malan had gone out of his way to explain how easy it was in South Africa to 'rouse a feeling of hate towards the Jew'. Prime Minister Hertzog, too, recognised the political potential of inflammatory anti-Jewish propaganda, including some empathy for it within his own party. The alleged Jewish boycott of German goods was of particular concern, as Germany was among South Africa's largest trading partners. Despite an absence of evidence that the boycott was impacting on them, wool farming interests were particularly anxious about potential damage, and persistently fingered the Jewish Board of Deputies as the villain behind the action.

The influx of German Jews (unaffected by the Quota Act of 1930, which targeted eastern European Jews only) fleeing Nazi Germany exacerbated anger, as did the upward mobility of Jews in South Africa. Led now for the most part by young Afrikaner intellectuals, protest meetings deemed the Jewish newcomers a threat to Afrikaner advancement. Jews had indeed moved into spaces hitherto the preserve of white Gentiles, where they challenged the largely English-speaking mercantile establishment and made their mark as traders and storekeepers. By the mid-1930s, a high proportion of Jewish men in Johannesburg were clustered in commerce, finance and insurance – just under 40 per cent of adult males compared to only 18 per cent in the general population. Significantly, over eight per cent of all adult Jewish males were in the professions, a percentage nearly double that of the general population.[3]

Exemplifying Jewish upward mobility was New York-born Isadore William Schlesinger, who pioneered the South African insurance and entertainment industries, together with a myriad of other innovative enterprises. Emerging out of long-standing hostility towards capitalism and a persistent anti-imperialism that dated back to the heyday of the Randlords and their perceived role in the Anglo-Boer War, Schlesinger was turned into a convenient symbol of international Jewish machinations. He reminded the Afrikaner of his alien and inferior place in the often abhorred capitalist order – graphically portrayed in the cartoon caricature Hoggenheimer. As late as 1944, Piet Meyer's *Die Stryd van die Afrikanerwerker* (The Struggle of the Afrikaner Worker) castigated big capital and spoke of the need for Afrikaner socialism as a result of unequal relations with English-speakers.[4] At the same time, Jewish labour activists were threatening established power relations. Afrikaner nationalists, in particular, feared an alliance between communist agitators and African workers that would fuel the push for racial equality. The 'Red Peril', writes Wessel Visser, was equated with the 'Black Peril', and, most importantly, the 'Jewish Peril' was conflated with both the 'Red Peril' and the 'Black Peril'.[5] Class politics ran counter to the organic orientation of *völkisch* thought in the 1930s and 1940s. For this reason, rival Afrikaner unions were formed, beginning with the Spoorbond in 1934.

The alien Jew also challenged an emerging sense of 'South Africanness' among English- and Afrikaans-speaking whites, who were considered to be the founding immigrants. While the United Party believed that a limited number of Jews could be absorbed, the breakaway 'Purified' National Party under Malan – grappling with nativist categories, manipulating notions of 'Nordicism' and sensing Jews as a race apart – unequivocally opposed a Jewish influx. Such thinking was the product of a *völkisch* mindset that viewed individuals primarily as members of organic communities.[6] However, many white South Africans (both English- and Afrikaans-speaking) shared concerns about Jews, believing that yet another racial group was being added to the already problematic Asiatic, Coloured and African mix. Malan had made this clear when he met with Jewish leaders in the wake of his controversial interview in *Die Burger* in 1931. Increasingly, he and his followers became more explicit: Jews were immutably unassimilable, thus posing a threat to what Peberdy describes as 'the delicate balance between the black and white populations of the Union as a result of their perceived difference' and contaminating 'the body of the nation itself'.[7] In this essentialist cast of mind, we have hints of a paradigm that would subsequently inform Nationalist thought about culture and ethnicity in general.[8] It was a cast of mind that underpinned the apartheid project in its aim to safeguard the values and standards of 'white civilisation'.[9] The 'Jewish Question' and the ways of dealing with it thus paralleled – and to some extent even presaged – apartheid ideology as it evolved from the mid-1930s.[10]

Some would argue that hostility towards Jews was classic xenophobia, based as it was on the distinctiveness of the eastern European Jew. Added to this was the Jew's upward mobility, perceived as a bulwark against Afrikaner advancement.[11] Jewish particularism and upward mobility, however, cannot alone explain the hostility;[12] prevailing discourses also need to be taken into account.[13] Just as modern European antisemitism was at least in part a response to the construction of the Jew over centuries, Jew hatred in South Africa owed much to domestic anti-Jewish stereotypes that had evolved from the late nineteenth century. Antisemites perceived Jews through a prism of familiar cultural patterns, and insofar as Jews had always been underdogs, the prospect of a reversal of power relations was disturbing.[14] However, the key to understanding the potency and depth of antisemitism in South Africa during the 1930s and 1940s lies in nascent *völkisch* Afrikaner Christian-Nationalism, in which the Jew was a threatening outsider. Many of the key theoreticians within the *völkisch* movement had studied in Germany, where they imbibed views of the corporate state, an idealist worldview and a sense of exclusivist nationalism. These ideas propelled a powerful republicanism rooted in notions of divine election, a leitmotif within the Afrikaners' civil religion.[15] Like their European counterparts on the right, Afrikaner nationalists were opposed to liberalism, Marxism and laissez-faire capitalism.[16] The last-mentioned, associated with British imperialism, was exemplified by Hoggenheimer, who was, as Moodie reminds us, 'English-speaking, imperialist and clearly Jewish'.[17] Thus the Jew became entangled in Afrikaner history in interesting and potentially dangerous ways.

By the late 1930s, antisemitism had become an integral part of *völkisch* Afrikaner nationalism. This ideological shift, generated beyond the Jew although not necessarily unrelated to the Jew, transformed the equation. Here the situation was comparable to other countries where exclusivist nationalism also impacted on the Jewish condition, sometimes in tandem with religion.[18] Such was the case in France and Poland in the interwar years, and especially in Canada, where fascist groups such as Adrien Arcand's Parti National Social Chrétien were at the forefront of scapegoating Jews. Besides highlighting the allegedly negative role of Jews in society, these extremists sought to redefine the nature of French Canada, and the Jew was a useful means of bolstering a Francophone identity rooted in confession and notions of race.[19]

Similarly, in South Africa in the 1930s and 1940s, calls to marginalise Jews were underpinned by the growth of Afrikaner Christian-Nationalism, subtly reinforced and informed by a neo-Calvinist (and neo-Kuyperian) tradition that tied culture to nation and sought to protect white Afrikaners, while infusing a strong sense of separation. Manifest in republicanism, and coupled with a sense of religious mission, *völkisch* Afrikaner Christian-Nationalism sharpened perceptions of the Jew as a quintessential alien, representing all that was foreign and oppressive. Being English-speakers for the most part, they were also political enemies; it was in fact often easier (as Hancock points out) to target the Jew – or append him to alleged British machinations – than to focus on the old enemy.[20] 'British-Jewish-liberal' democracy was a mantra of the radical right during the war years, when the appeal of fascism and the rhetoric of antisemitism were rampant. Importantly, the Jew helped to consolidate an all-embracing Afrikaner identity, with antisemitism papering over class divisions and antagonisms within Afrikaner society. The Afrikaner's inferior status in society and his poverty could be explained in racial or national terms. Moreover, by employing the discourse of 'race' to exclude and denigrate Jews, the Afrikaner was in turn elevated.[21] It is therefore no coincidence that antisemitism continued to suffuse specifically radical right Afrikaner political discourse and programmes, despite the upturn in the economy from the early 1930s.

It would be wrong, however, to suggest that there was a widespread consensus on the 'Jewish Question'. Many Jews enjoyed respect at the highest level and attained prominence in diverse fields, including public life. Few confronted naked antisemitism, as opposed to social snobbery, in everyday life. But across the party and language divide there remained an essentialist understanding of 'the Jew'. Even Jan Hofmeyr, a champion of the Jews, maintained that their entry into the country would be advisable only if they were part of a wider immigration stream of the 'stock of people from whom we have sprung'.[22] At the same time, however, relatively few South Africans shared an affinity with the conspiratorial notions of the radical right – most evident in the peddling of the *Protocols of the Elders of Zion* – and many felt a distinct discomfort with vulgar Jew-baiting. Electoral contests, too, showed little support for the radical right. Yet it needs to be noted that the National Party imported much of its rhetoric from that source and welcomed anti-Jewish extremists into its fold in the late 1930s. In fact, the National Party formally paid tribute to Weichardt's SANP in late 1937 for alerting South Africans to the Jewish problem.

These ambiguities in attitudes towards the Jew are captured to a certain extent by André van Deventer, who has argued that there were two schools of thought within the National Party when it came to the Jews: on the one hand DF Malan and Hans Strijdom, very much in line with the National Party, were concerned about the Jewish threat to South African economic life; on the other hand Eric Louw, Petrus van Nierop and Albertus Werth, while stressing Jewish domination of South African economic life, also emphasised in conspiratorial terms the allegiance of South African Jews to the nefarious aims of international Jewry.[23] Van Deventer maintains that when Malan did make occasional anti-Jewish comments, these were isolated,[24] and in fact the National Party leader often expressed discomfort in singling out the Jew alone. But the reality is more complex. Malan's rationalisation of the Quota Act in 1930, for example, was rooted in European Romanticism and infused with nativist assumptions. As time went on, he frequently identified the Jew as an additional racial problem and often lapsed into anti-Jewish conspiratorial fantasies, arguably *the* hallmark of antisemitism.[25] In this respect, Lindie Koorts appears to soft-peddle the issue when she suggests that Malan was a simple opportunist when it came to the 'Jewish Question'.[26] While opportunism was indeed a feature of his political style, and while some of his attacks were in all likelihood politically driven, too often he appeared consumed by imaginary Jewish machinations, especially when placed under pressure by the radical right. A demonstrable shift in his attitudes towards Jews is evident through the 1930s: Nordicism and economic concerns at the start of the decade mutate into the familiar stalking-horses of international Jewish communists and international Jewish bankers.[27] Importantly, any opportunism on Malan's part suggests a personal pandering to widespread anti-Jewish sentiment. Why else would he – the political opportunist *par excellence* – play the Jewish card?

Nevertheless, it needs to be acknowledged that Malan turned away from the 'Jewish Question' soon after the Second World War and refused to kowtow to Eric Louw, who persisted with Jew-baiting and did his best to pressurise the National Party to maintain its anti-Jewish policies. Indeed, soon after becoming Prime Minister, Malan assured the Board that the 'Jewish Question' was a thing of the past. He was, moreover, the first head of state to visit the newly created State of Israel. Yet Malan had many colleagues who were less ambiguous about Jews and who were happy to echo the radical right without so much as a word of censure. Important figures such as Hendrik Verwoerd, Hans Strijdom, Nico van der Merwe, Blackie Swart, Paul Sauer, Albertus Werth, Stephanus le Roux, Karl Bremer, Petrus van Nierop and Eric Louw all expressed raw antisemitic sentiments. Each voiced his concern about the stranglehold Jews were alleged to have over the economy. Verwoerd in fact pursued a crusade from his editorial desk at *Die Transvaler*, persistently calling for the introduction of business and professional quotas based on the proportion of Jews in the white population. These ideas had undoubted purchase in a party that represented so many aggrieved whites and which identified the Jew as a convenient explanation for all misfortunes.[28]

Importantly, even after German Jews had been prevented from entering South Africa by the Aliens Act of 1937, the 'Jewish Question' remained alive. It is not a case (as Moodie and, to a lesser extent, Furlong maintain) of grassroots anti-Jewish pressure informing the leaders.[29] Many high-ranking Nationalists – including senior bureaucrats – gave direction; many had a visceral dislike of Jews. And while it is true that Malan's Cape Province wing of the party refused to follow the example of the Transvaal in precluding Jewish membership of the party, it needs to be noted that Article One of the National Party constitution effectively excluded Jews.[30] It is also apparent that antisemitism was not, as Moodie claims, a marginal factor in the general election of 1938.[31] Throughout the campaign the 'Jewish Question' was employed as a stick with which to beat the United Party. Moodie does, however, make a fair point when he argues that Christian-Nationalism was hostile to all non-Calvinists, non-Christians and, of course, non-whites.[32] But it was only the Jew who was invested with malevolent and awesome powers, arguably a defining feature of classic antisemitism.[33] Here one must bear in mind the continuities of imagery and stereotyping that could be employed under the right circumstances, as indeed was the case in the 1930s and 1940s.[34] Only in this way can we begin to understand why so many on the radical right were prepared to engage an imaginary enemy. This was especially evident in the fascist agendas of the Nuwe Orde and the Ossewa-Brandwag. Both movements were adamant that Jews would at best enjoy a second-class status in South Africa.

For all that, it is fair to argue – as does Hermann Giliomee in his magisterial study of the Afrikaners – that only fringe groups, influenced by Nazi literature from abroad, fitted into that category of classical Jew-haters in South Africa in the 1930s and 1940s. Anti-Jewish feelings, he asserts, were located in economic frustration on the part of Afrikaners living in the cities, especially Johannesburg.[35] The importance of the 'Jewish Question' in South African public life during these years, however, should not be minimised. With racial obsessions mounting, the addition of yet another 'racial' group – especially a group perceived to be bent on undermining the status quo and thwarting Afrikaner mobility – was viewed with grave concern. Paul Sauer captured this when he warned the party faithful in 1939 that the country already faced a problem with 'kaffirs, Indians, and Coloureds' and did not need an additional Jewish problem.[36]

The Jewish presence in South Africa undoubtedly exercised the minds of many across the white political and language spectrum. This is apparent in government documents, church records, private papers, formal Jewish records, newspapers and memoirs. There was widespread concern about the putative power and subversive qualities of Jews. It needs to be noted, however, that at no time during these years did anti-Jewish discourse in South Africa approximate the language of exclusion and frenzy heard in some European countries. Beyond immigration prohibition, programmatic action was never likely in South Africa, even if the circumstances had been propitious. Nativism and economic jealousy, rather than deep-rooted fantasies, drove hostility. Indeed, *völkisch* Afrikaners paradoxically had a grudging respect for the 'unassimilable' Jews who had, after all, survived for millennia, despite their minority status. Malan captured this in his preface to Rabbi Abrahams' *The Birth of a Community*, in which he praised the Jews for the maintenance of racial identity and their ability to adapt and 'fit themselves into the national structure of the various countries in which they happen to live'.[37]

That Malan could become infatuated with, and effectively praise, 'unassimilability' – a term of abuse for over a decade – illustrates the contingency of Jew-hatred. Paradoxically, Jewish survival now served as a model for the Afrikaner, existentially threatened in a decolonising world. Grand apartheid would be a substitute for the Jewish spiritual fortress. Most importantly, the upwardly mobile Afrikaner no longer confronted the Jew as a threat. Within a few years, an emergent Afrikaner bourgeoisie – well educated, confident and more optimistic than its forebears – enjoyed the economic fruits of racist exploitation and political power. Afrikaners developed a newfound respect for enterprise and material success. As they began to experience power and social mobility, their sense of inferiority and fear of the Jew began to evaporate. Crass Jew-baiting was now restricted to a fringe ultra-right element. Although the government from time to time in the 1950s and 1960s reminded Jews that their disproportionate involvement in anti-apartheid activities was unwelcome, the Jewish community had little cause for discomfort.

With the celebration of cultural diversity after 1990 in the new post-apartheid democratic South Africa, the threat of crude antisemitism receded even further. Today it is easy to forget the mood of the 1930s and 1940s, when Jews were extremely worried and perplexed – and justifiably so. Under siege domestically, and helplessly observing the plight of their core-ligionists in Europe, not to mention the fate of trapped family and friends, they carefully monitored domestic politics. Even if their own reportage bordered at times on the alarmist, it is apparent – from a wide range of diverse sources – that for a great number of whites, both English- and Afrikaans-speakers, the Jew was an unwelcome challenge and a disturbing addition to society.

In my quest to explore and understand the 'Jewish Question' in South
Africa during the 1930s and 1940s, I have been assisted by numerous colleagues and friends. I owe a great deal to David Welsh, Adam Mendelsohn,
Hermann Giliomee and Siamon Gordon for ongoing scholarly exchanges
and for reading and commenting on parts of or on the whole manuscript. I
am particularly deeply indebted to Millie Pimstone who during her many
readings of the manuscript perceptively identified and corrected its errors.
Alfred LeMaitre added his astute editorial observations on behalf of the
publishers. I was also fortunate to benefit from the insights of scholars when
I presented aspects of my work at the Center for European Studies, Har-
vard University, and at conferences at the University of California, Santa
Cruz; Tel Aviv University; the University of Sydney; the University of British Columbia/Simon Fraser University; and the University of Cape Town.
In the final analysis, however, it was my dialogue with the printed word,
housed in a range of libraries and archives, both in South Africa and abroad,
that enabled me to reach the conclusions presented in this study. I wish
therefore to extend my thanks and appreciation to the following institutions: Special Collections and Archives, Jagger Library, University of Cape
Town; Government Publications Department and Interlibrary Loans Unit,
Chancellor Oppenheimer Library, University of Cape Town; The National
Archives, Public Record Office, London; Archives for Contemporary

Affairs, University of the Free State, Bloemfontein; National Archives and Record Service of South Africa, Pretoria; National Library of South Africa, Pretoria; National Library of South Africa, Cape Town; Western Cape Archives and Record Service, Cape Town; South African National Defence Force Archives, Pretoria; Hoover Institution Archives, Stanford University; Dutch Reformed Church in South Africa: Archive, Stellenbosch; DF Malan Collection, Manuscript Section, JS Gericke Library, University of Stellenbosch; Historical Papers Research Archives, South African Institute for Race Relations, University of the Witwatersrand, Johannesburg; Killie Campbell Archives and Manuscripts, University of KwaZulu-Natal; North-West University, Potchefstroom; Library of Parliament, Cape Town; Jewish Studies Library, Isaac and Jessie Kaplan Centre for Jewish Studies, University of Cape Town; Administration, Archives and Legal Services and Secretariat, Office of the Registrar, University of Cape Town; Jacob Gitlin Library, Cape Town; and the SA Rochlin Archives, South African Jewish Board of Deputies, Johannesburg.

A great number of individuals in the foregoing institutions generously assisted. In particular I would like to thank the following for their time and diligence: Leslie Hart, Clive Kirkwood, Renate Meyer, Sue Ogterop, Busi Khangala, Allegra Louw, Isaac Ntabankulu, Beverley Angus, Laureen Rushby, Stephen Herandien, Anita Visser, Rosie Watson, Juan-Paul Burke, Glynnis Lawrence, Marlene van Niekerk, Naomi Musiker, Lynn Fourie, Huibre Lombard and Sadeck Casoojee. I have also worked with a number of research assistants: Gina Fourie, Mauritz Preller, Jan Lanicek, Lindie Koorts, Gunther Pakendorf, Emile Coetzee, Cornelis Muller, Alana Baranov, Petrie le Roux, Sandy Shell, Hermione Müller, Derick Griessel, Hannah Belitz, Aniel Botha, Lauren Myers, Joshua Mendelsohn, Ruth Muller, Paul Weinberg and Sandra Kruger. Sandra Kruger, in particular, devoted many hours to chasing documents and tracing newspapers. I want also to acknowledge financial assistance from the National Research Foundation, and the University Research Committee at the University of Cape Town. Technical support from Janine Blumberg at the Isaac and Jessie Kaplan Centre for Jewish Studies and Research at the University of Cape Town was constantly forthcoming, and the Centre itself has provided an environment for reflection and engagement. Finally, I want to thank Jonathan Ball and Jeremy Boraine of Jonathan Ball Publishers for their encouragement and support.

Milton Shain
Cape Town
August 2015

INTRODUCTION

1 The 'Jewish Question' is the one issue where broader South African historiography intersects with South African Jewish historiography. For the rest, Jews are virtually ignored. When they do emerge in the standard secondary sources, it is invariably as *homo economicus*. Where Jews came from and how the community lived is hardly addressed. Understandably it is issues of race and class that have dominated historiographical paradigms. Yet for contemporaries the Jew loomed large: the British-journalist and intellectual JA Hobson, for example, blamed Jews and other financiers for the Anglo-Boer War, while a range of vicious antisemites – many of whom appear in this study – characterised the Jews as all-powerful and subversive.

2 See William Henry Vatcher, *White Laager: the Rise of Afrikaner Nationalism,* Frederick Praeger, New York and London, 1965; Brian Bunting, *The Rise of the South African Reich,* Penguin Books, Harmondsworth, Middlesex, 1969; Michael Cohen, 'Anti-Jewish Manifestations in the Union of South Africa during the Nineteen Thirties', unpublished BA (Hons) dissertation, University of Cape Town, 1968; FJ van Heerden, 'Nasionaal-Sosialisme as faktor in die Suid-Afrikaanse Politiek, 1933–1948', unpublished DPhil, University of the Orange Free State, 1972; Gideon Shimoni, *Jews and Zionism: The South African Experience 1910–1967,* Oxford University Press, Cape Town, 1980; Izak Hattingh, 'Nasionaal-Sosialisme en die Gryshemp-beweging in Suid-Afrika', unpublished DPhil, University of the Orange Free State, 1989; Charles Bloomberg, *Christian-Nationalism and the Rise of the Afrikaner Broederbond, 1918–48* (edited by Saul Dubow), Macmillan, Basingstoke, 1990; Patrick J Furlong, *Between*

Crown and Swastika: The Impact of the Radical Right on the Afrikaner Nationalist Movement in the Fascist Era, Wesleyan University Press, Middletown, CT, and Witwatersrand University Press, Johannesburg, 1991; and Michael Cohen, 'Anatomy of South African Antisemitism: Afrikaner Nationalism, the Radical Right and South African Jewry between the World Wars', unpublished PhD, Monash University, 2014.

3 See Dunbar T Moodie, *The Rise of Afrikanerdom: Power, Apartheid, and the Afrikaner Civil Religion,* University of California Press, Berkeley, 1975; Dan O'Meara, *Volkskapitalisme: Class, Capital and Ideology in the Development of Afrikaner Nationalism 1934–1948,* Ravan Press, Johannesburg, 1983; André van Deventer, 'Afrikaner Nationalist Politics and Anti-Communism, 1937 to 1945', unpublished MA dissertation, University of Stellenbosch, 1991; and Wessel Visser, 'The Production of Literature on the "Red Peril" and "Total Onslaught" in Twentieth Century South Africa', *Historia,* 49(2), 2004.

4 See Furlong, *Between Crown and Swastika,* Ch 1, *passim.*

5 *Cape Times,* 27 October 1933.

6 From time to time the Asian or Indian trader was also identified in negative terms.

7 Seemingly petty issues divided individuals, resulting in breakaways and the formation of new movements. See chapters one and four, *passim.* For a sense of infighting and bickering, see Weichardt Collection, PV 29, File 14.

8 For similar notions of uniformity underpinning antisemitism elsewhere, see Richard Levy, 'Political Antisemitism in Germany and Austria, 1848–1914', in Albert S Lindemann and Richard S Levy (eds), *Antisemitism: A History,* Oxford University Press, Oxford, 2010.

9 See Edna Bradlow, 'Immigration into the

Union 1910–1948: Policies and Attitudes',
unpublished PhD dissertation, University of
Cape Town, 1978, and Sally Peberdy, *Selecting
Immigrants: National Identity and South Africa's
Immigration Policies 1910–2008*, Witwatersrand
University Press, Johannesburg, 2009.

10 See Christoph Marx, *Oxwagon Sentinel:
Radical Afrikaner Nationalism and the History
of the Ossewabrandwag*, University of South
Africa Press, Pretoria, 2008, and P de Klerk,
'Die Ideologie van die Ossewa-brandwag',
in PF van der Schyff (ed), *Die Ossewa-
Brandwag: Vuurtjie in droë gras*, Potchefstroom,
1991.

11 See Vatcher, *White Laager*. For an extended
discussion on the impact of fascism and
National Socialism in South Africa, see
Van Heerden, 'Nasionaal-Sosialisme as
faktor in die Suid-Afrikaanse Politiek,
1933–1948'; Steven Uran, 'Afrikaner Fascism
and National Socialism in South Africa:
1933–1945', unpublished MA dissertation,
University of Wisconsin, 1975; Sipho
Mzimela, *Apartheid: South African Nazism*,
Vantage Press, New York, 1983; Hattingh,
'Nasionaal-Sosialismus en die Gryshemp-
beweging in Suid-Afrika'; and Jeff Guy,
'Fascism, Nazism, Nationalism and the
Foundation of Apartheid Ideology', in
Stein Ugelvik Larsen (ed), *Fascism Outside
Europe: The European Impulse Against
Domestic Conditions in the Diffusion of Global
Fascism*, Columbia University Press, New
York, 2001. For an overview of Afrikaner
nationalism during the first two-thirds of
the twentieth century, see Coenraad Jacobus
Juta, 'Aspects of Afrikaner Nationalism,
1900–1964: An Analysis', unpublished PhD
dissertation, University of Natal, 1966; for
the radical right and antisemitism during
the war years, see Michael Roberts and
AEG Trollip, *The South African Opposition
1939–1945: An Essay in Contemporary History*,
Longman, Green and Co, London, 1947;
and for a Marxist analysis of Afrikaner
fascism, see Howard Simson, *The Social
Origins of Afrikaner Fascism and its Apartheid
Policy*, Acta Universitatis, Uppsala Studies in
Economic History 21, Armqvist and Wiksell,
Stockholm, 1980.

12 Moodie, p. 167.

13 The 1936 census reported 90 645 Jews out
of a total white population of 2 003 857.
See *Office of the Census and Statistics, Sixth
Census, 5th May, 1936, Vol VI, Religions of the
Europeans, Asiatics and Coloured Population*,

Government Printer, Pretoria, UG No 28,
1941, p. vii.

14 See Allie A Dubb, *The Jewish Population of
South Africa: The 1991 Sociodemographic Survey*,
Jewish Publications – South Africa, Kaplan
Centre for Jewish Studies, University of
Cape Town, 1994, p. 7.

15 The absence of a genuine sense of common
nationhood is captured in George Calpin,
There are no South Africans, Nelson, London,
1941.

16 Of the 14 per cent of Jewish women
gainfully employed, seven in ten were
engaged in commerce, double the
proportion among non-Jewish white
women. A mere four per cent of Jews in
formal occupations were farmers, though
some Jewish traders in the countryside had
subsidiary farming interests. See Morris
de Saxe (ed), *The South African Jewish Year
Book, 1929*, South African Jewish Historical
Society, Johannesburg, nd, p. 41.

17 Nearly 40 per cent of graduands and
diplomats at the University of the
Witwatersrand at the end of the 1920s were
Jewish. At the University of Cape Town,
Jews often made up over 20 per cent of the
graduating classes in Arts, Law, Medicine
and Commerce. See Richard Mendelsohn
and Milton Shain, *The Jews in South
Africa: An Illustrated History*, Jonathan Ball
Publishers, Cape Town, 2014, p. 91.

18 See EA Mantzaris, 'Radical Community:
The Yiddish-speaking Branch of the
International Socialist League, 1980–1920',
in Belinda Bozzoli (ed), *Class, Community
and Conflict. South African Perspectives*, Ravan
Press, Johannesburg, 1987.

19 Hostility was already evident in the old
Cape Colony, where mounting opposition
to the influx of 'undesirable' eastern
European Jews led to the passing of the
Cape Immigration Act of 1902, which
sought to exclude eastern European
Jews (together with Indians) by way of a
language provision. See Milton Shain, *Jewry
and Cape Society: The Origins and Activities
of the Jewish Board of Deputies for the Cape
Colony*, Historical Publications Society, Cape
Town, 1983, chapter two.

20 For the emergence of scientific racism, see
Saul Dubow, *Illicit Union: Scientific Racism
in Modern South Africa*, Witwatersrand
University Press, Johannesburg, 1995.

21 For the history of South African Jewry, see
Mendelsohn and Shain, *The Jews in South*

Africa.

22 *Hansard*, 10 February 1930.

23 Peberdy, p. 76

24 Milton Shain, *The Roots of Antisemitism in South Africa*, University of Virginia Press, Charlottesville, and Witwatersrand University Press, Johannesburg, 1994.

25 See Todd M Endelman, 'Comparative Perspectives on Modern Anti-Semitism in the West', in David Berger (ed), *History and Hate: The Dimensions of Anti-Semitism*, Philadelphia, Jewish Publication Society, 1986, p. 104.

26 The few occasions Jews are mentioned, be it in positive or negative terms, will be examined in a planned new volume examining antisemitism in South Africa after 1948.

CHAPTER ONE

AN UNABSORBABLE MINORITY

1 Bethal Publicity Association, *Bethal: A Progressive Centre of the Eastern Transvaal*, Cape Times Limited, 1928.

2 Lithuanian-born Esrael Lazarus began life as a trader in the Bethal district. He established a chain of stores early in the century before turning to farming. See MJ Murray, 'Factories in the Fields: Capitalist Farming in the Bethal District, c. 1910–1950', in A Jeeves and J Crush (eds), *White Farms, Black Labour: The State and Agrarian Change in Southern Africa, 1910–1950*, Heinemann, Portsmouth, NH, 1997, p. 82. Later his prominence in the region and his desire for cheap African labour gained him some notoriety. See Helen Bradford, 'Getting Away With Murder: "Mealie Kings", the State and Foreigners in the Eastern Transvaal, c. 1918–1950', in Philip Bonner, Peter Delius and Deborah Posel (eds), *Apartheid's Genesis, 1935–1962*, Ravan Press and Witwatersrand University Press, Johannesburg, 2001, p. 104.

3 About four per cent of Jews in formal occupations were farmers at the time, though some Jewish traders in the countryside had subsidiary farming interests. See De Saxe, p. 41.

4 Most of the Jewish newcomers to South Africa gravitated towards the larger towns. According to the 1926 census, South Africa's Jewish population numbered 71 816, or 4.3 per cent of the total white population.

5 Britain was attempting to transform South Africa into an efficient capitalist link in the chain of Empire. Anglicisation underpinned the process of reconstruction, which would ensure black subordination to whites, both Afrikaner and English. See Shula Marks and Stanley Trapido, 'Lord Milner and the South African State', *History Workshop Journal*, 8(1), 1979.

6 Despite the town's name, meaning 'House of God' in Hebrew, the number of Jews in the town remained small. See De Saxe, p. 281. From earliest days, the Jews played a significant role in the town's commercial rather than local affairs.

7 According to Bension Hersch, the National Party's Oswald Pirow had told a Vrededorp audience a few months earlier that 'some kind of quota was bound to be introduced in parliament to restrict further [eastern European Jewish] immigration'. See the *South African Jewish Chronicle (SAJC)*, 10 October 1930. Also, early in 1929, in response to a question at the hustings, Pirow had hinted at an immigration quota system. See Marcia Gitlin, *Vision Amazing*, Menorah, Johannesburg, 1950, p. 303.

8 *Cape Times*, 21 October 1929.

9 The National Party held the Bethal seat by a mere 107 votes and Stellenbosch by 268. See BM Schoeman, *Parlementêre verkiesings in Suid-Afrika 1911–1976*, Aktuele Publikasies, 1977, pp. 157 and 169. The Stellenbosch Hebrew Congregation then numbered 40. But many more Jews lived in the constituency. See Adrienne Kollenberg, Joan Gentin, Phyllis Jowell and David Saks (eds), *Jewish Life in the South African Country Communities*, Vol II, South African Friends of Beth Hatefuzoth, Johannesburg, 2004, pp. 241–54.

10 *Cape Times*, 24 January 1930. Described thus by George Wilson, one-time editor. See GH Wilson, *Gone Down The Years*, Howard Timmins, Cape Town, nd, p. 218. It appears that efforts had been made by the National Party to have Morris Alexander, a prominent Jewish leader and independent parliamentarian, stand in the by-election for the party. See Enid Alexander, *Morris Alexander: A Biography*, Juta and Co Ltd, Cape Town and Johannesburg, 1953, p. 143.

11 See JJJ Scholtz, 'Oswald Pirow', *Dictionary of South African Biography*, Volume V, Human Sciences Research Council, Pretoria, 1987, pp. 594–96.

12 *SAJC*, 24 January 1930. Since the meeting took place on a Friday night, few Jews would have attended. But they surely would have received the message.

13 *Ibid.*

14 To be sure, in November 1929, WP Louw, private secretary to the Minister of the Interior, Dr Daniël François Malan, sent a 'Strictly Confidential' communication to the Minister of Lands, PGW Grobler, with an attached 'copy of the Immigration Quota Bill which Dr Malan proposes to introduce at the next Parliamentary Session. The Minister requests that the provisions of this draft Bill be kept strictly confidential' (emphasis in original). WP Louw to Malan/Grobler, 25 November 1929. DF Malan Collection, 1/1/859. See also Cohen, 'Anatomy of South African Antisemitism', pp. 72–74.

15 *Cape Times*, 16 August 1921.

16 *Ibid*, 21 October 1929. The notion of Nordic was part of a European intellectual tradition rooted in essentialist race thinking. See chapter four. The reference to two nations related to the Afrikaners and the English.

17 See Dubow, *Illicit Union*; Saul Dubow, 'Race, Civilisation and Culture: The Elaboration of Segregationist Discourse in the Inter-war years', in Shula Marks and Stanley Trapido (eds), *The Politics of Class, Race and Nationalism in Twentieth Century South Africa*, Longman, London and New York, 1987; Peberdy, pp. 57–63; and Rodney Reznek, 'Excluding the Jew: Antisemitism and Eugenics in South Africa before 1930', unpublished MA thesis, University of London, 2012.

18 *The Star*, 17 September 1925.

19 Two Jewish MPs, Emile Nathan and Morris Kentridge, expressed shock immediately after Malan gave notice of the Bill. See *Hansard*, 29 January 1930.

20 See Bradlow, 'Immigration into the Union 1910–1948', chapter XI, *passim*.

21 See Hermann Giliomee, *The Afrikaners: Biography of a People*, Tafelberg, Cape Town, 2003, p. 366. Malan had spelled out the 'sacred task' of Afrikaners decades earlier. See Moodie, p. 1. For a detailed account of Malan's political thought and the impact of theology on his worldview, see Lindie Koorts, *DF Malan and the Rise of Afrikaner Nationalism*, Tafelberg, Cape Town, 2014, chapters one to four.

22 See Shain, *The Roots of Antisemitism in South*

Africa, chapter six, *passim*.

23 *Daily Dispatch*, 3 February 1930. For further indications of support see *Die Burger*, 30 January 1930; *Sunday Times*, 2 February 1930; *The Cape Argus*, 7 February 1930; and the *Daily Representative*, 3 February 1930. The eastern European Jewish newcomers were widely looked upon as the wrong sort of immigrant, devoid of morals. See Shain, *The Roots of Antisemitism in South Africa*, pp. 99–102.

24 *Hansard*, 10 February 1930.

25 *Ibid.*

26 For Abraham Kuyper and 'Kuyperianism' see Richard Elphick, *The Equality of Believers: Protestant Missionaries and the Racial Politics of South Africa*, University of KwaZulu-Natal Press, Scottsville, 2012, chapter 15, *passim*; Bloomberg, *Christian-Nationalism and the Rise of the Afrikaner Broederbond in South Africa 1918–48*, pp. 10–12; and Dubow, *Illicit Union*, pp. 259–62. Kuyper had decidedly ambivalent attitudes towards Jews. See Jonathan Israel and Renier Salverda (eds), *Dutch Jewry: Its History and Secular Culture*, Brill, Leiden, 2002, pp. 6–7. For Herder, see Paul Lawrence Rose, *German Question/Jewish Question: Revolutionary Antisemitism from Kant to Wagner*, Princeton University Press, Princeton, NJ, 1990, p. 99. Herder certainly believed in a national 'essence' that needed protection and promotion. The nation was 'a living organism, not a collection of individuals ... All cultures were organic and unique totalities, with unique and inimitable languages, values, traditions, institutions, and customs.' See Zeev Sternhell, 'From Counter-Enlightenment to the Revolutions of the 20th Century', in Shlomo Avineri and Zeev Sternhel (eds), *Europe's Century of Discontent: The Legacies of Fascism, Nazism and Communism*, The Hebrew University Magnes Press, Jerusalem, 2003, p. 12. We will see how Afrikaner cultural determinism in its Herder-like formulation had within it the potential to, as Sternhell writes, 'end in racial determinism' (p. 10).

27 Other government spokesmen denied that the Bill insulted Jews and also acknowledged the important contribution they had made to South Africa, focusing in effect, if not intent, on their power. Interestingly, conspiracies and the power of international financiers peppered Malan's rhetoric during a speech in Oudtshoorn as

early as 1921. See the *Oudtshoorn Courant*, 26 January 1921.

28 *Hansard*, 10 February 1930.

29 *Ibid*, 12 February 1930.

30 *Ibid*.

31 *Ibid*.

32 See Alan Paton, *Hofmeyr*, Oxford University Press, Cape Town and London, 1964, p. 169.

33 *Hansard*, 10 February 1930. For comment on the ambivalence in Hofmeyr's speech, which was noted by his opponents, see Paton, *Hofmeyr*, pp. 169–70. For his general ambivalence with regard to the Jewish immigration questions, see Edna Bradlow, 'JH Hofmeyr, Liberalism and Jewish Immigration', *South African Historical Journal*, 40(1), 1999, pp. 120–21.

34 *Hansard*, 17 February 1930. See also Cohen, 'Anatomy of South African Antisemitism', pp. 81–82.

35 Gerald Shaw, *The Cape Times: An Informal History*, David Philip Publishers, Cape Town, 1999, p. 63.

36 See *Hansard*, 17 February 1930.

37 In a study dealing with law, mobility and nationality in South Africa, Jonathan Klaaren notes that the Quota Act of 1930 (and Section 3 of the Immigration [Amendment] Act 19 of 1933) was 'by no means solely responsive to anti-Jewish sentiment within the European population'. However, virtually the entire debate around the Quota Act involved the question of eastern European Jews. Section 3 of the Act simply blocked loopholes for 'European' agricultural and domestic workers that dated back to the 1913 Immigration Act. See Jonathan Eugene Klaaren, 'Migrating to Citizenship: Mobility, Law, and Nationality in South Africa, 1897–1937', unpublished PhD dissertation, Yale University, 2004, pp. 246–47. In examining the panoply of immigration legislation in the different components of pre-Union South Africa, Klaaren largely ignores the 'undesirable' eastern European Jews as targets of legislation, albeit not the sole or primary targets.

38 *Hansard*, 17 February 1930. Kentridge would join the South African Party in 1932.

39 *Ibid*.

40 *Ibid*, 10 February 1930. Similar concerns about eastern European Jews were raised in the Senate debate discussing the Bill, most notably by George Munnik and CJ Langenhoven. See Cohen, 'Anatomy of South African Antisemitism', pp. 91–92.

41 From April to December 1930, a mere 77 immigrants born in 'restricted' countries entered the country, whereas in the first three months of that year the number had been 1 890. In 1931 only 780 Jewish newcomers came from 'quota' countries and for the next five years the combined number of Jews from restricted countries totalled 2 669. See Peberdy, p. 62. For details on the proportion of Jewish immigrants into South Africa from 1926 to 1942, see Lotta M Stone, 'Seeking Asylum: German Jewish Refugees in South Africa 1933–1948, unpublished PhD dissertation, Clark University, 2010, p. 43.

42 *SAJC*, 10 January 1930.

43 *Ibid*. Malan had spoken in support of Morris Alexander standing as an independent against the South African Party in March 1929. Alexander had most recently been the founder and sole member of the Constitutional Democrat Party.

44 See *Zionist Record*, 7 February 1930. The Board encouraged these meetings. See South African Jewish Board of Deputies, Executive Committee Minutes, 30 January and 3 February 1930.

45 See Morris Alexander to Siegfried Raphaely, c. 11 February 1930. Alexander Papers BC160, List II, 2, Letter Books, 1925–1932, and South African Jewish Board of Deputies, Executive Minutes, 17 February 1930 and 23 February 1930. See also Cohen, 'Anatomy of South African Antisemitism', pp. 96–98. Alexander had hoped to postpone discussion until Smuts returned from abroad. As we have seen, his return late in the proceedings had little impact.

46 DF Malan, Letter to 'Amice', 10 June 1930. EH Louw Collection, PV4, Vol 2/4. See also Furlong, *Between Crown and Swastika*, p. 51, and PE van der Schyff, 'Eric H Louw in die Suid-Afrikaanse Politiek', unpublished DLitt dissertation, Potchefstroom Universiteit vir Christelike Onderwys, 1974.

47 See Shain, *The Roots of Antisemitism in South Africa*, p. 26.

48 See Legislative Assembly Debates, Cape of Good Hope, 8 August, 1893, and Shain, *The Roots of Antisemitism in South Africa*, pp. 22–26. The *plaasroman* (farm novel), idealising the countryside and shunning the city, which emerged in the 1920s as a genre of antimodernist and romantic writing, affirmed these observations. See

JM Coetzee, *White Writing: On the Culture of Letters in South Africa*, Yale University Press, New Haven and London, 1988, p. 78; and CN van der Merwe, *Breaking Barriers: Stereotypes and the Changing Values in Afrikaans Writings 1875–1990*, Rodopi, Amsterdam and Atlanta, 1994, pp. 18–22.

49 A pejorative term for the poor eastern European Jew. For etymologies see Mendelsohn and Shain, *The Jews in South Africa*, p. 45.

50 See Shain, *The Roots of Antisemitism in South Africa*, pp. 62–64.

51 *Ibid*, chapter five, *passim*.

52 Quoted in *The Star*, 16 March 1922.

53 The Anglo-Boer War had also aggravated the 'poor white' problem. About 30 000 Boer homesteads were destroyed, along with livestock and crops, during the conflict, uprooting thousands of Boer tenant farmers, or *bywoners*.

54 See David Welsh, 'The Growth of Towns', in Leonard Thompson and Monica Wilson (eds), *The Oxford History of South Africa*, Oxford University Press, London, 1971, p. 202.

55 WA de Klerk, *The Puritans in Africa: A story of Afrikanerdom*, Penguin Books, Harmondsworth, 1975, p. 199.

56 See O'Meara, *Volkskapitalisme*, p. 33.

57 De Klerk, *The Puritans in Africa*, p. 110.

58 *Cape Argus*, 21 October 1931.

59 Giliomee, *The Afrikaners*, p. 430. Already in 1930, Professor JF Burger of the University of Cape Town spoke of the Afrikaners in the cities living 'in the midst of a foreign environment' who had to be taught 'to remain Afrikaners in heart and soul'. See *Die Burger*, 17 December 1930.

60 The commission investigating the 'poor white' problem was established in 1928 under the auspices of the Carnegie Corporation, acting with the Dutch Reformed Church and the South African government. It was a multidisciplinary social science investigation. The report was published in December 1932. See JWF Grosskopf, *Poor White Problem in South Africa. Report of the Carnegie Commission*, Vol II, Stellenbosch, 1932, pp. 115 and 123, and Peberdy, p. 76. See also JR Albertyn, *The Poor White Society: Report of the Carnegie Commission*, Vol V, Stellenbosch, 1932, p. 35, and the autobiography of one of the commissioners, EG Malherbe, *Never A Dull Moment*, Howard Timmins Publishers, Cape Town, 1981, p. 128.

61 See *Cape Times*, 24 February 1930. For tensions between Jews and non-Jews in Brandfort, see also Adrienne Kollenberg and Rose Norwich, *Jewish Life in the South African Country Communities*, Vol V, South African Friends of Beth Hatefutzoth, Johannesburg, 2012, p. 449.

62 Even the Humane Slaughtering Bill, which questioned Jewish (and Muslim) methods of slaughter, managed to put Jewish parliamentarians on the defensive. See *Hansard*, 13 May 1930, and South African Jewish Board of Deputies, Report of the Executive Committee, December 1929 to November 1931. Four years later, the Jewish method of slaughter became the subject of debate in the Senate. See *Daily Dispatch*, 14 March 1934 and *Zionist Record*, 25 May 1934.

63 *SAJC*, 30 May 1930.

64 *Ibid*, 10 October 1930.

65 See Bradlow, 'Immigration into the Union 1910–1948', p. 247 and *Rand Daily Mail*, 28 March 1930.

66 See South African Jewish Board of Deputies, Executive Committee Minutes, 19 May 1930. As early as 1923 the Board reported that a publication with extracts from the *Protocols* had been distributed by *Die Burger*. See South African Jewish Board of Deputies, Report of the Executive Council, August 1921 to May 1923 to Fifth Congress, August 1923. For the spread of the *Protocols of the Elders of Zion*, see chapter two.

67 *Zionist Record*, 12 September 1930. Yet Pirow also claimed that there was no antisemitism in South Africa other than some trade jealousy on the part of English-speakers. See *Die Vaderland*, 9 September 1930.

68 *Rand Daily Mail*, 10 September 1930.

69 *Zionist Record*, 22 September 1930.

70 See *Zionist Record*, 16 January 1931.

71 The following year the Board of Deputies reported that defamatory anti-Jewish leaflets had been seen in Oudtshoorn. See *Zionist Record*, 15 May 1931.

72 Many Jews had enjoyed a comfortable relationship with the National Party in the 1920s. See Shimoni, pp. 92–96.

73 See also Paton, p. 189.

74 According to the *SAJC* (27 November 1931), the Jews of the North West Districts numbered a mere 643 souls out of a total population of 52 581. Six years later, Malan

told Maria Louw, his future wife, that Jews would not be as useful to Steenkamp in the wake of the fusion of the South African Party and the National Party. See DF Malan to Maria Louw (shortly before their marriage on 20 December 1937), Maria Malan Supplement, DF Malan Collection, No 1 KG67/347/31.

75 Patrick Duncan told Maud Selborne that Steenkamp was a great threat to the Nationalists, who 'are very concerned about him'. Duncan to Selborne, 20 February 1931. Duncan Papers, BC294, J1.9.7. Similarly, JH Hofmeyr recognised the importance of the 'Steenkamp movement'. See Minister JH Hofmeyr, Reutersberig in *Manchester Guardian*, 5 August 1931. DF Malan Collection 1/1/903. Conjecturing about what drove Malan's outburst, the *Zionist Record* (6 November 1931) hoped Malan's interview was not driven by more deep-seated anti-Jewish sentiments. If 'his statements were deliberate and calculated, made of set purpose and not under the stress of momentary feeling', it noted, 'then indeed we are faced with a grave and critical situation'.

76 *Die Burger*, 2 November 1931.
77 *The Star*, 3 November 1931.
78 *The Friend*, 4 November 1931.
79 *Cape Times*, 3 November 1931. See also Alexander, pp. 154–55.
80 *Ibid*, 4 November 1931. A distraught Herzl Schlosberg, a young advocate who had contested Patrick Duncan's Yeoville seat on behalf of the Nationalists in 1929 and would stand for the National Party in the Germiston by-election of 1932, wrote personally to Malan, expressing his assurances that very few Jews would be involved in 'the Steenkamp camp'. See HJ Schlosberg to DF Malan, 13 November 1931. DF Malan Collection, 1/1/916. A sense of concern is also evident in Ivan H Haarburger to JBM Hertzog, 4 November 1931. JBM Hertzog Collection, Box 62, A32.
81 See WP Louw to S Raphaely, 12 November 1931. DF Malan Collection, 1/1/915. For the full text of the meeting, see S Raphaely to DF Malan, 6 November 1931. DF Malan Collection, 1/1/914.
82 See *SAJC* and *Zionist Record*, 27 November 1931.
83 According to the Board, a notice in the *Government Gazette* had raised the fees from one pound ten shillings to five pounds. See

Zionist Record, 27 February 1931.
84 *Rand Daily Mail*, 21 November 1931.
85 *Ibid*, 21 November 1931.
86 *Ibid*. With regard to *The Riddle of the Jew's Success*, Malan's private secretary said the Minister had only made 'a cursory review of its contents' and had 'not read the book complained of, and on its merits and demerits he therefore did not and could not pass judgment'. See WH Louw to S Raphaely, 12 November 1931. DF Malan Collection, 1/1/915. For full text, see *SAJC*, 27 November 1931.
87 *Rand Daily Mail*, 21 November 1931.
88 *Die Burger*, 21 November 1931 and *Volksblad*, 21 November 1931.
89 *Ons Vaderland*, 20 November 1931.
90 An anti-Jewish leaflet, 'The Farmer and the Jew', was distributed in the Kroonstad district, and stickers defaming Jews were placed in library books in Cape Town. See South African Jewish Board of Deputies, Executive Committee Minutes, 29 November 1931.
91 *SAJC*, 11 December 1931.
92 *Zionist Record*, 27 November 1931.
93 *Ibid*.
94 See South African Jewish Board of Deputies, Report of the Executive Council for the period: December 1st 1929 to November 30th 1931.
95 For a full report, see *Zionist Record*, 8 and 15 January 1932.
96 Bohle was appointed to the South African College (forerunner to the University of Cape Town) in 1906. He was described as a 'Dogged and rabid old Nazi, notorious for his rough and unrefined behaviour'. See 'List of Dangerous Nazis'. Lawrence Papers, BC640, E3.266, and 'Nazi Activities in the Union of South Africa Before and During the War', December 1945. Lawrence Papers, BC640, E5.45.
97 Bohle, who had helped with war relief for the Germans, had been a founder member of the association and subsequently its leader. Sometimes the club is referred to as the Nationale Sozialistische Deutsche Arbeiter Partei, the Deutscher Bund or the Deutsche Verein. See also Otto von Strahl, *Seven Years as a Nazi Consul*, Unie-Volkspers Beperk, Port Elizabeth and Cape Town, 1944, chapter four, *passim*; and Furlong, *Between Crown and Swastika*, pp. 16–17. Furlong points out that, by the time Hitler came to power, Nazi organisational

structures in South Africa and South West Africa, had been in place since 1928. Bohle was the *Landesgruppenleiter* (country group leader) in South Africa, furthering Nazi aims from 1932 to 1934. From 1935 Nazi propaganda was given a boost by *Der Deutsche Afrikaner*, edited by Dr Wilhelm Stark. See Fankie Lucas Monama, 'Wartime Propaganda in the Union of South Africa, 1939–1945', unpublished PhD thesis, University of Stellenbosch, 2014, pp. 12–17.

98 See *SAJC*, 1 July 1932. The Deutsche Verein did attract attention in 1933 when Bohle strongly denied an accusation in the *Cape Times* (14 July 1933) that Hitler had Jewish ancestry. Morris Alexander expressed concern about Bohle in a letter to Hirsch Hillman in May 1932. See Morris Alexander to Hirsch Hillman, 10 May 1932. Alexander Papers, BC160, Letter Books, 1932–34. Bohle was closely monitored by the South African security establishment. See Major Colonel EA Gibbs to DECHIEF, 29 January 1941, 'Enquiries re Individuals', SADF Archives, CGS, War Box 249, File 53(4). The British High Commission was also concerned. See P Liesching to JM Thomas, 11 November 1933. High Commissioner (South Africa) Papers. Foreign Office, 371.

99 See Gustav Saron, 'Is the Conscience Clause On the Way Out?', *Jewish Affairs*, May 1959. The university was an outgrowth of the Gereformeerde Church Seminary at Potchefstroom, and was deeply informed by Kuyperian theology.

100 Alexander had been returned to parliament on a South African Party ticket in a by-election for the Woodstock seat on 5 January 1932. According to Enid Alexander, it was Malan's interview in *Die Burger* that led to his decision to return to the House. See Alexander, p. 153.

101 Morris Alexander to Mr Hillman, 15 March 1932, Alexander Papers, BC 160, List II, 2, Letter Books, 1925–1932.

102 *Cape Argus*, 16 April 1932.

103 *Hansard*, 15 April 1932.

104 *Ibid*.

105 *Zionist Record,* 30 September 1932. On the other hand, at the committee stage of the Potchefstroom University College Bill a year later, Alexander was more successful. See *Hansard*, 17 February 1933. Nevertheless, the *Zionist Record* (17 February 1933) remained unhappy.

106 See South African Jewish Board of Deputies, Executive Committee Minutes, 21 March 1932.

107 David Dainow (ed), *South African Rosh Hashana Annual 5693, 1932*, SA Zionist Federation, Technical Press, Johannesburg, 1932.

108 *Ibid*.

109 Dingaan's Day 'celebrated' the victory of the Voortrekkers over the Zulu in the Battle of Blood River in 1838.

110 This was not the first time Roos had challenged the political order. He had for some time sought to establish a Centrist Party. See Koorts, p. 248.

111 *Rand Daily Mail*, 31 December 1932.

112 See De Klerk, *The Puritans of Africa,* pp. 285ff.

113 See *Die Burger*, 4 and 29 January 1933. Boonzaier had given the appellation of 'Hoggenheimer' to his mining magnate cartoon in 1903. See Shain, *The Roots of Antisemitism in South Africa*, pp. 62–63. Another cartoon appeared in *Die Burger*, 18 February 1933. For the view of finance behind coalition and fusion, see At van Wyk, *Die Keeromstraatkliek: Die Burger en die politiek van koalisie an samesmelting 1932–1934*, Tafelberg, Cape Town, 1983.

114 See Aletta J Norval, *Deconstructing Apartheid Discourse*, Verso, London, 1996, p. 38.

115 He was confident that the real differences between the Nationalists and South African Party were minimal as a result of the important initiatives under the 'Pact' government. See also Moodie, p. 123.

116 See JC Smuts, *Greater South Africa: Plans for a Better World. The Speeches of JC Smuts*, The Truth Legion, Johannesburg, 1940, pp. 67ff.

117 The National Party won 75 of the 150 parliamentary seats, the South African Party 61.

118 See Koorts, pp. 264ff. Ironically, Smuts had assisted him at the hustings. Even so, he won by a mere 621 votes.

119 The National Party and the predominantly English Labour Party had compromised to lessen tensions around the key political issues of language and South Africa's relationship with Britain.

120 See, for example, *SAJC*, 10 April 1931. In April 1932, the writer Sarah Gertrude Millin wrote to Patrick Duncan explaining how Jews were suffering in Germany and criticising the Quota Act for its exclusionary principles. Sarah G Millin to Duncan, 16 April 1933. Duncan Papers, BC 294, D 9.1.23.

121 *SAJC*, 10 March 1933. One week later alarm bells were again sounded. In an editorial, 'The Plight of German Jews', the weekly warned that the predicament of German Jews could well spill over beyond Germany's borders. See *SAJC*, 17 March 1933.

122 *Ibid*, 31 March 1933.

123 *Zionist Record*, 31 March 1933.

124 See, for example, *Rand Daily Mail*, 31 January 1933. For further detail see Samuel McNally, 'Tracing Hitler, the Rise of Nazism and the Final Solution: Observations from the *Cape Times*, 1933–1945', unpublished MA (Minor) thesis, University of Cape Town, 2009.

125 *SAJC*, 31 March 1933.

126 *Zionist Record*, 28 April 1933.

127 *Rand Daily Mail*, 9 May 1933. In fact Hertzog issued an official statement deploring interference in the affairs of other countries and objecting to those driving an economic boycott of Germany. See Liesching to His Majesty's Government, 30 August 1933. High Commissioner (South Africa) Papers. Foreign Office, 371. It is interesting to note that Eric Louw informed Hertzog of a meeting with the German ambassador to South Africa, Dr Luther, a strong supporter of Hitler, who told him that Germany was being reborn (*her-geboorte*) and that the antisemitism was a product of Jewish commercial influence and Jewish communist activity since the First World War. Louw, EH 1933. Letter to General JBM Hertzog, 29 May 1937. EH Louw Collection, PV4, Vol 82/183. These comments must have resonated with Hertzog.

128 *Rand Daily Mail*, 9 May 1933. See also H Lester Smith to Dominion Office, 10 May 1933. High Commissioner (South Africa) Papers. Foreign Office, 371.

129 See *Zionist Record*, 19 May 1933.

130 *Die Vaderland*, 10 May 1933.

131 The issue of the alleged Jewish boycott would continue to fester. See, for example, letter from Karl Spilhaus, *Cape Times*, 28 September 1934. Events, closely monitored by the British High Commissioner, revealed that the South African Government was genuinely concerned about the threat of losing exports. According to a British High Commission report, it had requested journalists to tone down anti-German rhetoric. See P Liesching to JH Thomas, (Dominion Office), 30 August 1933. High Commissioner (South Africa) Papers. Foreign Office, 371.

132 *SAJC*, 2 June 1933.

133 See Saron, 'A History of South African Jewry', p. 621.

134 *SAJC*, 11 August 1933.

135 *Zionist Record*, 1 September 1933. The official statement was also noted in a communication from P Liesching to His Majesty's Government, 26 August 1933. High Commissioner (South Africa) Papers. Foreign Office, 302.

136 *SAJC*, 1 September 1933.

137 See *Official Year Book of the Union of South Africa 1934–35*. Office of the Census and Statistics, Pretoria, 1936, pp. 648–51. Hjalmar Schacht, President of the Reichsbank in Germany, stressed the 'ties of blood' between Germany and South Africa when he launched the *Pretoria*, a new vessel in the Woermann shipping line. He noted that Germany was South Africa's second-best customer, after Britain. See also Furlong, *Between Crown and Swastika*, p. 78, and Albrecht Hagemann, 'Very Special Relations: The "Third Reich" and the Union of South Africa, 1933–39', *South African Historical Journal*, 27(1), 1992, pp. 134–37. Calls for the boycott of its goods placed these trading ties under threat. To be sure, the German chargé d'affaires had bluntly told Dr Helgard Bodenstein, South Africa's Secretary for External Affairs, that German imports of South African goods would be halted in retaliation. See Liesching to His Majesty's Government, 26 August 1933. High Commissioner (South Africa) Papers. Foreign Office, 371.

138 See *SAJC*, 12 May 1933.

139 *Ibid*, 7 July 1933.

140 *Cape Times*, 3 August 1933.

141 Furlong, *Between Crown and Swastika*, p. 17.

142 See *Zionist Record*, 19 May 1933. Copy of the pamphlet in the Rudman Collection, PV160, File, 1/51/4/1. According to the copy in Rudman's file, the pamphlet was first printed in 1926.

143 *Zionist Record*, 19 May 1933.

144 See *SAJC*, 4 August 1933.

145 After completing his schooling at the South African College in Cape Town, Ernst Wilhelm Bohle left South Africa in 1920 to study in Germany. After studying Political Science and Commerce at the universities of Cologne and Berlin and spending several years in the import and export business,

he entered the Auslands-Abteilung and became close to Hitler, who decorated him in 1937. He was subsequently sentenced to five years' imprisonment at the Nuremberg trials after the war. See RW Guelke, 'Bohle, Hermann', in WJ de Kock and DW Krüger (eds), *Dictionary of South African Biography*, Vol II, Human Sciences Research Council, Pretoria, 1972, p. 68; Israel Gutman (ed), *Encyclopedia of the Holocaust*, Vol 1, Macmillan, New York and London, 1990, pp. 122–23, and 'Nazi Activities in the Union of South Africa Before and During the War'. For a thorough account of German activities in South West Africa, see 'Report on German Activities in SWA', Department of Foreign Affairs, BTS 1-18-6, AJ 1943.

146 See Gutman (ed), *Encyclopedia of the Holocaust*, Vol 1, pp. 122–23, and Ulrich Hutten, *South Africa is German*, anti-Hitler Publication, Johannesburg, 1942. The Hutten booklet was kindly provided by Richard Rosenthal from the collection of his father, Eric Rosenthal.

147 See *Report from South West Africa Commission*, UG No 26. 1936, Union of South Africa, Government Printer, Pretoria, 1936, pp. 54–64. These events drew the attention of the British High Commission in Pretoria. See Foreign Office, 371.

148 *SAJC*, 25 August 1933.

149 See Morris Alexander to Mr Niehaus, 9 September 1933. Alexander Papers, BC160, List II, 2, Letter Books 1932–34.

150 See I Goldblatt, *History of South West Africa, from the Beginning of the Nineteenth Century*, Juta & Co Ltd, Cape Town, 1971, p. 231.

151 This emerged after a speech given by Hofmeyr on the subject. See *SAJC*, 9 November 1934. For an overview, see 'Report on German Activities in SWA'. Department of Foreign Affairs, BTS 1-18-6, A J 1943.

152 See South African Jewish Board of Deputies, Executive Committee Minutes, 4 October 1933.

153 Van Heerden (p. 39) cites *Die Burger* reporting an obviously inflated crowd of 7000. An extract from a judgment by justices HS van Zyl and EF Watermeyer in the matter of *IJ Wilson* vs *Hairdresser's Supplies Ltd*, the latter under the control of Louis Weichardt, suggests that Weichardt had serious financial difficulties at the time and behaved improperly. See Appeal Case 12/1931 Cape of Good Hope Provincial Division. Copy in DF Malan Collection 1/1/894. At the time of his speech, Weichardt was chairman of the Hairdressers Apprenticeship Board, although he was not practising as a hairdresser according to an angry letter he penned to the *Cape Times* (28 October 1933). For further details on Weichardt, see chapter two.

154 Weichardt's speech was fully reported in the *Cape Times*, *Cape Argus* and *Die Burger* on 27 October 1933.

155 *Cape Times*, 27 October 1933.

156 *Cape Argus*, 27 October 1933.

157 *Natal Mercury*, 30 October 1933.

158 *Die Burger*, 27 October 1933.

159 The Dutch Reformed Church was often referred to as 'the National Party at prayer', but De Klerk suggests that description was not quite correct. 'It is more correct to say that the National Party was itself becoming, if not a church, then a party imbued with religion – a secular religion – at its very roots'. De Klerk, *Puritans in Africa*, p. 199. *Die Kerkbode* reached one in five Dutch Reformed Church households. See Elphick, p. 244.

160 *Die Kerkbode*, 8 November 1933. Yet only two years earlier a Dutch Reformed Church Synod report stated that the Jews 'were people who were strangers to the God of their forefathers, who have time and respect for nothing else but capital and capitalists, and who are clearly worshippers of Mammon'. See Cohen, 'Anatomy of South African Antisemitism', p. 111. The British High Commission, too, noted the Weichardt meeting. Percivale Leisching reported that 'it is too early to attempt an estimate of the strength of this anti-Jewish movement, or to judge whether an attempt to boycott Jewish traders is likely to be attended by any measure of success. There is little or no evidence of anti-Jewish propaganda in the Transvaal up to the present, whatever may be happening at the Cape.' P Liesching to JM Thomas, 30 October 1933, High Commissioner (South Africa) Papers. Foreign Office, 371. Patrick Duncan also noted the Weichardt meeting: 'Some foolish persons are trying or pretending to try to start a sort of Nazi movement here against the Jews by secret meetings and anonymous missives and the Jews, as is their wont, instead of treating it with contempt get up into the high places of publicity and shriek and rend their

garments.' Duncan to Selborne, 31 October 1933. Duncan Papers, BC 294, D5.25.37.

161 *SAJC*, 3 November 1933.

162 The meeting took place on 6 October 1933. See Alexander Papers, BC 160, List 1 C, 10 November 1933.

163 See South African Jewish Board of Deputies, Executive Committee Minutes, 23 October 1933, and Jocelyn Hellig, 'German-Jewish Immigration to South Africa during the 1930s: Revisiting the Charter of the SS *Stuttgart*', in James Jordan, Tony Kushner and Sarah Pearce (eds), *Jewish Journeys: From Philo to Hip Hop*, Vallentine Mitchell, London and Portland, 2010, pp. 151–52.

164 The *Zionist Record* (3 November 1933) was particularly pleased.

165 South African Jewish Board of Deputies, Executive Committee Minutes, 19 November 1933.

166 See South African Jewish Board of Deputies, Executive Committee Minutes, 20 November 1933.

167 *Cape Argus*, 27 October 1933. For the spread of propaganda, see also 'A Memorandum on Anti-Jewish Movements in South Africa'. Alexander Papers, BC160, List IV, 24.

168 *Cape Argus*, 27 October 1933. A flurry of correspondence in the *Cape Times* followed Weichardt's speech, not all of it hostile to the Greyshirt leader. See, for example, *Cape Times*, 1 and 6 November 1933. Ordination as a Reverend at Jews' College in London was possible without the advanced knowledge in Talmud that was necessary for the title of Rabbi.

169 See *Cape Times*, 28 October 1933. See also Morris Alexander to IM Goodman, 17 June 1933. Alexander Papers, BC160, List 1C, Letter Books 1932–1934.

170 See Special Committee report to Executive Council of Kimberley Conference Resolution. As Amended by Executive Council on June 21 1932. Alexander Papers, BC160, List IV, 24.

171 *Zionist Record*, 3 November 1933. In a letter to Hillman Hirsch, Morris Alexander expressed great concern about the spread of antisemitic propaganda. See Morris Alexander to Hillman Hirsch, 2 November 1933. Alexander Papers, BC160, Letter Books 1932–34.

172 *Cape Times*, 6 November 1933.

173 See South African Jewish Board of Deputies, Executive Committee Minutes, 29 January 1933 and 26 February 1933.

174 See P Liesching to JM Thomas, Dominion Office, 8 November 1933. High Commissioner (South Africa) Papers. Foreign Office, 371. Dold edited the journal *Industries of South Africa*.

175 Dold received only 53 votes in the by-election. According to Liesching, the Dolds 'were made to suffer for their sympathies during the war of 1914–1918'. See P Liesching to JM Thomas, Dominion Office, 8 November 1933. High Commissioner (South Africa) Papers. Foreign Office, 371. Dold denied any affiliations with the Nazi movement. See 'Mr Dold in South Africa, Say "heil" to Hitler', *Jewish Telegraphic Agency*, 17 December 1933. See also South African Jewish Board of Deputies, Executive Committee Minutes, 20 August 1934 and 'A Memorandum on Anti-Jewish Movements in South Africa'.

176 *Zionist Record*, 3 November 1933. This was certainly the case. Weichardt in the meantime received a letter (replete with letterhead and a swastika on the mast) from one GLL deFriedland, the 'Grand Master' of the Fascist League of South Africa. According to DeFriedland, the Fascist League had been founded in Cape Town two and a half years earlier (deFriedland to Weichardt, 28 November 1933, Weichardt Collection, PV 29, File 1/1). Writing earlier from Johannesburg, he told Weichardt that he had read reports of the new movement and suggested 'an exchange of ideas'. 'We are both convinced of the utter futility of the Democratic system of governing, and I believe that we both realise that if we wish to save this country for our own race, we shall have to scrap this system. The old politicians may try to do something in that direction themselves, but if so, I expect very little benefit to the country in general and the workers in particular, from any such move. We must make a clean sweep if we want to regenerate South Africa. None of the existing crowds will do, and neither the Nationalist Party, South African Party, Centre Party, Farmers and Workers Bond, or the Republican Bond are any good' (DeFriedland to Weichardt, 7 November 1933. Weichardt Collection, PV 29, File 1/1). In a further communication that revealed Weichardt had failed to reply, DeFriedland spoke of plans for a conference with 'leaders of all known bodies with Fascist ideals' in

Johannesburg (DeFriedland to Weichardt, 28 November 1933. Weichardt Collection, PV 29, File 1/1).

177 *The Friend*, 22 January 1934.
178 *Die Kerkbode*, 8 November 1933.
179 *Ibid*, 6 December 1933.
180 *Ibid*, 13 December 1933.
181 *The Friend*, 18 January 1934.
182 See Giliomee, *The Afrikaners*, pp. 405–406.
183 *Rand Daily Mail*, 16 January 1934. For swastika daubing, see *Rand Daily Mail*, 9 January 1934.
184 This was no doubt in response to a letter Alexander had written to John David Rheinhallt Jones at the Institute warning of the surge of antisemitism. 'It is too widespread to ignore,' he wrote. 'An attempt is being made to introduce the propaganda among the poor whites, the railway and other workers, the Coloured people, the Asiatics and the natives'. See Morris Alexander to Mr Jones, 28 November 1933, Hofmeyr Papers, 'Anti-Semitism' Collection, 88.6.1, Historical Papers Research Archives.
185 *Rand Daily Mail*, 24 January 1934.
186 As noted in the Introduction, the black majority in South Africa had never specifically identified Jews in their struggle for political rights. It was an issue of white exploitation and oppression.
187 *SAJC*, 26 January 1934. Alexander had been briefed by Hirsch Hillman, President of the Board, about a meeting he had had with Hertzog and Smuts. Smuts had assured him that the government 'was determined to put down any disturbances with a firm hand, but the movement had not yet reached the stage that the Government could take action and prevent free speech'. Hertzog was in agreement with Smuts. See South African Jewish Board of Deputies, Executive Committee Minutes, 5 February 1933. Alexander's letter books include a number of references at this time to rising antisemitism. He even noted Nazi swastikas on the headlights of a post office van in Cape Town. See 3 February 1934. Alexander Papers, BC 160, Letter Books, 1932–34.
188 See South African Jewish Board of Deputies, Executive Committee Minutes, 26 February 1934.
189 The movement had its own newspaper, *Ons Reg*, published in Ermelo. See South African Jewish Board of Deputies, 'The Anti-Jewish Movements in South Africa: The need for action', South African

Jewish Board of Deputies, July 1936. For the programme see 'The Programme of the South African National Democratic Movement', Morris Alexander Papers, BC 160, List III, 3c, 20 December 1933. Tielman Roos referred to Wessels as 'a bad egg'. See Morris Alexander to IM Goodman, 20 December 1933. Morris Alexander Papers, BC 160, List 1C, Letter Books, 1932–1934. According to Hattingh (pp. 136–37), the Suid-Afrikaanse Nasionale Demokratiese Beweging was born in the wake of the break-up of the Junior National Party in the Transvaal. Under the protection of the National Party, Havemann opposed the Greyshirts, whom he considered National Socialist and not democratic. He wanted to purify democracy of all influences that benefited the Jews at the cost of the Afrikaner and to see that the state controlled culture and not the capitalists. He was also against international capitalists and Jewish immigration and wanted to abolish citizen's rights of Jews. The Blackshirts were National Democratic and did not want a dictator (Weichardt Collection, PV 29, File 1). Another movement, *Die Volksbeweging* (The People's Movement), was established by HS Terblanche in Cape Town. See 'The Anti-Jewish Movements in South Africa', South African Jewish Board of Deputies, p. 4. In a letter to the *Cape Argus* (14 March 1934), Terblanche explained that he had been linked to Weichardt until he discovered a German element at work.

190 *Rand Daily Mail*, 1 February 1934.
191 For the speech, see *Rand Daily* Mail, 1 February 1934. In a communication six weeks earlier to Morris Alexander, IM Goodman complained that the *Protocols* were being circulated in 'Port Elizabeth and elsewhere'. See IM Goodman to Morris Alexander, 20 December 1933. Morris Alexander Papers BC 160, List III, 3c. On 27 October 1933, the *Cape* published 'A Devastating Conspiracy', an exposition of 'The Protocols of the Learned Elders of Zion' by J Robertson. Twenty-three so-called *Protocols* were listed. At the conclusion Robertson suggested that Social Credit, a movement founded in Britain by Major CH Douglas, was the only antidote to the *Protocols*. On 10 November, a letter appeared in the *Cape* from HG Cornish Bowden, Honorary Secretary of the Douglas Social Credit Study Circle, pointing

out that the Circle was non-racial and in no sense antisemitic. Bowden was concerned that a section of the community may have been pained by Robertson's article. See the *Cape*, 10 November 1933.

192 *Cape Times*, 16 February 1934.

193 See Alexander Papers BC 160, List 111 3c. IM Goodman to Morris Alexander, 20 December 1933, including the 'Programme of the South African National Democratic Movement'. Wessels soon embarked on a speaking tour of the Transvaal, with eight engagements in four days. See 'Anti-Semitism Correspondence, Part B 88.6.1, "Publieke Vergadering"', Historical Papers Research Archives, South African Institute for Race Relations.

194 *Cape Argus*, 18 January 1934.

195 *Zionist Record*, 19 January 1934. This is certainly borne out in the Greyshirt Case Papers, housed at the University of Cape Town. Schauder, a prominent Port Elizabeth Jewish leader, would soon be implicated in the 'Greyshirt Trial' in Grahamstown. See chapter two.

196 *Ibid*, 2 February 1934.

197 *Eastern Province Herald*, 30 January 1934.

198 *Ibid*, 30 January 1934. A protest meeting against Greyshirt activities was held in Port Elizabeth at which an organisation was founded to combat 'the spread of racialism in any form whatsoever'. See *Zionist Record*, 9 February 1934.

199 See Furlong, *Between Crown and Swastika*, p. 34.

200 See, for example, the *Rand Daily Mail*, 15 January 1934.

201 Riotous Assemblies and Criminal Law Amendment Act 27 of 1914. *Statutes of the Union of South Africa 1914*, Government Printer, Cape Town, 1914, p. 246.

202 *Hansard*, 2 February 1934. Shortly after this exchange, two young men in Port Elizabeth were charged with public violence. See *Zionist Record*, 23 February 1934.

203 Duncan to Selborne, 29 March 1934. Patrick Duncan Papers, BC294, D5.26.7. 'Fuhrer' was a reference to Louis Weichardt. At the time Duncan was writing, meetings were being held across the country. An anti-Jewish sermon delivered by the Reverend Gerrit Dirk Worst in Potchefstroom on 4 March 1934 claimed the Jews were no longer the 'Chosen People' because they rejected the creator. They traded all over the world in nefarious ways, he said, and the

Jewish guest was becoming the owner of the world and pushing out the host. Worst's speech was reported in full in *Die Weste*, 9 March 1934. See South African Jewish Board of Deputies, Executive Committee Minutes, 25 March 1934. A copy of *Die Weste* is included in the 'Anti-Semitism' Collection, 88.6.1, Historical Papers Research Archives.

204 In the 1920s a League of Gentiles had been established with a crude anti-Jewish manifesto. But it failed to get off the ground. See Shain, *The Roots of Antisemitism in South Africa*, pp. 120–25.

205 See, for example, Eric Louw's letter to JBM Hertzog, almost a year before South Africa left the gold standard, in Van der Schyff, 'Eric H Louw in die Suid-Afrikaanse Politiek tot 1948', p. 303. For the alleged power of Hoggenheimer in the tumultuous period leading to Fusion, see Van Wyk, *Die Keeromstraatkliek*.

206 *SAJC*, 20 April 1934. Six months later, the Sea Point Synagogue was daubed with swastikas. See *Zionist Record*, 19 October 1934.

207 See WK Hancock, *Smuts. Vol II: The Fields of Force, 1919–1950*, Cambridge University Press, Cambridge, 1968, pp. 269–70.

208 *SAJC*, 20 April 1934.

209 *Ibid*, 23 March 1934.

210 The merger was also unacceptable for the mainly Natal-based and English-speaking devolutionists in the South African Party. They formed the pro-Empire Dominion Party, under Colonel Charles Stallard in October 1934.

211 Paton, p. 197. See also *Die Burger*, 5 August 1933.

212 Four years later he characterised Afrikaner history as 'nothing other than the highest work of art of the centuries. We have a right to our nationhood because it was given to us by the Architect of the universe.' See *Die Burger*, 3 May 1937. From its inception the 'Purified' National Party was hostile to Jewish immigration and 'parasitism', a euphemism for Jewish middlemen. See National Party Cape. PV27 1/3/2/2/1/1.

213 See Furlong, *Between Crown and Swastika*, pp. 53–54.

214 See AN Pelzer, *Die Afrikaner-Broederbond: Eerste 50 Jaar*, Tafelberg, Cape Town, 1979; Bloomberg; and ELP Stals, Afrikaner Bond, Afrikaner Broederbond, *Geskiedenis van die Afrkaner-Broederbond 1918–1994*, Uitvoerende

Raad, 1998. In 1933 the Broederbond had already defined among its political ideals abolishing 'the exploitation by foreigners of the natural resources and population of South Africa', and the 'nationalisation of finance and the planned coordination of economic policy'. See *Die Volksblad*, 3 January 1945. See also Moodie, pp. 112–13, and Juta, pp. 46 and 52.

215 De Klerk, *The Puritans in Africa*, p. 107.

216 See Giliomee, *The Afrikaners*, p. 416.

217 See Moodie, pp. 147–49. The Handhawersbond looked to Malan for leadership, but with *samesmelting* and the conciliatory mood that followed, its popularity waned.

218 See *Zionist Record*, 3 November 1933.

219 *Die Burger*, 20 December 1934. As will be seen in chapter three, all these ideals would inform an exclusivist Afrikaner nationalism under Malan's 'Purified' National Party from the mid-1930s. See Joanne L Duffy, *The Politics of Ethnic Nationalism: Afrikaner Unity, the National Party, and the Radical Right in Stellenbosch, 1934–1948*, Routledge, New York and London, 2006, pp. 89–90. See also Furlong, *Between Crown and Swastika*, pp. 92–93.

220 See *Cape Times*, 14 June 1934; *Die Burger*, 14 June 1934; *Cape Argus*, 15 June 1934; and *Die Waarheid / The Truth*, 29 June 1934. Following the clash the Board issued an instruction that Jews were to ignore the Greyshirts, and those who took part in the battle were ordered to appear before the Board in Cape Town. See *Cape Argus*, 18 June 1934.

221 See South African Jewish Board of Deputies, Executive Committee Minutes, 14 May 1934.

222 Special Committee Report to Executive Council of Kimberley Conference Resolution. As Amended by Executive Council on June 21st 1932. Alexander Papers, BC160, List IV, 24.

223 A full report of speech was sent by the *Natal Witness* to the Board of Deputies, 17 June 1934. See South African Jewish Board of Deputies, Executive Committee Minutes, 27 June 1934. Rudman had been a member of the SA Horse IX Regiment and the SA Motor Cycle Corps during the First World War. Rudman Collection, PV 160, File 33. For the full text of the speech see 'Antisemitism, Documents and Speeches', Historical Papers Research Archives.

224 South African Jewish Board of Deputies, Executive Committee Minutes, 26 June 1934.

225 *Ibid*, 3 June 1934.

226 *Ibid*, 27 June 1934. For examples of other clashes between Jews and Greyshirts, see *The Friend*, 20 October 1934 and 5 November 1934.

227 Maritz was convicted of high treason, having returned to South Africa ten years after his involvement in the 1914 Afrikaner Rebellion.

228 'Herinneringe', Dr AL Geyer. Cape Archives, A 1890, Vol 1, No 3 (6 July 1934). Some months later, Geyer defined 'Hoggenheimer' as the chief enemy of the Afrikaner nationalist struggle. 'The Dark Money-Power is a tumour in the body of the capitalist system,' he wrote. See *Die Burger*, 15 November 1934 and Furlong, *Between Crown and Swastika*, p. 36. For the role of *Die Burger* in South African politics, see Jurie Jacobus Joubert, '*Die Burger* se Rol in die Suid-Afrikaanse Partypolitiek, 1934–1948', unpublished DLitt et Phil, University of South Africa, 1990.

CHAPTER TWO

THE RADICAL RIGHT

1 Louis Weichardt's father, Carl Heinrich Wilhelm, was a stationmaster at Lady Grey Bridge station in Paarl. He died shortly after Louis' birth. These details appeared in the applications of Louis and Carl Weichardt for British passports after the Great War. They were provided in a court case, *Louis Theodore Weichardt* vs *Argus Printing and Publishing Company*, 1943, Supreme Court of South Africa, Cape of Good Hope Provincial Division.

2 Although Van Heerden (p. 36) and Hattingh (p. 42) and a Greyshirt propaganda pamphlet claimed Weichardt attended an English high school in Natal before departing for Germany in 1912 (see Isak le Grange, 'Die Plan en Die Man vir die Volk van Suid Afrika', Suid-Afrikaanse Nasionaal-Sosialistiese Bond, Kaapstad, 1941/2), an affidavit signed by Weichardt in his case against the *Argus* notes that he left for Germany in 1906 at the age of twelve. This accords with the record of his schooling at the Neu-Hannover Schule. Under 'Child's Parent or Guardian', his school record notes

Mrs J Weichardt and her address is given as 'Pretoria'. It is also noted that he had come from the German School in Pretoria. He was at Neu-Hannover Schule for one year only. I wish to thank Erich Vorwerk for assisting me in obtaining the school registration record. Le Grange does not mention the Neu-Hannover Schule period. Significantly Weichardt had a passport issued to him in Nuremberg in 1912 according to the affidavit.

3 See 'Composition of Anti-Jewish Movements', 'Antisemitism 1933–42', SA Rochlin Archives, circa November 1934, 210.1.

4 See Van Heerden, p. 36. Little information on Weichardt's personal life is included in Van Heerden's account. For an overview of his life see the obituary by Willem Steenkamp (*Cape Times*, 29 October 1985). In an interview with Hattingh (p. 42) conducted in 1983, Weichardt claimed that his maternal grandfather had been a missionary in Jerusalem for twenty years before emigrating to Paul Kruger's republic.

5 *Natal Mercury*, 29 October 1985.

6 See *Louis Theodore Weichardt* vs *Argus Printing and Publishing Company*, 1943.

7 *Ibid*. Weichardt told Hattingh that he had joined the German army in 1913 for six months to learn about German military practices and had been in the army during what he anticipated would be a short war. He claimed to have been wounded three times. Soon after returning to South Africa, Weichardt said he had been arrested for treason, only to be released following his uncle's intervention with Smuts. He had further legal complications but these, according to Weichardt, were sorted out. See Hattingh, pp. 43–44. See also *Die Waarheid/The Truth*, 11 January 1935, for an account of Weichardt's war experience.

8 Frikkie Jacobus du Toit, 'A Short Biography of a Great Leader', *Die Waarheid/The Truth*, 3 January 1936, and Le Grange, 'Die Man en die Plan vir die Volk van Suid Afrika'. *Die Waarheid/The Truth* was published between 1934 and 1938. See also 'Re: *LT Weichardt* vs *The Argus Printing & Publishing Co*', Weichardt Collection. PV29, File 163.

9 See Du Toit, 'A Short Biography of a Great Leader'.

10 See *Louis Theodore Weichardt* vs *Argus Printing and Publishing Company*, 1943. Weichardt named his house in Mowbray (Cape Town)

'Solingen'. He married a German woman from the town.

11 Du Toit. See also LT Weichardt, 'National Socialism in South Africa', *Fascist Quarterly*, 2(4), 1936; Van Heerden, 'A Short Biography of a Great Leader', pp. 36–37, and Hattingh, pp. 44–45. While Weichardt objected to all 'parasites', he identified Jews as especially adept at exploitation. See Hattingh, p. 61, n. 49.

12 Weichardt was also irritated by Malan's tepid handling of the Quota Act of 1930 and the boycott campaign against Germany. See Van Heerden, p. 38. He maintained his original motivation twelve years later. As he explained, he left the National Party in 1933 'not because he did not share its "national convictions", but because he had a "deeper conviction": the *Boerevolk* had to be anchored in *race*; an Afrikaner is not someone who merely joins the NP, for then Jews could be Afrikaners as well. "Afrikanerhood" had to be purified of its illegitimate elements …' See Norval, p. 50.

13 See Van Heerden, p. 41. According to Van Heerden (p. 40), the movement was created a few days after the Koffiehuis meeting at the behest of enthusiasts who had attended the occasion. This is confirmed in Hattingh, (p. 48). Weichardt initially planned to call the movement the Green Shirts but he had been asked to change it to the Greyshirts. He was particularly proud that of the 13 original members, all remained on board. This was not the case for the original seven Nazis in Germany, he said. See Weichardt Collection, PV 29, File 117.

14 Weichardt claimed the SANP was established in late 1933. It was in fact 1934. Van Heerden (pp. 46–47) argues that the name change was a deliberate move to play a new role in the wake of coalition and fusion and because of the birth of the Oranjehemde, a National Party shirt-movement initiative (see below). It was also claimed that the movement was changed into a party so as to prevent meetings being banned by the government. Weichardt made it clear that he would contest as many constituencies as possible and would have nothing to do with other parties. See Hattingh, p. 63.

15 Weichardt, 'National Socialism in South Africa', pp. 557–58.

16 Hattingh, p. 57.

17 This was certainly a far-fetched claim.

However, Weichardt did receive hostile mail.
See Weichardt Collection, PV 29, File 1/1
and Hattingh, pp. 46–48.

18 See David M Scher, 'Louis T Weichardt and
the South African Greyshirt Movement',
Kleio, 18(1), 1986; Van Heerden, chapter
two, *passim*; Hattingh, chapter two, *passim*
and Uran, chapter five, *passim*. Interviewed
in the *Cape Times* in 1966, Weichardt
denied ever being a fascist or a Nazi. 'I am,
and always have been, a national socialist;
socialist because I oppose the capitalist
system, and nationalist because I have only
one love – South Africa.' See obituary, *Cape
Times*, 29 October 1985.

19 See Hattingh, pp. 51–52.

20 Not all members of the party were
Greyshirts but all Greyshirts were members
of the party. See Weichardt Collection,
PV29, File 117. For Greyshirt structure and
organisation see Van Heerden, pp. 42–45,
and Hattingh, pp. 51–54. The members
also wore a black jacket with a swastika
which, according to Weichardt, represented
the unity of the four provinces and dated
back a decade before Hitler came to
power in Germany. See Hattingh, p. 52.
Die Waarheid / The Truth, on the other hand
claimed that the swastika was 'the symbol
of the Nordic races and always has been
from the beginning of Sunworship. It does
not belong to Germany although Hitler
could not have chosen a more appropriate
symbol'. See Uran, p. 193.

21 This support was strongly denied by
Weichardt, who said he would be willing
to fight against Germany notwithstanding
the pride he took in his German ancestry.
See Hattingh, pp. 53, 56, 75–76. Evidence
gathered after a raid on the Nazi offices in
Windhoek on 12 July 1934 tells a different
story.

22 Van Heerden, p. 44. From the start,
Weichardt was supported by English-
speaking and Afrikaner businessmen. See
Hattingh, p. 48.

23 See 'Composition of Anti-Jewish
Movements'. Weichardt told Hattingh
(p. 62) that membership by the end of
1933 was 3 000. The EG Malherbe Papers
indicate over 7 000 by 1937. See Monama,
p. 38. Malherbe served a director of military
intelligence for most of the Second World
War.

24 According to Van Heerden (personal
communication), his English betrayed a

German accent. At the first SANP Congress
in December 1934, a Mr de Bruyn was
upset that the SANP leader did not address
the gathering in Afrikaans. Weichardt
assured him he would master the language
within six months. See Congress Report,
Weichardt Collection, PV29, File 117. In his
interview with Hattingh (p. 45), Weichardt
said he wanted Afrikaans to be the official
language in South Africa and hoped English,
as a remnant of European colonialism,
would disappear.

25 See Van Heerden, p. 65 and *Die Waarheid /
The Truth*, 19 February 1937.

26 Weichardt believed that Afrikaners saw
his movement as a means of dealing with
the 'poor white' problem, while English-
speakers supported him in order to
challenge the traditional English business
establishment. See Van Heerden, p. 45 and
Hattingh, p. 100. One observer, J Conradie,
reported to the South African Institute for
Race Relations that most of those attending
Greyshirt meetings were 'tramdrivers,
railway workers, unskilled labourers,
shopwalkers etc'. Conradie viewed the
emergence of the Greyshirts in a very
serious light, noting that audiences were
not simply attending meetings 'out of sheer
curiosity'. See Hofmeyr Papers, J Conradie
to JD Rheinallt-Jones, 25 June 1934.
South African Institute of Race Relations,
Records, Part B 88.6.1.

27 Wylie's efforts as editor were carried out
secretly, presumably because of his position
at the University of Cape Town. See
Weichardt to JHH de Waal, 24 October
1934, Weichardt Collection, PV 29, File
1/1/117. HC Dashwood Browne, another
English-speaker, also served as editor.

28 Wylie held degrees from Edinburgh and
London. He took up a position at the
University of Cape Town at the age of 40
in 1924. See *Cape Times*, 22 June 1948. In
addition to alerting the government to
the problem of antisemitism, the Board
did its best to gain support in important
places. Thus the secretary to the Executive
Council of the Board, IM Goodman, asked
the Reverend AP Bender, a Professor of
Hebrew at the University of Cape Town,
as well as the spiritual leader of the Cape
Town Hebrew Congregation, to alert the
university to the activities of Wylie. He
'has openly associated himself with the
activities of the Grey Shirt Movement',

Goodman informed Bender. Wylie was writing editorials for *Die Waarheid/The Truth*, which did not befit 'a gentleman holding a responsible educational position in the University', noted Goodman (IM Goodman to Bender, 22 January 1935). Personal File, JK Wylie 4.4.2 (382). Human Resources Department, Registry, Personal Files, University of Cape Town.

29 *Die Waarheid/The Truth*, 23 February 1934.

30 For a copy of the constitution of the South African National Party, see Rudman Collection, PV 160, File 1/69/2/1. See also Van Heerden, chapter two, *passim* and Hattingh, pp. 70–75. For 'Nordicism', see chapter four.

31 See Hattingh, pp. 65–70.

32 Clause 9: Definite Immigration Laws to exclude all Alien Races who are unable by reason of their character to be assimilated by the white races of South Africa.
a) South African Nationality shall not be granted to any such Aliens who entered South Africa after 1st November 1918.
b) Should South African Nationality already have been granted to any such Aliens, same to be declared null and void.
Clause 17 spelled out the great enemies of the country: 'National welfare in the first place, and consider international Socialism, Communism, and International Capitalism as enemies of the State. As an independent member of the Commonwealth of Nations, we will do our share in promoting world peace along economic and political lines. HAIL SOUTH AFRICA.' See *Die Waarheid/The Truth*, 23 February 1934, and Van Heerden, pp. 56–82. In 1935 the constitution was amended: Jews would be treated 'merely as temporary denizens of the country' and their positions regulated 'by special statutory provisions'. Under no circumstances would a Jew enjoy South African nationality; they could not hold official positions and their professional activity would be limited and regulated. See HH Morris to IM Abrahams, IM Goodman Collection, BC805.

33 See, for example, *Die Waarheid/The Truth*, 28 February 1936; 24 April 1936; 19 February 1937 and 5 March 1937. See also cartoon, 17 January 1936.

34 *Die Waarheid/The Truth*, 8 February 1935.

35 See, for example, 'Die Sionistiese Protokolle', in *Die Waarheid/The Truth*, 4 May 1934. The question of the *Protocols of the Elders of Zion* would become the subject of a major court case. See below.

36 See Van Heerden, pp. 78–80.

37 *Die Waarheid/The Truth*, 10 July 1936.

38 *Ibid*, 13 July 1934.

39 *Ibid*, 24 March 1936.

40 This was not a new accusation and can be traced to JA Hobson, the pro-Boer English intellectual. See Shain, *The Roots of Antisemitism in South Africa*, pp. 42–44. Weichardt's family allegedly suffered financially in what Weichardt referred to as 'the Jew-made Anglo-Boer War of 1899–1902'. See Du Toit, 'A Short Biography of a Great Leader'.

41 See Van Heerden, pp. 57–70.

42 *Ibid*, pp. 80–81.

43 See Shain, *The Roots of Antisemitism in South Africa*, pp. 12–16 and 22–26.

44 *SAJC*, 20 July 1934.

45 At its highpoint in the 1930s there were only 36 families. See Adrienne Kollenberg and Rose Norwich, *Jewish Life in the South African Country Communities*, Vol III, The South African Friends of Beth Hatefutsoth, Johannesburg, 2007.

46 He alleged this was because of a bribe from a 'Jewish notable'. See below.

47 See Mark Lazarus, *The Challenge*, Mercantile Press, Port Elizabeth, 1935, p. 120.

48 *Ibid*, p. 17.

49 See 'Composition of Anti-Jewish Movements'. According to Hattingh (p. 81), Weichardt met Inch at a National Party congress and Inch introduced Von Moltke to Weichardt. Von Moltke was happy to support Weichardt's initiative so long as he did not establish a formal political party.

50 See 'Transcript of the Greyshirt Trial', University of Cape Town.

51 It later turned out that the lettering spelled out 'Kosher lepesach' (Pesach accredited).

52 See *Die Rapport*, 6 April 1934.

53 *Die Rapport* published a range of viciously anti-Jewish articles, focusing on Jewish conspiracies. Much of the material emanated from abroad, including from *The Fascist,* the official organ of the Imperial Fascist League of England.

54 *Die Rapport* subsequently had 'Official Organ of the South African Gentile National Socialist Movement' on its masthead and Olivier was appointed Greyshirt leader in Aberdeen. See Olivier's invitation to Johannes von Strauss von Moltke, 17 February 1934; Olivier to Von

Moltke, 26 February 1934; and 'Greyshirt Case'. Von Moltke was happy to write articles for the newspaper at no cost.

55 'Transcript of the Greyshirt Trial'.

56 It was published in Afrikaans on 6 April 1934 and in English on 13 April 1934, but now using Von Moltke's speech at the Feather Market Hall. See below.

57 *Die Rapport*, 6 April 1934.

58 Quoted on the cover of Lazarus, *The Challenge*.

59 *Die Rapport*, 13 April 1934.

60 *SAJC*, 4 May 1934. See also Gustav Saron, 'Four Eventful Decades', in *Jewish Affairs*, June 1953, pp. 33–35, and the South African Jewish Board of Deputies, Executive Committee Minutes, 3 July 1934. In terms of South African libel law, an attack on the community as a whole could not be considered libellous; identifying an individual could be.

61 *SAJC*, 20 April 1934.

62 *Ibid*, 27 April 1934. Full affidavits were published in *Die Rapport*, 18 May 1934. The distributor of *Die Rapport*, Alfred King, also known as Koening, was also named in the suit but he settled out of court. See *Zionist Record*, 3 August 1934.

63 See 'Greyshirt Case'.

64 For a classic account of the evolution and history of this forgery, see Norman Cohn, *Warrant for Genocide: The Myth of the Jewish World-conspiracy and the Protocols of the Elders of Zion*, Eyre & Spottiswoode, London, 1967.

65 *Die Waarheid / The Truth*, 4 May 1934.

66 See Hadassa Ben-Itto, *The Lie That Wouldn't Die: The Protocols of the Elders of Zion*, Vallentine Mitchell, London and Portland, 2005, p. 231.

67 As attorney general in the old Cape Colony, Graham had received a deputation of Jewish leaders (an embryonic Jewish Board of Deputies for the Cape Colony) to discuss discriminatory language provisions in the Cape Immigration Restriction Act of 1902. See Shain, *Jewry and Cape Society*, pp. 59–60.

68 *Zionist Record*, 13 July 1934.

69 *Ibid*.

70 They were instructed by B Smulian of Port Elizabeth. See South African Jewish Board of Deputies, Executive Committee Minutes, 26 August 1934.

71 See Ben-Itto, pp. 237ff.

72 See Lazarus, *The Challenge*, p. 52 and *Zionist Record*, 20 July 1934.

73 *Zionist Record*, 20 July 1934. 'Kahal' refers to a governing body of a pre-modern European Jewish community administering religious, legal and communal affairs.

74 See Von Moltke to Beamish, 5 May 1934. 'Greyshirt Case'. In this letter one gets the sense that Von Moltke believed his own conspiratorial worldview.

75 This claim was questioned in a document produced by the Board. See 'Composition of Anti-Jewish Movements'.

76 See Gisela C Lebzelter, *Political Anti-Semitism in England 1918–1939*, Holmes & Meier, New York, 1978, p. 2; Barry A Kosmin, 'Colonial Careers for Marginal Fascists – A Portrait of Hamilton Beamish', in *Wiener Library Bulletin*, 28(30–31), 1973–74; and Giesela C Lebzelter, 'Henry Hamilton Beamish and the Britons: Champions of Anti-Semitism', in Kenneth Lunn and Richard C Thurlow (eds), *British Fascism: Essays on the Radical Right in Interwar Britain*, Croom Helm, London, 1980.

77 *The Times*, 2 December 1919.

78 See Lebzelter, *Political Anti-Semitism in England*, pp. 21–22.

79 See the evidence of Beamish in Lazarus, *The Challenge*, pp. 77–97, and *Zionist Record*, 20 July 1934. Beamish appears to have genuinely believed in Jewish conspiracies. See letter to Mrs Bird. HH Beamish to Mrs Bird, 29 July 1934, Rudman Collection, PV 160, File 1/80/B1.

80 Jews at the time comprised about 4.5 per cent of the white population.

81 *Zionist Record*, 24 August 1934. Olivier subsequently recanted with an article in *Die Rapport* and Inch was tried for making false statements in affidavits and for perjury. He was sentenced to six years and three months to prison, with hard labour. See 'Truth will Prevail', Council of Natal Jewry, February 1935. A petition organised by Weichardt subsequently led to a reduction in the sentence to three years and three months, with hard labour. See Furlong, *Between Crown and Swastika*, p. 42, and Hattingh, pp. 89–93. Matthys Strijdom (brother of Hans) was involved in the case but was acquitted. See Hattingh, p. 92.

82 See *Zionist Record*, 24 August 1934 and Supreme Court of South Africa. Eastern Districts Local Division. Between Abraham Levy and Johannes von Strauss von Moltke, Harry Victor Inch, David Hermanus Olivier (Junior).

83 Supreme Court of South Africa. Eastern

Districts Local Division.

84 *Zionist Record*, 24 August 1934.

85 *SAJC*, 24 August 1934.

86 *The Friend*, 23 August 1934.

87 Cited in *SAJC*, 31 August 1934.

88 See, for example, 'From the South African Gentile National Movement. South African National Party, Compiled and Presented by: R Rudman'. RK Rudman Collection, PV160, File, 1/69/2/1.

89 *Zionist Record*, 19 October 1934.

90 JHH de Waal (Jnr) and FJ du Toit were the joint organising secretaries. In the main, the SANP attracted Afrikaans-speakers disillusioned with the National Party under Hertzog. See 'Composition of Anti-Jewish Movements'. Du Toit was a lead writer and driving force of *Die Waarheid/The Truth*.

91 PM de Waal, a brother of the Greyshirt organising secretary in the Cape, was secretary. On 17 November 1934 a Constable Davidson of Vryheid had asked members of the police mess in Pietermaritzburg to indicate their feelings about the Greyshirts. There was unanimous support for the movement. See 'Composition of Anti-Jewish Movements'.

92 The inaugural meeting was addressed by HA (Manie) Wessels at Vrededorp on 23 August 1934. See *Rand Daily Mail*, 24 August 1934. General Manie Maritz and Johannes von Strauss von Moltke – 'whose activities have in no way apparently been checked by judgment delivered against him in the recent libel action' – were members. See *Zionist Record*, 19 October 1934.

93 See South African Jewish Board of Deputies, Executive Committee Minutes, 7 October 1934. Bruwer was a disillusioned and Marx-inspired economist. The Brownshirts dissolved in 1936. See Hattingh, p. 138. In 1937 Bruwer attacked Malan's brand of nationalism and his scapegoating of the Jews. See *Independent*, 14 May 1937. Four years later he was highly critical of Nazi propaganda. See *Die Vrystater*, 6 June 1941.

94 Born in 1900, Stoffberg was the son of Senator Theunis Christoffel Stoffberg. After completing his dentistry degree at the University of the Witwatersrand in 1921 he went on to study in Michigan in 1925. Three years later he returned to South Africa and settled with his wife in Vryheid. See Hattingh, p. 174, n 43.

95 *Cape Times*, 12 September 1934.

96 JHH de Waal (Jnr) referred to the Oranjehemde at a meeting in Cape Town in June 1934, making it clear that the Greyshirts wanted nothing to do with them. See *Cape Argus*, 12 June 1934.

97 The major radical right players appeared to know one another. See L Kunze to Weichardt, 25 May 1934 and 29 May 1934, Weichardt Collection, PV 29, File, 1/1. Lothar Kunze was editor of *Die Deutsche-Afrika Post*, a German-language newspaper in Johannesburg. He had stated that Weichardt was the accepted leader of the Nazi movement in South Africa. 'Composition of Anti-Jewish Movements'.

98 See *Rand Daily Mail*, 30 October 1934 and *Natal Mercury*, 30 October 1934 for an assault on a Jew by RK Rudman and Peter de Waal.

99 See, for example, the *Paarl Post*, 22 June 1934, which indicated that it did not wish to report on political meetings. In some cases, meetings were prohibited by local magistrates. See chapter three.

100 See South African Jewish Board of Deputies, Executive Committee Minutes, 7 October 1934.

101 *Ibid*.

102 *Cape Argus,* 8 August 1934. The correspondent was Professor Bohle.

103 *Ibid*.

104 *SAJC*, 28 September 1934. Greyshirt meetings certainly attracted attention in the smaller rural towns. See Hattingh, pp. 101–102.

105 See SN Herman, *The Reaction of Jews to Anti-Semitism: A Social Psychological Study based upon Attitudes of a Group of South African Jewish Students*, Witwatersrand University Press, Johannesburg, 1945, pp. 29–31. An examination of stereotypes held by English-speaking university students, undertaken at this time by ID MacCrone, clearly illustrated the association of Jews with business. See ID MacCrone, 'A Quantitative Study of Race Stereotypes', *South African Journal of Science*, XXXIII, March 1937.

106 *Zionist Record*, 19 October 1934.

107 *The Newcastle Advertiser and Northern Post,* 3 November 1934 (Copy). Adendorff Collection PV 136: File 2/1/1/3.

108 In 1933, 204 German Jews entered the country; 452 entered in 1934. See Bradlow, 'Immigration into the Union', p. 251, and Peberdy, p. 65.

109 JHH de Waal to Hillel Schulgasser, 3 September 1934. I wish to thank Richard

Freedman for alerting me to the letter, which was in his personal possession.

110 *Rand Daily Mail*, 27 October 1934. The *SAJC* (9 November 1934) took exception to a suggestion made by Hofmeyr that the Jewish boycott of German goods was adding fuel to the hostility. For the spread of antisemitism, see Furlong, *Between Crown and Swastika*, p. 37.

111 The congress proceedings were reported in the press and a typescript of proceedings is available in the Weichardt Collection, PV 29 File 117. Reportage of the proceedings is based largely on the typescript with additional quotes from the *Cape Argus*. *Die Burger* (19 December 1934) reported that only 25 delegates were present, with about 15 members of the public attending.

112 *Cape Argus*, 18 December 1934.

113 It appears that Von Moltke had stolen money (see 'Composition of Anti-Jewish Movements'), although Hattingh (pp. 83–85) maintains Weichardt was furious with Von Moltke for releasing the 'Jewish plot' document and betraying Inch. (See F van Hasselt to Von Moltke, 30 January 1935. Weichardt Collection, PV 29, File 49, and Hattingh, p. 96). This resulted in the eastern Cape Province Greyshirts under Von Moltke establishing a separate movement (see Hattingh, pp. 83–85) and the subsequent formation of the South African Fascists under Von Moltke, supported by Olivier's *Rapport* and later by *Patria*, which was financially assisted by Bruckner de Villiers, the National Party MP for Stellenbosch. Weichardt also had problems with Manie Maritz, whom he believed had deserted the 'Cause'. But the 1914 Rebellion leader's anti-Jewish credentials were not in question, according to Weichardt. It is quite apparent that much infighting took place within the movement. See Hattingh, pp. 106–107.

114 See 'Composition of Anti-Jewish Movements', and Dashwood Browne to Weichardt, 11 November 1934; Adeliza Marshall to Weichardt, 20 October 1934, and A Marshall to Weichardt, 20 October 1934, Weichardt Collection, PV 29 File 1.

115 *Cape Argus*, 18 December 1934. For the full text of Wiechardt's speech, see Weichardt Collection, PV 29, File 117.

116 Seemingly untouched by the Greyshirt trial, Harry Inch added his voice in support of Weichardt, whom, he said, had stood by him at the time of the trial after he had been

misled by others. Philip Salzwedel (known as the 'Greyshirt Storm Trooper') of the Free State added his support for Weichardt, followed by Mr Els from Cradock and Mr Bruyns from Wolmaranstad in the Orange Free State.

117 Weichardt noted that there were non-Jewish aliens who would have to be removed, and erroneously fingered among them Solly Sachs, secretary general of the Garment Workers' Union, who was in fact Jewish. For indications of Jewish influence among unionists, see HJ Simons and RE Simons, *Class and Colour in South Africa*, Penguin Books, Harmondsworth, Middlesex, 1969, p. 470, and *Die Burger*, 19 December 1934.

118 *Cape Argus*, 21 December 1934.

119 South African Jewish Board of Deputies, Executive Committee Minutes, 5 January 1935.

120 *Ibid*, 7 January 1935.

121 'A Memorandum on the Anti-Jewish Movements in South Africa'. De Waal wished to focus on the 'Jewish Question' only and was unhappy with the SANP's National Socialism. See Hattingh, pp. 113–14. Hattingh (pp. 61–62) also notes that De Waal objected to parliamentary politics. See also Hattingh, pp. 82 and 111, and interview with LC Botha in 1973 (p. 80).

122 *Zionist Record*, 8 March 1935.

123 *Die Burger*, 31 May 1935.

124 See South Africa Jewish Board of Deputies. Executive Committee Minutes, 24 June 1935.

125 *Zionist Record*, 15 and 22 March 1935.

126 See South African Jewish Board of Deputies. Executive Committee Minutes, 30 June 1935. According to Hattingh (p. 112), 13 branches were established by April 1935, each with on average 40 members.

127 Jan Hendrik Hofmeyr de Waal, *My Ontwaking*, Cape Town, nd.

128 *Zionist Record*, 29 March 1935. The newspaper anticipated that De Waal's *My Ontwaking* would soon be translated into English.

129 In an interview with Hattingh (p. 82), Von Moltke recalled that the South African Fascists (sometimes known as the South African Fascist League) and the SANP shared the same basic ideas. The League, he said, had ties to the Imperial Fascist League and the League of Rhodesian Fascists, as well as connections with HH Beamish. See 'A Memorandum on the anti-Jewish

Movements in South Africa'.

130 See Van Heerden, p. 100. D de Flemingh (whom it will be recalled communicated with Weichardt shortly after the Greyshirt leader had launched his movement) was prominent in Havemann's Blackshirt movement, which appealed to many Nationalists.

131 Report by 'Vlam', 16 March 1935. In the author's personal possession.

132 *Zionist Record*, 15 and 22 March 1935.

133 See South Africa Jewish Board of Deputies. Executive Committee Minutes, 24 June 1935.

134 See Hattingh, pp. 77 and 119, and *Pretoria News*, 22 May 1935. Weichardt wrote an angry letter to Prime Minister Hertzog expressing disgust at Morris Alexander and the Board for pressurising magistrates to refuse venues for the SANP. See Louis Weichardt to JBM Hertzog, 24 August 1935, Weichardt Collection, PV29, File 1/69/2/1. According to Weichardt, Jews threatened non-Jewish tenants in their rented offices. See Van Heerden, pp. 47–48. Von Moltke and Inch also wrote an open letter in pamphlet form to Smuts deploring the outlawing of Greyshirt meetings in Paarl and Cradock. The nefarious hand of the Jew, they asserted, was manipulating South Africa, as it had done since the Jameson Raid. J von Moltke and H Inch to Jan Smuts, 15 June 1934. Weichardt Collection, PV 160, File 1/69/2/1.

135 See South African Jewish Board of Deputies. Executive Committee Minutes, 24 June 1935.

136 Verbatim report of speech made on 2 May 1935. See 'The Anti-Jewish Movements in South Africa', p. 24.

137 *Zionist Record*, 17 May 1935.

138 *Ibid*, 24 May 1935. Smuts also assured the Jewish leadership that 'if there was no improvement in the near future, the Government will not hesitate to take effective measures to stop this Anti-Jewish agitation'. See South African Jewish Board of Deputies. Executive Committee Minutes, 24 June 1935. See also Stone, pp. 65–66. The Board also told Smuts of graffiti placed outside the Wolmarans Synagogue on 21 July 1935. See Stone, p. 68.

139 *Zionist Record*, 17 May 1935. On the same day the *North Western Press Prieska* (17 May 1935) reported a tirade by Zuidmeer in which he castigated Jews from beginning

to end. A new heaven and earth 'will come when Jews are gone and the National Socialists (not communists by any manner of means) have got into power'. The government, said Zuidmeer, was mostly in the pay of Jews.

140 See Giliomee, *The Afrikaners*, p. 406.

141 See Norval, p. 12.

142 *Cape Argus*, 3 October 1934.

143 *Ibid*, 4 October 1934.

144 See Koorts, p. 300.

145 Giliomee, *The Afrikaners*, p. 347.

146 Early in his career, the Dutch-born scholar had turned his attention to public policy issues and wider politics, focusing especially on the Afrikaner 'poor white' problem. For Verwoerd's studies in Germany see Christoph Marx, 'Hendrik Verwoerd and the Leipzig School of Psychology in 1926', *Historia*, 58(2), 2013.

147 Of course the depression had also caused massive poverty for the majority African population.

148 See Alexander Hepple, *Verwoerd*, Penguin, Harmondsworth, Middlesex, 1967, p. 27, and Henry Kenny, *Architect of Apartheid: HF Verwoerd – An Appraisal*, Jonathan Ball Publishers, Johannesburg, 1980, pp. 28–32. Roberta Miller takes issue with Hepple. See Roberta Balstad Miller, 'Science and Society in the Early Career of HF Verwoerd', *Journal of Southern African Studies*, 19(4), 1993, p. 654.

149 *Zionist Record*, 15 and 22 March 1935.

150 See Ivor Wilkins and Hans Strydom, *The Super-Afrikaners*, Jonathan Ball Publishers, Johannesburg, 1978, p. 54; René de Villiers, 'Afrikaner Nationalism', in Leonard Thompson and Monica Wilson (eds), *The Oxford History of South Africa*, p. 398; and *The Friend*, 8 November 1935.

151 De Villiers, p. 397. See also Moodie, chapter six, *passim*.

152 See Norval, p. 38.

153 *Cape Argus*, 25 March 1935. The National Party had been formed in the period 1914–15 after Hertzog split from the South African Party, which he believed had failed to respect Afrikaner interests.

154 See Simons and Simons, p. 470.

155 *Ibid*, and Giliomee, *The Afrikaners*, pp. 426–27. The Great Depression had seen thousands of Afrikaner women moving into the labour market. See Louise Vincent, 'Bread and Honour: White Working Class Women and Afrikaner Nationalism in the 1930s', *Journal of Southern African Studies*,

26(1), 2000.

156 Simons and Simons, p. 471. For fears of an alliance between the 'Jewish Peril' and the 'Black Peril', see Visser, 'The Production of Literature on the "Red Peril" and "Total Onslaught" in Twentieth Century South Africa'.

157 See Moodie, p. 17.

158 *Wapenskou*, November 1935. By then the Greyshirts had established a foothold in the university town (Duffy, p. 81) and a student branch was established in August 1935. In the same month Weichardt and his colleague, Zuidmeer, attracted a large audience when they spoke in the old power station building. See Duffy, pp. 81–82.

159 Moodie, p. 156. In his doctoral dissertation 'Vom Leiden und Dulden' (On Suffering and Patience) Diederichs rejected liberal rationalism. 'Only in the nation as the most total, most inclusive human community can man realise himself in full', writes Diederichs. 'The nation is the fulfillment of the individual life.' See N Diederichs, *Nasionalisme as lewensbeskouing en sy verhouding tot internasionalisme*, Nasionale Pers, Bloemfontein, 1936.

160 See Moodie, pp. 156–57; Dubow, *Illicit Union*, p. 263, and Bloomberg, pp. 115–16.

161 See, for example, the writings of Lodewicus (Wicus) Johannes du Plessis, a Professor of Constitutional Law at Potchefstroom. See also Moodie, pp. 161–62.

162 Hermann Giliomee, 'The Growth of Afrikaner Identity', in Heribert Adam and Hermann Giliomee (eds), *The Rise and Crisis of Afrikaner Power*, David Philip, Cape Town, 1979, p. 112.

163 See Elphick, p. 280.

164 *Die Volksblad*, 10 July 1935.

165 See Van Heerden, chapter two, *passim*.

166 To be sure, Isak le Grange, former editor of *Die Brandwag* and a key Greyshirt ideologue in the early 1940s, captured the close intellectual ties between the National Party and the Greyshirts. See Uran, pp. 169–74. Although the views of the Greyshirts were considered too extreme for official ties with mainstream Afrikaner nationalists, ordinary Nationalists did give financial donations, and electoral pacts between Nationalists and the Greyshirts were established in a number of constituencies over time. See below.

167 *Zionist Record*, 17 April 1935.

168 *Ibid*, 12 July 1935.

169 *Ibid*, 16 August 1935. A similar line was followed by *Die Republikein* (17 July 1934), a new Nationalist-supporting newspaper (formerly *Die Weste*). In its first editorial the newspaper explained that it stood against British imperialism, not the English, and against parasitism and liberalism but not the Jew as such.

170 'The Party recognises the sovereignty and guidance of the Almighty God and seeks the development of our national life along Christian-national lines'. See 'Programme of Principles of the National Party of South Africa', in The National Party of the Cape Province. Programme of Principles, National Party, Cape Town,

171 See, for example, *Zionist Record*, 17 April 1935.

172 See *Zionist Record*, 12 July 1935.

173 See South African Jewish Board of Deputies, Executive Committee Minutes, 25 August 1935.

174 *Zionist Record*, 12 July 1935.

175 Van Zyl Commission, UG No 26, 1936. See also Vernon A Barber, 'Nazi Activity in South Africa', *The National Review*, CVII, 1936.

176 For an overview, see 'Nazi Activities in South West Africa'; 'Report on German Activities in South West Africa', Department of Foreign Affairs, BTS 1-18-6, AJ, 1943; 'Nazi Activities in South West Africa'. Friends of Europe – Publication No 43, South African Jewish Board of Deputies, Archives, 308.2; and Anon, 'It Did Happen Here', *Common Sense*, February 1940.

177 Letter dated 27 May 1934. Cited in 'It Did Happen Here'.

178 See Hattingh, pp. 114–16. Weichardt did not dispute that he was on good terms with the Germans but claimed his loyalty was to South Africa. He did, however, send copies of *Die Waarheid/The Truth* to the Berlin Deutsche Koloniale Gesellschaft, which worked in South West Africa and exchanged *Die Waarheid/The Truth* with *Die Deutsche-Afrikaner*. See Furlong, *Between Crown and Swastika*, p. 23.

179 Von Lossnitzer informs 'Comrade Sens' that he 'would like to particularly draw your attention to the Greyshirt movement in the Union, whose leader is a German front ranker Weichardt in Cape Town. Weigel thinks that if these people were granted financial assistance to the amount of £500 a good and useful working combination with the NSDAP would be attainable.' Von Lossnitzer went on, *inter alia*, to mention the

Landsgruppenleiter, Professor Bohle in Cape Town, who was looking after their interests. Von Lossnitzer to Comrade Sens, Windhoek, 25 June 1934. 'Nazi Activities in South West Africa', Vol 2, BT51-18-6.

180 *Zionist Record*, 2 August 1935. See also 'Executive's Memo' on a meeting of the Board's executive with Mr Taljaard, a South West African MP, and Colonel Papert, a Windhoek farmer. Alexander Papers, BC160: List IV, 24.

181 Letter dated 11 June 1934. Cited in 'It Did Happen Here'. According to 'A Memorandum on anti-Jewish Movements in South Africa' this was a letter from E Muller, group leader in Sanfeld to Weigel. Weichardt certainly seems to have had financial resources at his disposal. Despite going bankrupt, he bought a very comfortable house in a fashionable Cape Town suburb and seemingly had endless funds for campaign journeys and the running of myriad offices. More than that, his senior colleagues also bought cars. See 'It Did Happen Here'. See also 'Analysis of Documents Relating to the Greyshirt Movement in South Africa', SADF Archives, File UWH 279. The secrecy is also evident in a confidential letter from Lothar Kunze to Weichardt. See L Kunze to Weichardt, 25 May 1934, PV 29, File 1.

182 See also 'OB and Kindred Activities – With a Comparison of the Report of Un-American Propaganda Activities in the United States' (cited in Uran, p. 164). The report claimed Weichardt was an associate of Hermann Goering and Edward Bohle. (This was presumably Ernst Wilhelm Bohle, son of the University of Cape Town professor.) According to the report, these consulates were the source of German propaganda. See Uran, p. 164.

183 See 'It Did Happen Here'. Dutch Reformed Church clergy received pamphlets on the 'Jew Bolshevist' threat. The Nazis rapidly gained control of *Die Deutsche-Afrikaner*, which functioned as a key propaganda organ for the German-speaking community and as a sorting house for the flood of propaganda from Germany. See 'Nazi Activities in the Union of South Africa Before and During the War, December 1945', Lawrence Papers, BC640, E5.45, and 'Nazi Activities and Nazi Propaganda in the Union of South Africa from the year 1933 until the Outbreak of War, September 1939, Vol 5. Lawrence

Papers BC640, E5.44.4. *Die Deutsche-Afrikaner* (22 November 1934) suggested that Afrikaners look to Germany for friendship, adopt antisemitism and support pro-German policy in South West Africa. See Furlong, *Between Crown and Swastika*, pp. 75–76. The Deutscher Fichte Bund advertised in *Die Waarheid/the Truth*. See Uran, p. 163.

184 See Von Strahl, pp. 108–27. In 1934–35 Professor Graf von Duerckheim-Montmartin visited South Africa under educational auspices. His meetings included a meeting with the Broederbond. On his return to Germany he informed the German government that he anticipated anti-Jewish and anti-British sentiment increasing. See 'Duerckheim Rapport. Offisele Dokumente oor Nazi Komplot in die Unie: Beoogde Anneksasie', Unie Eenheid-Waarheiddiens, Annam-Huis, Johannesburg. Pam 308, SA Rochlin Archives.

185 *Zionist Record*, 2 August 1935. In its 'Report on Nazi Activities of the NSDAP', the attorney general, EG Rosenow, writes that Professor Bohle had connected himself to the South West African Movement. An unsigned letter from Bohle, the 'Local Leader at Swakopmund', was noted. It explained that Weichardt was a true German, and a fanatical Nazi who advocated the secret introduction of the Greyshirt newspaper into South West Africa, and the cooperation of South West African Nazis with the Union Movement for election purposes, so that a Nazi could be introduced into the House of Assembly. Evidence suggested close cooperation between the radical right and pro-Nazi activists in South West Africa and the desire for secrecy. See Attorney General EG Rosenow to Secretary for South West Africa, 19 July 1934. 'Nazi Activities in SWA'. Department of Foreign Affairs, BTS 1-18-6, Vol 2, 107.

186 Letter dated 29 April 1934. See 'The Anti-Jewish Movements in South Africa', p. 21.

187 See South African Jewish Board of Deputies, Executive Committee Minutes, 30 June 1935.

188 *Ibid*, 24 June 1935.

189 See *Cape Times*, 2 September 1935.

190 *Ibid*, 3 September 1935. Of course the Jewish identity of Nelson was also stressed by Zuidmeer. See *Paarl Post*, 30 August 1935.

191 *Ibid*, 19 August 1935. According to WP Steenkamp, Jews had been warned by

Nationalists not to vote. See *Cape Argus*, 23 August 1935. Even flu victims left their beds to cast a vote. See *Cape Times*, 14 August 1935.

192 *Ibid*, 19 August 1935.

193 SW Schneider, General Merchant of Molteno, to the Board of Deputies. See South African Jewish Board of Deputies, Executive Committee Minutes, 22 July 1935.

194 See *Zionist Record*, 6 September 1935.

195 SA Rochlin Archives, ARCH 321.2.

196 See South African Jewish Board of Deputies, Executive Committee Minutes, 2 December 1935.

197 See, for example, *Die Republikein*, 28 September and 7 December 1934.

198 See South African Jewish Board of Deputies, Executive Committee Minutes, 3 December 1935.

199 Simons and Simons, pp. 475 and 478.

200 Hermann Giliomee and Bernard Mbenga, *New History of South Africa*, Tafelberg, Cape Town, 2007, p. 287.

201 *Die Waarheid/The Truth*, 13 December 1935.

CHAPTER THREE

THE JEWISH QUESTION MOVES TO THE CENTRE

1 *Eastern Province Herald*, 7 January 1936.

2 *Die Burger*, 9 January 1936.

3 According to the Board, Weichardt had indicated Retief's past Greyshirt sympathies. Retief was 'challenged to make an unequivocal disavowal of his Grey Shirt sympathies, but had so far not done so'. See South African Jewish Board of Deputies, Executive Committee Minutes, 15 January 1936.

4 See the *Cape Times*, 20 January 1936.

5 *Die Waarheid/The Truth*, 17 January 1936

6 *Eastern Province Herald*, 18 January 1936.

7 This was even less than W Stuart, the Dominion Party candidate, who hardly featured in the campaign. He polled 1 682 votes.

8 *Die Waarheid/The Truth*, 7 February 1936.

9 *Ibid*, 3 January 1936.

10 See, for example, *Die Waarheid/The Truth*, 9 and 24 April, and 8 May 1936. For reports on Weichardt's public lectures in the Transvaal and Orange Free State, see South African Jewish Board of Deputies, Executive Committee Minutes, 26 April 1936.

11 *Die Waarheid/The Truth*, 10 September 1936.

12 For an example of the language employed, see *Die Waarheid/The Truth*, 8 May 1936. See also editorial, 'The New South African Nationalism', *Die Waarheid/The Truth*, 24 April 1936, and *Die Waarheid/The Truth*, 8 May 1936.

13 See South African Jewish Board of Deputies, Executive Committee Minutes, 1 and 24 March 1936.

14 *Ibid*, 1 March 1936.

15 *Zionist Record*, 10 April 1936.

16 See South African Jewish Board of Deputies, Executive Committee Minutes, 26 April 1936.

17 See 'The Jew', a poem distributed by Die Volksbeweging. See 'The Anti-Jewish Movements in South Africa', p. 26.

18 See South African Jewish Board of Deputies, Executive Committee Minutes, 26 April 1936. Terblanche was booed by the audience in Kimberley. See *Diamond Fields Advertiser*, 21 February 1936.

19 See 'It Did Happen Here'.

20 South African Jewish Board of Deputies, Executive Committee Minutes, 28 March 1936.

21 *Ibid*, 29 March 1936.

22 See 'The Anti-Jewish Movements in South Africa', pp. 8–9. The medieval blood libel charge accused Jews of using the blood of Christians for ritual purposes. Despite its historicity being questioned by scholars, Purim celebrates the deliverance of the Jews from the designs of Haman in ancient Persia. Schechitah refers to the kosher slaughtering of animals.

23 'The Anti-Jewish Movements in South Africa', p. 13.

24 South African Jewish Board of Deputies, Executive Committee Minutes, 24 March 1936.

25 See *Die Waarheid/The Truth*, 9 April 1936. For Weichardt's speech, see 'Report of speech by LT Weichardt. Grand Parade, Cape Town, 2 April 1936'. Shorthand note and transcript by anonymous author for Cape Committee, SA Rochlin Archives. See also Rebecca Hodes, 'Free fight on the Grand Parade: Jewish resistance to the Greyshirts in 1930s South Africa', *International Journal of African Historical Studies*, 46(3), 2013.

26 See South African Jewish Board of Deputies, Executive Committee Minutes, 21 and 26 April 1936. According to the Board, the pamphlet was written by Dr Joseph

Goebbels.

27 Hertzog's legal advisers were distinctly cool towards such legislation. They examined comparative examples but found them problematic. See Department of Justice, JUS 1359, Ref: 1-153-35. Ultimately Hertzog envisaged anti-defamation law as forming part of a series of control measures, including the press, which aroused opposition and resulted in no Bill ever coming before parliament. See South African Jewish Board of Deputies, Report of the Executive Council, June 1937 to May 1940.

28 South African Jewish Board of Deputies, Executive Committee Minutes, 26 April 1936.

29 L Weichardt to Frikkie, 20 April 1936. Weichardt Collection, PV 29, File 3.

30 South African Jewish Board of Deputies, Executive Committee Minutes, 26 April 1936. See also *Pretoria News*, 20 April 1936.

31 Rooipoort and Ventersdorp (8 April); Taalbosbult and Potchefstroom (9 April); Pretoria (14 April); Pretoria (15 April); Pretoria West and Daspoort (16 April); Honingsfontein and Nylstroom (17 April); Vereeniging and Gezina (18 April); Boshoek and Rustenburg (20 April); Koster (24 April); Sanieshof (27 April); Vryburg (28 April); Schweizer Reneke (29 April); Vleeschkraal (30 April); Maquassi (1 May); Wolmaranstad (2 May); Christiana (4 May); Hertzogville (5 May); Hoopstad (6 May); Wesselsbron (7 May); Bothaville (two meetings, 8 May). See 'The Anti-Jewish Movements in South Africa', p. 14.

32 See, for example, Sunday Express Clippings, 2 August 1936. Lawrence Papers, BC640.

33 See Bill Freund, 'South Africa: the Union Years, 1910–1948 – Political and Economic Foundations' in Robert Ross, Anne Kelk Mager and Bill Nasson (eds), *The Cambridge History of South Africa, Volume 2, 1885–1994*, Cambridge University Press, Cambridge, 2012, pp. 227–28.

34 South African Jewish Board of Deputies, Executive Committee Minutes, 9 May 1936. According to the Board, an attorney, a schoolteacher and a shopkeeper in Bothaville had actively assisted the Greyshirt cause. See South African Jewish Board of Deputies, Executive Committee Minutes, 20 May 1936.

35 South African Jewish Board of Deputies, Executive Committee Minutes, 20 May

1936. The councillor who introduced the business licence motion in Lichtenburg was ruled out of order by the mayor but asked for permission to explain reasons for the motion and followed this with a violent speech against the Jews. South African Jewish Board of Deputies, Executive Committee Minutes, 31 May 1936.

36 *Die Burger*, 6 May 1936. See also South African Jewish Board of Deputies, Executive Committee Minutes, 20 May 1936.

37 *Zionist Record*, 1 May 1936.

38 *Ibid*.

39 See South African Jewish Board of Deputies, Executive Committee Minutes, 26 April 1936. Havemann's Blackshirts would soon subsume Terreblanche's Volksbeweging and become known as the Blackshirts or Patriotte. See Chairman to JBM Hertzog, 25 March 1937, Department of Justice Archives: 1359, Ref 1-153-235. See also South African Jewish Board of Deputies, Report of the Executive Council, 21 May 1935 to 31 May 1937. For the programme of principles, see 'SA Nasionale Volksbeweging (Patriotte)', Hertzog Collection, A32. The focus was exclusively on Jews.

40 *Zionist Record*, 1 May 1936.

41 IM Goodman to Bender, 22 January 1935. Interestingly, the Board was alerted in the late 1920s to a *numerus clausus* operating at College House, one of the university residences. See Cohen, 'Anatomy of South African Antisemitism', p. 63.

42 Personal File, JK Wylie.

43 J Kerr Wylie to Principal, 7 May 1936. Personal File, JK Wylie. Beattie pointed out in reply that Wylie could not separate himself from the university and that he was unwilling to participate in 'loud mouthed' extremism.

44 See *SAJC*, 5 June 1936.

45 South African Jewish Board of Deputies, Executive Committee Minutes, 31 May 1936.

46 'The general atmosphere pervading in the House of Assembly on the Jewish question was anything but pleasant,' reported Max Geffen, chairman of the Law Committee of the Board of Deputies, following a visit to Cape Town and a meeting with the Cape Committee of the Board. See South African Jewish Board of Deputies, Executive Committee Minutes, 31 May 1936.

47 See Bradlow, 'Immigration into the Union', p. 251. Furlong (p. 55) puts the figure

for 1935 at 421, and Peberdy at 410. See
Furlong, *Between Crown and Swastika*, p. 55,
and Peberdy, p. 65.

48 South African Jewish Board of Deputies,
Executive Committee Minutes, 31 May
1936.

49 See WFC Morton, Minute, 1 May 1933.
Department of Interior, BNS, Box 464, File
212(74), Vol 1, 'Jewish and other refugees
from Germany'. It needs to be noted that
opposition to Jewish immigration was not
confined to Afrikaners. As early as October
1933, Patrick Duncan told Maud Selborne
that although many Jews in South Africa
were accepted, there were 'many others
who are a really bad element' in the Jewish
community. Duncan then trotted out
the standard anti-Jewish stereotypes. See
Duncan to Selborne, 31 October 1933.
Duncan Papers, BC 294, D5.25.37. See
also F Brehmer (Consulate of the Union
of South Africa, Hamburg) to Dr HB van
Broekhuizen, 14 April 1934. Department of
the Interior, BNS, Box 464 File 212(74).

50 SFN Gie to HDJ Bodenstein. Department
of Interior, BNS, Box 464, File 212(74),
Vol 1, 'Jewish and other refugees from
Germany'. See also SFN Gie to HDJ
Bodenstein, 22 October 1935. Department
of the Interior, BNS 1-1-386. Ref 212-74,
Part A. Gie complained that a great number
of Jews visiting the offices in Berlin
to inquire about immigration. They did
not make a favourable impression and
he suspected many were communists.
Even the better class posed a danger,
he said. For Gie's Germanophilism and
Bodenstein's dominant role in external
affairs, see Michael Graham Fry, 'Agents
and Structures: the Dominions and
Czechoslovak Crisis, September 1938', in
Igor Lukes and Erik Goldstein (eds), *The
Munich Crisis, 1938: Prelude to World War II*,
Frank Cass, London, 1999, pp. 297–99.

51 See EH Louw to Malan, 2 February 1936.
DF Malan Collection, 1/1/1168. See also
Hertzog Collection, Vol 62. Louw had
already written to all the ambassadors in
1935, expressing concern about the number
of applications the South African office in
Paris was getting from German Jews. See
Peberdy, p. 66.

52 See Bradlow, 'Immigration into the Union',
p. 256.

53 'Memorandum – Immigration': Jan
Hofmeyr Papers, A1/Dh, File 1 'Anti-
Semitism and Immigration'.

54 *Die Burger*, 21 April 1936.

55 *Ibid*, 24 April 1936.

56 *Hansard*, 20 April 1936. *Die Burger* published
interviews denying the persecution of Jews
in Germany. See Paton, p. 255.

57 *SAJC*, 1 May 1936. See also South African
Jewish Board of Deputies, Executive
Committee Minutes, 31 May 1936. *Die
Vaderland* (12 May 1936) claimed Jews were
secretly getting requests for financial aid to
campaign against anti-Jewish organisations.

58 *Hansard*, 20 April 1936.

59 *Ibid*, 7 May, 19 1936. The boycott issue
exercised the minds of civil servants in the
Department of Justice. See, for example,
HDJ Bodenstein to Secretary for Justice,
13 November 1936. Department of Justice
Collection, JUS 1359, Ref 1/153/35. For
wide-ranging concern, see Department of
Justice Collection, JUS 1359, Ref 1/1/35.

60 *Hansard*, 29 May 1936. These figures were
disputed. See *The Star*, 10 September 1936,
and *Cape Argus*, 15 September 1936. For
concerns about wool exports, see also *Die
Waarheid/The Truth*, 8 May 1936. Reference
was also made to the Johannesburg City
Council refusing to purchase from firms
that did business with Germany. See
Hattingh, p. 118. The Cape Town City
Council was similarly wary.

61 *Hansard*, 29 May 1936.

62 *Zionist Record*, 15 May 1936. Much
discussion on the question of free speech
and liberty ensued in the press. See, for
example, interview with Morris Kentridge,
Zionist Record, 15 May 1936 and the editorial
in the *Natal Witness*, 9 May 1936.

63 *Zionist Record*, 5 June 1936.

64 *Cape Argus*, 30 May 1936.

65 Just over 1 000 Jews immigrated in 1934
(24 per cent of total immigration) and
1935 (16.5 per cent of total immigration).
Before the Quota Act the figures had been
much higher. South African Jewish Board
of Deputies, Executive Committee Minutes,
31 May 1936.

66 *Hansard*, 28 April 1936.

67 *Cape Argus*, 4 May 1936. See also South
African Jewish Board of Deputies to J
Hofmeyr, 2 June 1936. Alexander Papers,
BC160, Folder 1-29.

68 See South African Jewish Board of
Deputies, Executive Committee Minutes,
26 July 1936. There was substantial debate
about this in the Board. See Stone,

pp. 71ff. The Bill tabled in May would have amended section 6 of the Quota Act of 1930 and in effect would have (a) conferred upon the Minister of the Interior a discretion in recognising a document of identity for the purposes of the entry of its holder into South Africa, and (b) made it a necessary condition of such a recognised document of identity that it should be valid for the return of its holder to the country in which it was issued. See South African Jewish Board of Deputies, Report of Executive Council, 21 May 1935 to 31 May 1937.

69 See South African Jewish Board of Deputies, Executive Committee Minutes, 26 July 1936.

70 *Hansard*, 16 and 19 June 1936.

71 The Bill was tabled in May and then seemingly withdrawn.

72 *Hansard*, 17 June 1936. There was genuine concern on the part of government that South African Jews were assisting with the immigration of German Jews. See South African Jewish Board of Deputies, Executive Committee Minutes, 30 August 1931, and Stone, p. 71. The *Zionist Record* (19 June 1936) took some comfort that Malan had distanced himself from any anti-Jewish prejudice.

73 The committee was comprised of Dr HDJ Bodenstein (chairman); PI Hoogenhout (Secretary for the Interior); Dr JF van Rensburg (Secretary for Justice); Dr AA Schoch (Law Advisor, Department of Justice); A Broeksma (Law Advisor, Department of External Affairs) and PF Kincaid (Commissioner for Immigration and Asiatic Affairs).

74 (a) Any person or class of persons deemed by the Minister on economic grounds or on account of standard or habits of life to be unsuited to the requirements of the Union or any particular province thereof; (b) any person who is unable, by reason of deficient education, to read and write any European language to the satisfaction of an immigration officer or, in case of an appeal, to the satisfaction of the board; and for the purposes of this paragraph Yiddish shall be regarded as a European language; (c) any person who is likely to become a public charge, by reason of infirmity of mind or body, or because he is not in possession for his own use of sufficient means to support himself and such of his dependants as he shall bring or has brought with him into the Union.

75 Dr HDJ Bodenstein to Private Secretary, Minister of Finance, 8 June 1936 (Memorandum, 8 June 1936). Smuts Collection, Vol 123, File 46. In addition, the committee recommended that naturalisation processes be reconsidered, especially with regard to deportation, which it deemed problematic when it came to non-British-born individuals.

76 Dr HDJ Bodenstein to Private Secretary, Minister of Finance, 7 July 1936 (Memorandum, 8 June 1936). Smuts Collection, Vol 123, File 46.

77 See Private Secretary to Prime Minister, 24 July 1936 (Memorandum). Smuts Collection, Vol 123, File 48.

78 See, for example, *Die Waarheid / The Truth*, 31 July 1936.

79 *Die Waarheid / The Truth*, 10 July 1936.

80 *SAJC*, 7 August 1936. A number of leading clerics and politicians would establish the South African Society of Jews and Christians in late 1937 to combat anti-Jewish propaganda. See Sandra Braude, 'Combatting Anti-Jewish Propaganda: The South African Society of Jews and Christians 1937–1951', *Jewish Affairs*, October/November 1991.

81 South African Jewish Board of Deputies to Prime Minister, 1 July 1936. Smuts Collection, Vol 123, A1, 1936. Ironically, there was legislation to this effect in the case of whites and Africans: see the Native Administration Act 38 of 1927 (section 29(1)), *Government Gazette* Extraordinary No 1645, 5 July 1927.

82 HDJ Bodenstein to Board, 19 August 1936. Smuts Collection, Vol 123, A1, File 53.

83 See South African Jewish Board of Deputies, Executive Committee Minutes, 26 August 1936.

84 *Die Burger*, 19 August 1936.

85 See South African Jewish Board of Deputies, Executive Committee Minutes, 30 August 1936.

86 See Daniel Coetzee, 'From Immigrants to Citizens: Civil Integration and Acculturation of Jews into Oudtshoorn Society, 1874–1999', unpublished MA thesis, University of Cape Town, 2000, p. 121.

87 See South African Jewish Board of Deputies, Executive Committee Minutes, 30 August 1936. Ultimately, it was resolved that the Free State Agricultural Union

would request the government to oppose the present movement to boycott the goods of countries trading with South Africa and that it was 'absolutely essential to maintain good relations with nations like Germany which were buying agricultural produce'. See *Farmers Weekly*, 23 September 1936.

88 For resolutions, see *Cape Argus*, 22 September 1936. For Congress, see *Die Burger*, 30 September, and 3 and 4 October 1936.

89 See South African Jewish Board of Deputies, Executive Committee Minutes, 30 August 1936.

90 See *Die Volksblad*, 21 August 1936.

91 *Zionist Record*, 14 August 1936.

92 See South African Jewish Board of Deputies, Executive Committee Minutes, 23 September 1936. During September, Weichardt addressed meetings in Woodstock, Philadelphia, Reitz, Pietrusteyn, Warden and Vrede. See South African Jewish Board of Deputies, Executive Committee Minutes, 23 September 1936.

93 South African Jewish Board of Deputies, Executive Committee Minutes, 27 September 1936.

94 *Ibid.*

95 *Ibid.*

96 See South African Jewish Board of Deputies, Report of the Executive Council, 21 May 1935 to 31 May 1937.

97 See South African Jewish Board of Deputies, Executive Committee Minutes, 27 September 1936.

98 *Ibid.*

99 See *Sunday Express*, 27 September 1936.

100 South African Jewish Board of Deputies, Executive Committee Minutes, 27 September 1936.

101 *Fascist Quarterly*.

102 Duncan to Selborne, 26 August 1936. Duncan Papers, BC 294, D5.28.28. His figures were erroneous and far in excess of the paltry number of Jews entering South Africa.

103 For his hostile sentiments towards eastern European Jews in the mid-1920s, see Bradlow, 'Immigration into the Union', pp. 195-222.

104 The Board wrote to the Jewish Refugee Committee in London and the Hilfsverein in Berlin (a German welfare organisation assisting Jews wishing to emigrate) urging these two organisations to reduce the volume of Jewish immigration to South

Africa. See South African Jewish Board of Deputies, Executive Committee Minutes, 30 August 1936 and Stone, p. 73.

105 See South African Jewish Board of Deputies, Executive Committee Minutes, 30 August 1936. The cabinet discussed immigration on 24 August 1936. See Hofmeyr Papers, Files 'Immigration', 18.8.36.

106 A Broeksma to Prime Minister (Memorandum – Immigration). Smuts Collection, Vol 123, A1, File, 52 [author's emphasis].

107 Duncan explained to Maud Selborne that Jews were easily able to comply with the guarantee rules with support from local Jews. See Duncan to Selborne, 7 October 1936. Duncan Papers, BC294, D5.28.34

108 Acting Secretary for the Interior, AB Smit, to Board of Deputies, 5 September 1936. South African Jewish Board of Deputies, Executive Committee Minutes, 9 September 1936.

109 *Die Kerkbode*, 29 July 1936.

110 See, for example, *Die Burger*, 26 August 1936.

111 See *Die Republikein*, 4 September 1936, and *Die Volksblad*, 4 September 1936.

112 *Die Burger*, 4 September 1936.

113 *Die Republikein*, 18 September 1936.

114 *Die Waarheid* (11 September 1936) published a full list of his meetings.

115 *Natal Witness*, 23 October 1936.

116 'Publicity Committee Report', South African Jewish Board of Deputies, Executive Committee Minutes, 25 October 1936.

117 Also known as the Deutsche Verein. The association initially had Jewish members.

118 See 'Publicity Committee Report', South African Jewish Board of Deputies, Executive Committee, 25 October 1936.

119 Letter from Bodenstein to Board, 23 September 1936. Smuts Collection, Vol 123, File 153. See also Jocelyn Hellig, 'German-Jewish Immigration to South Africa during the 1930s: Revisiting the Charter of the SS *Stuttgart*'.

120 See Siegfried Raphaely to JBM Hertzog, 13 October 1936. A1 Smuts Collection, Vol 123, File 57.

121 See *Cape Argus*, 3 September 1936. The information was formally published in the *Government Gazette*, 25 September 1936. See Regulations made under Immigration Quota Act, 1930, *Government Gazette*, No 1456, 25 September 1936.

122 See Stone, p. 44.

123 See Bradlow, 'Immigration into the Union',

p. 264.

124 *Die Burger,* 21 September 1936.

125 See, for example, *Die Waarheid / The Truth,* 2 October 1936. Weichardt, too, went beyond the question of immigration in a speech at Ladysmith. See *Natal Witness,* 23 October 1936.

126 *Die Waarheid / The Truth,* 23 October 1936.

127 *Die Volksblad,* 23 September 1936.

128 *Ibid,* 21 October 1936. This message was regularly repeated by Malan. See *Cape Argus,* 8 October 1936, and *Die Volksblad,* 23 October 1936.

129 For details, see Stone, chapter three, *passim.* Although the *Stuttgart* passengers were by now on their way to a new life in South Africa, at the official level the Jewish community had faced an unenviable moral conundrum at the time of the Aliens Act. They knew only too well the circumstances under which their coreligionists lived in Germany, but they also recognised that South Africa confronted a 'Jewish Question'. Reluctantly, an anguished Board of Deputies had chosen to advise German Jews considering emigration to South Africa to seek an alternative destination. See Linda Coetzee, Myra Osrin and Millie Pimstone, *Seeking Refuge: German Jewish Immigration to the Cape in the 1930s, Including Aspects of Germany Confronting its Past,* Cape Town Holocaust Centre, 2003, and Stone, pp. 86–88.

130 See Bradlow, 'Immigration into the Union', p. 266; *Cape Argus,* 17 October 1936; *Die Burger,* 17, 18, 20, 21, 26, 30 October, 3 November 1936 and *The Star,* 19 October 1936.

131 Duncan to Selborne, 7 October 1936. Duncan Papers, BC294 D5.28.34.

132 They were joined by the students of 'Dagbreek', a residence at the University of Stellenbosch. *Die Burger* (20 October 1936) reported that the students considered a March to the docks.

133 See Duffy, pp. 84ff. Duffy also names AC Cilliers, CGS de Villiers and JA Wiid. All had been named by Hofmeyr in a letter critical of their involvement in the immigration issue. See Duffy, p. 84. See also Jacobus Johannes Broodryk, 'Stellenbosch Akademici en die Politieke Problematiek in Suid-Afrika, 1934–1948', unpublished MA dissertation, University of Stellenbosch, 1991, pp. 111–21. Broodryk includes Frans Joubert among the academics opposed to Jewish

immigration. There is no record of Joubert as an academic but there is a Frans Joubert who wrote the music for the flag song.

134 O'Meara, *Volkskapitalisme,* pp. 110–12.

135 See O'Meara, *Volkskapitalisme,* pp. 111–16 and Giliomee, *The Afrikaners,* p. 437.

136 See Hepple, p. 27, and Kenny, pp. 28–33.

137 See 'Publicity Committee Report', South African Jewish Board of Deputies, Executive Committee Minutes, 25 October 1936. *Die Burger* (28 October 1936) reported an attendance of 3 000 and *Die Volksblad* (28 October 1936) 1 500. I am indebted to John Matisonn for informing me of the mood within the ANS at this time.

138 *Die Volksblad,* 28 October 1936.

139 *The Star,* 28 October 1936.

140 See *Die Vaderland,* 30 October 1936.

141 *SAJT,* 23 October 1936. According to Harry Lawrence, Stiller arranged for Nazi films to be shown to Stellenbosch professors. See Monama, p. 19.

142 See *Die Burger,* 21 October 1936.

143 See *Cape Times,* 28 October 1936, and Duncan to Selborne, 28 October 1936. Duncan Papers, BC294, D5.28.37. 'We have a Greyshirt movement here of young men who go about in semi-uniform dress in imitation of the Fascists and Nazis but their objects do not seem to go beyond baiting the Jews. They have a good deal of support in the country and small towns and they have almost captured the Malan party.'

144 See Coetzee, Osrin and Pimstone, pp. 15–29.

145 *Zionist Record,* 23 October 1936.

146 *SAJC,* 30 October 1936.

147 *Ibid,* 6 November 1936.

148 See South African Jewish Board of Deputies, Executive Committee Minutes, 11 November 1936.

149 An ironic comment, given the massive legal and normative discrimination towards Africans, Coloureds and Asians.

150 See South African Jewish Board of Deputies, Executive Committee Minutes, 11 and 23 November 1936.

151 *Die Volksblad,* 12 November 1936.

152 *Ibid,* 28 October 1936. Malan expressed satisfaction at the outcome of the Transvaal congress, noting that Transvalers felt the same as everyone else when it came to the Jewish influx. See *Die Volksblad,* 31 October 1936.

153 See Leibl Feldman, *Oudtshoorn: Jerusalem of Africa* (translated by Lilian Dubb and Sheila Barkusky and edited by Joseph Sherman),

Friends of the Library, University of the Witwatersrand, Johannesburg, 1989, and Sarah Abrevaya Stein, *Plumes: Ostrich Feathers, Jews, and a Lost World of Global Commerce,* Yale University Press, New Haven, 2008, pp. 28–53.

154 See *Hansard,* 17 February and 26 March 1930.

155 *Die Volksblad,* 12 November 1936. Effectively they said only a Christian republican could join the party.

156 Peberdy, p. 82. For a wider perspective on issues of nationality and citizenship within the British Empire, see Audie Klotz, *Migration and National Identity in South Africa, 1860–2010,* Cambridge University Press, New York, 2013. Klotz argues that nation-building in South Africa cannot be divorced from imperial contestations over nationality and other forms of identity.

157 Dubow, *Illicit Union,* pp. 180–89.

158 *Die Burger,* 27 November 1936. Grant was a renowned American eugenicist and very influential in the anti-immigrant movement in the United States.

159 Similarly, essentialist notions of culture (evident in physical differences) would be employed by the anthropologist Werner Eiselen to justify apartheid. See Dubow, *Illicit Union,* pp. 277–78.

160 See Saul Dubow, 'South Africa and South Africans: Nationality, Belonging, Citizenship', in Robert Ross, Anne Kelk Mager and Bill Nasson (eds), *The Cambridge History of South Africa, Volume 2, 1885–1994.*

161 See *Die Volksblad,* 12 November 1936.

162 South African Jewish Board of Deputies, Executive Committee Minutes, 29 November 1936.

163 *Die Burger,* 9 November 1936. See also *Die Republikein,* 27 November 1936. Geyer, the editor of *Die Burger,* recognised the wave of antisemitism sweeping over the country which he blamed on the government for doing nothing about the organised influx of Jewish immigrants. See *Die Burger,* 28 October 1936.

164 *Die Volksblad* (2 November 1936) held similar views. It warned of the wave of antisemitism sweeping the country. What had happened in Germany could recur in South Africa, the newspaper asserted.

165 See, for example, *Die Burger,* 4 November 1936.

166 See, for example, *Die Burger,* 12, 16, 17 and 26 November 1936.

167 Moodie, p. 166.

168 South African Jewish Board of Deputies, Executive Committee Minutes, 23 November 1936. See *Die Volksblad,* 5 November 1936 and *Die Burger,* 5 November 1936. *Die Waarheid/The Truth,* 13 November 1936.

169 South African Jewish Board of Deputies, Executive Committee Minutes, 29 November 1936.

170 *Die Burger,* 5 November 1936. Significantly, in a private communication to Frikkie du Toit, Weichardt, who was on the road, spoke of the need for more finances. See Weichardt to Frikkie, 16 November 1936. Weichardt Collection P29, File 3.

171 See Duffy, pp. 85–86.

172 South African Jewish Board of Deputies, Executive Committee Minutes, 29 November 1936.

173 DF Malan to Amice, 9 December 1936. Eric Louw Papers, PV4, File 2. The King's 'antics' was a reference to Edward VIII's entanglement with Wallis Simpson, which would cost him his throne.

174 *SAJT,* 27 November 1936. *Die Volksblad* blamed Hofmeyr for not heeding the warning signs of hostility. See editorial, 'Rookskerms', *Die Volksblad,* 24 November 1936. The professors hit back at Hofmeyr, supported by Professor Kerr Wylie in a letter to *Die Burger,* 23 November 1936.

175 See, for example Stuttaford (*Zionist Record,* 11 December 1936).

176 South African Jewish Board of Deputies, Executive Committee Minutes, 16 November 1936.

177 See *SAJC,* 11 December 1936.

178 *Cape Times,* 17 December 1936.

179 *Cape Argus,* 17 December 1936.

180 *Zionist Record,* 11 December 1936. Stuttaford replaced Hofmeyr as Minister of the Interior when Hofmeyr became Minister of Mines following Patrick Duncan's appointment as Governor General. There were whispers that the change was because of Hofmeyr's views on immigration legislation, but this was denied by Hofmeyr. See Paton, pp. 256–58.

181 See comments by Sir Carruthers Beattie at December graduation at the University of Cape Town (*Cape Argus,* 10 December 1936) and Smuts' speech at Roodebank, reported in *SAJC,* 4 December 1936.

182 See Stone, p. 64.

183 Sarah Gertrude Millin, *The Measure of My*

Days, Central News Agency Ltd, South Africa and Kingstons Limited, Bulawayo, 1955, pp. 159–60.

184 *Die Waarheid/The Truth*, 25 December 1936.

CHAPTER FOUR

FELLOW TRAVELLERS ALONG THE NAZI DIRT TRACK

1 'Aliens' Bill, South African Government, *Government Gazette Extraordinary Bill No 2400*, 28 December 1936.

2 For this special recognition of Yiddish, see Shain, *Jewry and Cape Society*, chapter two, *passim*.

3 WH Clark to the Right Honourable Malcolm MacMonald, MP, Dominion Office, 31 December 1936. High Commissioner (South Africa) Papers. Foreign Office, 371.

4 *Hansard*, 12 January 1937.

5 *Ibid*.

6 *Ibid*.

7 *Ibid*.

8 See Stone, pp. 97–98.

9 The Cape Committee of the Board met with Stuttaford on 18 January 1937 to discuss the definition of assimilability within the guidelines of the Bill and the possibilities for appeal. He made it clear that their concerns had been considered in cabinet and it had been agreed that any changes would open them up for attacks from the Malanites. See Bradlow, 'Immigration into the Union', p. 287. On 15 March 1937 Hofmeyr (Acting Minister of the Interior) introduced the Immigration Amendment Bill, which, although intended to facilitate the recruitment and importation of mine labour, had implications for Jewish immigration. Under the new legislation, the minister was able to refuse entry to someone not possessing a valid return to the country that issued the document. This was a means of dealing with the small number of immigrants holding so-called Nansen and McDonald passports, which dated back to territorial adjustments after the First World War. Many Jews had acquired these passports after Hitler came to power and Malan had pushed for some time to have them declared invalid for entry to South Africa. By opening the possibility of ministerial discretion in the Immigration Amendment Act, the United Party had taken the middle road.

See Bradlow, 'Immigration into the Union', pp. 297–301.

10 *Hansard*, 18 January 1937.

11 *Ibid*, 14 January 1937. During the debate, Du Toit reminded the House of the so-called Christian Clause at the time of the Potchefstroom University College debate, in 1932.

12 See *Hansard*, 18 January 1937.

13 *Ibid*, 27 January 1937.

14 See South African Jewish Board of Deputies, Executive Committee Minutes, 16, 18, 19, 20, 21 and 26 January 1937.

15 *Hansard*, 18 January 1937.

16 *Ibid*, 20 January 1937. Malan's wish was reiterated by Johannes de Waal *père*, who bemoaned the possibility that an English-born Jew could enter the country, while this would not be possible for the Afrikaner's 'Christian kinsmen in Germany, Holland and France'. *Hansard*, 20 January 1937.

17 See Goverment Notice 665 of 1937 (Form D(1)(10), Clause 5(b)) and South African Jewish Board of Deputies, Executive Committee Minutes, 28 February 1937. The Board was concerned about the guiding principles and the operations of the Immigrant Selection Board. See South African Jewish Board of Deputies, Executive Committee Minutes, throughout 1937. A few months after the introduction of the Aliens Act, the Board wanted to investigate the use of category 'Hebrew' in Govt Notice 665 of 1937 (Form D(1)(10), Clause 5(b)) and generally to investigate the use of 'Hebrew' in government documents. See South African Jewish Board of Deputies, Executive Committee Minutes, 25 June 1937.

18 Cuthbertson claims that Hofmeyr had drafted the Bill long before Malan's Bill was introduced at the end of 1936. This was confirmed by Stuttaford during the debate. See *Hansard*, 12 January 1937 and GC Cuthbertson, 'Jewish Immigration as an Issue in South African Politics, 1937–39', *Historia*, 26(2) 1981, p. 119.

19 Presumably taking aim at Hofmeyr, who had been critical of the behaviour of the Stellenbosch academics during the *Stuttgart* affair, Malan offered a special word of thanks 'to the little circle of Professors at Stellenbosch … who took their courage in their hands … and tried to arouse the people in regard to the question.' 'Purified' Nationalists such as Frans Erasmus did

not believe the Bill would curtail the
Jewish influx. 'I say that the door is being
completely opened,' explained Erasmus.
'What are the people asking for? They
ask the Government actually to close the
door to the inrush of immigrants, but the
Government introduces a measure which
in any case opens the door to such an
extent to immigrants from Eastern Europe,
if it does not entirely open it, that people
can come in without control.' *Hansard*,
18 January 1937.

20 *Hansard*, 27 January 1937.
21 *Zionist Record*, 22 January 1937.
22 WH Clark to the Right Honourable
Malcolm MacDonald, MP, Dominion
Office, 21 January 1936 [sic]. High
Commissioner (South Africa) Papers.
Foreign Office, 371. The date 1936 was an
error and should have been 1937, as evident
from the discussion.
23 See also *Die Burger*, 28 January 1937.
24 *Die Waarheid/The Truth*, 22 January 1937.
25 Paton, pp. 258–59.
26 South African Jewish Board of Deputies,
Executive Minutes, 28 February 1937. See
also *Die Volksblad*, 3 February 1937.
27 *Die Volksblad*, 3 February 1937.
28 See *SAJT*, 26 February 1937 and *Rand Daily
Mail*, 19 April 1937.
29 See *Die Volksblad*, 16 February 1937, and
Suiderstem, 3 May 1937.
30 See *Die Volksblad*, 1 March 1937.
31 See South African Jewish Board of Deputies,
Executive Committee Minutes, 25 April
1937.
32 Giliomee, *The Afrikaners*, p. 409.
33 See Koorts, p. 311.
34 Hancock, p. 290.
35 *Die Burger*, 24 February 1937. See also the
SAJT, 26 February 1937 and *Rand Daily
Mail*, 24 February 1937.
36 The idealisation of the Nordic race, or
'Nordicism', had a long pedigree, with
strong ties to racial anthropology, Romantic
'folk' nationalism and, from the late
nineteenth century, European racism.
With race underpinning its categorisation,
'Nordicism' was connected in complicated
ways with 'Aryanism' and European fascism,
especially Nazism. Within this *Weltanschaung*,
Jews were a people apart from the 'Nordic'
peoples and an ever-present threat. See
Christopher M Hutton, *Race and the Third
Reich: Linguistics, Racial Anthropology and
Genetics in the Dialectic of Volk*, Polity Press,

Cambridge, 2005, chapter seven, *passim*.
37 See South African Jewish Board of Deputies,
Executive Committee Minutes, 28 February
1937.
38 *SAJC*, 5 March 1937.
39 *Cape Argus*, 24 February 1937. See also *Cape
Argus*, 27 February 1937.
40 *Natal Advertiser*, 27 February 1937.
41 *The Star*, 26 March, 1937.
42 See O'Meara, *Volkskapitalisme*, pp. 69–73
43 The Broederbond wished to organise
Afrikaner workers under the banner of
'Christian-National trade unionism'. For
the Broederbond and trade unionism, see
also Giliomee, *The Afrikaners, p.* 423 and
Bloomberg, pp. 112–14.
44 See Van Deventer, p. 55.
45 Marx, *Oxwagon Sentinel*, p. 234.
46 See Bloomberg, p. 114
47 See Van Deventer, pp 58–59 and South
African Jewish Board of Deputies, Executive
Minutes, 14 and 25 April 1937, and *SAJC*,
23 April 1937.
48 See Marx, *Oxwagon Sentinel*, p. 236. Charles
Harris, a mineworkers' union leader, who
was Jewish, was killed by a fanatic. In a note
to himself, Albert Hertzog refers to one
Mr P Whiteley identifying who was who
among the conglomerates. It is not without
significance that Hertzog indicates who
is a Jew at every opportunity. See Albert
Hertzog Collection, PV 451 1/190/1/1.
'Jode', 8 October 1936.
49 *Hansard*, 8 April 1937.
50 *Ibid*.
51 *Ibid*.
52 See LJ du Plessis, 'Christelik-Nasionale
Organisasie van Afrikanerwerkers',
Koers, June 1937. In July 1936 an Afrikaans
organisation, *Die Rasse Afrikaner Kultuur*
(Racial Afrikaans Culture), accused Jewish
trade unionists of spreading materialistic
values among Afrikaner workers. See
Cohen, 'Anatomy of South African
Antisemitism', p. 131.
53 Dan O'Meara, 'Analysing Afrikaner
Nationalism: The "Christian National"
Assault on White Trade Unionism in South
Africa, 1934–1948', *African Affairs*, 77(306),
1978, p. 55. See also Van Deventer, p. 55.
54 This 'Jewish influence' was thus never far
from the surface. During a parliamentary
debate in early 1937, Smuts was vilified
by the opposition benches for not forcing
Solly Sachs and Issy Diamond, two leading
Jewish labour activists, to pay their legal

costs when they were found guilty of
using 'riotous language' during a protest.
Nationalists accused the government of
excessive sympathy for communists and
Jews, insofar as there was no proof to Smuts'
claim that the 'two Jews' could not pay. See
Hansard, 15 February 1937 and the South
African Jewish Board of Deputies, Executive
Committee Minutes, 22 February 1937.
See also *Die Burger* (16 February 1937) for
comment on Kantorowitch (Kentridge).
For a vicious letter to Sachs, see Norval,
pp. 42–43.

55 See Edward Roux, *Time Longer than Rope:
The Black Man's Struggle for Freedom in
South Africa*, University of Wisconsin Press,
Madison, 1964, pp. 480–83.

56 Duncan to Selborne, 15 April 1937. Duncan
Papers (Political Notebooks), BC294,
C15.4.5.

57 See Simons and Simons, pp. 470–71.

58 Van Deventer, p. 272.

59 *Ibid*, p. 30.

60 This popular association of Jews with
communism was a growing concern
recognised by the Board. See South African
Jewish Board of Deputies, Executive
Committee Minutes, 25 July 1937.

61 Van Deventer, p. 273.

62 *Hansard*, 29 April 1937.

63 *Die Waarheid/The Truth*, 23 July 1937. *Die
Kerkbode* also used this trope. See the South
African Jewish Board of Deputies, Executive
Committee Minutes, 25 July 1937.

64 *Die Waarheid/The Truth*, 6 August 1937.

65 *SAJT*, 26 February 1937.

66 South African Jewish Board of Deputies,
Executive Committee Minutes, 22 February
1937.

67 Weichardt addressed 3 000 at Bethlehem
on 25 January. He also spoke at Reitz
(26 January), Tweeling (27 January),
Frankfort (28 January), Villiers (30 January),
Heilbron (1 February) and Lindsay
(5 February). Jews in Reitz were feeling
the economic pinch. The Greyshirts also
spoke in Beaufort West on 20 February.
The Blackshirts' Havemann and Kritzinger
spoke in Boksburg on 5 February, with 400
present. There were other meetings on the
Witwatersrand, including Germiston on
26 February 1937.

68 *Die Volksblad*, 3 February 1937.

69 See, for example, *Die Waarheid*, 26 March
1937.

70 *Ibid*, 26 March 1937.

71 *Ibid*.

72 *Ibid*.

73 *Ibid*, 19 February 1937.

74 See, for example, *Die Waarheid/The Truth*,
19 February 1937, 20 August 1937 and
10 September 1937.

75 South African Jewish Board of Deputies,
Executive Committee Minutes, 21 January
1937.

76 *Ibid*.

77 *Patria*, 19 February 1937. In the same edition,
Patria carried a full-page article, 'The
Anglo-Boer War was caused by Jews!' Even
after the Second World War, Wiid remained
perplexed about the 'Jewish Question'. See
Die OB, 17 April 1946.

78 South African Jewish Board of Deputies,
Executive Committee Minutes, 22 February
1937. Von Moltke acknowledged sending
Patria to friends with a hope of encouraging
them to take up the anti-Jewish cause and
not move into the fusionist camp, which
was the case with some of his old friends.
See Johannes von Strauss von Moltke
to JF van der Merwe, 11 March 1937
and Johannes von Strauss von Moltke to
Antonie van Dyk, 11 March 1937. Johannes
von Strauss von Moltke Collection, PV103.
File 2/1/1/1.

79 South African Jewish Board of Deputies,
Executive Committee Minutes, 17 February
1937.

80 See South African Jewish Board of
Deputies, Executive Committee Minutes, 28
and 30 April 1937 and 19 May 1937. For the
judgment, see the *SAJC*, 25 February 1938.

81 See South African Jewish Board of Deputies,
Executive Committee Minutes, 18 and
29 August 1937.

82 *Ibid*, 22 February 1937.

83 *Ibid*, 10 March 1937.

84 See G Saron to JH Hofmeyr, 17 March
1937. See South African Jewish Board of
Deputies, Executive Committee Minutes,
24 March 1937. A similar letter was written
to Hertzog, focusing on Von Moltke and
Patria, the Greyshirts, the importation
of propaganda material and the Suid-
Afrikaanse Volksbeweging (Blackshirts)
under Havemann, now including
Terblanche's movement. See Chairman to
JBM Hertzog, 25 March 1937. Department
of Justice, JUS 1359, Ref 1-153-235.

85 He also indicated that even *Patria*, which
he saw for the first time at the meeting,
would not fall within 'the purview of group

defamation'. See South African Jewish Board of Deputies, Executive Committee Minutes, 7 April 1937.

86 Proclamation No 51, *Government Gazette*, No 2462, 2 April 1937.

87 See telegram, Sir E Phipps (Berlin), 5 April 1937. See also WH Clark to Right Honourable Malcolm MacDonald, MP, 29 April 1937, and RA Wiseman to Strang, 10 April 1937, High Commissioner (South Africa) Papers. Foreign Office, 371.

88 *Die Waarheid / The Truth*, 14 May 1937.

89 *Hansard*, 6 April 1937.

90 The German government took great exception to these developments.

91 *SAJC*, 9 April 1937. For the role of Welt-Dienst, see Hanno Plass, '*Der Welt-Dienst*: International Antisemitic Propaganda', *The Jewish Quarterly Review*, 103(4), 2013.

92 The Nazi organisation was made up of 'Landesgruppe' (territorial groups), which controlled the functions of lesser groups (in order of importance): Kreisleitung, Ortsgruppe and Stutzpunkt. There was close monitoring of German affairs in South Africa as well as secret communications, including a special telegraph code known as AO (Auslands-Organisation). See 'Nazi Activities in the Union of South Africa Before and During the War'.

93 See Von Strahl, pp. 12, 126–27.

94 Von Strahl's secondment to Durban was unsuccessfully opposed by Ernst Bohle, who considered him less than lukewarm in his support for the Reich.

95 See *SAJC*, 30 April 1937 and South African Jewish Board of Deputies, Executive Minutes, 8 March 1937.

96 See *SAJC*, 30 April 1937.

97 See *Die Volksblad*, 26 April 1937.

98 *SAJC*, 30 April 1937.

99 *Cape Times*, 12 April 1937, and *Die Burger*, 12 April 1937.

100 *Cape Argus,* 16 April 1937. See also *Die Suiderstem*, 16 April 1937.

101 This was indeed the case. See chapter one.

102 *SAJC*, 16 April 1937.

103 It was Tielman Roos who persuaded the young Van Rensburg to change his academic direction from the study of German Language and Literature to Law. Van Rensburg went on to become private secretary to Roos. See Marx, *Oxwagon Sentinel*, p. 389. For Van Rensburg's infatuation with Nazi Germany, see Albrecht Hagemann, *Südafrika und das 'Dritte Reich':*

Rassenpolitische Affinität und machtpolitische Rivalität, Campus Verlag, Frankfurt and New York, 1980, pp. 261–71.

104 Marx, *Oxwagon Sentinel, p.* 388. See also JFJ van Rensburg, *Their Paths Crossed Mine: Memoirs of the Commandant-General of the Ossewa-Brandwag*, Central News Agency, South Africa, 1956, pp. 101–116, and Uran, pp. 295–301.

105 In the text of the speech he referred to 'Jew Communism'. Perhaps this was excised following the furore around Malan's speech. The following was also absent when delivering the speech. '[The socialist leaders] in Russia, Germany, Austria, France and Hungary were never Russians, Germans, Austrians, French or Hungarian, but always Jews. In my mind everything that the Jew follows is international and everything that is international is Jewish. They are a tight National unit that took a tactical international position. The one organised army in the international chaos.' For original text, see JFJ van Rensburg Collection A174, 4/33. The original text of the speech is dated February 1937, but it was delivered in April 1937. For a further report see *Die Volksblad*, 19 April 1937.

106 *Die Waarheid / The Truth*, 14 May 1937.

107 See Furlong, *Between Crown and Swastika*, p. 79.

108 *Die Waarheid / The Truth*, 14 May 1937.

109 See *Die Burger,* 22 May 1937. The notion of Jews blocking the advance of Afrikaners was a common theme. See, for example, *Die Burger,* 2 February 1937, and the South African Jewish Board of Deputies, Executive Committee Minutes, 22 February 1937. Malan valued the 'organised will of the people'. See Moodie, p. 129.

110 *Die Waarheid / The Truth*, 11 June 1937.

111 *Ibid*. In the opinion of *Die Waarheid / The Truth*, Jews were not afraid of Malan and they knew that, even if he came to power, nothing would change. As for the 'Smelters', (the United Party), they existed for the benefit of the 'International Money Power'.

112 *Die Waarheid / The Truth*, 16 April 1937.

113 He identified Von Moltke's behaviour and the manipulation of Inch as hurting the party.

114 See Hattingh, pp. 146-149. Weichardt told Hattingh that participating was a means of enhancing solidarity. He was prepared to use the system to gain control and thereafter to introduce National Socialism. See Hattingh,

p. 129.

115 *Die Volksblad*, 13 April 1937. The National Party denied it was seeking a compromise with Weichardt. See *Die Volksblad*, 14 April 1937. Weichardt continued to rave against the Jews. See, for example, *Die Waarheid/ The Truth*, 14 May 1937. See also South African Jewish Board of Deputies, Executive Committee Minutes, 16 April 1937.

116 *Die Waarheid/The Truth*, 23 July 1937.

117 See South African Jewish Board of Deputies, Executive Committee Minutes, 25 July 1937.

118 See, for example, *Die Burger*, 20 and 29 July 1937.

119 See South African Jewish Board of Deputies, Executive Committee Minutes, 25 July 1937. *The Leader* was first published on 31 December 1936. See 'Antisemitism', 1933–1945, ARCH 200.1, File 2, South African Jewish Board of Deputies, February 1937.

120 See *Rand Daily Mail*, 9 August 1937.

121 *SAJC*, 28 May 1937. The Jewish community might have drawn some comfort from the United Party's concern about the political mood. At a conference in Johannesburg the government was urged 'immediately to investigate the activities of all Shirt movements in South Africa and to consider it desirable to introduce legislation, should it be found that such movements endanger the welfare of South Africa'. Press Report 56: 1937. South African Jewish Board of Deputies, SA Rochlin Archives.

122 *SAJC*, 28 May 1937.

123 In an interview with the *Diamond Fields Advertiser* (3 June 1937), Rabbi Judah Landau spoke of 'the regrettable spirit of Nazism which is pervading the country …'

124 See Giliomee, *The Afrikaners*, pp. 415–17. Giliomee argues that most of these intellectuals were not informed by Nazism. For a harsher assessment, see Furlong, *Between Crown and Swastika*, pp. 105–10. On the other hand, Hagemann maintains that Diederichs and Meyer were strongly identified with Nazi Germany. See Hagemann, *Südafrika und das 'Dritte Reich'*, pp. 233–35; and Lawrence Papers, BC640, 'Nazi Anti-Semitism and Nazi Propaganda in the Union of South Africa from the Year 1933 until the Outbreak of War in September 1939', E3.266.

125 See Moodie, p. 154.

126 *Ibid*, pp. 157–59.

127 *Ibid*, pp. 157–65.

128 *Die Suiderstem*, 19 August 1937, and *Die Burger*, 19 August 1937. The resolution was also tied to the Jewish communist threat. See Van Deventer, p. 70. Soon after he had returned from Europe, Louw declared that unwanted aliens and those involved in communist propaganda ought to be deported immediately. See *Die Burger*, 4 and 19 August 1937, and the South African Jewish Board of Deputies, Executive Committee Minutes, 29 August 1937.

129 See *Eastern Province Herald*, 19 August 1937.

130 *The Friend*, 28 July 1937.

131 *Rand Daily Mail*, 29 July 1937, and *Die Burger*, 29 July 1937. At question time Malan denied that there had been an agreement with the Greyshirts.

132 *Die Burger*, 30 July 1937. Malan praised Mussolini and Hitler because, he claimed, they did not believe in 'dictatorship by one man'. He believed in 'dictatorship by the people'. See Press Report 53: 1937; and WH Clark to Right Honourable Malcolm MacDonald, MP, 13 August 1937. High Commissioner (South Africa) Papers. Foreign Office, 371.

133 See *Rand Daily Mail*, 3 August 1937.

134 *The Friend*, 14 September 1937.

135 *Cape Times*, 13 September 1937.

136 *Die Burger*, 15 September 1937.

137 WH Clark, High Commissioner, to the Right Honourable Malcolm MacDonald, MP, Dominion Office, 13 August 1937. High Commissioner (South Africa) Papers. Foreign Office, 371. As far as the United Party was concerned, Clark said it was accused of being 'pro-Jew' since they depended on Jewish support', while Mr Hofmeyr was described as 'the self-admitted champion of the Jews as well as of the natives'. Malan reiterated his ideas in numerous speeches. See *The Friend,* 14 September 1937, and *Die Burger*, 15 September 1937.

138 See Daniel Coetzee, 'Fires and Feathers: Acculturation, Arson and the Jewish Community in Oudtshoorn, South Africa, 1914–1948', *Jewish History*, 19(2), 2005, pp. 158–59. For the 'Jerusalem of South Africa', see Israel Abrahams, *The Birth of a Community*, Cape Town Hebrew Congregation, Cape Town, 1955, p. 70. Yet Jews supplied credit to Afrikaners when necessary during the Great Depression and some even rose to prominence in civic affairs.

139 *Oudtshoorn Observer*, 5 August 1937.

140 See Coetzee, 'From Immigrants to Citizens', p. 136.

141 See South African Jewish Board of Deputies, Executive Committee Minutes, 29 August 1937. On his release from prison Inch described himself as coming 'out of the darkness into light, more determined than ever to fight the cause of National Socialism in South Africa and make it triumph'. See *Die Waarheid/The Truth*, 14 May 1937.

142 *Ibid*, 25 July 1937.

143 See O'Meara, *Volkskapitalisme*, pp. 89–95.

144 *Die Vaderland*, 6 July 1937. Dönges, too, voiced concerns about the threat of communism penetrating South Africa and called on the FAK to emulate Hitler's example and bring the Afrikaner worker into the national fold. For the centrality of concerns about communism see Van Deventer, pp. 256–63, and O'Meara, *Volkskapitalisme*, p. 64.

145 *SAJC*, 20 August 1937. Two months later, Malan lashed out at the proliferation of unions, 'the members of which were natives or coloured, often of the lowest type, and the controllers of which neither belong to the trade unions nor the industry concerned and all of whom are Jews.' *Rand Daily Mail*, 6 October 1937.

146 See South African Jewish Board of Deputies, Executive Committee Minutes, 29 August 1937.

147 See *Die Burger*, 28 August 1937.

148 WH Clark, High Commissioner, to the Right Honourable Malcolm Macdonald, MP, Dominion Office, 27 August 1937. High Commissioner (South Africa) Papers. Foreign Office, 372.

149 See Roux, *Time Longer than Rope*, pp. 295–98.

150 *Die Burger*, 13 February 1937, and *Eastern Province Herald*, 13 March 1937.

151 *Die Waarheid/The Truth*, 16 April 1937.

152 See South African Jewish Board of Deputies, Executive Committee Minutes, 25 April 1937. The *Afrikaans-Duitse Kultuur-Unie* (Afrikaner-German Cultural Union) and other Nazi bodies organised trips to Germany for leading Afrikaner politicians and intellectuals. See Patrick J Furlong, 'The National Party of South Africa: A Transnational Perspective', in Martin Durham and Margaret Power (eds), *New Perspectives on the Transnational Right*, Palgrave Macmillan, New York, 2010, pp. 69–70.

153 Speaking at an SANP congress in early 1937, Weichardt claimed the National Party had approached him with a request to reach a compromise with the Greyshirts. He had turned this down. Asked by *Die Burger* (14 April 1937) if this was indeed the case, Malan said the allegation was unsubstantiated. No one, he said, from his party had approached Weichardt 'directly or indirectly'.

154 See Koorts, p. 311. The assertion is based on Laubscher's response to Erasmus, which refers to the informal approach. The Laubscher communications with Erasmus were discussed on an ongoing basis within the 'Dagbestuur' of the National Party. See NP Federal, PV 27, File 1/3/2/2/1/1.

155 Letters all drafted by Malan, and then typed and set by Laubscher. See Koorts, pp. 311–12. See WR Laubscher to Erasmus, 13 July 1937, Cape National Party Collection, PV 27, File 2/12/III.

156 FC Erasmus to WR Laubscher, 1 September 1937, Cape National Party Collection, PV27, File 2/12/1/1/1.

157 WR Laubscher to F Erasmus, 22 September 1937, Cape National Party Collection, PV27, File 2/12/1/1/1. Erasmus and Jan Haywood had suggested the Greyshirts had been bought by Jewish gold. See *Die Volksblad*, 5 July 1937 and *Die Waarheid/The Truth*, 20 December 1937.

158 WR Laubscher to F Erasmus 28 September 1937, Cape National Party Collection, PV27, file 2/12/1/1/1. As far as Malan was concerned, the discussion between the two organisations was at an end – there was nothing to be gained from an agreement between them. Addition to DF Malan Collection: DF Malan to Maria Louw, 27 September 1937. At this point Laubscher updated Weichardt on the negotiations, suggesting that it was the Greyshirts' strength that led to Erasmus' approach. He expressed anger at Erasmus's last letter, which contained 'the old Jewish lies about German Movements and Dictatorship'. Laubscher also indicated that he would write a noncommittal response to Erasmus while awaiting Weichardt's instructions. WR Laubscher to LT Weichardt, 13 October 1937. Weichardt Collection, PV29.

159 FC Erasmus to WR Laubscher, 15 October 1937, Cape National Party Collection, PV27, File 2/12/1/1/1.

160 FC Erasmus to WR Laubscher, 25 October

1937, Cape National Party Collection, PV27, File 2/12/1/1/1.

161 WR Laubscher to FC Erasmus, 1 November 1937, Cape National Party Collection, PV27, File 2/12/1/1/1, F.C.

162 An editorial in *Die Transvaler* (3 November 1937) made it clear that the breakdown arose over the Fascist and Nazi mindset of the Greyshirts, with its emphasis on the Leader. *Die Burger* (3 November 1937) went further, referring to the SANP imitating the Nazi Party and wishing to destroy democracy.

163 See *SAJC*, 13 August 1937. Antisemitism in South Africa, the pamphlet explained, was because of a 'racial affinity' between 'a certain section of the Afrikaans-speaking population and the Germans'. Despite Malan's confidence, he was surely aware of mileage to be gained by exploiting the Jewish Question. In October 1937 one M Kotze, a Pretoria Greyshirt, wrote to his friend, Willie Laubscher, the Greyshirt secretary in Cape Town, that Weichardt wanted him to keep a friendly stance towards the Nationalists. 'The Nationalists are courting us seriously here in the Transvaal,' he wrote, 'but it is just because of the attitude we are taking up towards the National Party ... We now have gained old Nationalists as members of our party and they inform one that they are tired of the standpoint of the federal council regarding Jews as members of the National Party.' See M Kotze to Weichardt, 20 October 1937. Weichardt Collection, PV29. Greyshirt Records, File 3.

164 See South African Jewish Board of Deputies, Executive Committee Minutes, 25 June 1937, and *Rand Daily Mail*, 29 June 1937. Speaking in support of Vermeulen, Jan Haywood urged his followers to follow the example of Hitler. See *Rand Daily Mail*, 29 June 1937.

165 The price of gold had moved up from £4.25 to £6.23, and in 1939 to £7.70. See Giliomee, *The Afrikaners*, p. 410.

166 See Giliomee, *The Afrikaners*, p. 410, BJ Liebenberg, 'From the Statute of Westminster to the Republic of South Africa, 1931–1961', in CFJ Muller, *Five Hundred Years: A History of South Africa*, Academia, Pretoria and Cape Town, 1969, p. 372; and William Beinart, *Twentieth Century South Africa*, Oxford University Press, Oxford, 1994, chapter five, *passim*.

167 Giliomee, *The Afrikaners*, p. 409.

168 South African Jewish Board of Deputies. Report of the Executive Committee Council, June 1937 to May 1940. For the full statement, see Malan Collection, Briewe, 26 November 1937 and 15 December 1937, 1/1/1258 (C).

CHAPTER FIVE

ANNUS HORRIBILIS: A BARRAGE OF ANTISEMITISM

1 *Die Transvaler* soon agreed to exchange copies with *Die Waarheid / The Truth*. See Furlong, *Between Crown and Swastika*, p. 38.

2 *Die Transvaler*, 1 October 1937. Translation by Jan Schaafsma and James Myburgh at www.politicsweb.co.za. See also South African Jewish Board of Deputies, Executive Minutes, 1 October 1937 and Hepple, pp. 222ff. One of the articles in *Die Transvaler's* first edition reported a talk by Professor AJ van der Walt to an ANS congress, in which he maintained that liberalism falsely argued that the Jews are not a people. As long as there were only a few Jews in a country, said Van der Walt, there were no problems. As soon as numbers increased there were problems.

3 For Verwoerd's early thinking on race, see Miller, 'Science and Society in the Early Career of HF Verwoerd'.

4 See South African Jewish Board of Deputies, Executive Committee Minutes, 12 October 1937.

5 *Die Transvaler*, 18 November 1937. Cited in *SAJC*, 26 November 1937.

6 It also resulted in a critical reaction from *The Star* (27 November 1937) and the *SAJC* (3 December 1937). The exchange was published in full in the *SAJC* (10 December 1937).

7 See *SAJT*, 8 October 1937.

8 Ibid, 3 December 1937. See also AJ van Zyl to The Secretary, Jewish Board of Deputies, 12 October 1937. Malan Collection, 1/1/1240.

9 See *SAJT*, 3 December 1937.

10 It was not only in Afrikaans circles that relations were problematical. The *SAJT* (22 October 1937) reported that the newly formed, English-dominated Cape Town City Council harboured antisemites.

11 See *Cape Argus*, 15 October 1937.

12 See South African Jewish Board of Deputies, Executive Committee Minutes, 31 October

1937.

13 It was also reported that the Natal Congress of the HNP resolved that Jews could not become members of the Party in Natal. See *Die Vaderland*, 9 January 1941.

14 See *Die Transvaler*, 20 November 1937, and South African Jewish Board of Deputies, Executive Committee Minutes, 31 October 1937.

15 South African Jewish Board of Deputies, Executive Committee Minutes, 8 November 1937.

16 *Ibid*, 28 November 1937.

17 *Ibid*, and *The Star*, 10 November 1937.

18 *Die Transvaler*, 24 November 1937. See South African Jewish Board of Deputies, Executive Committee Minutes, 26 November 1937, and Gustav Saron to DF Malan, Briewe, 26 November 1937, 1/1/1258 (D).

19 See JL Bridgen to ME Antrobus, 25 October 1937 (forwarded by ME Antrobus to RA Wiseman, 2 November 1937). This information was contained in a letter forwarded to the High Commission claiming that the National Party had many German sympathisers and that one of the resolutions passed at a recent Nationalist conference advocated the return of Germany's confiscated colonies. High Commissioner (South Africa) Papers. Foreign Office, 371.

20 See, for example, *Die Transvaler*, 4 October 1937 and Press Report: 1937.

21 Cited in Furlong, *Between Crown and Swastika*, pp. 85–86.

22 *SAJC*, 5 November 1937.

23 *Die Transvaler*, 3 November 1937. See also South African Jewish Board of Deputies, Executive Committee Minutes, 28 November 1937.

24 A perusal of the press, the Board noted, revealed that the Union 'was becoming more alive to the dangers of the free importation of such propaganda'. See South African Jewish Board of Deputies, Executive Committee Minutes, 31 October 1937 and 8 November 1937.

25 See *Die Waarheid/The Truth*, 29 October 1937.

26 Hertzog suggested that the Board should continue with its policy, but subject to one qualification: that 'special circumstances might well make it desirable for the Board to answer certain allegations'.

27 'Notes on Interview with Prime Minister' (written by M Franks), 25 November 1937.

See South African Jewish Board of Deputies, Executive Committee Minutes, 8 November 1937.

28 *Ibid*. Gustav Saron did write to Malan on 15 December 1937, expressing the 'deep regret and concern' felt by the Jewish citizens of South Africa with regard to 'the expressions of unfriendliness towards them which have been voiced during the past months by the leaders and the press of the Nationalist Party, and in resolutions adopted at its conference'. Gustav Saron to Dr DF Malan, 15 December 1937, DF Malan Collection, Briewe, 1/1/1258 (A).

29 *SAJC*, 26 November 1937.

30 *SAJT*, 19 November 1937, and *SAJC*, 26 November 1937.

31 *SAJC*, 26 November 1937.

32 Press Report 68: 1937.

33 *Die Vaderland*, 25 November 1937.

34 See Sinodale Kommissie vir Sending onder Israel, KS 2117, Kaap, Rekordinhoud: Notules, 1924–1967. Dutch Reformed Church in South Africa: Archives. The resolution was welcomed by the *SAJC* (3 December 1937) as it seemed to herald a move away from the National Party's programme of antisemitism among the more intelligent members of the party.

35 See 'Twee-en-Dertigste Vergadering van die Hoog-Eerw.-Sinode van die Gereformeerde Kerk in die Oranje-Vrystaat gehou te Bloemfontein op 8 April 1937 en volgende dae'. Dutch Reformed Church in South Africa: Archives.

36 *Die Transvaler*, 26 November 1937. The communist menace was increasingly being discussed. See, for example, *Die Huisgenoot*, 17 December 1937.

37 *Sunday Express*, 28 November 1937.

38 See *SAJC*, 3 December 1937 and letter from Board (*The Star*, 27 November 1937).

39 Gustav Saron to National Party, 26 November 1937. DF Malan Collection, 1/1/1258. The notion of a Jewish boycott persisted, even in English circles. See, for example, *Rand Daily Mail*, 9 December 1937.

40 See *SAJC*, 17 December 1937.

41 *Ibid*, 26 November 1937.

42 *Sunday Times*, 12 December 1937, and *Yiddischer Zeitung*, 24 December 1937. Press Report 71: 1937.

43 *SAJC*, 17 December 1937.

44 *Cape Argus*, 9 December 1937. Although Odendaal resigned from the Waterberg branch, he stated that he would continue

to support the National Party, but he could not associate himself with 'Jew-baiting'. 'That principle of anti-Semitism may yet cause the Malanites serious embarrassment is becoming clear,' he said. 'Some of the younger hotheads, more particularly those in economically dependent positions, are endeavouring to force the Party leaders into a definite programme of anti-Semitism, but since a report of the Dutch Reformed Church Synod of the Cape Province has expressed strong disapproval of this policy and has characterised it as unchristian, there has been a general hesitation among the more intelligent members of the party.' *Rand Daily Mail*, 27 November 1937.

45 In certain quarters the United Party was criticised for having 'not generally adopted a sufficiently militant attitude on this subject'. At the Labour Party's December congress it adopted a short-term policy aiming, *inter alia*, at the prohibition of (a) the wearing of political uniforms and (b) the importation of Nazi propaganda literature. See South African Jewish Board of Deputies, Executive Committee Minutes, 30 January 1938.

46 Da Flemingh stood as a candidate in Vrededorp, where he captured 37.4 per cent of the vote, only eight per cent less than the winner, Carolina Badenhorst.

47 *Die Transvaler*, 29 November 1937.

48 See *SAJC*, 21 January 1938; *The Leader*, 6 January 1938; and Press Report 73: 1938.

49 South African Jewish Board of Deputies, Executive Committee Minutes, 8 November 1937. Even a Dingaan's Day celebration in Moordrift used the occasion to attack the Empire, Jews and 'coolies'. See *SAJT*, 31 December 1937.

50 Kollenberg and Norwich, *Jewish Life in the South African Country Communities*, Volume II, p. 432.

51 In a letter to Maria Louw, Malan's future wife, the Cape National Party leader wrote of the Jewish presence in the area. DF Malan Collection, KG 67/347/31. DF Malan to Maria Louw, 20 December 1937.

52 *Die Burger*, 25 January 1938. Malan's problem was that his party's exploration of ties with the Greyshirts was on record; all knew that the National Party had praised the Greyshirts for bringing 'the Jewish problem' to the notice of South Africa. For a perceptive analysis, see *SAJC*, 28 January 1938. See also the *Cape Argus*, 24 January 1938, and South African Jewish Board of Deputies, Executive

Committee Minutes, 30 January 1938.

53 In the early twentieth century there had been an outburst against the Jewish newcomers. See *The Owl*, 21 January 1905.

54 *Die Burger*, 22 January 1938.

55 *Die Transvaler*, 26 January 1938. See also South African Jewish Board of Deputies, Executive Committee Minutes, 30 January 1938.

56 See *SAJC*, 14 January 1938. An outcry followed the invitation from the Sons of England Society, with the *Sunday Times* (16 January 1938) leading the charge.

57 Hattingh, p. 131.

58 Even a late attempt by *Die Waarheid / The Truth* (14 January 1938) to mock *Die Transvaler* for complaining about the absence of Jewish advertisements made no difference.

59 *Die Burger*, 4 February 1938.

60 *Sunday Times*, 6 February 1938. See also South African Jewish Board of Deputies, Executive Committee Minutes, 6 March 1938. *Die Republikein* (18 February 1938) had similar views, noting that this was because all the Shirt movements tried to imitate the Nazis.

61 *Die Waarheid / The Truth*, 11 February 1938.

62 *Ibid.*

63 *Ibid.*

64 Britain's *Daily Express* (15 January 1938) similarly reported on German spies operating in South Africa. According to the newspaper, documents supporting this were in the hands of the British Secret Service. Press Report 74: 1938.

65 'Nazi Anti-Semitism and Nazi Propaganda in the Union of South Africa from the Year 1933 until the Outbreak of War in September 1939'.

66 Herr Kroenart (Transvaal); Herr Vogel (Johannesburg); Herr Heydenreich (Pretoria) Herr Debertshauser (Cape Town); Herr Schmaedecke (Durban); Herr Genter (East London); Herr von Delft (Bloemfontein and Stutterheim); Herr H Wedemann (Port Elizabeth).

67 The Merensky farm had been reported on before. Press Report 60: 1937.

68 See *Cape Argus*, 27 and 28 January 1938. See also 'Nazi Anti-Semitism and Nazi Propaganda in the Union of South Africa from the Year 1933 until the Outbreak of War in September 1939'.

69 *Cape Argus*, 10 February 1938.

70 See South African Jewish Board of

Deputies, Executive Committee Minutes,
6 March 1938. German residents of Durban
denied the allegations. *Daily Express*,
31 January 1938. See also *Sunday Times*,
20 February 1938.

71 *Cape Argus*, 10 February 1938. *The Forward*
(25 March 1938) had a lengthy report based
on the revelations of the Nazi menace in
South Africa.

72 *SAJC*, 4 February 1938. A few months later
the anthropologist, Audrey Richards, wrote
of Nazi agents pouring into the country 'in
recent years, determined on getting German
South-West. The Afrikaner element
is rather in favour of them,' she notes.
Audrey Richards/Dame Isabel Richards,
29 November 1938, Johannesburg. Raymond
Firth, 'Audrey Richards 1899–1984, *Man*,
20(2), 1985, p. 343. I am indebted to Andrew
Bank for drawing my attention to the
comment. See his forthcoming *Pioneers of
the Field: South Africa's Women Anthropologists*,
Cambridge University Press in association
with the International African Institute.

73 Hansard, 18 February 1938.

74 High Commissioner WH Clark to Sir
Harry Batterbee (Most secret), 24 February
1938. Foreign Office, 371.

75 *Ibid.*

76 Sir Henry Batterbee to O Sargent,
25 March 1938. 'In view of Gauleiter Bohle's
connection with South Africa,' wrote
Batterbee, 'it is natural that the Auslands-
Organisation should be particularly active
there.' High Commissioner (South Africa
Papers). Foreign Office, 371.

77 See South African Jewish Board of
Deputies, Executive Committee Minutes,
23 February 1938.

78 *Die Transvaler*, 28 February 1938. According
to the *Sunday Express* (27 February 1938),
3 500 people attended the meeting.

79 *Die Volksblad*, 14 May 1938.

80 *Die Waarheid / The Truth*, 1 April 1938.
See *Die Waarheid / The Truth*, 4 March
1938. In line with this sort of journalism,
WB Robinson of Grahamstown praised
National Socialism, while a correspondent
to *Die Waarheid / The Truth* (4 March 1938)
lauded Alfred Rosenberg's infamous *The
Myth of the Twentieth Century*, a foundational
Nazi text that was riddled with racial and
social Darwinist ideas.

81 See South African Jewish Board of Deputies,
Executive Committee Minutes, 6 March
1938.

82 *Ibid.*

83 *Die Burger*, 25 February 1938.

84 See *SAJC* (4 March 1938) linking Von
Moltke's switch due to his 'political
bankruptcy' in the wake of the Centlivres
judgment.

85 Shortly after the Centlivres judgment,
Von Moltke had dissolved his movement
and signalled his intention to merge with
the National Party. 'The Nationalist Party
has unequivocally given proof that it is
protecting the interest of the people and
that it wants a "race-pure" Afrikaner nation
which will rule its own country.' He was
happy that the Nationalists recognised the
democratic system in South Africa was full
of flaws and should be changed. See *Die
Burger*, 25 February 1938.

86 See South African Jewish Board of
Deputies, Executive Committee Minutes,
6 March 1938, and *Daily Express*,
28 February 1938.

87 The *Sunday Express* (6 March 1938) reported
that the 'Jewish Problem' was adopted
by the National Party as a 'vote-catching
device' but was beginning to affect the party
adversely. According to *The Star* (29 January
1938), Malan's reticence to make a statement
on his party's programme was because the
Jewish question had not yet 'received its
finishing touches'. It was anticipated that
emphasis would be on the Jewish 'system'
rather than on Jews as such. A few Cape
Nationalists even spoke of dropping Jewish
issues if assurances were given that no
further Jewish immigration would take
place. Cited in *SAJC*, 18 February 1938.

88 *Die Transvaler*, 12 March 1938. Verwoerd's
comments in this instance were provoked by
those Dutch Reformed Church ministers
that belonged to the Society for Christians
and Jews and sought to build bridges
between the two faiths.

89 *Die Transvaler*, 30 March 1938.

90 See comments made by Frederick William
Beyers, (former Appeal Court judge). South
African Jewish Board of Deputies, Executive
Minutes, 6 March 1938 and 12 March 1938.

91 See, for example, South African Jewish
Board of Deputies, Executive Committee
Minutes, 6 March 1938.

92 Press Report 84: 1938.

93 *The Star*, 16 March 1938.

94 See South African Jewish Board of
Deputies, Executive Committee Minutes,
6 March 1938. Havemann believed the

Blackshirts were the first to open the eyes of the Afrikaners to the Jewish problem.

95 According to Van Heerden (p. 80), they did not fight Newcastle.

96 *Die Burger*, 25 March 1938.

97 A *Cape Times* editorial (25 March 1938) suggested that the Greyshirts and Malanites appeared to be reconciled with regard to their approach to the 'Jewish Question' and their tactics. See also *The Star*, 21 March 1938, and South African Jewish Board of Deputies, Executive Committee Minutes, 10 April 1938.

98 See South African Jewish Board of Deputies, Executive Committee Minutes, 10 April 1938. See also *Die Waarheid/The Truth*, 22 April 1938.

99 *Die Waarheid/The Truth*, 8 April 1938.

100 *Ibid*.

101 See WA Kleynhans, *SA Algemene Verkiesingsmanifeste. SA General Elections Manifestos 1910–1981*, University of South Africa, Sigma Press, 1981, p. 278, and Furlong, *Between Crown and Swastika*, p. 66.

102 See South African Jewish Board of Deputies, Executive Committee Minutes, 10 April 1938 and Kleynhans, *SA Algemene Verkiesingsmanifeste*, p. 278.

103 Koorts, p. 371. See also Koorts, pp. 278–79, and Newell M Stultz, *Afrikaner Politics in South Africa, 1934–1948*, University of California Press, Berkeley, 1974, pp. 56–59.

104 *SAJC*, 8 April 1938. Jewish leaders were asked by the *SAJC* to maintain, rather than undermine, 'the courage, fortitude and dignity of the Jewish community …'

105 *Die Transvaler*, 9 April 1938.

106 *Ibid*.

107 *Die Waarheid/The Truth*, 22 April 1938.

108 *Rand Daily Mail*, 26 March 1938.

109 *Cape Argus*, 5 April 1938.

110 *Die Vaderland*, 7 April 1938.

111 See, for example, *SAJC* and *Rand Daily Mail*, 22 April 1938, *Die Transvaler*, 6 May 1938, and *Die Volksblad*, 2 May 1938.

112 *Die Transvaler*, 9 April 1938.

113 *Ibid*, 25 April 1938.

114 *Ibid*, 21 May 1938 and 29 April 1938. *Die Waarheid/The Truth* (22 April 1938) wrote of 'Jochanan' Smuts backing 'Moses Cantorowitz' Kentridge.

115 *Die Transvaler*, 27 April 1938.

116 *Ibid*, 14 April 1938.

117 *Cape Argus*, 5 April 1938. Furlong notes that, prior to the split, the former Administrator of South West Africa, Albertus Werth,

had felt Malan had feet of clay and was vacillating on the decision to break away. See Furlong, *Between Crown and Swastika*, p. 33.

118 *SAJC*, 8 April 1938. *Die Burger*, 30 March 1938.

119 See *Die Burger*, 28 March 1938 and *SAJC*, 8 April 1938.

120 See Press Report 86: 1938.

121 Press Report 87: 1938. Sauer also attacked the Jews during a speech at Gamtoos-Stasie. See *Die Oosterlig*, 2 May 1938. See also JG 'Kaalkop' van der Merwe's attack on Jews (*Die Volksblad*, 15 April and 14 May 1938).

122 See South African Jewish Board of Deputies, Executive Committee Minutes, 10 April 1938. The Board also pointed out that the issue of Jewish firms not placing advertisements in Nationalist newspapers was being resurrected by hecklers at National Party meetings. Allied to this was *Die Transvaler*'s encouragement to its readers to purchase only from those firms that advertised in its columns.

123 See *Die Vaderland*, 2 May 1938, and *Die Transvaler*, 25 April 1938. See also comments made by Dr Carl Potgieter (*Rand Daily Mail*, 21 April 1938) and a pamphlet distributed at one of his meetings in Benoni (*Die Vaderland*, 22 April 1938).

124 See Eric Louw speech at Queenstown, *Die Burger*, 22 April 1938. See also *Die Volksblad*, 18 May 1938.

125 *Die Transvaler*, 30 April 1938.

126 *Ibid*. See also Brill's speech at the Christiana Town Hall. *The Star*, 30 April 1938.

127 *Die Vaderland*, 2 May 1938.

128 *SAJC*, 22 April 1938.

129 *Eastern Province Herald*, 27 April 1938.

130 *The Star*, 25 April 1938, and *SAJC*, 29 April 1938.

131 *Rand Daily Mail*, 14 April 1938.

132 See also *SAJC*, 6 May 1938. Smuts in fact spoke out on more than one occasion against the twin dangers of antisemitism and fascism, as did other members of the United Party.

133 South African Jewish Board of Deputies, Executive Committee Minutes, 28 April 1938.

134 *SAJT*, 29 April 1938.

135 *Rand Daily Mail*, 30 April 1938 and *SAJC*, 6 May 1938.

136 *Die Volksblad*, 30 April 1938. These sentiments were shared by *Die Burger* (28 April 1938), which pointed out that

the National Party leader could not have anticipated the extent of German-Jewish immigration at the time he introduced the Quota Act in 1930. *Ons Vaderland* (29 April 1938) similarly supported the wish to halt the influx of Jews.

137 *Die Transvaler*, 3 May 1938.
138 *Die Volksblad*, 2 May 1938.
139 *Die Transvaler*, 6 May 1938.
140 See the South African Jewish Board of Deputies, Executive Minutes, 28 April 1938. In one or two constituencies the Blackshirts campaigned under the Nationalist banner.
141 *Daily Tribune*, 7 May 1938.
142 *Rand Daily Mail*, 5 May 1938. For the Blackshirts, see *SAJC*, 20 May 1939, and South African Jewish Board of Deputies, Executive Minutes, 12 June 1938.
143 *SAJC*, 13 May 1938.
144 See, for example, Dr Carl Potgieter. Press Report 92: 1938.
145 *Die Transvaler*, 4 May 1938.
146 See Patrick Furlong, *The Mixed Marriages Act: An Historical and Theological Study*, Centre for African Studies, University of Cape Town 1983.
147 *Die Transvaler*, 12 May 1938. See also Moodie, p. 246, and Jonathan Hyslop, 'White Working-Class Women and the Invention of Apartheid: "Purified"' Afrikaner Nationalist Agitation for Legislation Against "Mixed" Marriages, 1934–9', *Journal of African History*, 36(1), 1995. Hyslop argues that the essence of the campaign revolved around the poster and was tied to Afrikaner males losing their patriarchal power over white Afrikaner women who had entered the workplace. Placing the campaign in a wider context, it is obvious that the Jewish question loomed at least as large as any others. For the Afrikaner women in the workplace, see also Elsabe Brink, 'The Afrikaner Women of the Garment Workers' Union, 1918–1938', unpublished MA dissertation, University of the Witwatersrand, 1986.
148 See Hyslop, p. 77.
149 *Die Transvaler*, 12 May 1938.
150 *Ibid.* See also *Die Transvaler*, 13 May 1938.
151 *Die Volksblad*, 13 May 1938.
152 *Die Transvaler*, 11 May 1938.
153 *Die Volksblad*, 12 May 1938.
154 *Die Transvaler*, 16 May 1938.
155 *Die Volksblad*, 11 May 1938.
156 *Die Transvaler*, 16 May 1938.
157 *Ibid.*
158 For example, the notion of the Boer being

diddled by the Jews was a theme in Stephen Black's play, 'Helena's Hope', produced in 1910. See Shain, *The Roots of Antisemitism in South Africa*, pp. 72–73.
159 According to *Die Transvaler* (14 May 1938), an organised Jewish gang had precipitated the violence, which left the pavement stained with blood. See also *Die Volksblad*, 14 May 1938.
160 *Die Transvaler*, 18 May 1938. Meetings were often violent, with Jews targeted by the Nationalists and the radical right. See *Daily News*, 14 and 18 May 1938, and *Die Transvaler*, 18 May 1938, for clashes in Vrededorp.
161 *Die Vaderland*, 18 May 1938.
162 *The Star*, 18 May 1938. On the eve of the election a crowd of Blackshirts led by Havemann prevented Solly Sachs from addressing a Labour Party meeting in Germiston. See *Die Transvaler*, 18 May 1938.
163 *Die Transvaler*, 17 May 1938.
164 *SAJC*, 13 May 1938.
165 The Natal-based and essentially English-speaking Dominion Party, with a strong imperial orientation, obtained eight seats, Labour three, and the Socialist Party a paltry one.
166 Hepple, p. 49.
167 *Die Transvaler*, 20 May 1938.
168 *SAJC*, 20 May 1938.
169 *Ibid*, 27 May 1938.
170 *Die Transvaler*, 20 May 1938.
171 *Die Burger*, 23 May 1938.
172 *Die Transvaler*, 21 May 1938.
173 *Die Burger*, 27 May 1938.
174 See, for example, *Die Transvaler*, 25 May 1938.
175 Press Report 92: 1938.
176 *Die Transvaler*, 21 May 1938.
177 The pernicious action of Jewish business was also noted. Twenty Afrikaner girls, according to *Die Transvaler* (25 May 1938), were dismissed from a factory in Germiston because they worked and voted for the National Party. The newspaper further alleged that Solly Sachs had threatened with dismissal every girl who voted for the National Party.
178 See *SAJC*, 3 June 1938.
179 *Ibid*, 20 May 1939 and South African Jewish Board of Deputies, Executive Committee Minutes, 12 June 1938.
180 Press Report 92: 1938.
181 The document from the Broederbond Collection is: Broederbond Archives, 2/3/8/2, Uitvoerende Raad, Notule, Bylae

B, UR Vergadering, 24 and 25 June 1938.
1938/6/24. I am indebted to Christoph
Marx for bringing these minutes to my
attention. For concerns about the 'Jewish
Question' within the Broederbond, see
also Stals, Afrikaner Bond, Afrikaner
Broederbond, *Geskiedenis van die Afrikaner-
Broederbond*, pp. 128–29.

CHAPTER SIX

IN THE CROSSFIRE OF
AFRIKANERDOM'S BATTLES

1 See Moodie, chaper nine, *passim*. For the
importance of the Eeufees in Afrikaner
nationalist mythology, see Leonard
Thompson, *The Political Mythology of
Apartheid*, Yale University Press, New Haven
and London, 1985, chapters two and five,
passim.
2 See *Die Burger*, 19 December 1938.
3 See Marx, *Oxwagon Sentinel*, pp. 268–275;
Norval, pp. 39–40; and Giliomee and
Mbenga, *New History of South Africa*, p. 290
4 Moodie, p. 180.
5 See Hancock, p. 296. Hertzog did not even
attend, while Smuts, who was present at the
Pretoria celebration, did not speak.
6 Koorts, p. 328.
7 See Philip Bonner, 'South African Society
and Culture, 1910–1948,' in Robert Ross,
Anne Kelk Mager and Bill Nasson (eds),
*The Cambridge History of South Africa,
Volume 2, 1885–1994*, p. 307. *Gelykstelling*, or
equalisation with blacks, was a major worry
for Christian-National theologians.
8 Duffy, p. 97.
9 Even the singing of 'God Save the King' was
dropped from the original programme.
10 *The Friend*, 26 October 1938.
11 Norval, p. 40.
12 *Die Volksblad*, 7 November 1938.
13 *Die Transvaler*, 21 November 1938.
14 Cited in Van Heerden, p. 111.
15 South African Jewish Board of Deputies,
Executive Committee Minutes, 30 October
1938.
16 *Ibid*. As non-Christians, Jews were also
barred from festivities in Springfontein.
See *Sunday Times*, 18 September 1938. An
official pamphlet (*Liga vir die Instandhouding
van Volksregering, Die Eeufees*, p. 27) asked
rhetorically if, a century after the Great
Trek, the *volk* would allow itself 'to be
trampled underfoot by "foreign ideas" and

"outside elements" [*uitlandse elemente*]?' See
Vincent, p. 75.
17 See S Gill and D Humphriss, *One Man and
His Town*, Juta and Co, 1985, pp. 59–60, and
Rand Daily Mail, 18 November 1938. There
were some moderate voices – for example,
the Moderator of the Dutch Reformed
Church, the Reverend William Nicol. See
Die Vaderland, 5 December 1938.
18 South African Jewish Board of Deputies,
Executive Committee Minutes,
22 December 1938.
19 *SAJC*, 9 December 1938.
20 *Ibid*, 19 August 1938.
21 *Cape Times*, 22 July 1938.
22 *Ibid*, 23 July 1938. See also *Cape Times*, 25,
26, 28, 29 July 1938.
23 *Ibid*, 25 July 1938. See 'Summary of Nazi
Activities in South West Africa – 1934–
1939', AH Jonker Collection. PV 42, File
129.
24 Some months later, Smuts informed J
Martin that the Commissioner of Police had
visited the territory and had returned with
a disturbing report about conditions there.
See Jan Smuts to JC Martin, 3 August 1939.
Cited in Jean van der Poel (ed), *Selections
from the Smuts Papers, Volume VI, December
1934–August 1945*, Cambridge University
Press, Cambridge, 1973, p. 468.
25 *Die Waarheid / The Truth*, 8 July 1938.
26 See Hattingh, pp. 149–51. Much time
was spent on the washing of dirty linen
and financial issues. For full details of the
conference, see 'Notule van Suid-Afrikaanse
Nasionale Party (Gryshemde) Konferènsie
gehou te Pretoria op 19 en 20 Augustus
1938', Weichardt Collection, PV 29, File 115.
27 *Die Burger*, 6 July 1938. See also *SAJC*,
22 July 1938. At a meeting in Parow, one
of the leading members of the Greyshirts
in the Cape Peninsula, DJ Kotze, also
announced his defection to the Nationalists,
claiming that there were others in Paarl,
Parow and Southfield who had done so.
See *SAJC*, 22 July 1938, and *Die Burger*,
6 July 1938. Three months later, CCJ
Els of Cradock published a letter in *Die
Oosterlig* (17 October 1938) saying he and
his wife had left the Greyshirts and joined
the National Party. He called on their
65 Greyshirt followers in Cradock to do
likewise. The Blackshirts, too, struggled to
get an audience in Benoni. See *Rand Daily
Mail*, 6 September 1938.
28 *Die Burger*, 15 August 1938.

29 *Ibid*, 20 August 1938.

30 *Hansard*, 14 September 1938.

31 *Ibid*, 21 September 1938, and *Rand Daily Mail*, 23 September 1938.

32 See, for example, *Die Burger*, 1 September and 5 October 1938, and *Die Oosterlig*, 2 September 1938.

33 *Die Burger*, 23 September 1938.

34 *Die Transvaler*, 28 September 1938.

35 *Sunday Tribune*, 4 September 1938, and *Sunday Express*, 4 September 1938. The shelving of the already drafted Bill, suggested the two newspapers, 'was a confession that an anti-Semitic policy is doomed to failure in South Africa'.

36 *Sunday Tribune*, 4 September 1938. Montgomery was described as a National Party 'urban organiser'.

37 *Daily Express*, 3 October 1938.

38 *Die Burger*, 19 October 1938. The Nationalist press, according to the *SAJC* (28 October 1938), had a slightly different version of the speech, which concluded: 'Unless we get another Government than the present one which is under the thumb of the Jews and coloureds – it is they who are in great measure responsible for the victory of the Government in the general elections – I see a dark future for South Africa.' See also *Daily Express*, 17 October 1938.

39 See, for example, the clash at the Germiston Town Hall between white mineworkers and the Blackshirts. *The Star*, 4 August 1938. Board President Cecil Lyons met with Smuts and Senator Charles Francis Clarkson, Minister of the Interior, on 29, 30 November and 1 December, respectively, to discuss the Johannesburg riot and immigration. See South African Jewish Board of Deputies, Executive Committee Minutes, 12 February 1939.

40 See *Daily Express*, 30 September 1938.

41 *Die Transvaler* (30 November 1938) deplored suggestions of Nationalist involvement.

42 *SAJC*, 11 November 1938. See also Van Heerden, p. 112.

43 See Elphick, pp. 239–41, and Bloomberg, pp. 78–85.

44 *The Star*, 11 November 1938.

45 See *Rand Daily Mail*, 20 October 1938, and *The Star*, 20 October 1938.

46 It is perhaps because of Article One that some claimed the Orange Free State joined the Transvaal in precluding Jewish membership. Malan actually told a meeting some time later that Jews were not allowed to join the Orange Free State National Party. See Press Report 89: 1938.

47 *Rand Daily Mail*, 20 October 1938 and *The Star*, 20 October 1938.

48 *Die Burger*, 10 November 1938.

49 *Ibid*, 11 November 1938.

50 See *Pretoria News*, 14 February 1939, and *SAJC*, 10 March 1939.

51 *The Star*, 16 February 1939.

52 *Pretoria News*, 14 February 1939.

53 For Lichtenburg see, for example, *Die Volksblad*, 22 February 1939.

54 *Natal Witness*, 16 March 1939. Three months later, Hugo joined Van Nierop in a discussion in Paarl billed 'Have we a Jewish Problem'. Specific questions were posed in the advert for the meeting that clearly threatened South African Jewry.

55 See *Rand Daily Mail*, *Die Burger*, *Die Transvaler* and *Die Volksblad*, 15 April 1939.

56 *The Star*, 10 February 1939, and *Die Burger*, 9 February 1939.

57 *Daily Tribune*, 10 March 1939. On the stump, Smuts accused the National Party of becoming a Nazi party and a menace to democracy and Christian principles. See *Pretoria News*, 6 March 1939. Davis won the election with 2 193 votes, while Van den Heever obtained 2 003 and the Dominion Party's RS Cook 728.

58 *Pretoria News*, 9 March 1939.

59 *Die Volksblad*, 5 January 1939.

60 South Africa, Aliens (Amendment) Immigration Bill, *Government Gazette*, No 2596 (6 January 1939), Government Printer, Pretoria, 1939. Louw's speech was published as a booklet in the United States by the far-right 'Nationalist Press Association of New York'. See 'Mr Louw's American Friends', *Common Sense*, November 1940.

61 *The Star*, 10 January 1939.

62 *Independent*, 18 January 1939. The newspaper also reported that Nazi agents in the disguise of 'pen friends' were sending propaganda to South African schoolchildren.

63 *Cape Argus*, 9 January 1939.

64 *Die Suiderstem*, 12 January 1939.

65 *SAJC*, 13 January 1939. The Nuremberg Laws, introduced in Germany in 1935, classified and defined who was a Jew.

66 *SAJC*, 31 March 1939.

67 See, for example, *The Friend*, 26 January 1939.

68 See *Cape Times*, 10 January 1939.

69 See, for example, *Die Burger*, 21, 23, 26, 27 and 30 January 1939.

70 *Cape Argus*, 13 January 1939. Two weeks later, Fanie Brand, the secretary of the Greyshirts, stated that the movement would continue to operate along non-party lines. See *Die Burger*, 27 January 1939. See also Weichardt letter to *Die Burger*, 13 January 1939.

71 *Die Burger*, 13 January 1939. At a National Party meeting in Vryheid, three weeks later, Professor A du Toit expressed his appreciation to the Greyshirts 'for the exposure of the Jewish menace'. One of the Greyshirt stalwarts, Dr Louis Stoffberg, was welcomed to the platform to shake hands with the dignitaries. *Natal Mercury*, 3 February 1939.

72 *The Star*, 21 January 1939, and *Die Volksblad*, 21 January 1939.

73 *Die Vaderland*, 19 January 1939. On the other hand, Zuidmeer wondered why it had taken so long for the Nationalists to tackle the question of Jewish immigration. In his view, dealing with the Jews was even more important, given their stranglehold on commerce. See *Die Burger*, 31 January 1939.

74 See *Die Burger*, 18 January 1939, and *Die Vaderland*, 18 January 1939.

75 *SAJC*, 20 January 1939. The authoritian tendencies of the National Party in the late 1930s are explored in Furlong, *Between Crown and Swastika*, chapter four, *passim*.

76 *Die Burger*, 19 January 1939, and *Die Transvaler*, 19 January 1939.

77 Eric Louw's parliamentary speech in support of his Private Member's Bill was published as a pamphlet: 'Die Jodevraagstuk in Suid-Afrika/The Jewish Problem in South Africa', Nasionale Pers, Cape Town, 1939. Louw would remind Malan of this speech and its publication by the party at the time Malan was considering changing policies towards Jews in late 1947. See chapter seven.

78 *Hansard*, 24 February 1939. Presumably, in his understanding, the Talmud allowed for double standards when dealing with non-Jews.

79 *Ibid*. Hofmeyr's defence (in the best traditions of philosemitism) failed to convince Albertus Werth, who supported Louw. According to Werth, the Jew had abused his position in South Africa and this had resulted in rising resentment. 'The history of the last six years especially,' he explained, 'shows us that the Jew is prepared at a critical moment in our national history to abuse the citizenship which we have given him in South Africa.' Werth reiterated much of what Louw had said, adding the charge that Jews lacked patriotism and reinforcing the notion that communist Jews were inciting the black population.

80 *Rand Daily Mail*, 27 February 1939.

81 *Natal Daily News*, 25 February 1939. See also *Cape Times*, 25 February 1939, and *Cape Argus*, 25 February 1939. Louw had no problems in reconciling this apparent paradox. Like the capitalists, the communists wanted control of production and distribution. See *Hansard*, 14 April 1939.

82 *Die Burger*, 27 February 1939.

83 *Die Transvaler*, 28 February 1939.

84 In fact numbers had dwindled. In 1936, the high point of German-Jewish immigration, 3 330 Jews had entered the country; in 1937, 954; and in 1938, 566. See Peberdy, p. 65.

85 *Hansard*, 17 March 1939. In his speech Malan wondered what the difference was between Jews and Indians, the latter not being allowed to immigrate to South Africa.

86 *Die Suiderstem*, 27 March 1939. In 1941 Jonker would publish (with the support of the Board) *The Scapegoat of History* (Central News Agency, South Africa, 1941). In 1956 he joined the National Party.

87 In the interview Weichardt made it clear that he still disagreed with the National Party insofar as they advocated the maintenance of democracy. As far as party politics were concerned, he intended to throw the weight of the Greyshirt movement behind the National Party, but he would continue to work on constitutional and non-party lines for the establishment of fascism in South Africa. See *Daily Express*, 21 March 1939.

88 *Daily Express*, 25 March 1939, and *Oosterlig*, 27 March 1939. According to a report in the *Natal Mercury* (23 May 1940), the Greyshirt movement was being reorganised and old members were invited to rejoin.

89 Hattingh, pp. 157–58. Weichardt, meanwhile, emulated Hitler in dress style and would be met by a stage-managed procession of appropriately dressed woman and youths, arms outstretched, shouting 'Heil'. See *Cape Argus*, 10 November 1938.

90 Hattingh, p. 160.

91 See 'It Did Happen Here'. 'The eternal Jew' appeared under the name of the Blackshirts' HS Terblanche and comprised a collection of leaflets issued over time by the

movement. See South African Jewish Board of Deputies, Executive Committee Minutes, 16 January 1939. Similarly, *Die Nuwe Tyd*, a weekly published in Aberdeen and edited by H Postma, carried antisemitic observations. See *SAJC*, 7 July 1939. Manie Maritz wrote a letter to *Die Nuwe Tyd* calling on readers to inform him of their negative experiences with Jews. See *SAJC*, 21 July 1939. For reported anti-Jewish incidents, see South African Jewish Board of Deputies, Executive Committee Minutes, 14 March 1939, 5 June 1939 and 17 July 1939.

92 South African Jewish Board of Deputies, Executive Committee Minutes, 17 July 1939. The Board was concerned about Dutch Reformed Church insinuations that Jews were associated 'with Communistic influences'. See *SAJC*, 7 July 1939.

93 *Mossel Bay Advertiser*, 6 May 1939. Here he was repeating arguments he had made in parliament a few weeks earlier. See *Hansard*, 14 April 1939. See also *SAJC*, 11 August 1939.

94 *Die Oosterlig*, 17 July 1939.

95 *Die Burger*, 5 April 1939, and Hattingh, p. 160.

96 South African Jewish Board of Deputies, Press Report 130: 1939. One year earlier he had sent a message to the Welt-Dienst congress in Erfurt, where he indicated that 'there should be no difficulty in forming a united front throughout the world in order that Judah may be put in his place.' For the full text, see Botschaft von Louis T Weichardt an den internationalem 'Welt-Dienst-Kongress, Erfurt'. Weichardt Papers, PV29, and 'It Did Happen Here'. See also Hattingh, p. 161.

97 The *Sunday Times* and *Daily Express* accused Weichardt of encouraging Hitler to start a war. However, a letter to Hitler from Weichardt proved that this was not the case. See Hattingh, p. 164. For Weichardt's accusations that Jews were communists, see *Natal Mercury*, 27 January 1937.

98 See *Sunday Times*, 25 June 1939. On appeal, the sentence was suspended by the Cape Supreme Court for a period of two years on condition Weichardt did not reoffend against the Act again. See *Rand Daily Mail*, 5 December 1939.

99 See Hattingh, pp. 162–63.

100 *The Star*, 15 July 1938. Maritz even established the short-lived 'Maritz's Fighting Commando' in Vredendal. See *Die Burger*, 3 November 1938.

101 *Sunday Times*, 13 November 1938. He too had been refused a hall for a meeting a few months earlier. See *Cape Argus*, 15 July 1938.

102 The meeting took place on 28 June 1939. See *SAJC*, 21 July and 11 August 1939. See also Roberts and Trollip, p. 70.

103 Following his death, his widow, together with Col Laas, who was expelled from the OB (see below), founded Die Boerenasie. Laas fell out and established Die Boerevolk. See *Rand Daily Mail*, 26 March 1941. Shortly before his death, Maritz delivered a vicious diatribe against Jews in Kroonstad. See *SAJC*, 6 December 1940.

104 See South African Jewish Board of Deputies, Executive Committee Minutes, 12 February 1939. According to the Board, the book made use of material from the Nazi Fichtebund. The Board also reported that the book was on sale at the offices of *Die Transvaler*. See South African Jewish Board of Deputies, Executive Committee Minutes, 14 March 1939.

105 See, for example, the comments on Lionel Phillips and Alfred Beit, p. 118 and comments on the press, p. 129.

106 Manie Maritz, *My Lewe en Strewe*, Johannesburg, 1938.

107 See South African Jewish Board of Deputies, Executive Committee Minutes, 12 February 1939. The book became a major matter of concern for the Board. See South African Jewish Board of Deputies, Executive Committee Minutes, 29 March 1939. South African law precluded attempts to have *My Lewe en Strewe* banned. However, when the book began to circulate in South West Africa the law allowed for its banning on the grounds that it promoted 'feelings of hostility between different races of the community' (Section 4, Criminal Amendment Act 13 of 1934). See South African Jewish Board of Deputies, Executive Committee Minutes, 29 March 1939.

108 See Gustav Saron, unpublished manuscript, p. 656 ARCH. This was probably a reference to the Kristelike Nasionale Bond, a movement with possible links to the Broederbond or perhaps to the League of Gentiles, which was reported on in the press in the 1920s. See Bloomberg, p. 41, and Shain, *The Roots of Antisemitism in South Africa*, pp. 121–23.

109 See Shain, *The Roots of Antisemitism in South Africa*, pp. 114–15.

110 *Ibid*, pp. 41–43.

111 *Zionist Record*, 25 August 1939.

112 See the *Zionist Record*, 25 August 1939 and *Die Transvaler*, 25 August 1939. Letters of sympathy and offers to pay the fine were sent to *Die Transvaler* (25 August 1939). Before the trial, Maritz focused his activities on the town of Aberdeen, supported by *Die Nuwe Tyd*. There he tried to elicit from the public experiences with Jews that would support his case. See *SAJC*, 21 July 1939.

113 *Die Volksblad*, 18 September 1939. Maritz was fined £75 with an alternative of nine months in prison.

114 *The Star*, 2 September 1939.

115 *Die Volksblad*, 22 September 1939.

116 *Die Volk* (14 February 1941) exposed the falsehoods in *My Lewe en Strewe* and protested against its circulation. It was subsequently banned. See *Zionist Record*, 14 March 1941.

117 *Die Transvaler*, 7 August 1939.

118 *Ibid*, 8 August 1939.

119 *Ibid*.

120 The focus was on Jewish immigration. See *Die Transvaler*, 27 September 1939. See also *SAJC*, 13 October 1939.

121 These were pogroms across Germany orchestrated by Joseph Goebbels, with Hitler's support, in the wake of the assassination in Paris of a German diplomat by a young Jew.

122 See McNally, p. 17.

123 *Die Burger*, 25 November 1938. For a full discussion of *Die Burger's* attitude towards the Nazis and the 'Final Solution', see Sharon Lynne Friedman, 'Jews, Germans and Afrikaners: Nationalist Press reaction to the Final Solution', unpublished Hons dissertation, University of Cape Town, 1982. See also Furlong, *Between Crown and Swastika* (pp. 153–54) for examples of popular support for Hitler and hostility towards Jews.

124 See Jan Smuts to MC Gillet, 19 April 1936. Cited in Van der Poel, p. 35.

125 Antony Lentin, *Jan Smuts: Man of Courage and Vision*, Jonathan Ball, Cape Town, 2010, pp. 129–33.

126 Leslie Blackwell, *Blackwell Remembers … An Autobiography*, Howard Timmins, Cape Town, 1971, p. 75. See also Fry, 'Agents and Structures'.

127 Hertzog also repudiated any German plans for 'world domination'. See *Hansard*, 4 September 1939.

128 *Die Vaderland*, 18 October 1939.

129 *Die Burger*, 13 September 1939. See also *SAJC*, 6 October 1939.

130 *Die Transvaler*, 18 October 1939. According to the British High Commissioner, WH Clark, the term was taken directly from the German propaganda station at Zeesen. See dispatch from High Commissioner in the Union of South Africa to His Majesty's Government in the United Kingdom. Dispatch 91/279, 19 October 1939. Foreign Office, 371. Malan also used the phrase 'Janowitz Smutsowitz' at the Transvaal congress of the National Party in September 1939. See *Die Transvaler*, 27 September 1939.

131 Paton, *Hofmeyr*, p. 329.

132 See Furlong, *Between Crown and Swastika*, p. 132, and Monama, p. 145.

133 *Die Volksblad*, 7 November 1939. Certainly Eric Louw had taken this view shortly before the outbreak of war. See *Rand Daily Mail*, 8 August 1939.

134 *Rand Daily Mail*, 18 September 1939.

135 See, for example, *Die Transvaler*, 7 October 1939, *Die Burger*, 10 October 1939, and *Die Transvaler*, 13 October 1939.

136 See Koorts, p. 384. These meetings were driven by the Prime Minister's son, Albert Hertzog. See South African Jewish Board of Deputies, Executive Committee Minutes, 5 April 1939. Further efforts at *hereniging* were driven by Professor AC Cilliers and a number of his colleagues at Stellenbosch University. The drama surrounding Smuts' decision to enter the war and the polarisation it brought along language lines ignited a sense of urgency to the negotiations on *hereniging*. Grundlingh has noted that about half the fighting forces were Afrikaners. Most, however, signed up for financial rather than for idealistic reasons. See Albert Grundlingh, 'The King's Afrikaners: Enlistment and Ethnic Identity in the Union of South Africa's Defence Force in the Second World War', *Journal of African History*, 44(3), 1999, p. 360.

137 South African Jewish Board of Deputies, Executive Committee Minutes, 29 October 1939. See also 'Two Kinds of Nationhood', *SAJC*, 1 December 1939.

138 *Die Transvaler* (30 January 1940) ominously noted that the Jewish question involved more than simple immigration. Ten days earlier (on 20 January 1939), it had discussed divisions in the National Party, including the significant presence of those with allegiance

to the Greyshirts following Weichardt's decision to join the party.

139 See Rodney Davenport and Christopher Saunders, *South Africa: A Modern History*, fifth edition, Macmillan Press, London, 2000, p. 331.

140 See Furlong, *Between Crown and Swastika*, p. 136.

141 South African Jewish Board of Deputies, Report of Executive Council, June 1937 to May 1940. Nico van der Merwe indeed told a Bloemfontein audience that the National Party was not in favour of persecuting Jews, but that they were opposed to further Jewish immigration. See *SAJC*, 1 December 1939.

142 Holm had founded a German choral society in Durban, whose musical activities served to conceal its propaganda aims. See 'List of Dangerous Nazis'. Lawrence Papers, BC640, E3.2.66. For further information see *The Star*, 30 October 1939, *Rand Daily Mail*, 31 October 1939, and *Sunday Times*, 10 December 1939.

143 See Christoph Marx, 'Dear Listeners in South Africa: German Propaganda Broadcasts to South Africa, 1940–1941', *South African Historical Journal*, 27(1), 1992, and Monama, pp. 28–30. According to Monama (pp. 64–65), the station had a number of Afrikaner broadcasters.

144 Jan Smuts to MC Gillet, 21 September 1939. Cited in Van der Poel, pp. 193–94.

145 Bill Nasson, *South Africa at War*, Jacana, Pretoria, p. 65. See also, for example, the confidential letter from Pierie to D Pyne Mercier, 17 January 1940. SANDF Archives, CGS, War Box 223, File 49(1).

146 Nasson, p. 74. See also Kent Fedorowich, 'German Espionage and British Counter-Intelligence in South Africa and Mozambique, 1939–1944', *Historical Journal*, 48(1), 2005.

147 South African Jewish Board of Deputies, Executive Committee Minutes, 28 January 1940. The Board also reported that the 'interning of Union citizens will result in antisemitism unlike any which has preceded it'. South African Jewish Board of Deputies, Executive Committee Minutes, 28 January 1940. On 11 September 1939 an Aliens Registration Act came into force. An 'alien' was defined as a person 'who is not a natural-born British subject or Union National'. See *SAJC*, 22 September 1939. See also Furlong, *Between Crown and Swastika*, pp. 131–34. For internments, see

FD Tothill, 'The 1943 Election', unpublished MA thesis, University of South Africa, 1987, pp. 89–90.

148 The *SAJC* (10 November 1939) reported on comment in the general press regarding Nazi plots and sabotage in the Union, including the mobilisation of the Blackshirts for a March on Johannesburg. Nazi activity was taken seriously by the British High Commission. See 'Nazi Activities in South Africa', from Dominion Office, C19831, 6 December 1939. Foreign Office, 371. For individuals under surveillance, see 'Internal Security Measures'. SANDF Archives, CGS, Box 93, File 169(6). The government, too, took the threat of subversion seriously, with Pirow and Van Rensburg closely monitored. See also Fortnightly Reports, SANDF Archives, CGS, Box 93, File 169/7; and 'News Letter', No 77, 28 March 1940, Published by News Research Service, Los Angeles, California.

149 See *Die Volksblad*, 20 July 1940.

150 *SAJC*, 10 May 1940.

151 See Roberts and Trollip, p. 41.

152 See *Zionist Record*, 12 December 1940. Later, Strijdom spoke of the need not to imitate the 'British-Jewish capitalist system'. *Die Transvaler*, 26 May 1941.

153 See, for example, Van Nierop, who blamed Jews for the Versailles Treaty and for causing wars. *Die Burger*, 8 February 1941.

154 See South African Jewish Board of Deputies, Executive Committee Minutes, 20 October 1941.

155 South African Jewish Board of Deputies, Executive Minutes, 24 September 1940. See also Gustav Saron, 'Nazi Propaganda and South African Imitations', *Hasholom: Rosh Hashana Annual 5702*.

156 See South African Jewish Board of Deputies, Executive Committee Minutes, 10 December 1940.

157 *Ibid*, 16 December 1940.

158 See, for example, *Die Oosterlig*, 6 September 1940.

159 See South African Jewish Board of Deputies, Executive Committee Minutes, 25 June 1940. See also letter from S Berger (*Die Oosterlig*, 16 September 1940).

160 SANDF Archives, SAP-349, 36-29-42, Bylaag. See *Rand Daily Mail*, 22 December 1941.

161 See Coetzee, 'Fires and Feathers', pp. 164–65: arson against Jewish stores began in November 1940. See also Coetzee, 'From

Immigrants to Citizens', p. 153. Swastikas were also painted on the wall of the Paarl Synagogue. See *Rand Daily Mail*, 30 July 1940.

162 See South African Jewish Board of Deputies, Report of the Executive Council, June 1937 to May 1940.

163 In 1937 a *Nasionaal-Republikeinse Eenheidsfront* (National Republican Unity Front) was founded and was followed by the creation of a Christian Republican Party. Although of no political significance, the Nasionaal-Republikeinse Eenheidsfront sought to establish a Christian republic in which 'British-Jewish Imperialistic Capitalism' would be targeted, as well as the 'parasitic middleman', and immigration controls implemented. See South African Jewish Board of Deputies, Executive Committee Minutes, 28 February 1937; *Die Republikein*, 23 January 1937; Moodie, p. 144; De Villiers, 'Afrikaner Nationalism', pp. 392ff; *Zionist Record*, 3 May 1940 and *Die Vaderland*, 17 March 1937. *Die Republikein* had long punted a National Socialist republic and glorified everything in Nazi Germany. In 1938 it ceased publication.

164 See Marx, *Oxwagon Sentinel*, chapter seventeen, *passim*; O'Meara, *Volkskapitalisme*, chapter ten, *passim*; and Giliomee, *The Afrikaners*, pp. 436–39.

165 Giliomee, *The Afrikaners*, p. 437.

166 See CGW Schumann, 'Die Nuwe Duitsland', *Die Huisgenoot*, 15 and 22 July 1938.

167 *Die Vaderland*, 4 October 1939.

168 *Ibid*, 6 October 1939.

169 See Giliomee, *The Afrikaners*, p. 438; O'Meara, *Volkskapitalisme*, pp. 147–53; and Cohen, 'Anatomy of South African Anti-Semitism', p. 129.

170 *Zionist Record*, 3 May 1940.

171 *Ibid*, 8 March 1940.

172 See Fortnightly Intelligence Report, No 42, 11 August 1943. SANDF Archives, CGS GP2, Holder 93, File 169/7. From the outset, noted an official report of the war years, in its collection activities, the Reddingsdaabond never disclosed to Jews and English-speakers that money collected would only go to Afrikaner businesses. See Major to Deputy Commissioner SAP, Commanding SWA, to the Commissioner of South African Police, Pretoria, 'SA Police, Official History of the War, 1939 to 1945', 30 June 1947. South African Police Archives,

391-2-4-47. As late as 1947, Jewish sources reported that the Reddingsdaadbond was harming English and Jewish business on the platteland. See *Zionist Record*, 4 July 1947.

173 *The Star*, 6 February 1939. Christoph Marx explores the possibility that the OB was founded by the Broederbond. See Marx, *Oxwagon Sentinel*, pp. 299–303.

174 Duffy, p. 97.

175 *Cape Argus*, 6 March 1939. For the OB military structure, see Marx, *Oxwagon Sentinel*, pp. 307–309. For Broederbond support, see Furlong, *Between Crown and Swastika*, p. 139.

176 Jan Smuts to JC Martin, 3 August 1939. Cited in Van der Poel, p. 468.

177 See, for example, Fortnightly Intelligence Report. SANDF Archives, CGS, GP2, Holder 93, File 169/7.

178 See 'Secret Report', Deputy Commissioner, SA Police Headquarters to Commissioner, 21 February 1940. Smuts Collection, A1, Vol 142, File 36. The mysterious De Friedlander (mentioned in chapter one as a Fascist leader) also appeared, together with his wife. For some time Havemann had claimed the OB had no Jewish policy because it was under Jewish influence. See report of Havemann's speech. JD Jerling Collection, PV158, File 11, 11/141.

179 Marx, *Oxwagon Sentinel*, p. 320.

180 SANDF Archives, PP59, 1st Reserve Brigade Headquarters, 5 June 1941.

181 See Marx, *Oxwagon Sentinel*, p. 320. Less than two years later, an intelligence report noted that Terblanche and Havemann were reviving their activities. A printed circular was distributed with a swastika and 'a violent tirade against Jewish elements in this country'. Fortnightly Intelligence Report, No 15, 4 April 1941. SANDF Archives, CGS, Box 93, File 169/7.

182 See comments by Laas in *Die Transvaler*, 26 February 1940. The *SAJT* (1 March 1940) blasted Laas and the OB for its exclusionary policies. See discussion in *Die Oosterlig*, 11 March 1940.

183 Marx, *Oxwagon Sentinel*, p. 320. See also South African Jewish Board of Deputies. Report of Executive Council, August 1942 to May 1945.

184 Marx, *Oxwagon Sentinel*, pp. 331 and 337. See also Van Heerden, pp. 125 and 129.

185 See Van Heerden, p. 132. A draft republican constitution, published by the Transvaal OB in April 1940, spoke of settling the

'Jewish Question' as well as the 'poor white' and 'coloured' questions without delay. A precondition for citizenship in the envisaged republic would be 'pure white descent and service to the Afrikaans ethnic calling and incorporation into organic ethnic life would be a first requirement'. *Die Volkstem*, 5 October 1940.

186 See Marx, *Oxwagon Sentinel*, pp. 310–13, 316–18, 324 and 327.

187 See Roberts and Trollip, p. 74. Initially women, too, were tasked with building the nation. For the role and place of women in the OB, see Charl Blignaut, '*Die hand aan die weeg regeer die land* [The hand that rocks the cradle rules the land]: Exploring the Agency and Identity of Women in the Ossewa-Brandwag, 1939–1954', *South African Historical Journal*, 16(1), 2015.

188 In late 1940, Ben Schoeman told a National Party congress that the German victories would speed things up, allow for negotiations with the Nazis and ensure a republic. 'The whole future of Afrikanerdom was dependent on a German victory,' he told the congress in November 1940. See Nasson, p. 65. Fortnightly Intelligence Reports, No 15, 4 April 1941. SANDF Archives, CGS, Box 93, File 169/7.

189 Marx, *Oxwagon Sentinel*, pp. 328 and 346–47.

190 It is difficult to date exactly the formation of the Stormjaers. See Marx, *Oxwagon Sentinel*, p. 353.

191 In 1941, an intelligence report noted that the HNP, OB and NO 'are agreed on being anti-British, anti-Smuts, anti-Semitic and anti-war, but for the rest there are no points of contact'. See Fortnightly Intelligence Report, No 13, 15 September 1941. SANDF Archives, CGS GP2, Holder 93, File 169/7.

192 Marx, *Oxwagon Sentinel*, p. 384. Weichardt would not accept the Cradock Agreement and left the National Party. See chapter seven.

193 Oswald Pirow, *Nuwe Orde vir Suid-Afrika*, Christelike Republikeinse Suid-Afrikaanse Nasionaal-Sosialistiese Studiekring, Pretoria, 1940.

194 JHO Du Plessis, *Die Nuwe Suid-Afrika – Die Rewolusie van die Twintigste Eeu*, Die Nasionale Pers, 1940. See Van Heerden, pp. 157–61. See also Roberts and Trollip, pp. 79–80.

195 See Shimoni, pp. 132–33.

196 See chapter seven. Democracy was labelled a sham and a guild system was proposed,

much in line with Italian fascism. See Van Heerden, pp. 163–88.

197 Hertzog's moderation did not have full support. Verwoerd, for example, was adamant that Jews would not enjoy full rights within the polity he envisaged. He told the annual congress of the *Nasionale Jeugbond* (National Youth Organisation) that 'it need have no doubt of the preparedness of the HNP to look the Jewish problem in the face, nor need it fear that Jews would suddenly be allowed to become members of the HNP in the Transvaal'. See South African Jewish Board of Deputies, Executive Committee Minutes, 16 December 1940.

198 See his speech to the Orange Free State congress (*Die Burger*, 6 November 1940). See also *Zionist Record*, 15 November 1940. Such divisions ensured Hertzog could anticipate dirty infighting. This was evident when he and his loyal colleague, Havenga, were linked to a fabricated, sinister Jewish-inspired Freemason plot to establish an English-dominated republic. See Marx, *Oxwagon Sentinel*, pp. 374–75. Described as the 'Freemason Letters Affair', the highly regarded Bloemfontein Dutch Reformed minister, the Rev Christiaan Kotzé, (later chairman of the Grootraad of the OB), claimed that Jews had founded 'the secret world organisation of Freemasonry, which they control and which in every country acts as a link between Jewry and the government of the country'. Here Kotzé was tapping into a European trope with a long pedigree. Disturbingly, the Dutch Reformed Church and Nationalist youth, including students, were impressed with these ideas. See Marx, *Oxwagon Sentinel*, pp. 374–75.

199 'Notule van Vergadering van die Federale Raad van die Nasionale Party gehou in Kaapstad op 20 Februarie 1940'. National Party, Federal Council, PV54, File 2-2.

200 South African Jewish Board of Deputies, Report to the Executive Council, July 1940 to July 1942, p. 7. For the 1941 'Programme of Principles, Programme of Action and Constitution', see Shimoni, p. 134. See also Hepple, *Verwoerd*, pp. 84–86.

201 See the 'general review' submitted to the meeting of the Board, 24 November 1940. See also Hepple, *Verwoerd*, p. 85 and *Die Transvaler*, 5 December 1940.

202 *Die Transvaler*, 3 December 1940.

203 As Smuts told Margaret Gillet, Havenga and

Hertzog resigned their seats 'in protest at the scurvy treatment meted out to Hertzog by the reunited Nat party'. See JC Smuts to MC Gillet, 30 December 1940. Cited in Van der Poel, p. 268.

204 CM van den Heever, *Generaal JBM Hertzog*, AP Boekhandel, Johannesburg, 1946, pp. 295–96. See also Oswald Pirow, *James Barry Munnik Hertzog*, Howard Timmins, Cape Town. nd, p. 259.

205 It would appear that Hertzog had even approached the Nazi regime to establish his genealogy, and was told by Hitler that he had no Jewish blood. I wish to thank David Welsh for drawing my attention to this. Piet Meiring, *Generaal Hertzog–50 Jaar Daarna*, Perskor-Uitgewers, Johannesburg and Cape Town, 1986, pp. 196–97. For reflections on Hertzog's political inclinations, see also Furlong, *Between Crown and Swastika*, pp. 154–55 and Van Heerden, pp. 273–77.

206 Fortnightly Intelligence Report, No 15, 1 November 1941. SANDF Archives, CGS GP2, Holder 93, File 169/7.

207 See Sir William Clark to Sir E Harding, 7 December 1938 (From Mr Garrett, Dominion Office, to Mr Makins, 29 December 1938). Foreign Office, 371. Clark also reported that Smuts agreed with the view that the Union had reached saturation point for Jewish settlement, as did the Board of Deputies as conveyed by Smuts. For reflections on Hertzog's worldview, as understood by Hans van Rensburg (writing in 1966), see 'Generaal Hertzog en Die Nasionaal-Sosialisme'. JFJ van Rensburg Collection, PV70, File 1, 4/4/3/5. I am indebted to Tony Kushner for alerting me to this document.

208 *Die Transvaler*, 16 January 1941. See also *Die Burger*, 16 January 1941. Van Rensburg shared all the classic canards about Jews and infatuation with Nazism. See, for example, Juta, p. 284.

209 *Die Transvaler*, 16 January 1941. Smuts told his friend, the British politician LS Amery, that he was watching the 'semi-military' Ossewa-Brandwag closely. It was formed 'somewhat on Hitler lines', and he anticipated that the movement 'may finally take their place as a militant political party.' See Smuts to LS Amery, 18 February 1941, in Van der Poel, p. 280. Smuts also warned Van Rensburg not to use 'young school children' in the OB. See Smuts to JF van Rensburg, 23 April 1941, in Van der Poel,

p. 294.

210 Koorts, pp. 353–54.

211 Fortnightly Intelligence Report, No 8, 31 May 1941. SANDF Archives, CGS GP2, Holder 93, File 169/7.

212 See Paton, p. 342.

213 For the violence, see George Cloete Visser, *OB: Traitors or Patriots?*, Macmillan South Africa, Cape Town, 1976, chapter five, *passim*.

214 *Die Transvaler*, 26 May 1941.

215 Nasson, pp. 85–88. Already in April 1941 Smuts was informed that the Germans were plotting a coup. See Tothill, p. 105.

216 See Annexure to Fortnightly Intelligence Report, No 36, 20 March 1943. SANDF Archives, CGS GP2, Holder 93, File 169/7. In his statement to the court, Leibbrandt denied any connection to the Nazis and Hitler, but revealed a belief in the *Protocols of the Elders of Zion*. He was clearly antisemitic and in fact supportive of National Socialism. See SR Leibbrandt Collection, PV 228 3/1/1/1.

217 Roberts and Trollip, p. 85.

218 See Roberts and Trollip, pp. 82–91. The Afrikanereenheidskomitee was composed, *inter alia*, of leaders of the HNP, OB, FAK and Reddingsdaadbond.

219 OB Archives: GR 1/1/1: Rassevraagstuk: Algemene Uitgangspunt. Undated document. Cited in Van Deventer, p. 277.

220 See Koorts, p. 353. Van Rensburg's *Kenmerke van die Nuwe Staat* illustrated the OB's vision of an organic society, its hostility to liberalism, its *völkisch* impulses, its racial worldview and its opposition to unassimilable Jewish immigration. See Van Heerden, p. 136.

221 Koorts, pp. 359–60.

222 See, for example, *Die OB*, 19 May 1943. Shortly after the formation of the OB, South African intelligence noted that it was modelled on Nazi doctrines. See Annexure to Fortnightly Intelligence Report No 1, 25 January 1941. See also Fortnightly Intelligence Report No 27, 18 August 1942. SANDF Archives, CGS GP2, Holder 93, File 169/7.

223 See, for example, *Die OB*, 7 January 1942, 12 August 1942, 9 September 1942, 30 September 1942, 18 November 1942, 25 November 1942, 9 December 1942, 6 January 1943, 17 March 1943, 19 May 1943 and 20 October 1943.

224 See *Zionist Record*, 26 December 1941. For visceral anti-communism, see also *Die Matie*,

29 May 1942.

225 Stultz, *Afrikaner Politics in South Africa*, p. 82. See also South African Jewish Board of Deputies. Report of Executive Council, August 1942 to May 1945.

226 *Hansard*, 2 February 1942. See also Hepple, p. 96.

227 For *Die Transvaler* and the OB, see Dioné Prinsloo, 'Dr HF Verwoerd en die Ossewa-Brandwag, 1938–1952', *Kleio*, 17(1), 1985.

228 *Rand Daily Mail*, 16 March 1942. See also Visser, *OB: Traitors or Patriots*, p. 17.

229 South African Jewish Board of Deputies Report to Congress, 1942. For broader policies, see Van Heerden, p. 138.

230 See Fortnightly Intelligence Report No 32, 16 December 1942. SANDF Archives, CGS GP2, Holder 93, File 169/7.

231 Cited in Marx, *Oxwagon Sentinel*, p. 399.

232 Visser, *OB: Traitor or Patriots?*, pp. 168–69. Interestingly, Van Rensburg told Dr J Harris of the American Embassy that Hertzog was an antisemite who had described Roosevelt as 'a second-rate Dutch Jew' after the United States entered the war.

233 Marx, *Oxwagon Sentinel*, p. 357 and Visser, *OB: Traitors or Patriots?*, p. 201.

234 Visser, *OB: Traitors or Patriots?*, p. 29.

235 Koorts, p. 356.

236 See *Die Burger*, 22 September 1941, and *Die Oosterlig*, 22 September 1941.

237 Marx, *Oxwagon Sentinel*, p. 481. See also South African Jewish Board of Deputies. Report of Executive Council, August 1942 to May 1945.

238 See De Klerk, 'Die ideologie van die Ossewa-Brandwag'.

239 *Ibid*. Notwithstanding this array of prejudice, De Klerk minimises OB antisemitism, which he seemingly measures against a Hitlerian yardstick. In De Klerk's view, antisemitism was not too strong a presence in the OB insofar as it did not share a Nazi *herrenvolk* mentality. Typical of the OB's anti-Jewish mindset is an article by 'General' FD du Toit in *Die OB* that defined the movement as combating all forces undermining the *volk*, particularly the 'democratic party-system, the liberal press, organised Jewry and other influences that are the consequence of the maldistribution of power and wealth in our land'. See *Zionist Record*, 26 December 1941. See also Theodor H Gaster, 'British Commonwealth: South Africa', in Harry Schneiderman (ed), *American Jewish Year Book*, Vol 45, 1943,

p. 224. For concerns with race-mixing, see *Die OB*, 24 February 1943.

240 Marx, *Oxwagon Sentinel*, p. 509.

241 Shimoni, p. 128.

242 Marx, *Oxwagon Sentinel*, p. 488.

243 See Stultz, *Afrikaner Politics in South Africa*, p. 77. See also Van Heerden, chapter four, *passim*.

244 See Shimoni, p. 131, and *Die Oosterlig*, 20 March 1942.

245 Shimoni, p. 130.

246 With interesting foresight, *Die Waarheid/ The Truth* (26 March 1937) suggested that Pirow was a closet National Socialist but was fearful of his pro-Jewish colleagues. He had also told the National Party's Frans Erasmus that the Malanites were simply trying to snatch votes by imitating the policy of the Greyshirts. 'I read carefully,' he said, 'every issue of the Greyshirt organ, *Die Waarheid*. The Greyshirts are thoroughly honest and I admire them. You are thoroughly dishonest. The Greyshirts deliberately accuse you of stealing from them.' See *Die Waarheid/The Truth*, 26 March 1937.

247 At the same time Pirow did make plans to protect key facilities in the Union and to ensure sufficient powers for police in the event of an emergency.

248 See Nasson, p. 38. In 1934 he had declared himself in favour of a republican system. See *Die Republikein*, 19 October 1934. Pirow had met Hitler in August 1933. See Marx, *Oxwagon Sentinel*, pp. 264–65.

249 *Nuwe Orde Correspondence Course*, Lecture No 14, 'The Problem of the Jew', South African Jewish Board of Deputies Archives, No 313.2. See also Shimoni, pp. 130–32. According to a Fortnightly Intelligence Report, Professor HM van der Westhuysen, Chair of Afrikaans at the University of Pretoria, was one of the leading intellectuals of the combined OB-NO and was involved in preparing the NO lectures. These had been broadcast throughout the country 'by such ardent Pirowites as Dr Piet Meyer, Professors LC du Plessis, van der Walt [of Potchefstroom University] and a few lesser lights'. See Fortnightly Intelligence Report, No 39, 1 June 1943. SANDF Archives, CGS GP2, Holder 93, File 169/7.

250 *Die Burger*, 13 March 1941.

251 See *Zionist Record* (20 June 1941) for details and *Die Transvaler*, 16 June 1941.

252 See *Die Oosterlig*, 2 May 1941. Even so, Verwoerd's attitude to the war was seen to

be supportive of the Nazi cause. Following a hard-hitting editorial in *The Star* (31 October 1941), Verwoerd sued the editor and proprietor for defamation. The case was dismissed with costs by Justice Philip Millin. See Kenny, p. 63–64.

253 Stultz, pp. 77–78.

254 *Ibid*, p. 78. The Nuwe Orde operated its own office within the National Party.

255 Vatcher, p. 69. Du Plessis's thesis, writes Vatcher (p. 69), 'was accepted as expressing the ideology of the OB, and the *Draft Constitution* and the *Social and Economic Policy* were patterned after it'. See also *Die Oosterlig* (18 November 1940) for the Dutch Reformed Church's concern about Freemasons, allegedly controlled by Jews.

256 Vatcher, p. 70. See also Furlong, *Between Crown and Swastika*, pp. 182–200.

257 Vatcher, p. 70.

258 *The Star*, 12 January 1942, and *Die Transvaler*, 13 January 1942. Cited in Vatcher, p. 70.

259 *Eastern Province Herald*, 24 January 1942.

260 The draft constitution was never approved by an HNP congress. See Furlong, *Between Crown and Swastika*, pp. 186–89. This pandering to the radical right never resulted in Malan's supporting fascism or Nazism as ideology. Indeed, following accusations of spying for Germany in what was known as the 'Denk Affair', Malan was exonerated. See Koorts, p. 351. For a differing interpretation, see Furlong, *Between Crown and Swastika*, pp. 175–80.

261 At one youth congress in Potchefstroom, Wicus du Plesssis told students that full citizenship should be based on 'Afrikanership' and that commerce and 'harmful influences' would be purged. See *Die Volksblad*, 23 December 1941.

262 See Furlong, *Between Crown and Swastika*, pp. 167–70.

263 See Moodie, p. 227, and *SAJC*, 6 March 1942.

264 South African Jewish Board of Deputies Executive Committee Minutes, 11 November 1942. See also 'General Review' by Gustav Saron, *SAJC*, 11 September 1942. See also Louw's speech in the Strand. *Die Oosterlig*, 12 January 1943.

265 See Van Deventer, p. 83.

266 See Fortnightly Intelligence Reports 1942, 1943. SANDF Archives, CGS GP2, Holder 93, File 169/7.

267 See Van Deventer, pp. 86–87.

268 *Hansard*, 26 January 1943.

269 *Ibid*, 12 February 1943. See also *Zionist Record*, 19 February 1943.

270 *Die Transvaler*, 1 May 1943. For concerns about the 'Jew-Communist' bogey in the Nationalist press, see also South African Jewish Board of Deputies, Executive Committee Minutes, 22 February 1943.

271 See *Die Oosterlig*, 31 March 1941, *SAJC*, 10 April 1941, and South African Jewish Board of Deputies, Report of the Executive Council, June 1940 to July 1942. Dr DR Snyman (who voted with the minority) considered it dangerous for the Church to express itself on the 'Jewish Question'. 'I hold a diametrically opposite opinion to that expressed in this report, moreover, the matter is very closely related to the politics of the country – everbody knows that' (*SAJC*, 10 April 1941). The Orange Free State Synod had taken this decision in 1934, but coupled the decision with the statement that Jews were not to be pursued.

272 See, for example, Ds JAS Oberholster. 'Wat van die Jood', *Die Kerkbode*, 18 January 1939. Oberholster acknowledged that Jews were a religious and political problem, as well as the treatment of them according to the prophecies. Through persecution, the Jew will find belief in Christ. Still, he who rejected the Jew was rejecting God.

273 HG Stoker, *Die Stryd om die Ordes*, Caxton Drukkery, Pretoria, 1941, pp. 117–18, 157–58. See also HG Stoker, *Die Kerkblad*, 17 January 1941.

CHAPTER SEVEN

ANTISEMITISM: WAXING AND WANING

1 *Die Transvaler*, 2 April 1943.

2 *Ibid*.

3 See *Jewish Affairs*, June 1943.

4 See Milton Shain, 'South Africa', in David Wyman (ed), *The World Reacts to the Holocaust*, The Johns Hopkins University Press, Baltimore, 1996, p. 676; and Michael Anthony Green, 'South African Jewish Responses to the Holocaust 1941–1948', unpublished MA dissertation, University of South Africa, March 1987, chapters two and three, *passim*.

5 *SAJT*, 1 January 1943.

6 One of his young organisers, the twenty-six-year-old Pieter Willem Botha (a future prime minister), claimed atrocity talk was

all anti-Nazi propaganda. See *Cape Times*, 31 December 1942, and *Die Burger*, 1 January 1943.

7 One of the 12 Afrikaner Party candidates was a Nuwe Orde MP and one was a member of the OB. Under pressure from the HNP, five of these candidates withdrew before the poll. See Stultz, p. 85. The Afrikaner Party wanted to attract 'national-minded' Afrikaners outside the HNP, but it enjoyed little traction and had been losing support to both the United Party and HNP for some time. During the campaign Havenga made it clear that his party would not discriminate against Jews. See *Die Volksblad*, 3 July 1943.

8 *Cape Argus*, 2 June 1943.

9 See DW Krüger, *The Making of a Nation: A History of the Union of South Africa, 1910–1961*, Macmillan, Johannesburg, 1969, p. 215.

10 *Sunday Times*, 23 May 1943.

11 See *Zionist Record*, 2 July 1943. Some months earlier, *Die Burger* had published a few articles on Jews penetrating the property market. See, for example, *Die Burger*, 1 June 1943.

12 The *Rand Daily Mail* (20 March 1943) even reported that the HNP planned to win Jewish support. Yet Malan was at times happy to pander to anti-Jewish rhetoric in public. When complaining about the cost of the war and being told by someone in the audience that 'the Jews will have to pay', he replied that the United Party government would 'see to it that they do not pay'. *Eastern Province Herald*, 27 May 1943. When asked, during an address in Heilbron, whether it was not the Jews who had given the world Christianity, Malan replied instead that it was they who had crucified Christ. See *Die Volksblad*, 3 July 1943.

13 See *The Friend*, 21 June 1943.

14 *Die Burger*, 26 May 1943.

15 Ibid.

16 See, for example, *Die Transvaler*, 24 June 1943.

17 South African Jewish Board of Deputies, Executive Committee Minutes, 19 July 1943.

18 *Rand Daily Mail*, 26 May 1943.

19 South African Jewish Board of Deputies, Executive Committee Minutes, 19 July 1943.

20 See *Zionist Record*, 2 July 1943, and *Die Burger*, 25 June 1943.

21 *Daily Dispatch*, 10 June 1943. He obtained only 11.6 per cent of the total vote.

22 *Die Burger*, 24 May 1943. Perceived ties between Jews and communists were in fact

so strong that the United Party warned Jewish voters not to feed into Eric Louw's vision by voting communist. See also South African Jewish Board of Deputies, Executive Report, 21 June 1943.

23 *Die Volksblad*, 18 May 1943. For accusations of Jewish funding for the campaign, see *Zionist Record*, 5 March 1948. Van Rensburg told a meeting after the election that he did not want to blame people for their voting choice: 'Even a man who voted for the United Party is still an Afrikaner and therefore better than a Jew or a Turk.' See *Die Volksblad*, 13 August 1943.

24 See South African Jewish Board of Deputies, Executive Committee Minutes, 19 July 1943. At one point Radio Zeesen alleged that the HNP was receiving 'Jewish' money from an American bank. See Tothill, p. 253. See also 'Zeesen instructs South Africa', *Jewish Affairs*, June 1943. Interestingly, the *SAJC* (2 July 1943) noted that within the United Party there had been manifestations of antisemitism, albeit not in accordance with party policy.

25 Hancock, p. 383. For a detailed analysis of the election see JL Gray, 'How the Nation Voted', *Common Sense*, August 1943, and Tothill, chapter six.

26 See *Zionist Record*, 2 July 1943.

27 'Lessons of the General Election', *Jewish Affairs*, August 1943. 'Not a day passes without its tirade against the Smuts Government and the Jews', commented a listener to Radio Zeesen. 'If the war lasts another four or five years', life in South Africa will be 'under Jewish bosses and Bolshevist agents', warned its announcer. 'The Jew is the link between the two poles of Bolshevism and Plutocracy. The Jew will, of course, never support a really nationalist political party, but he will support a party which sacrifices national interests for the sake of international interests – that is why he supports the present South African Government'. 'Afrikaans soldiers,' asked Zeesen, 'do you support the negrophile policy of Smuts and the Jews?' See 'Zeesen Instructs South Africa', *Jewish Affairs*, June 1943.

28 *SAJC*, 1 October 1943. See also, South African Jewish Board of Deputies, Executive Committee Minutes, 26 February 1943 and 10 March 1943.

29 South African Jewish Board of Deputies Executive Committee Minutes,

13 September 1943.

30 *Ibid*, 21 September 1943.

31 See speeches by Lt Col Willem Adriaan Booysen (*Hansard*, 11 April 1944) and Gerard Bekker, (*Hansard*, 12 April 1944). See also South African Jewish Board of Deputies, Executive Committee Minutes, 25 January, 16 August and 21 September 1943, and 'The Fight Against Antisemitism', *Jewish Affairs*, September 1943, p. 23. For an overview, see South African Jewish Board of Deputies. Report of Executive Council, August 1942 to May 1945. As early as February 1941, AL Badenhorst, National Party MP for Riversdale, had declared that two Jewish factories in South Africa were producing all the khaki clothing for the war effort. It was not strange that the Jews were warmongers, he said. See *Die Burger*, 28 February 1941.

32 *Hansard*, 11 April 1944.

33 *Ibid*, 24 March 1944.

34 *Die OB*, 20 December 1944.

35 *Ibid*, 3 June 1945.

36 *Ibid*, 13 June 1945.

37 See *Die Ossewa-Brandwag: Vanwaar en Waarheen*, Die Afrikaanse Pers Beperk, Johannesburg, 1942, pp. 35–39, and 'Die OB-Arbeidslaer' (editorial), *Die OB*, 5 January 1944.

38 Die Raad van die Kerke (Church Council) also continued to engage with the 'Jewish Question'. See 'Handelinge van die Agtiende Vergadering van die Raad van die Kerke, gehou op Bloemfontein, 31 March 1943'. The report was issued to the federal council of the Dutch Reformed Church in April 1944, under the rubric of the 'Commission for Current Questions'. The Church penned the following letter to *Die Burger*: 'The Church further desires to call upon the Afrikaner volk to keep away from all bitterness and hatred which so frequently characterise the party political struggle, and wishes to awaken the people to treat each other in mutual respect, love and tolerance even where there are differences'. *Die Burger*, 15 April 1943.

39 Israel Abrahams, 'Die Ned. Geref. Kerk en Anti-Semitisme', *Common Sense*, May 1943. (Published also as 'An Open Letter to the Dutch Reformed Churches', *Jewish Affairs*, May 1943.)

40 Coetzee, 'From Immigrants to Citizens', p. 154.

41 *Ibid*, p. 155

42 *Oudtshoorn Observer*, 28 September 1944. For further examples, see Coetzee, 'Fires and Feathers'.

43 *Cape Times*, 27 September 1944, and *Oudtshoorn Observer*, 28 September 1944 and 5 October 1944.

44 *Hansard*, 29 February 1944. In his speech Louw accused Morris Alexander of telling a lie in 1937 when he had adamantly denied that Jews were helping the immigrants. In fact, very few Jews were given permits for permanent residence between 1939 and 1944: 1 109 (1939); 10 (1940): 43 (1941); 33 (1942); 19 (1943); 24 (1944). See Bradlow, 'Immigration into the Union 1910–1948', pp. 306–307.

45 *Ibid*.

46 *Ibid*, and *Zionist Record*, 21 April 1944.

47 *Ibid*, 10 April 1944.

48 *Ibid*. In fact, very few Jews entered the country. See *Zionist Record*, 2 March 1945.

49 See *Natal Witness*, 9 October 1944, and *Zionist Record*, 13 October 1944. See also Louw's speech in Pietermaritzburg. *Die Oosterlig*, 9 October 1944. Some months earlier, Abraham Jonker had warned of alarming antisemitism among English-speakers. See *SAJC*, 23 April 1943.

50 See 'Current Comment', *Jewish Affairs*, September 1944, p. 1.

51 See *Natal Mercury*, 9 November 1944, and South African Jewish Board of Deputies, Executive Committee Minutes, 11 November 1944.

52 See South African Jewish Board of Deputies, Executive Committee Minutes, 1 November 1944. See also *SAJC*, 17 November 1944, and 'Current Comment', *Jewish Affairs*, November 1944, p. 2.

53 Col Malherbe's Notes Written at the Request of General Smuts on General Attitude of South African Soldiers to Current Affairs (Lieut Olivier's Memo). EG Malherbe Papers, File 44/11, KCM 56974(907). Complaints about English-speaking and Jewish officers often found their way to the Prime Minister's Department through the United Party officer. See Tothill, p. 304.

54 The lecture was named in honour of Reinhold Friedrich Alfred Hoernlé, a South African philosopher and social reformer and Chairman of the South African Institute of Race Relations.

55 See EG Malherbe, 'Race Attitudes and

Education', Hoernlé Memorial Lecture, South African Institute of Race Relations, Johannesburg, 1946. Even though Jews numbered over four per cent, the implications remain.

56 Anonymous, Report on a Survey of Antisemitism, late 1944/early 1945; 31 pages typed in English. UNISA, Pretoria, United Party Archive, Division of Information, subject file: antisemitism. Full copy in Albrecht Hagemann, 'Antisemitism in South Africa During World War II: A Documentation', *Simon Wiesenthal Centre Annual, Volume 4*, Krauss International Publications, New York, 1987. Some time later, CR Swart, speaking at Barkly West, claimed the National Party was the only party that could solve the Jewish question. 'In the corridors, some United Party members attacked the Jews, but they did not have the courage to say the same things in the House,' he contended. See *Die Transvaler*, 27 August 1945.

57 See *Rand Daily Mail*, 8 September 1944. Gustav Saron had sensed the anti-Jewish mood. In an article in the *Zionist Record* (8 September 1944), he noted that a good deal was being heard in South Africa 'about alleged domination of Jews in commerce and the professions, business malpractices, inadequate support for the war effort and so on'. See also *Zionist Record*, 15 September 1944.

58 *Zionist Record*, 8 August and 29 August 1947. See Lauren Singer, 'The South African Jewish Press and the Problem of Palestine 1945–1948', unpublished History Additional Essay, University of Cape Town, 1985.

59 See, for example, *Natal Mercury*, 2 August 1947.

60 Section 2 (subsection 2). Three years later, Louw reiterated these recommendations in parliament. *Hansard*, 25 February 1947. See also *The social and economic policy of the National Party*, 1944, which stressed a form of central planning in industry, agriculture and labour. Trade licences would be issues so that completion would be controlled and 'superfluous trading entities and undesirable elements are to be eliminated'. See *The Social and Economic Policy of the National Party*, Federal Council of the National Party, Nasionale Pers [n.d.], and Vatcher, p. 74.

61 See AR Ravenscroft, 'The Geographical Distribution of Medical Practitioners in the Union', *South African Medical Journal*, 22 January 1944. Ravenscroft revealed that Jews comprised 46.5 per cent of the doctors and surgeons who had qualified in South Africa, and made up 57 per cent of the medical students at the University of the Witwatersrand and 38 per cent at University of Cape Town. See also, Howard Phillips, *The University of Cape Town 1918–1948: The Formative* Years, University of Cape Town and UCT Press, 1993, p. 339.

62 Report of the Committee on Medical Training in South Africa, UG 25 of 1939, Government Printer, Pretoria, 1939, pp. 51–52. This report put the figure at 42 per cent. See also *Zionist Record*, 2 September 1942. Two years later, *Die Transvaler* (23 April 1941) reported that of the 478 doctors in Johannesburg, 271 were Jews. See also *Die Transvaler*, 24 April 1941.

63 Report by HF Pentz on a Scheme of Free Hospitalisation, Government Printer, Pretoria, 1942, pp. 41–42, and Report of the National Health Services Commission on the Provision of an Organised National Health Service for all Sections of the People of the Union of South Africa 1942–1944, UG 30 of 1944, Government Printer, Pretoria, 1944. See also *Zionist Record*, 4 September 1942, and South African Jewish Board of Deputies, Report of Executive Council, August 1942 to May 1945.

64 Pentz's report was not intended to be hostile to Jews; it merely wanted to avoid problems for them. See *Die Transvaler*, 18 September 1942. A year later the HNP announced its intention to limit Jewish options in the professions. See Edgar Bernstein, 'Union of South Africa', in Harry Schneiderman (ed), *American Jewish Year Book*, 1944, Vol 45, p. 224. The issue would not go away. To be sure, according to its own figures, the University of the Witwatersrand reported that in 1944 Jews made up 25 per cent of males in the Arts, 36 per cent in Science, 45 per cent in Medicine, 34 per cent in Engineering, 47 per cent in Commerce and 39 per cent in Law. See Bruce K Murray, *Wits: The 'Open' Years. A History of the University of the Witwatersrand, Johannesburg 1939–1959*, Witwatersrand University Press, Johannesburg, 1997, p. 16.

65 Report of the Committee on the Admission of Students to the Medical Schools of South Africa, UG 26 of 1943, Government Printer, Pretoria, 1943.

66 See *Die Volksblad*, 9 April 1943.

67 *Die Transvaler*, 20 November 1944. See South African Jewish Board of Deputies, Executive Committee Minutes, 11 November 1944. As early as 1936 a resolution was adopted at a National Party meeting urging the Department of Public Health to remove a Jewish district surgeon. See *Die Burger*, 21 November 1936. For ongoing concern about Jewish domination of sectors of the economy, see *New Era*, 19 April 1945.

68 See *Zionist Record* (24 November 1944) for hostile attitudes toward Jews in *Die Transvaler*.

69 *Hansard*, 22 February 1945. Louw's claims were challenged by Abraham Goldberg, Dominion Party MP for Durban (Umlazi). See *Zionist Record*, 2 March 1945.

70 *Ibid*, 22 February 1945.

71 See, for example, *Die Kruithoring*, 3 January 1945, *Die Volksblad*, 3 January 1945, and *Daily Dispatch*, 12 January 1945. See also South African Jewish Board of Deputies, Executive Committee Minutes, 10 January 1945.

72 *Die Volksblad*, 23 February 1945.

73 As was the case a year earlier, the Federal Council of the Church would only accept the report 'vir kennisgewing'. See 'Handelinge van die Negentiende Vergadering van die Raad van die Kerke, Gehou in Kaapstad, 11 April 1945'.

74 South African Jewish Board of Deputies, Executive Committee Minutes, 21 February 1944. Weichardt was quite prepared to refer to himself as a 'National Socialist' and remained opposed to 'British-Jewish politics'. See *Die Vaderland*, 22 February 1943. Rudman had followed Weichardt into the National Party in 1939 and subsequently became Adjutant General of the OB in Natal.

75 See *Die Volksblad*, 2 November 1940 and Scher, p. 63. His old comrade Stoffberg was appointed deputy leader. For a sense of SANSB views, see Weichardt to Geagte Kameraad & Vriend, 26 November 1941. 'SA Nasionale Sosialistiese Bond', Hertzog Collection, Box 51, A 32.

76 See Scher, p. 63. See also *Die Volksblad*, 2 November 1940, and Hattingh, pp. 166–68.

77 Weichardt had been a target of Smuts for many years.

78 As a tactic for dealing with the radical right, Jewish leaders did their best to convince the government that attacks on Jews were the 'spearhead of the anti-democratic

movements' and as such had to be treated as a threat to society as a whole.

79 *SAJC*, 16 February 1945. In fact it was not long before the HNP blamed Jews for the housing shortage. Nor did it hesitate to use the 'Jewish angle' in its anti-communist crusade. See *SAJC*, 7 September 1945, and Press Report 442: 1945.

80 *Die OB* (2 May 1945) accused *Die Burger* of failing to comment on these lies. See also *Die OB*, 13 June 1945. *Die Burger* had indeed ignored the revelations. See Friedman, 'Jews, Germans and Afrikaners', p. 31.

81 See *Die Transvaler*, 24 and 25 April 1945 and *Die Matie*, 1 June 1945.

82 *Hansard*, 24 May 1945. See also his comments regarding debate on communist propaganda and agitation in South Africa (*Hansard*, 25 May 1945) and *Die OB*, 2 May 1945.

83 *Die Vaderland*, 24 November 1945.

84 See *Wapenskou*, 11 October 1946.

85 *Ibid*, 13 September 1946.

86 *Die Kerkbode*, 16 October 1946. Wicus du Plessis more sensibly condemned Nazi behaviour as pagan, but warned against characterising all Germans as evil. See *Koers*, December 1946.

87 *Die Matie*, 25 October 1946.

88 *Die Nuwe Orde*, 4 October 1945.

89 *Ibid*, 4 October 1947. See also *Zionist Record*, 14 November 1947. *Die Nuwe Orde* was outspokenly antisemitic, although Pirow asserted that he had explored with Neville Chamberlain and Jewish leaders in England, as well as with Hitler, the possible emigration of Jews from Germany to an alternative territory (not Palestine) shortly before the war. *Die Nuwe Orde*, 4 October 1945. See also *SAJT*, 19 October 1945.

90 See *Die Matie*, 25 October 1946, and *New Era*, 3 October 1946.

91 *Hansard*, 29 March 1946.

92 See South African Jewish Board of Deputies, Executive Committee Minutes, 22 October 1945.

93 See Lindie Korf, 'DF Malan: A Political Biography', unpublished PhD dissertation, University of Stellenbosch, 2009, p. 416. See also *Die Transvaler*, 24 and 25 June 1941, and *Die Burger*, 21 January 1943.

94 Indeed, as the *Zionist Record* recalled in 1947, this had been a hallmark of the war years, when anti-war groups had conducted a 'bitter campaign' against communism and 'Communistic agitators' – a campaign

linked to 'the charge that Communism aims at black-white equality in this country'. The slogan 'Jewish Bolshevism', popularised by the Nazis, explained the *Zionist Record*, 'expressly or implicitly' reinforced the campaign against the 'British-Jewish democracy'. See *Zionist Record*, 25 May 1947. It should be noted that it was not only the HNP and radical right that feared Bolshevism. As early as 1934, Smuts equated Bolshevism with Nazism and fascism. See Irina Filatova and Apollon Davidson, *The Hidden Thread: Russia and South Africa in the Soviet Era*, Jonathan Ball Publishers, Cape Town, 2013, p. 165.

95 Eric Louw, *The Communist Danger*. Publications of the Enlightenment Service of the Reunited Nationalist Party, No 5.

96 *Die OB*, 19 July 1944.

97 *Ibid*, 10 May 1944.

98 *Die Matie*, 16 June 1944. See also *Die Matie*, 9 June 1944.

99 *Hansard*, 22 February 1945. As early as April 1936, Bremer had expressed concern about communist propaganda in the Union. See *Hansard*, 20 April 1936. For Nationalist propaganda against 'Jewish Communism', see 'Reckless Nationalist Propaganda', *Jewish Affairs*, October 1945.

100 *New Era*, 20 September 1945. See also *New Era*, 3 May 1945.

101 See also *Die OB*, 17 April, 12 June and 4 July 1946. *Wapenskou* (November 1944) also discussed the preponderance of Jews among the Bolsheviks.

102 *New Era*, 22 August 1946.

103 *Ibid*, 26 April 1945. Jews were indeed prominent on the left, both at the University of the Witwatersrand (together with Indians) and the University of Cape Town. See, especially, Murray, pp. 96ff. As early as 1938, *Die Transvaler* (9 April) was complaining about the preponderance of Jews on the Students' Representative Council at the University of the Witwatersrand.

104 *Die OB*, 28 August 1946. See also *New Era*, 15 March and 27 September 1945, and South African Jewish Board of Deputies, Report of the Executive Council, June 1945 to July 1947.

105 Van Rensburg, p. 242.

106 *Die Burger*, 19 September 1945. See also *Die OB*, 12 June 1946.

107 See *Jewish Affairs*, October 1945.

108 See Saul Dubow, 'Afrikaner Nationalism, Apartheid and the Conceptualization of Race', *Journal of African History*, 33, 1992, pp. 216–17, and *Inspan*, October 1944.

109 *Hansard*, 22 February 1945. The speech caused some debate. See, for example, *Die Burger*, 2 March 1945, and *Zionist Record*, 2 March 1945.

110 *New Era*, 8 February 1945.

111 *Ibid*, 12 April 1945. In its first issues the *New Era* was silent on the 'Jewish Question'.

112 *Ibid*, 19 April 1945. For this reason, explained the *New Era*, the National Party supported a National Home for the Jews in Palestine and insisted that all Jewish immigration into South Africa cease.

113 *New Era*, 27 September 1945.

114 *Zionist Record*, 28 September 1945.

115 *New Era*, 18 July 1946.

116 *Hansard*, 22 March 1946.

117 *Ibid*.

118 *Die Kerkbode*, 6 November 1946.

119 *Hansard*, 14 April 1947. See South African Jewish Board of Deputies, Executive Committee Minutes, 15 April 1947.

120 *Ibid*, 3 March 1947. See *Zionist Record*, 2 May 1947. Occasional ugly epithets were hurled at Jews. See *Zionist Record*, 12 September 1947.

121 *Hansard*, 3 June 1947. See also *Zionist Record*, 2, 9 and 13 May 1947.

122 See *Jewish Affairs*, November 1947, pp. 6–7.

123 See *Zionist Record*, 24 October 1947. The Board, however, did manage to get a number of Afrikaans newspapers to repudiate the forgery. See South African Jewish Board of Deputies, Executive Committee Minutes, 21 January 1946. Rudman had claimed to hold the copyright of the *Protocols*. See *Zionist Record*, 27 February 1947. Pirow's weekly, *Die Nuwe Orde* (which he edited), bore all the hallmarks of conspiratorial thinking. By way of example, it identified Jews, together with Churchill, Atlee and the Labour Party, Roosevelt, the British press, certain British economic interests and members of the British military establishment as primarily responsible for causing the war. See *Die Nuwe Orde*, 19 September 1946.

124 See Van Rensburg, pp. 225–26, and Marx, *Oxwagon Sentinel*, chapter 31, *passim*. Pirow's career was resuscitated when he was appointed chief prosecutor in the 1956–61 Treason Trial.

125 See Van Heerden, p. 381.

126 DF Malan to J Nossel, 6 February 1947. Malan Papers, 1/1/2225.

127 *Hansard*, 14 February 1947.
128 *Ibid*, 25 February 1947.
129 *Ibid*. He reiterated this in parliament on 1
     May 1947. See Van Heerden, p. 381.
130 *Hansard*, 1 May 1947.
131 See I Frank to DF Malan, 28 July 1947.
     Malan Papers, 1/1/2313; and Shimoni,
     pp. 163–64. *Die Transvaler* (8 October 1947)
     refused to believe Malan could change the
     party's policy towards Jews.
132 *Die Oosterlig,* 3 November 1947.
133 *Die Transvaler*, 8 October 1947. Predictably
     the Blanke Werkersparty of South Africa
     and Rudman's supporters in the Boerenasie
     expressed support for Louw.
134 Eric Louw to Blackie Swart, 12 October
     1947. Swart Collection, PV18, File
     3-1-49. Louw had some reason to be
     concerned. Swart himself had told a
     meeting in Winburg that the HNP would
     not discriminate against Jews (*Zionist
     Record*, 26 September 1947) and Johannes
     Hendrikus Viljoen (Afrikaner Party) had
     explained that there was nothing to stop
     Jews joining the HNP or the Afrikaner
     Party. See *Zionist Record,* 17 October 1947.
135 *Cape Times*, 15 October 1947.
136 *Ibid*.
137 *Ibid*, 17 October 1947. The National Party
     Information Office officially denied being
     anti-Jewish, or indeed opposed to any
     other group, but reaffirmed its concern
     about the number of Jews in South
     Africa. It also expressed opposition to all
     parasites and all exploiters. See 'Nasionale
     Party-Inligtingskantoor', Jaargang 1, No 9
     (October 1947). Swart Collection, PV18,
     File 3-1-50.
138 *Ibid*, 16 October 1947. In response to Louw's
     letter to the *Cape Times*, Nossel wrote to
     Malan asking him to clarify the National
     Party's position on the Jews. 'You will realise
     that I have been violently criticised, abused,
     attacked, denounced, and belittled for my
     effort by the opponents, to create a better
     understanding between the Nationalist
     Party and South African Jews,' he wrote. 'I
     hope you will give this matter your earliest
     attention.' J Nossel to DF Malan, 15 October
     1947. Malan Collection, 1/1/2333.
139 Eric Louw to Blackie Swart, 26 October
     1947. Swart Collection, PV18, File 3-1-49.
140 We have no record of this, but Louw had
     clearly upset some colleagues with his letter.
141 EH Louw to DF Malan, 26 October 1947.
     Malan Collection, 1/1/2337.

142 *SAJT*, 24 October 1947.
143 *Die Burger*, 30 October 1947.
144 *Cape Times*, 30 October 1947.
145 *Die Suiderstem*, 30 October 1947.
146 *Zionist Record*, 7 November 1947. See also
     'Editorial', *Jewish Affairs*, November 1947.
147 *SAJT*, 7 November 1947.
148 *Die Dagbreek*, 2 November 1947.
149 JG Strijdom to F Erasmus, 10 November
     1947. Swart Collection, PV18 File 3-1-51.
     Strijdom too received a letter from Nossel
     asking for clarification on the question of
     Jewish membership. He did not bother to
     reply. Swart Collection, PV18 File 3-1-51.
     See also Van Heerden, pp. 382–83.
150 F Erasmus to JG Strijdom, 29 November
     1947. Erasmus Collection, PV97, Items 1–5.
151 JG Strijdom to F Erasmus, 3 December 1947.
     Erasmus Collection, PV97, Items 1–5.
152 F Erasmus to JG Strijdom, 8 December
     1947. Erasmus Collection, PV97, Items 1–5.
     While the question of Jewish membership
     remained moot, the National Party's
     propaganda focused on immigration,
     highlighting Smuts' wish to open the
     doors of South Africa to immigrants. See
     Nasionale Party – Propaganda, March 1947,
     PV 18.
153 CFJ Muller, *Sonop in die Suide: Geboorte
     en Groei van die Nasionale Pers 1915–1948*,
     Nasionale Boekhandel, 1990, p. 681. See
     Strijdom to Blackie Swart, 19 November
     1947, Swart Collection, PV18, File 3-1-51.
     Even Louw conceded that the Jewish
     question would no longer be on the
     table because two members of the Cape
     National Party 'Hoofraad' [Head Council]
     had contradicted party policy. Eric Louw
     to FC Erasmus, 17 November 1947. Swart
     Collection, PV18, File 3-1-51.
154 See Koorts, pp. 374–76.
155 Stultz, p. 131.
156 See Hattingh, p. 217, and *Die Vaderland*, 20
     May 1946. Indeed, Weichardt supported the
     Zionist movement, which was obviously a
     means of ridding South Africa of its Jews.
     See *Sunday Express*, 10 March 1946.
157 *Die Burger*, 15 June 1946. Weichardt's
     strategic return to mainstream politics was
     accompanied by his long-promised alliance
     with the Nuwe Orde. Van Rensburg, too,
     sought to unify opposition elements in
     'a common parliamentary front against
     common dangers, more especially against
     the threat of communism'. See *Zionist
     Record*, 13 April 1945. But his target was

to incorporate Malan. The HNP leader, however, was wary of the OB's National Socialist agenda and rejected overtures. On the other hand, Malan was happy to keep avowed antisemites within his party and in fact claimed that the Nuwe Orde was superfluous because the HNP programme already encapsulated most of Pirow's ideas. See *Die Nuwe Orde*, 7 March 1946. *Die Nuwe Orde* (August 1947) persisted with its focus on the Jewish question and its claim that a 'Jewish-jingo' plot had been behind the war and that Britain and America had betrayed 'Western civilisation'.

158 Hattingh, p. 185.

159 *Ibid*, p. 190.

160 *Die Transvaler*, 25 February 1948. Weichardt did have some concerns about his place within the National Party and Afrikaner Party, but he was happy to see how this played out after the election. See *Die Transvaler*, 10 March 1948.

161 Hattingh, p. 188. The new party founded a new newspaper, *Die Blanke Front* (The White Front), but had difficulty attracting an editor and closed down in May 1948.

162 *Ibid*, p. 190.

163 Hattingh, p. 189. Even though Weichardt had distanced himself from the party political system, he made it clear that he would support the HNP in order to overthrow the government. While he might have soft-pedalled for a while on anti-Jewish rhetoric, the Blanke Werkersparty of South Africa made no secret of its credo that there was no place for Jews in South Africa. See Hattingh, pp. 191–93. Between 13 April and 25 May he travelled 11 200 kilometres to attend meetings. Weichardt was ultimately rewarded with a seat in the Senate under Prime Minister JG Strydom. Von Moltke, too, entered parliament as a South West Africa representative in 1950.

164 See Philip Bonner, Peter Delius and Deborah Posel, 'The Shaping of Apartheid: Contradiction, Continuity and Popular Struggles', in Philip Bonner, Peter Delius and Deborah Posel (eds), *Apartheid's Genesis, 1935–1962*, Ravan Press and Witwatersrand University Press, Johannesburg, 1993.

165 See Bonner, 'South African Society and Culture, 1910–1948', pp. 315–17.

166 See Dan O'Meara, *Forty Lost Years: The Apartheid State and the Politics of the National Party, 1948–1994*, Ravan Press, Johannesburg, and Ohio University Press, Athens, 1996,

p. 32.

167 In 1943 the ANC had drafted a policy document, *Africans' Claims*, which suggested a new populist turn in black politics, evident also in the emergence of the Congress Youth League. See also Dubow, 'Afrikaner Nationalism, Apartheid and the Conceptualization of Race', p. 211.

168 Stultz, p. 113.

169 See Stultz, p. 113. Giliomee points out that apartheid as such hardly featured in the campaign. See Giliomee, *The Afrikaners*, pp. 480–81.

170 See Giliomee, *The Afrikaners*, chapter 13, *passim*, and Saul Dubow, *Apartheid 1948–1994*, Oxford University Press, Oxford, 2014, p. 30.

171 Stultz, p. 130. Meanwhile, *Die OB* (12 November 1947) harped on alleged Jewish immigrants streaming into the country.

172 These, according to the Board, emanated from Eineat Abeg of Sweden. See South African Jewish Board of Deputies, Executive Committee Minutes, 19 January 1948.

173 See *Zionist Record*, 23 January 1948.

174 *Die Burger*, 15 Janauary 1948.

175 See *Zionist Record*, 9 April 1948.

176 *Zionist Record*, 7 May 1948. There were a few moments when Jews were mentioned. For example, RH McLeod, the United Party candidate for South Peninsula, blamed a 'Haganah gang' for 'tearing down my posters as soon as I put them up. I am not interested in the Jews. I do not want the Jewish vote and my eyes have been opened to their insidious methods. The Jewish candidate Max Sonnenberg won the seat handsomely. See *Zionist Record*, 11 June 1948. Michiel Daniël Christiaan de Wet Nel seemingly believed that the Jewish card had political traction when he claimed that the name of his opponent in the Wonderboom constituency, Jan Maritz, was Maritzky. See *Zionist Record*, 14 May 1948.

177 See 'The "Jewish Question" in SA Politics,' *Jewish Affairs*, May 1949.

178 In fact Smuts misread divisions within Afrikanerdom and was oblivious to the depth of 'institutional mobilisation'. See Dubow, *Apartheid 1948–1994*, p. 31.

179 See Hancock, p. 498.

180 EG Malherbe, *Never a Dull Moment*, pp. 281–82.

181 See *Zionist Record* (21 May 1948) for some concerns.

182 Gus Saron, 'After the Election', *Jewish*

Affairs, June 1948, p. 9.

183 *Zionist Record*, 21 May 1948.

184 See 'The Government and the Jews', *Jewish Affairs*, July 1948, p. 2; Shimoni, p. 207; Edgar Bernstein, 'Union of South Africa', in Harry Schneiderman and Morris Fine (eds), *American Jewish Year Book*, 1950, Volume 50, The Jewish Publication Society of America, Philadelphia, 1950, p. 304; and South African Jewish Board of Deputies, Report of the Executive Council, August 1947 to May 1949.

185 Malan assured Jews in October 1948 that blood relatives of Jews in the Union would be admitted on humanitarian grounds, and there would be 'no stumbling-blocks in the way of providing for the cultural and religious requirements of the Jewish community'. See South African Jewish Board of Deputies, Report of the Executive Council, August 1947 to May 1949.

186 *Die Vaderland*, 19 September 1951 and *Die Transvaler*, 19 September 1951. There was, however, a long-standing struggle within the party over the issue. See South African Jewish Board of Deputies, Report of the Executive Council, August 1947 to May 1949. There were also concerns among Jews about 'Christian National Education' being contemplated within the National Party. See Phyllis Lewsen, 'The Threat of "Christian National" Education', *Jewish Affairs*, February 1949. Gustav Saron had already alerted the Board to this initiative in 1941. See *SAJC*, 2 May 1941.

187 See 'Anti-Semitic Manifestations', *Jewish Affairs*, May 1951, p. 43.

188 Abrahams, *The Birth of a Community*, pp. xii–xiii. With great irony, Abrahams (p. xvi) expressed his appreciation for 'the deeply significant words of this great Elder Statesman of our country' that would, he was sure, 'long be remembered as a notable contribution to better race relations, among all sections of the population'.

CONCLUSION

1 *Die Blanke Front*, 6 February 1948.

2 See Carnegie Commission of Investigation on the Poor White Question in South Africa.

3 See H Sonnabend, 'Notes on a Demographic Survey of a Johannesburg Group', *South African Journal of Science*, 33, March 1937. This professional ratio was reversed among Jewish women where 2.51 per cent of all adult females were in the professions, as opposed to 4.33 per cent among the 'general population'.

4 See Norval, p. 84.

5 See Visser, 'The Production of Literature on the "Red Peril" and "Total Onslaught"'. Visser notes that communist principles were considered 'irreconcilable with Christian beliefs and a threat to Afrikaner cohesion'.

6 Wicus du Plessis is an exemplar within the framework of *völkisch* ideologues. See Christoph Marx, 'From Trusteeship to Self-determination: LJ du Plessis' Thinking on Apartheid and his Conflict with HF Verwoerd', *Historia*, 55(2), 2010, p. 57.

7 Peberdy, p. 82.

8 The essentialising of culture was reflected in *Volkekunde*, a branch of social anthropology developed at major Afrikaans universities from the 1930s. Here culture was a special object of study, neatly connected to Christian–National ideology. See John Sharp, 'The Roots and Development of *Volkekunde* in South Africa', *Journal of Southern African Studies*, 8(1), 1981. It is no coincidence that the Suid-Afrikaanse Bond vir Rassestudie was established in 1935.

9 See Dubow, *Apartheid 1948–1994*, pp. 9–16, and 'Afrikaner Nationalism, Apartheid and the Conceptualization of Race'.

10 See Dubow, 'A definitive study of the Ossewabrandwag', *Historia*, 55(1), 2010, p. 158 (review of Christoph Marx, *Oxwagon Sentinel*). Deborah Posel argues that ideas were as important as material factors in the evolution of racial essentialism. Certainly, debates about the Jew support this insofar as Jews were considered both a race apart and a bulwark against Afrikaner economic advancement. For the evolution of apartheid, see Deborah Posel, *The Making of Apartheid, 1948–1962: Conflict and Compromise*, Clarendon Press, Oxford, 1991.

11 Such upward mobility similarly drove anti-Jewish hostility in Europe in the late nineteenth and early twentieth centuries. For an overview, see Albert S Lindemann, *Esau's Tears: Modern Anti-Semitism and the Rise of the Jews*, Cambridge University Press, Cambridge, 1997.

12 While not discounting the important structural underpinnings of antisemitism,

including 'cultural clashes' between alien Jewish immigrants and the host society in the context of industrialisation and social transformation, it needs to be pointed out that there was often antipathy towards the non-identifiable or assimilated Jew. For the German case, see Steven E Aschheim, 'Caftan and Cravat: the *Ostjude* as a Cultural Symbol in the Development of German Anti-Semitism', in S Drescher, D Sabean and A Sharlin (eds), *Political Symbolism in Modern Europe*, Transaction Books, New Brunswick, NJ, 1982.

13 As Todd Endelman argues, if Jewish particularism was a primary variable, antisemitism in Europe would have been most virulent in Great Britain and the United States, where London and New York had highly visible and alien Jewish communities at the end of the nineteenth century. Endelman's stress on ideology is a salutary warning to those like Lindemann, who, through an 'interactionist' perspective, seek to locate antisemitism essentially in 'rational' material or cultural clashes. See Endelman, p. 104, and Bryan Cheyette, 'Hilaire Belloc and the "Marconi Scandal" 1900–1914: A Reassessment of the Interactionist Model of Racial Hatred', *Immigrants and Minorities*, 8(1–2), 1989. The point at issue is that preconceptions about Jews precede attitudes and actions. For example, those worried about disproportionate Jewish representation in banking feel as they do only because of a preconceived notion that Jews are dangerous and harmful. A finding that 90 per cent of all newspaper editors are blondes, contends Guenter Lewy, would not provoke an anti-blonde movement. See Guenther Lewy, *The Catholic Church and Nazi Germany*, McGraw-Hill, New York, 1965, p. 272. For a critical overview of various approaches, see Milton Shain, *Antisemitism*, Bowerdean Press, London, 1998.

14 For a similar critique with regard to Europe, see Albert S Lindemann and Richard S Levy (eds), *Antisemitism: A History*, Oxford University Press, Oxford, 2010, p. 255.

15 See Moodie, p. 21. Christoph Marx has perceptively observed that radical nationalism in South Africa has its roots in times prior to the early 1930s and that the absorption of radical overseas 'nationalist and fascist ideological tendencies and elements' must be understood 'in the affirmative attitude which Afrikaner Nationalism took, from the 1930s onwards, towards urbanisation and modernisation, and also in its foundation on culture'. One should thus be cautious, he argues, when referring to the 'absorption of fascist ideas by an already radicalised nationalism'. The adoption of fascist ideas should be seen, he adds, 'as a *result* rather than a *cause*: If one narrowly concentrates on ideology there is always a danger of explaining radicalisation in terms of an 'importation' of radical ideas and ideologies ... overlooked in the process are the existent social and institutional conditions. But it is the latter which make possible – and really explain – ideologies.' Christoph Marx, 'The Ossewabrandwag as a Mass Movement, 1939–1941', *Journal of Southern African Studies*, 20(2), 1994, p. 3.

16 They did, however, believe in parliamentary government, which was patently not the case for the radical right.

17 Moodie, p. 15.

18 See Shmuel Almog, *Nationalism & Antisemitism in Europe 1815–1945*, Pergamon Press, Oxford, 1990, p. 121.

19 See Irving Abella, 'Antisemitism in Canada in the Interwar Years', in Moses Rischin (ed), *The Jews of North America*, Wayne State University Press, Detroit, 1987, p. 244; and Pierre Anctil, 'Interlude of Hostility: Judeo-Christian Relations in Quebec in the Interwar Period, 1919–39', in Alan Davies (ed), *Antisemitism in Canada: History and Interpretation*, Wilfrid Laurier University, Waterloo, Ontario, 1992, p. 153.

20 See Hancock, pp. 289–90.

21 See Robert Miles, *Racism*, Routledge, London and New York, 1989, p. 39.

22 *Hansard*, 10 February 1930.

23 Van Deventer, pp. 257–58. Van Nierop blamed Jews for the Anglo-Boer War and accused them of trying to buy off the old Transvaal Volksraad (parliament). See *Hansard*, 4 April 1939.

24 Van Deventer, p. 258, n12.

25 Here I am referring to the work of Gavin Langmuir, who defines antisemitism as delusional fantasies about the Jews as opposed to anti-Judaism which he argues is rational disagreement about Jewish texts and understandings. See Gavin Langmuir, *Toward a Definition of Antisemitism*, University of California Press, Berkeley and Los Angeles, 1990, pp. 4–6. Malan, as we have seen, always reverted to the argument, expounded

by some international Jewish leaders, that conflict between Jew and non-Jew was inevitable when Jews exceeded a certain proportion of the population.

26 Koorts, p. 314. Interestingly, Emil Wiehl, the German Minister Plenipotentiary in South Africa, felt Malan's antisemitism was utilitarian. See Cohen, 'Anatomy of South African Anti-Semitism', pp. 148–49. Ben Schoeman, a former colleague, suggested that Malan was afraid of having his party labelled anti-Jewish but nevertheless allowed the Transvaal to formally discriminate against Jews. See Ben Schoeman, *My Lewe in die Politiek*, Perskor, Johannesburg, 1978, p. 131.

27 Furlong, *Between Crown and Swastika*, p. 54. On the other hand, the *SAJC* (16 April 1937) saw Malan as a product of his times. 'Some people are born anti-semitic, some achieve anti-semitism, others have anti-semitism thrust upon them', it noted in early 1937. 'It would only be charitable to Dr Malan, in view of his past attitude, to assume that he falls into the last category. There was, of course, also an overlap between Malan's 'Nordicism' (albeit underpinned by *völkisch* Afrikaner ambitions) and Weichardt's 'Christian-Aryanism'.

28 For Verwoerd's editorial endeavours, see Dioné Prinsloo, 'Die Johannesburg-Periode in Dr HF Verwoerd se Loopbaan', unpublished DPhil, Rand Afrikaans University, 1979.

29 See Moodie, p. 167, and Furlong, *Between Crown and Swastika*, p. 54. Cohen shares a similar assessment. See 'Anatomy of South African Antisemitism', p. 15. Moodie (p. 165) notes that, following the collapse of Wall Street in 1929, the small-town Jews were 'the targets of antipathy as the most visible agents of the industrial economy, with its emphasis on profit, production, and credit with interest'.

30 Moodie (p. 162) writes that the Transvaal, Orange Free State and Natal excluded Jewish membership, citing an article by CWM du Toit in *Die Vaderland* (10 October 1937) as evidence. Jewish sources note only the Transvaal and, in some cases, the Orange Free State. Natal is never mentioned.

31 Moodie, p. 167. Moodie asserts that Malan was embarrassed by antisemitism, but does acknowledge that the Cape rural membership of the National Party may have welcomed it. See Moodie, pp. 165–68.

32 In Germany, writes Moodie, 'it was impossible to be fully National Socialist without violent anti-Semitism; but for Afrikaners, Christian Nationalism excluded non-Calvinists as well as non-Christians (and, of course, non-whites). Hence, insofar as Afrikaner intellectuals were anti-Semitic, they were elaborating a personal prejudice and not an integral aspect of Christian National ideology.' See Moodie, p. 168.

33 See Langmuir, chapter one, *passim*.

34 Contemporaries such as Jan Smuts and Jan Hofmeyr ignored growing hostility towards Jews before 1930 and understood antisemitism as an imported product. Hofmeyr spelled this out early in 1945 when he described Nazi antisemitism as 'an article meant for export' and explained that the 'seeds of this evil thing were blown over the oceans' where it was 'sometimes skilfully adapted to our local circumstances, and anti-Semitism grew apace'. Jan Hofmeyr, *Christian Principles and Race Problems*, Hoernlé Memorial Lecture, South African Institute of Race Relations, Johannesburg, 1945. Bunting and Vatcher similarly perceived antisemitism as an import to South Africa, comingling with wider racial ideas. See Bunting, *The Rise of the South African Reich*, and Vatcher.

35 See Giliomee, *The Afrikaners*, p. 418.

36 *Die Transvaler*, 7 August 1939.

37 Abrahams, *Birth of a Community*, p. xiii.

Archival Collections and Manuscript Sources

Special Collections, University of Cape Town

Morris Alexander Papers, BC 160

Patrick Duncan Papers, BC 294

Isaac Meyer Goodman Collection, BC 805

H.E. Lawrence Papers, BC 640

Greyshirt Case Papers, BC 1105

Supreme Court of South Africa, Eastern Districts Local Division. Between Abraham Levy
and Johannes von Strauss von Moltke, Harry Victor Inch, David Hermanus Olivier
(Junior), certified copy of judgment, South African Jewish Board of Deputies, BC 792

The National Party of the Cape Province. Programme of Principles, National Party, Cape
Town.

Transcript of the Greyshirt Trial. Supreme Court Case, Grahamstown, 10 July 1934, BC 792.

Human Resources Department, Registry Personal Files, Administration Archives and Legal Services and Secretariat, Office of the Registrar, University of Cape Town

Personal File, J K Wylie

University of Cape Town, Finance and General Programmes

Archives for Contemporary Affairs, University of the Free State, Bloemfontein

JCC Adendorff Collection, PV 136

F Erasmus Collection, PV 97

Albert Hertzog Collection, PV 451

JD Jerling Collection PV 158

AH Jonker Collection, PV 42

SR Leibbrandt Collection, PV 228

EH Louw Collection, PV 4

RK Rudman Collection, PV 160

Swart Collection, PV 18

J von S von Moltke Collection, PV 31

LT Weichardt Collection, PV 29

National Party Federal, PV 54

National Party Cape Collection, PV 27

National Party Transvaal, PV 2

National Archives and Record Service of South Africa, Pretoria
JBM Hertzog Collection A2; A3
JC Smuts Collection A1
Department of Justice Collection JUS
Department of the Interior Collection BNS
Department of Foreign Affairs Collection BTS

Government Publications Department, Chancellor Oppenheimer Library, University of Cape Town
Hansard
Legislative Assembly Debates, Cape Colony

The National Archives, Public Record Office, London
High Commissioner (South Africa) Papers

Library of Parliament, Cape Town
Police Commissioner Reports, 1930–48

Western Cape Provincial Archives and Record Service, Cape Town
AL Geyer Collection
Louis Weichardt vs *Argus Printing and Publishing Company*, 1943, Supreme Court of South
    Africa, Cape of Good Hope Provincial Division

South African National Defence Force Archives, Pretoria
Fortnightly Reports
CGS War Box

Hoover Institution Archives, Stanford University
William H Vatcher Papers

Manuscript Section, JS Gericke Library, Stellenbosch University
DF Malan Collection

Historical Papers Research Archives, South African Institute for Race Relations, University of the Witwatersrand, Johannesburg
Jan Hendrik Hofmeyr Papers

SA Rochlin Archives, South African Jewish Board of Deputies, Johannesburg
Antisemitism, 1933–1945, ARCH 200.1
'Composition of Anti-Jewish Movements', Antisemitism 1933–42
'Duerckheim Rapport. Offisiele Dokumente oor Nazi Komplot in die Unie: Beoogde
    Anneksasie', Unie eenheid-Waarheiddiens, Annam-Huis, Johannesburg. Pam 308
Nuwe Orde Correspondence Course
Report of Speech by LT Weichardt. Grand Parade, Cape Town, 2 April 1936, 399
South African Jewish Board of Deputies, Executive Committee Minutes, 1930–48

South African Jewish Board of Deputies, Report of the Executive Council, 1921; 1925; 1927; 1930; 1932; 1933; 1935; 1937; 1940; 1943; 1947

Press Reports: 1930–1948.

Gustav Saron, *History of South African Jewry subsequent to 1910*. Unpublished Manuscript, 1977, ARCH 117

Killie Campbell Archives and Manuscripts, University of KwaZulu-Natal, Durban

Ernst Gideon Malherbe Papers

North-West University, Potchefstroom

JFJ van Rensburg Collection, North-West University, A174

Dutch Reformed Church in South Africa: Archive, Stellenbosch

Government Publications and Reports, Official Publications and Printed Government Documents

Carnegie Commission of Investigation on the Poor White Question in South Africa, *The Poor White Problem in South Africa: A Report*, Pro-Ecclesia-drukkery, Stellenbosch, 1932.

Federal Council of the National Party, The social and economic policy of the National Party. Cape Town: Nasionale Pers [n.d.].

Native Administration Act 38 of 1927, *Government Gazette* Extraordinary No 1645, 5 July 1927.

Office of the Census and Statistics, Sixth Census, 5th May, 1936, Vol VI, Religions of the Europeans, Asiatics and Coloured Population, Government Printer, Pretoria, UG No 28, 1941.

Official Year Book of the Union of South Africa 1934–35, Office of the Census and Statistics, Pretoria, 1936.

Proclamation No 51, *Government Gazette*, No 2462, 2 April 1937.

Report by HF Pentz on a Scheme of Free Hospitalisation, Government Printer, Pretoria, 1942.

Report of the Committee on Medical Training in South Africa, UG 25 of 1939, Government Printer, Pretoria, 1939.

Report of the Committee on the Admission of Students to the Medical Schools of South Africa, UG 26 of 1943, Government Printer, Pretoria, 1943.

Report of the National Health Services Commission on the Provision of an Organized National Health Service for all sections of the People of the Union of South Africa 1942–1944, UG 30 of 1944, Government Printer, Pretoria, 1944.

Report of the South West Africa Commission, UG No 26, 1936, Union of South Africa, Government Printer, Pretoria, 1936.

Riotous Assemblies and Criminal Law Amendment Act 27 of 1914. *Statutes of the Union of South Africa 1914*, Government Printer, Cape Town, 1914.

South Africa, Aliens (Amendment) Immigration Bill, *Government Gazette*, No 2596.

Statutes of the Union of South Africa 1914, Government Printer, Cape Town, 1914.

Contemporary Books, Documents, Reports and Articles

Anon, 'It did Happen Here: How the Nazis Conducted Propaganda in South Africa', *Common Sense*, January 1940.

Anon, 'News Letter' No 77, 28 March 1940, News Research Service, Los Angeles, California.

'Anti-Semitic Manifestations', *Jewish Affairs*, May 1951.

Abrahams, Israel, 'Die Ned. Geref. Kerk en Anti-Semitisme, *Common Sense*, May 1943.

Albertyn, JR, *The Poor White Society. Report of the Carnegie Commission*, Vol V, Stellenbosch, 1932.

Barber, Vernon A, 'Nazi Activity in South Africa', *The National Review*, CVII, 1936.

Bethal Publicity Association, *Bethal: A Progressive Centre of the Eastern Transvaal*, Cape Times, 1928.

Calpin, George, *There are no South Africans*, Nelson, London, 1941.

De Waal, Jan Hendrik Hofmeyr, *My Ontwaking*, Cape Town, n.d.

Die Ossewa-Brandwag: Vanwaar en Waarheen, Die Afrikaanse Pers Beperk, Johannesburg, 1942.

Diederichs, N, *Nasionalisme as lewensbeskouing en sy verhouding tot internasionalisme*, Nasionale Pers, Bloemfontein, 1936.

Du Plessis, JHO, *Die Nuwe Suid-Afrika – Die Rewolusie van die Twintigste Eeu*, Die Nasionale Pers, 1940.

Du Toit, Frikkie Jacobus, 'A Short Biography of a Great Leader', *Die Waarheid/the Truth*, 3 January 1936.

Gray, JL, 'How the Nation Voted', *Common Sense*, August 1943.

Grosskopf, JWF, *The Poor White Problem in South Africa. Report of the Carnegie Commission*, Vol II, Stellenbosch, 1932.

Herman, SN, *The Reaction of Jews to Anti-Semitism: A Social Psychological Study Based upon Attitudes of a Group of South African Jewish Students*, Witwatersrand University Press, Johannesburg, 1945.

Hofmeyr, Jan, *Christian Principles and Race Problems*, Hoernlé Memorial Lecture, South African Institute of Race Relations, Johannesburg, 1945.

Hutten, Ulrich, *South Africa is German*, Anti-Hitler Publication, Johannesburg, 1942.

Jonker, Abraham, *The Scapegoat of History*, Central News Agency, South Africa, 1941.

Lazarus, Mark, *The Challenge*, Mercantile Press, Port Elizabeth, 1935.

Le Grange, Isak, 'Die Plan en Die Man vir die Volk van Suid Afrika', Suid-Afrikaanse Nasionaal-Sosialistiese Bond, Kaapstad, 1941/2.

Lewsen, Phyllis, 'The Threat of "Christian National" Education', *Jewish Affairs*, February, 1949.

Louw, Eric, '*Die Jodevraagstuk in Suid-Afrika/The Jewish Problem in South Africa*', Nasionale Pers, Cape Town, 1939.

Louw, Eric, *The Communist Danger*, Publications of the Enlightenment Service of the Reunited Nationalist Party, No 5, 1943.

MacCrone, ID, 'A Quantitative Study of Race Stereotypes', *South African Journal of Science*, 38, March 1937.

Malherbe, EG, *Race Attitudes and Education,* Hoernlé Memorial Lecture, South African Institute of Race Relations, Johannesburg, 1946.

Maritz, Manie, *My Lewe en Strewe*, Johannesburg, 1938.

Pirow, Oswald, *Nuwe Orde vir Suid-Afrika*, Christelike Republikeinsa Suid-Afrikaanse Nasionaal-Sosialistiese Studiekring, Pretoria, 1940.

Ravenscroft, AR, 'The Geographical Distribution of Medical Practitioners in the Union', *South African Medical Journal*, 22 January 1944.

Saron, Gus, 'Four Eventful Decades', *Jewish Affairs*, June, 1953.

Saron, Gustav, 'Nazi Propaganda and South African Imitations', *Hasholom, Rosh Hashana Annual 5702*.

Saron, Gustav, 'After the Election', *Jewish Affairs*, June 1948.

Sonnabend, H, 'Notes on a Demographic Survey of a Johannesburg Group', *South African Journal of Science*, 33, March 1937.

Stoker, HG, *Die Stryd om die Ordes*, Caxton Drukkery, Pretoria, 1941.

The Anti-Jewish Movements in South Africa: The Need for Action, South Africa Jewish Board of Deputies, Johannesburg, 1936.

'Truth will Prevail', Council of Natal Jewry, February 1935.

Von Strahl, Otto, *Seven Years as a Nazi Consul*, Unie-Volkspers Beperk, Port Elizabeth and Cape Town, 1944.

Weichardt, LT, 'National Socialism in South Africa', *Fascist Quarterly*, 2(4), October 1936.

Secondary Sources

Reference Works

Bernstein, Edgar, 'Union of South Africa', in Harry Schneiderman (ed), *American Jewish Year Book*, 1944, Volume 45, The Jewish Publication Society of America, Philadelphia, 1945.

Bernstein, Edgar, 'Union of South Africa', in Harry Schneiderman and Morris Fine (eds), *American Jewish Year Book*, 1950, Volume 50, The Jewish Publication Society of America, Philadelphia, 1950.

Dainow, David (ed), *South African Rosh Hahana Annual 5693/1932*, SA Zionist Federation, Technical Press, Johannesburg, 1932.

De Saxe, Morris (ed), *The South African Jewish Year Book, 1929*, South African Jewish Historical Society, Johannesburg, nd,

Gaster, Theodor H, 'British Commonwealth. South Africa', in Harry Schneiderman (ed), *American Jewish Year Book*, Volume 43, The Jewish Publication Society of America, Philadelphia, 1943.

Guelke, R, 'Bohle, Hermann' in WJ De Kock, and DW Krüger (eds), *Dictionary of South African Biography*, Vol II, Human Sciences Research Council, Pretoria, 1972.

Gutman, Israel (editor in chief), *Encyclopedia of the Holocaust*, Vol 1, Macmillan Publishing Company, New York and London, 1990.

Kollenberg, Adrienne and Norwich, Rose, *Jewish Life in the South African Country Communities*, Vol III, The South African Friends of Beth Hatefutzoth, Johannesburg, 2007.

Kollenberg, Adrienne, Norwich, Rose, Gentin, Joan, Jowell, Phyllis and Saks, David, *Jewish Life in the South African Country Communities*, Vol II, The South African Friends of Beth Hatefutzoth, Johannesburg, 2004.

Scholtz, JJJ, 'Pirow' Oswald, in CJ Beyers and JC Basson (eds), *Dictionary of South African Biography*, Vol V, Human Sciences Research Council, Pretoria, 1987.

Journal Articles

Blignaut, Charl, 'Die hand aan die wieg regeer die land [The hand that rocks the cradle rules the land]': Exploring the Agency and Identity of Women in the Ossewa-Brandwag, 1939–1954', South African Historical Journal, 67(1), 2015.

Bradlow, Edna, 'JH Hofmeyr, Liberalism and Jewish Immigration', in South African Historical Journal, 40, May 1999.

Braude, Sandra, 'Combating Anti-Jewish Propaganda. The South African Society of Jews and Christians 1937–1951', Jewish Affairs, October/November, 1991.

Cheyette, Bryan, 'Hillaire Belloc and the "Marconi Scandal" 1900–1914: A Reassessment of the Interactionist Model of Racial Hatred', in Immigrants and Minorities, 8(1–2), 1989.

Coetzee, Daniel, 'Fires and feathers: Acculturation, arson and the Jewish community in Oudtshoorn, South Africa, 1914–1948', Jewish History, 19(2), 2005.

Cuthbertson, GC, 'Jewish Immigration as an Issue in South African Politics, 1937–39', Historia, 26 (2) 1981.

Dubow, Saul, 'A definitive study of the Ossewabrandwag', Historia, 55(1), 2010.

Dubow, Saul, 'Afrikaner Nationalism, Apartheid and the Conceptualization of Race, Journal of African History, 33, 1992.

Fedorowich, Kent, 'German Espionage and British Counter-Intelligence in South Africa and Mozambique, 1939-1944', in The Historical Journal, 48(1), 2005.

Furlong, Patrick J, 'Apartheid, Afrikaner Nationalism and the Radical Right: Historical Revisionism in Hermann Giliomee's The Afrikaners', South African Historical Journal, 49(1) 2003.

Furlong, Patrick J, 'Fascism, the Third Reich and Afrikaner Nationalism: an Assessment of the Historiography', in South African Historical Journal, 27(1), 1992.

Grundlingh, Albert, 'The King's Afrikaners: Enlistment and Ethnic Identity in the Union of South Africa's Defence Force in the Second World War', Journal of African History, 44(3), 1999.

Hagemann, Albrecht, 'Antisemitism in South Africa During World War II: A Documentation', Simon Wiesenthal Centre Annual, Volume 4, Krauss International Publications, New York, 1987.

Hagemann, Albrecht, 'Very Special Relations: The "Third Reich" and the Union of South Africa, 1933–39', South African Historical Journal, 27(1), 1992.

Hodes, Rebecca, 'Free Fight on the Grand Parade: Jewish Resistance to the Greyshirts in 1930s South Africa', International Journal of African Historical Studies, 46(3), 2013.

Hyslop, Jonathan, 'White Working-Class Women and the Invention of Apartheid: "Purified" Afrikaner Nationalist Agitation for Legislation Against "Mixed" Marriages, 1934–9' in Journal of African History, 36(1), 1995.

Kienzle, William, 'German-South African Trade Relations, in the Nazi Era', African Affairs, 78(310), 1979.

Kosmin, Barry A, 'Colonial Careers for Marginal Fascists: A Portrait of Hamilton Beamish', in Wiener Library Bulletin, 28(30–31), 1973–74.

Mantzaris, EA, 'Radical Community: The Yiddish-speaking Branch of the International Socialist League, 1980–1920' in Belinda Bozzoli (ed), Class, Community and Conflict: South African Perspectives, Ravan Press, Johannesburg, 1987.

Marks, Shula and Trapido, Stanley, 'Lord Milner and the South African State', History Workshop Journal, 8(1), 1979.

Marx, Christoph, 'Dear Listeners in South Africa: German Propaganda Broadcasts to South Africa, 1940–1941', in *South African Historical Journal*, 27(1), 1992.

Marx, Christoph, 'From trusteeship to self-determination: LJ du Plessis' Thinking on Apartheid and his Conflict with HF Verwoerd', *Historia*, 55(2), 2010.

Marx, Christoph, 'Hendrik Verwoerd and the Leipzig School of Psychology in 1926', *Historia*, 58(2), 2013.

Marx, Christoph, 'The Ossewabrandwag as a Mass Movement, 1939–1941', *Journal of Southern African Studies*, 20(2), 1994.

Miller, Roberta Balstad, 'Science and Society in the Early Career of HF Verwoerd', *Journal of Southern African Studies*, 19(4), 1993.

Minnaar, Anthony, 'The Great Depression 1929-1934', Adverse Exchange Rates and the South African Wool Farmer', *South African Journal of Economic History*, 5(1), 1990.

O'Meara, Dan, 'Analysing Afrikaner Nationalism. The "Christian National" assault on white trade unionism in South Africa, 1934–1948', *African Affairs*, 77(306), 1978.

Plass, Hanno, '*Der Welt-Dienst*: International Anti-Semitic Propaganda', *The Jewish Quarterly Review*, 103(4), 2013.

Plass, Hanno, '*Der Welt-Dienst*: International Antisemitic Propaganda', *The Jewish Quarterly Review*, 103(4), 2013.

Prinsloo, Dioné, 'Dr HF Verwoerd en die Ossewa-brandwag, 1938–1952', *Kleio*, 17(1), 1985.

Saron, Gustav, 'Is the Conscience Clause On the Way Out?', *Jewish Affairs*, May 1959.

Schellack, Werner, 'The Afrikaners' Nazi Links Revisited', *South African Historical Journal*, 27, 1992.

Scher, David M, 'Louis T Weichardt and the South African Greyshirt Movement', *Kleio*, 18(1), 1986.

Sharp, John, 'The Roots and Development of *Volkekunde* in South Africa, *Journal of Southern African Studies*, 8(1), 1981.

Vincent, Louise, 'Bread and Honour: White Working Class Women and Afrikaner Nationalism in the 1930s', *Journal of Southern African Studies*, 26(1), 2000.

Visser, Wessel, 'The Production of Literature on the "Red Peril" and "Total Onslaught" in Twentieth Century South Africa', *Historia*, 49(2), 2004.

Books and Book Chapters

Abella, Irving, 'Antisemitism in Canada in the Interwar Years' in Moses Rischin (ed), *The Jews of North America*, Wayne State University Press, Detroit, 1987.

Abrahams, Israel, *The Birth of a Community*, Cape Town Hebrew Congregation, Cape Town, 1955.

Alexander, Enid, *Morris Alexander: A Biography*, Juta and Co Limited, Cape Town and Johannesburg, 1953.

Almog, Shmuel, *Nationalism & Antisemitism in Europe 1815–1945*, Pergamon Press, Oxford, 1990.

Aly, Götz, *Why the Germans? Why the Jews?: Envy, Race Hatred and the Pre-History of the Holocaust*, Metropolitan Books, New York, 2014.

Anctil, Pierre, 'Interlude of Hostility: Judeo-Christian Relations in Quebec in the Interwar Period, 1919–39' in Alan Davies (ed), *Antisemitism in Canada. History and Interpretation*, Wilfred Laurier University, Waterloo, Ontario, 1992.

Aschheim, Steven E, 'Caftan and Cravat: the *Ostjude* as a Cultural Symbol in the

Development of German Anti-Semitism', in S Drescher, D Sabean and A Sharlin (eds), *Political Symbolism in Modern Europe*, Transaction Books, New Brunswick, 1982.

Barlow, Arthur G, *That We May Tread Safely*, Tafelberg, Cape Town, 1960.

Beinart, William, *Twentieth Century South Africa*, Oxford University Press, 1994.

Ben-Itto, Hadassa, *The Lie That Wouldn't Die: The Protocols of the Elders of Zion*, Vallentine Mitchell, London, 2005.

Blackwell, Leslie, *Blackwell Remembers … An Autobiography*, Howard Timmins, Cape Town, 1971.

Bloomberg, Charles, *Christian-Nationalism and the Rise of the Afrikaner Broederbond, 1918–48* (edited by Saul Dubow), Macmillan, Basingstoke, 1990.

Bonner, Philip, 'South African Society and Culture, 1910–1948', in Robert Ross, Anne Kelk Mager and Nasson, Bill (eds), *The Cambridge History of South Africa, Volume 2, 1885–1994*, Cambridge University Press, New York, 2012.

Bonner, Philip, Delius, Peter and Posel, Deborah, 'The Shaping of Apartheid. Contradiction, Continuity and Popular Struggles', in Philip Bonner, Peter, Delius, Deborah Posel (eds), *Apartheid's Genesis, 1935–1962*, Ravan Press and Witwatersrand University Press, Johannesburg, 1993.

Bradford, Helen, 'Getting Away With Murder: "Mealie Kings", the State and Foreigners in the Eastern Transvaal, c. 1918–1950', in Philip Bonner, Peter Delius and Deborah Posel (eds), *Apartheid's Genesis, 1935–1962*, Ravan Press and Witwatersrand University Press, 2001.

Bunting, Brian, *The Rise of the South African Reich*, Penguin Books, Harmondsworth, Middlesex, 1969.

Coetzee, JM, *White Writing: On the Culture of Letters in South Africa*, Yale University Press, New Haven and London, 1988.

Coetzee, Linda, Osrin, Myra and Pimstone, Millie, *Seeking Refuge: German Jewish Immigration to the Cape in the 1930s including aspects of Germany confronting its past*, Cape Town Holocaust Centre, 2003.

Cohn, Norman, *Warrant for Genocide. The Myth of the Jewish World-Conspiracy and the Protocols of the Elders of Zion*, Eyre & Spottiswood, London, 1967.

Davenport, Rodney and Saunders, Christopher, *South Africa: A Modern History*, fifth edition, Macmillan Press, London, 2000.

De Klerk, P, 'Die Ideologie van die Ossewa-brandwag', in PF van der Schyff (ed), *Die Ossewa-Brandwag: Vuurtjie in droë gras*, Potchefstroom, 1991.

De Klerk, WA, *The Puritans in Africa. A story of Afrikanerdom*, Penguin Books, Harmondsworth, Middlesex, 1975.

De Villiers, René, 'Afrikaner Nationalism', in Leonard Thompson and Monica Wilson (eds), *The Oxford History of South Africa*, Oxford University Press, London, 1971.

Dubb, Allie A, *The Jewish Population of South Africa: The 1991 Sociodemographic Survey*, Jewish Publications – South Africa, Kaplan Centre for Jewish Studies, University of Cape Town, 1994.

Dubow, Saul, 'Race, Civilisation and Culture: The Elaboration of Segregationist Discourse in the Inter-war years', in Shula Marks and Trapido, Stanley (eds), *The Politics of Class, Race and Nationalism in Twentieth Century South Africa*, Longman, London and New York, 1987.

Dubow, Saul, 'South Africa and South Africans: Nationality, Belonging, Citizenship', in

Robert Ross, Anne Kelk Mager and Bill Nasson (eds), *The Cambridge History of South Africa, Volume 2, 1885–1994*, Cambridge University Press, Cambridge, 2012.

Dubow, Saul, *Apartheid 1948–1994*, Oxford University Press, Oxford, 2014.

Dubow, Saul, *Illicit Union. Scientific Racism in Modern South Africa*, Witwatersrand University Press, 1995.

Duffy, Joanne L, *The Politics of Ethnic Nationalism: Afrikaner Unity, the National Party, and the Radical Right in Stellenbosch, 1934–1948*, Routledge, New York and London, 2006.

Elphick, Richard, *The Equality of Believers. Protestant Missionaries and the Racial Politics of South Africa*, University of KwaZulu-Natal Press, Scottsville, 2012.

Endelman, Todd M, 'Comparative Perspectives on Modern Anti-Semitism in the West' in David Berger (ed), *History and Hate: The Dimensions of Anti-Semitism*, Philadelphia, Jewish Publication Society, 1986.

Feldman, Leibl, *Oudtshoorn, Jerusalem of Africa* (translated by Lilian Dubb and Sheila Barkusky and edited by Joseph Sherman), Johannesburg, Friends of the Library, University of the Witwatersrand, 1989.

Filatova, Irina and Davidson, Apollon, *The Hidden Thread: Russia and South Africa in the Soviet Era*, Jonathan Ball Publishers, Cape Town, 2013.

Freund, Bill, 'South Africa: The Union Years, 1910–1948 – Political and Economic Foundations', in Robert Ross, Anne Kelk Mager and Bill Nasson (eds), *The Cambridge History of South Africa, Volume 2, 1885–1994*, Cambridge University Press, Cambridge, 2012.

Fry, Michael Graham, 'Agents and Structures: the Dominions and Czechoslovak Crisis, September 1938', in Igor Lukes and Erik Goldstein (eds), *The Munich Crisis, 1938. Prelude to World War II*, Frank Cass, Great Britian, 1999.

Furlong, Patrick J, 'The National Party of South Africa: A Transnational Perspective', in Martin Durham and Margaret Power (eds), *New Perspectives on the Transnational Right*, Palgrave Macmillan, New York, 2010.

Furlong, Patrick J, *Between Crown and Swastika: The Impact of the Radical Right on the Afrikaner Nationalist Movement in the Fascist Era*, Wesleyan University Press and Witwatersrand University Press, Johannesburg, 1991.

Furlong, Patrick J, *The Mixed Marriages Act: An Historical and Theological Study*, University of Cape Town, 1983.

Giliomee, Hermann and Mbenga, Bernard, *New History of South Africa*, Tafelberg, Cape Town, 2007.

Giliomee, Hermann, 'The Growth of Afrikaner Identity', in Heribert Adam and Hermann Giliomee (eds), *The Rise and Crisis of Afrikaner Power*, David Philip, Cape Town, 1979.

Giliomee, Hermann, *The Afrikaners: Biography of a People*, Tafelberg, Cape Town, 2003.

Gill, S and Humphriss, D, *One Man and His Town*, Juta and Co, Cape Town, 1985.

Gitlin, Marcia, *Vision Amazing*, Menorah, Johannesburg, 1950.

Goldblatt, I, *History of South West Africa, from the Beginning of the Nineteenth Century*, Juta & Company, Cape Town, 1971.

Guy, Jeff, 'Fascism, Nazism, Nationalism and the Foundation of Apartheid Ideology', in Stein Ugelvik Larsen, *Fascism Outside Europe: The European Impulse Against Domestic Conditions in the Diffusion of Global Fascism,* Columbia University Press, New York, 2001.

Hagemann, Albrecht, *Südafrika und das 'Dritte Reich': Rassenpolitische Affinitat und machtpolitische Rivalität*, Frankfurt and New York, Campus Verlag, 1980.

Hancock, WK, *Smuts. Vol 2: The Fields of Force, 1919–1950*, Cambridge University Press, Cambridge, 1968.

Hellig, Jocelyn, 'German-Jewish Immigration to South Africa during the 1930s: Revisiting the Charter of the SS *Stuttgart*', in James Jordan, Tony Kushner and Sarah Pearce (eds), *Jewish Journeys: From Philo to Hip Hop*, Vallentine Mitchell, London and Portland, 2010.

Hepple, Alexander, *Verwoerd*, Penguin, Harmondsworth, Middlesex, 1967.

Hutton, Christopher M, *Race and the Third Reich: Linguistics, Racial Anthroplogy and Genetics in the Dialectic of Volk*, Polity Press, Cambridge, 2005.

Kenny, Henry, *Architect of Apartheid: HF Verwoerd – An Appraisal*, Jonathan Ball Publishers, Johannesburg, 1980.

Kleynhans, WA, *SA Algemene Verkiesingsmanifeste: SA General Elections Manifestos 1910–1981*, University of South Africa, Sigma Press, 1981.

Klotz, Audie, *Migration and National Identity in South Africa, 1860–2010*, Cambridge University Press, 2013.

Koorts, Lindie, *DF Malan and the Rise of Afrikaner Nationalism*, Tafelberg, Cape Town, 2014.

Krüger, DW, *The Making of a Nation. A History of the Union of South Africa, 1910–1961*, Macmillan, Johannesburg, 1969.

Langmuir, Gavin, *Toward a Definition of Antisemitism*, University of California Press, Berkeley and Los Angeles, 1990.

Le Roux, JH, 'Die "gesuiwerde" Nasionale Party, 1934–1940', in PW Coetzer (ed), *Die Nasionale Party*, Instituut vir Eietydse Geskiedenis, University of the Orange Free State, 1975.

Lebzelter, Gisela C, 'Henry Hamilton Beamish and the Britons: Champions of Anti-Semitism', in Kenneth Lunn and Richard C Thurlow (eds), *British Fascism: Essays on the Radical Right in Inter-war Britain*, Croom Helm, London, 1980.

Lebzelter, Gisela C, *Political Anti-Semitism in England 1918–1939*, Holmes & Meier, New York, 1978.

Lentin, Antony, *Jan Smuts: Man of Courage and Vision*, Jonathan Ball, Cape Town, 2010.

Levy, Richard, 'Political Antisemitism in Germany and Austria, 1848–1914', in Albert S Lindemann and Richard S Levy (eds), *Antisemitism: A History*, Oxford University Press, Oxford, 2010.

Lewy, Guenther, *The Catholic Church and Nazi Germany*, McGraw-Hill, New York, 1965.

Liebenberg, BJ, 'From the Statute of Westminster to the Republic of South Africa, 1931–1961', in CFJ Muller, *Five Hundred Years: A History of South Africa*, Academia, Pretoria and Cape Town, 1969.

Lindemann, Albert S and Levy, Richard S (eds), *Antisemitism: A History*, Oxford University Press, Oxford, 2010.

Lindemann, Albert S, *Esau's Tears: Modern Anti-Semitism and the Rise of the Jews*, Cambridge University Press, Cambridge, 1997.

Malherbe, EG, *Never A Dull Moment*, Howard Timmins Publishers, Cape Town, 1981.

Marx, Christoph, *Oxwagon Sentinel: Radical Afrikaner Nationalism and the History of the Ossewabrandwag*, University of South Africa Press, Pretoria, 2008.

Meiring, Piet, *Generaal Hertzog – 50 Jaar Daarna*, Perskor-Uitgewery, Johannesburg and Cape Town, 1986.

Mendelsohn, Richard and Shain, Milton, *The Jews in South Africa: An Illustrated History*, Jonathan Ball, Cape Town, 2008.

Miles, Robert, *Racism*, Routledge, London and New York, 1989.

Millin, Sarah Gertrude, *The Measure of my Days,* Central News Agency Ltd, South Africa and Kingstons Limited, Bulawayo, 1955.

Moodie, Dunbar T, *The Rise of Afrikanerdom: Power, Apartheid, and the Afrikaner Civil Religion*, University of California Press, Berkeley, 1975.

Muller, CFJ, *Sonop in die Suide: Geboorte en Groei van die Nasionale Pers 1915–1948*, Nasionale Boekhandel, 1990.

Murray, Bruce K, *Wits. The 'Open' Years. A History of the University of the Witwatersrand, Johannesburg 1939–1959*, Witwatersrand University Press, 1997.

Murray, MJ, 'Factories in the Fields: Capitalist Farming in the Bethal District, c1910–1950', in A Jeeves and J Crush (eds), *White Farms, Black Labour: The State and Agrarian Change in Southern Africa, 1910–1950*, Heinemann, Portsmouth, NH, 1997.

Mzimela, Sipho, *Apartheid: South African Nazism*, Vantage Press, New York, 1983.

Nasson, Bill, *South Africa at War, 1939–1945*, Jacana, Johannesburg, 2012.

Norval, Aletta J, *Deconstructing Apartheid Discourse*, Verso, London, 1996.

O'Meara, Dan, *Forty Lost Years: The Apartheid State and the Politics of the National Party, 1948–1994*, Ravan Press, Johannesburg, and Ohio University Press, Athens, 1996.

O'Meara, Dan, *Volkskapitalisme: Class, Capital and Ideology in the Development of Afrikaner Nationalism 1934–1948*, Ravan Press, Johannesburg, 1983.

Paton, Alan, *Hofmeyr*, Oxford University Press, Cape Town and London, 1964.

Peberdy, Sally, *Selecting Immigrants: National Identity and South Africa's Immigration Policies 1910–2008*, Witwatersrand University Press, Johannesburg, 2009.

Pelzer, AN, *Die Afrikaner-Broederbond: Eerste 50 Jaar*, Tafelberg, Cape Town, 1979.

Phillips, Howard, *The University of Cape Town 1918–1948: The Formative Years*, University of Cape Town and UCT Press, 1993.

Pirow, Oswald, *James Barry Munnik Hertzog*, Howard Timmins, Cape Town. n.d.

Reitz, Deneys, *No Outspan*, Faber and Faber, London, 1942.

Roberts, Michael and Trollip, AEG, *The South African Opposition 1939–1945: An Essay in Contemporary History*, Longman, Green and Co, London, 1947.

Rose, Paul Lawrence, *German Question/Jewish Question: Revolutionary Antisemitism from Kant to Wagner*, Princeton University Press, Princeton, NJ, 1990.

Roux, Edward, *Time Longer than Rope: The Black Man's Struggle for Freedom in South Africa*, University of Wisconsin Press, Madison, 1964.

Saron, Gustav, *The Jews of South Africa: An Illustrated History to 1953* (edited by Naomi Musiker), Scarecrow Books in association with the South African Jewish Board of Deputies, 2001.

Schoeman, Ben, *My Lewe in die Politiek*, Perskor, Johannesburg, 1978.

Schoeman, BM, *Parlementêre verkiesings in Suid-Afrika 1911–1976*, Aktuele Publikasies, 1977.

Shain, Milton, 'South Africa', in David Wyman (ed), *The World Reacts to the Holocaust*, The Johns Hopkins University Press, Baltimore, 1996.

Shain, Milton, *Antisemitism*, Bowerdean Press, London, 1998.

Shain, Milton, *Jewry and Cape Society: The Origins and Activities of the Jewish Board of Deputies for the Cape Colony*, Historical Publication Society, 1983.

Shain, Milton, *The Roots of Antisemitism in South Africa*, University of Virginia Press,

Charlottesville, and Witwatersrand University Press, Johannesburg, 1994.

Shaw, Gerald, *The Cape Times: An Informal History*, David Philip Publishers, Cape Town, 1999.

Shimoni, Gideon, *Jews and Zionism: The South African Experience 1910–1967*, Oxford University Press, Cape Town, 1980.

Simons, HJ and Simons, RE, *Class and Colour in South Africa*, Penguin Books, Harmondsworth, Middlesex, 1969.

Simson, Howard, *The Social Origins of Afrikaner Fascism and its Apartheid Policy*, Acta Universitatis Upsalensis, Uppsala Studies in Economic History 21, Armqvist and Wiksell, Stockholm, 1980.

Smuts, JC, *Greater South Africa: Plans for a Better World. The Speeches of JC Smuts*, The Truth Legion, Johannesburg, 1940.

Stals, ELP, *Afrikaner Bond, Afrikaner Broederbond, Geskiedenis van die Afrikaner-Broederbond 1918–1994*, 1998.

Stein, Sarah Abrevaya, *Plumes: Ostrich Feathers, Jews, and a Lost World of Global Commerce*, Yale University Press, New Haven, 2008.

Sternhell, Zeev, 'From Counter-Enlightenment to the Revolutions of the 20th Century', in Shlomo Avineri and Zeev Sternhell (eds), *Europe's Century of Discontent: The Legacies of Fascism, Nazism and Communism*, The Hebrew University Magnes Press, Jerusalem, 2003.

Stultz, Newell M, *Afrikaner Politics in South Africa, 1934–1948*, University of California Press, Berkeley, 1974.

Thompson, Leonard, *The Political Mythology of Apartheid*, Yale University Press, New Haven and London, 1985.

Van den Heever, CM, *Generaal JBM Hertzog*, APB Boekhandel, Johannesburg, 1946.

Van der Merwe, CN, *Breaking Barriers: Stereotypes and the Changing Values in Afrikaans Writings 1875–1990*, Rodopi, Amsterdam and Atlanta, 1994.

Van der Poel, Jean (ed), *Selections from the Smuts Papers, Volume VI, December 1934–August 1945*, Cambridge University Press, Cambridge, 1973.

Van Rensburg, JFJ, *Their Paths Crossed Mine: Memoirs of the Commandant-General of the Ossewa-Brandwag*, Central News Agency, South Africa, 1956.

Van Wyk, At, *Die Keeromstraatkliek: Die Burger en die politiek van koaliesie en samesmelting 1932–1934*, Tafelberg, Cape Town, 1983.

Vatcher, William Henry, *White Laager: the Rise of Afrikaner Nationalism*, Frederick Praeger, New York and London, 1965.

Visser, George Cloete, *OB: Traitors or Patriots?*, Macmillan South Africa, Cape Town, 1976.

Welsh, David, 'The Growth of Towns' in Leonard Thompson and Monica Wilson (eds), *The Oxford History of South Africa*, Oxford University Press, Oxford, 1971.

Wilkins, Ivor and Strydom, Hans, *The Super-Afrikaners*, Jonathan Ball, Johannesburg, 1978.

Wilson, GH, *Gone Down The Years*, Howard Timmins, Cape Town, n.d.

Theses and Dissertations

Bradlow, Edna, 'Immigration into the Union 1910–1948: Policies and Attitudes', unpublished PhD dissertation, University of Cape Town, 1978.

Brink, Elsabe, 'The Afrikaner Women of the Garment Workers' Union, 1918–1938', unpublished MA dissertation, University of the Witwatersrand, 1986.

Broodryk, Jacobus Johannes, 'Stellenbosse Akademici en die Politieke Problematiek in Suid

Afrika, 1934–1948', unpublished MA dissertation, University of Stellenbosch, 1991.

Coetzee, Daniel, 'From Immigrants to Citizens: Civil Integration and Acculturation of Jews into Oudtshoorn Society, 1874–1999', unpublished MA thesis, University of Cape Town, 2000.

Cohen, Michael, 'Anti-Jewish Manifestations in the Union of South Africa during the Nineteen Thirties', unpublished BA (Hons) dissertation, University of Cape Town, 1968.

Cohen, Michael, 'Anatomy of South African Antisemitism: Afrikaner Nationalism, the Radical Right and South African Jewry between the World Wars', unpublished PhD, Monash University, 2014.

Friedman, Sharon Lynne, 'Jews, Germans and Afrikaners: Nationalist Press Reaction to the Final Solution', unpublished Honours dissertation, University of Cape Town, 1982.

Green, Michael Anthony, 'South African Jewish Responses to the Holocaust 1941–1948', unpublished MA dissertation, University of South Africa, 1987.

Hattingh, Izak, 'Nasionaal-Sosialismus en die Gryshemp-beweging in Suid-Afrika', unpublished DPhil, University of the Orange Free State, 1972, 1989.

Joubert, Jurie Jacobus, 'Die Burger se Rol in die Suid-Afrikaanse Partypolitiek, 1934–1948', unpublished DLitt et Phil, University of South Africa, 1990.

Juta, Coenraad Jacobus, 'Aspects of Afrikaner Nationalism, 1900–1964: An Analysis', unpublished PhD dissertation, University of Natal, 1966.

Klaaren, Jonathan Eugene, 'Migrating to Citizenship: Mobility, Law, and Nationality in South Africa, 1897–1937', unpublished PhD dissertation, Yale University, 2004.

Korf, Lindie, 'DF Malan: A Political Biography', unpublished PhD dissertation, University of Stellenbosch, 2009.

McNally, Samuel, 'Tracing Hitler, the Rise of Nazism and the Final Solution: Observations from the Cape Times, 1933–1945', unpublished MA (Minor) thesis, University of Cape Town, 2009.

Monama, Fankie Lucas, 'Wartime Propaganda in the Union of South Africa, 1939–1945', unpublished PhD thesis, University of Stellenbosch, 2014.

Prinsloo, Dioné, 'Die Johannesburg-Periode in Dr HF Verwoerd se Loopbaan', unpublished DPhil, Rand Afrikaans University, 1979.

Reznek, Rodney, 'Excluding the Jew: Antisemitism and Eugenics in South Africa before 1930', unpublished MA thesis, University of London, 2012.

Singer, Lauren, 'The South African Jewish Press and the Problem of Palestine 1945–1948', unpublished History Additional Essay, University of Cape Town, 1985.

Stone, Lotta M, 'Seeking Asylum: German Jewish Refugees in South Africa 1933–1948, unpublished PhD dissertation, Clark University, 2010.

Tothill, FD, 'The 1943 Election', unpublished MA thesis, University of South Africa, 1987.

Uran, Steven, 'Afrikaner Fascism and National Socialism in South Africa: 1933–1945', unpublished MA dissertation, University of Wisconsin, 1975.

Van der Schyff, PE, 'Eric H Louw in die Suid-Afrikaanse Politiek tot 1948', unpublished DLitt dissertation, Potchefstroom Universiteit vir Christelike Onderwys, 1974.

Van Deventer, André, 'Afrikaner Nationalist Politics and Anti-Communism, 1937 to 1945', unpublished MA dissertation, University of Stellenbosch, 1991.

Van Heerden, FJ, 'Nasionaal-Sosialisme as faktor in die Suid-Afrikaanse Politiek, 1933–1948', unpublished DPhil, University of the Orange Free State, 1972.

Newspapers and Periodicals

Die Burger
Cape Argus
The Cape
Cape Guardian
Cape Standard
Cape Times
Common Sense
Daily Express (Britain)
Daily Representative
Daily Tribune
Diamond Fields Advertiser
East London Daily Dispatch
Eastern Province Herald
Farmers Weekly
Fascist Quarterly
The Forward
The Friend
Die Huisgenoot
Independent
Inspan
Jewish Affairs
Jewish Telegraphic Agency
Die Kerkbode
Koers
Die Kruithoring
The Leader
Die Matie
The/Die Monitor
Mossel Bay Advertiser
Natal Daily News
Natal Mercury
Natal Witness
The Newcastle Advertiser and Northern Post
New Era
Die Nuwe Orde
Die Nuwe Tyd
Die OB
Die Oosterlig
Ons Vaderland
Oudtshoorn Courant
Oudtshoorn Observer
The Owl
Paarl Post
Patria
Pretoria News

Rand Daily Mail
Die Republikein
South African Jewish Chronicle (SAJC)
South African Jewish Times (SAJT)
The Star
Die Suiderstem
Sunday Express
Sunday Times
Sunday Tribune
Die Transvaler
Die Vaderland
Vlam
Die Volk
Die Volksblad
Volkstem
Die Vrystater
Die Waarheid / The Truth
Wapenskou
Yiddischer Zeitung
Zionist Record